EYEWITNESS ◉ HANDBOOKS

TREES

TREES

ALLEN J. COOMBES

Photography by
MATTHEW WARD

A DK PUBLISHING BOOK

Editor Gillian Roberts
Art Editor Vicki James
Design Coordinator Spencer Holbrook
Editorial Consultant Roy Lancaster
Production Caroline Webber
US Consultant Fred C. Galle
US Editor Charles A. Wills

Tree illustrations commissioned by
Mustafa Sami

Plant material photographed at
Sir Harold Hillier Gardens and Arboretum,
Ampfield, Hampshire, England

First American Edition, 1992
8 10 9
Published in the United States by
DK Publishing, Inc.
95 Madison Avenue,
New York, NY 10016

ISBN 1-56458-075-X
ISBN 1-56458-072-5 [Flexibinding]

Library of Congress Catalog
Card Number 92-52782

Computer page makeup done in Great Britain
by The Cooling Brown Partnership.

Text film output done in Great Britain
by The Right Type.

Reproduced in Singapore by Colourscan.

Printed and bound in Singapore
by Kyodo Printing Co.

CONTENTS

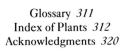

LOOKING AT TREES

Whether standing in isolation on a windy hillside, crowded together in dense forest, or lining a city street, trees form an important element of nearly every landscape. The almost infinite variation of trees through the seasons – not only in shape, size, color, and texture, but also in the finer details of leaves, flowers, fruit, and bark – makes the study of these familiar plants an ever-changing, yet enduring, source of delight.

THE FACT THAT trees survive almost everywhere means that you can appreciate and study them wherever you happen to be. In the countryside, they grow, it is hoped but not always, as nature intends; in urban environments, planted along streets, and in parks and public gardens, they give solace among man-made structures. Of course, while there is nothing to compare with seeing trees growing wild in their natural habitat, towns and cities are still excellent places for observing and learning more about them.

THE TREE SELECTION

This book includes only those species of tree that grow wild in the temperate regions of the world. In the northern hemisphere, this covers most of Asia, North America, Europe south to the Mediterranean, the Himalayas, and most of China; in the southern hemisphere, it includes South America, the cooler regions of Australia, and New Zealand. From within this extensive area, I have made a selection of plants that illustrates the amazing diversity of trees that can be found throughout the world. At the same time, I have tried to include most of the species that you are likely to find planted in gardens and along streets, as well as a few that are unusual or more rare.

BEECH WOOD IN AUTUMN
An English beech wood is one of the glories of autumn. Its densely leafy canopy allows little light to penetrate, with the result that little else can grow beneath it.

ORIENTAL BEECH (*Fagus orientalis*)

CONSERVATION ISSUES

In recent years, the destruction of the tropical forests has excited a good deal of attention, and rightly so: these last great areas of natural diversity are home to numerous plants and animals, whose continuing existence may be of vital importance to mankind. Faced with so large a debate, it is easy to forget that most forests in temperate zones have already suffered the fate that is threatening those in tropical regions. In the developed world, extensive areas of natural woodland have been lost through man's demand for paper, building materials, and other wood-based products, as well as through the need for agricultural land, creating the relatively unnatural countryside we see today.

CHINESE CHESTNUT (C. mollissima)

In developing parts of the world, temperate woods are still under threat in places like the Himalayas and South America. Particularly in areas of heavy rainfall, the felling of trees – with scant regard to the far-reaching consequences of this action – causes problems such as flooding and mud landslides, when the vegetation that once stabilized entire hillsides is gone.

The majority of species are distributed over a wide enough area to be able to endure partial felling and survive without the danger of extinction. Some have a much more limited range, however. One

THREATENED SPECIES
Diseases can nearly destroy a species. Chestnut blight from East Asia has killed all but a few wild American chestnuts (Castanea dentata, *p.149). The Chinese chestnut* (C. mollissima, *p.149) is being used to help breed resistant trees.*

single example is the Spanish fir *(Abies pinsapo,* see p.56), which grows wild on very few mountainsides in a small area of southern Spain. Years ago, its timber was a valuable local resource. Now, any further cutting might extinguish these glorious forests forever. We must make special efforts to protect this and other such endangered species.

SURVIVOR FROM CHINA
The bark of Magnolia officinalis *var.* biloba *was once harvested to produce medicines, causing the species to become extinct in the wild. Cultivation has ensured that it still grows in gardens.*

ADAPTATION FOR SURVIVAL
The larches (Larix, see pp.60–61) grow wild under the harshest conditions. They produce their foliage on short side shoots – an adaptation that allows them to take advantage of favorable conditions as they come into leaf.

HABITAT AND ENVIRONMENT

By adapting to an extensive range of environmental conditions, trees are able to grow in many different habitats. Generally speaking, it is the conifers that inhabit the most hostile situations. Their slender shape minimizes damage by snow; evergreen leaves make the best use of a growing season that may be short and mean that the plant can survive extended periods of drought when the ground is frozen; wind pollination eliminates the need for insect visitors, which may be sparse or nonexistent in unfavorable habitats.

Friendlier habitats produce a longer growing season and encourage decidu-ous species. Here, the plant has time to produce new leaves, and shed old ones, every year in a continuous cycle of regeneration. In shady places, large leaves are needed to intercept as much sunlight as can filter through; in wet areas, tapered tips allow for the rapid shedding of water; in dry areas, gray or silvery leaves reduce water loss; and fragrant or showy flowers ensure a good chance of pollination by insects.

ILEX X
KOEHNEANA ▷

◁ LUSTERLEAF
HOLLY (*Ilex
latifolia*)

HYBRID PLANTS
A hybrid is produced when two different species cross together. The plant that results usually shows characteristics that are intermediate between the two parents. Some hybrids occur only through cultivation in gardens, because the parent plants do not grow together in the wild.

△ PARENT ONE
Lusterleaf holly (Ilex latifolia, see p.112) has rather large leaves, which are toothed at the margin but not spiny.

◁ ENGLISH HOLLY
(Ilex aquifolium)

THE HYBRID ▷
Ilex x koehneana *(see p.112)* has the large leaves of I. latifolia. The spiny margin of the leaves is inherited from I. aquifolium.

△ PARENT TWO
The familiar English holly (Ilex aquifolium, see p.109) has leaves that are typically edged with spiny teeth.

A FAMILY TREE

ROSACEAE

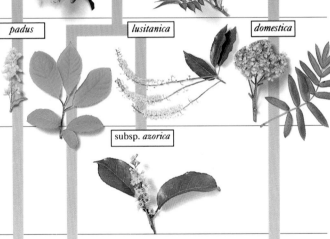

Family
A family contains a single genus or several related genera. The family name is always written in roman type, e.g., Rosaceae.

Prunus

Sorbus

Genus, Genera
A genus contains a single species or several related species. The genus element is always written in italic type, e.g., *Prunus, Sorbus*.

padus

lusitanica

domestica

Species
A species is one unit. It denotes a specific plant. The species element is always written in italic type, e.g., *padus, lusitanica, domestica*.

subsp. *azorica*

Subspecies
A subspecies is a major division of a species. The two elements are always written in roman and italic type, e.g., subsp. *azorica*.

var. *pomifera*

var. *pyrifera*

Variety & Forma
Variety (var.) and forma (f.) are minor divisions of a species. The two elements are always written in roman and italic type, e.g., var. *pomifera*.

'Amanogawa'

Cultivar
A cultivar is a form selected and named for its garden merit. The name is written in roman type, with quotation marks, e.g., 'Watereri.'

'Watereri'

OBSERVING AND RECORDING TREES

Keeping written notes about the trees you see is not only an enjoyable activity at the time: it also makes interesting reading at a later date. Choose half a dozen favorite trees close to where you live or work. Visit each one several times during the four seasons and build up a fact file that records their special features at different times of the year.

MAKING BARK IMPRESSIONS

Rubbing bark can be an effective way of capturing its diverse patterns and textures. Hold a piece of paper flat to the surface of the trunk, and rub lightly with a wax crayon. Label your rubbing with the date, the tree's name, and its location.

TAKING FIELD NOTES

Jot down the tree's height, the circumference of its trunk, and the color and texture of the bark. Note details of its leaves, flowers, and fruit (depending on the time of year), its location, and the date. Expand your notes at home.

MEASURING A TREE'S HEIGHT

Cut a straight piece of stick that is the same length as the distance between your eye and your fist. Hold it vertically at arm's length and walk toward or away from the tree to align the top of the stick with the top of the tree and the base of the stick with the base of the tree. Mark the point at which you are now standing and measure the distance on the ground to the base of the trunk. This distance equals the height of the tree.

long, 100 ft (30 m) tape for measuring height, and trunk circumference

colored pencils for making sketches

small sketch-book for visual notetaking

reference photographs

wax crayon and paper for making bark impressions

cut specimen to take home for more detailed examination

magnifying glass

label with string tie for cut specimens

HOW THIS BOOK WORKS

THE BOOK IS ARRANGED according to the major groups of tree: Conifers and their Allies, and Broadleaves. The groups are divided, alphabetically, into families. A short introduction to each family tells you how many genera and species it contains, and describes the general characteristics and features of the plants that belong to it. The entries that follow are arranged alphabetically by genus and by species within each

genus. They give detailed information, in words and pictures, about selected species that are found in that family.

Each entry begins with the common name, or the scientific name if there is no single, accepted common name for that plant. Many plants do not have a common name: indeed, they are well enough known under their scientific name to not need one. This example shows how a typical entry is organized.

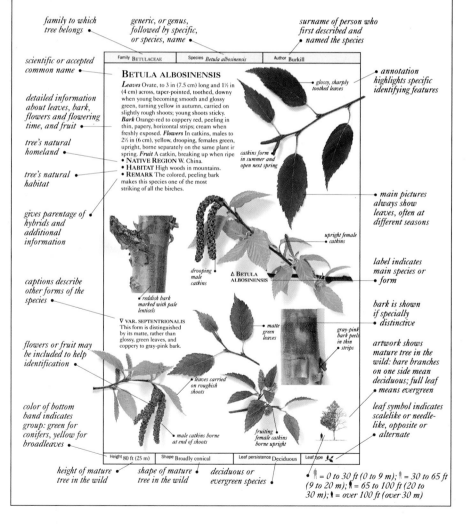

family to which tree belongs •

generic, or genus, followed by specific, or species, name •

surname of person who first described and • named the species

scientific or accepted common name •

| Family BETULACEAE | Species *Betula albosinensis* | Author Burkill |

BETULA ALBOSINENSIS

detailed information about leaves, bark, flowers and flowering time, and fruit •

Leaves Ovate, to 3 in (7.5 cm) long and 1½ in (4 cm) wide, taper-pointed, toothed, downy when young becoming smooth and glossy green, turning yellow in autumn, carried on slightly rough shoots; young shoots sticky. **Bark** Orange-red to coppery red, peeling in thin, papery, horizontal strips; cream when freshly exposed. **Flowers** In catkins, males to 2½ in (6 cm), yellow, drooping, females green, upright, borne separately on the same plant in spring. **Fruit** A catkin, breaking up when ripe

tree's natural homeland •

• NATIVE REGION W. China.

tree's natural habitat •

• HABITAT High woods in mountains.

gives parentage of hybrids and additional information •

• REMARK The colored, peeling bark makes this species one of the most striking of all the birches.

• glossy, sharply toothed leaves

annotation highlights specific • identifying features

catkins form • in summer and open next spring

main pictures always show • leaves, often at different seasons

upright female • catkins

drooping male catkins

△ BETULA ALBOSINENSIS

label indicates main species or • form

• reddish bark marked with pale lenticels

bark is shown if specially • distinctive

captions describe other forms of the species •

▽ VAR. SEPTENTRIONALIS This form is distinguished by its matte, rather than glossy, green leaves, and coppery to gray-pink bark.

• matte green leaves

gray-pink bark peels in thin • strips

artwork shows mature tree in the wild: bare branches on one side mean deciduous; full leaf • means evergreen

flowers or fruit may be included to help identification •

• leaves carried on roughish shoots

color of bottom band indicates group: green for conifers, yellow for broadleaves •

• male catkins borne at end of shoots

fruiting female catkins borne upright

leaf symbol indicates scalelike or needle-like, opposite or • alternate

| Height 80 ft (25 m) | Shape Broadly conical | Leaf persistence Deciduous | Leaf type 🗲 |

height of mature • tree in the wild

shape of mature • tree in the wild

deciduous or • evergreen species

• 🗍 = 0 to 30 ft (0 to 9 m); 🗍 = 30 to 65 ft (9 to 20 m); 🗍 = 65 to 100 ft (20 to 30 m); 🗍 = over 100 ft (over 30 m)

WHAT IS A TREE?

A TREE IS a living thing. It has a woody stem, a root system, and branches that are clothed in season with leaves. It may have flowers and, later, fruit.

Size and habit distinguish a tree from a shrub. A tree usually attains at least 17 ft (5 m) and has a single stem that may divide; a shrub is usually smaller and has many stems growing from the base. Habit is related to habitat. A species that is a tallish tree in a fertile valley may be only a low shrub on an exposed hillside. Open situations allow the plant to develop a spreading crown; in dense forest, where the trees are crowded, it may form a narrower shape.

chlorophyll may be obscured by other pigments

a flat leaf surface works most efficiently

leaf veins conduct water and nutrients

all leaf types have the same function

variegated leaves have areas that lack chlorophyll

LEAVES
Chlorophyll is the pigment that makes leaves green. It enables the plant to convert water and carbon dioxide into sugars and oxygen, using the energy from sunlight (photosynthesis).

TRUNK AND BARK
The trunk conducts water and food to the leaves, and nutrients from the leaves to the roots. It supports the branches and their foliage. The layer of bark on the outside protects the delicate living tissues beneath.

bark is composed of dead cells

growth rings in the trunk show annual increase in size

ROOT SYSTEM
A mature tree has large, main roots that anchor it into the ground and support it. The surrounding network of very fine roots takes up water and minerals for transporting to its actively growing parts.

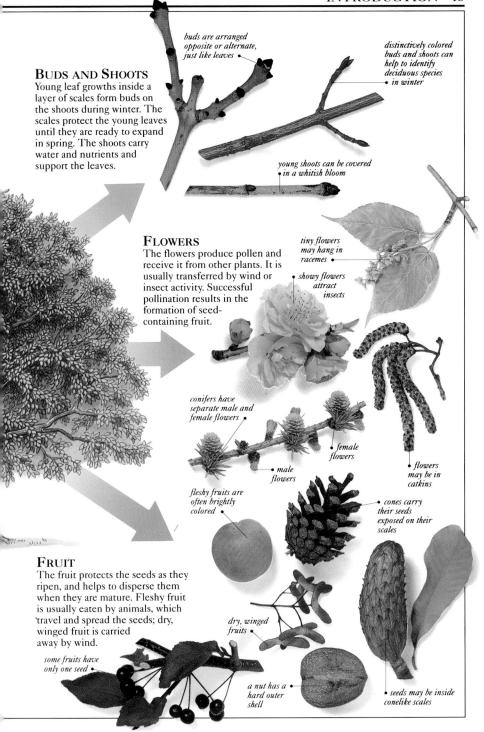

BUDS AND SHOOTS

Young leaf growths inside a layer of scales form buds on the shoots during winter. The scales protect the young leaves until they are ready to expand in spring. The shoots carry water and nutrients and support the leaves.

buds are arranged opposite or alternate, just like leaves

distinctively colored buds and shoots can help to identify deciduous species in winter

young shoots can be covered in a whitish bloom

FLOWERS

The flowers produce pollen and receive it from other plants. It is usually transferred by wind or insect activity. Successful pollination results in the formation of seed-containing fruit.

tiny flowers may hang in racemes

showy flowers attract insects

conifers have separate male and female flowers

female flowers

male flowers

flowers may be in catkins

FRUIT

The fruit protects the seeds as they ripen, and helps to disperse them when they are mature. Fleshy fruit is usually eaten by animals, which travel and spread the seeds; dry, winged fruit is carried away by wind.

fleshy fruits are often brightly colored

cones carry their seeds exposed on their scales

dry, winged fruits

some fruits have only one seed

a nut has a hard outer shell

seeds may be inside conelike scales

THE PARTS OF A TREE

BECOMING FAMILIAR with the principal parts of a tree, and their variety, can help you identify trees at any season of the year; and it is useful to recognize the special words that describe them.

These pages illustrate typical leaves, flowers, fruit, and bark. If you can relate the words to the pictures, you can see in your mind what the parts of the tree look like as you read the entries.

TEN BASIC LEAF SHAPES

Leaves occur in a great variety of shapes; each also has variations within its basic shape. Every leaf may not fit exactly into one of the shapes shown below: it may be between two different ones. These shapes apply not only to simple leaves, but also to the individual leaflets of compound leaves. A simple leaf is one that is not divided into separate parts. A compound leaf is divided into two or more parts: each separate division is known as a leaflet.

Needlelike leaves are parallel-sided and taper-pointed.

Linear leaves are parallel-sided and have a blunt tip.

Rounded leaves are more or less circular in outline.

Oblong leaves are parallel-sided or nearly so.

Elliptic leaves are broad, narrowing at each end.

Heart-shaped leaves have a deep notch at the base.

Ovate leaves are widest below the middle.

Obovate leaves are widest above the middle.

Lanceolate leaves are slender and widest below the middle.

Oblanceolate leaves are slender and widest above the middle.

THE PARTS OF A FLOWER

Whereas leaves may vary greatly within any one genus, the flowers of related species and genera are usually similar, at least in structure. Those found on trees are often small, sometimes insignificant and without petals, or even inconspicuous; alternatively, they can be large and showy. Some tree flowers are fragrant; some smell unpleasant; some have no scent at all. How they are borne – singly or together in clusters – is also a notable identifying feature.

each anther is borne on a thin filament

each style ends in a stigma

petals are not distinct from sepals

petals are often showy

sepals look like petals

ADVANCED FLOWER ▷
Most flowers are of this type. They have petals that are usually distinct from the sepals.

sepals do not look like petals

PRIMITIVE FLOWER ▷
These flowers have no very clear distinction between the petals and sepals, which are known collectively as tepals.

stigmas are arranged spirally

anthers split to release pollen

TYPES OF FRUIT

Fruits develop from flowers, and so it follows that – as with flowers – the type of fruit a tree bears is characteristic of the genus or even the family to which it belongs. Most fruits originate from a single flower. Others, such as the fig *(Ficus carica, see p.219)*, are derived from several flowers, which fuse together to form multiple fruits.

WALNUT *(Juglans regia)* ▽

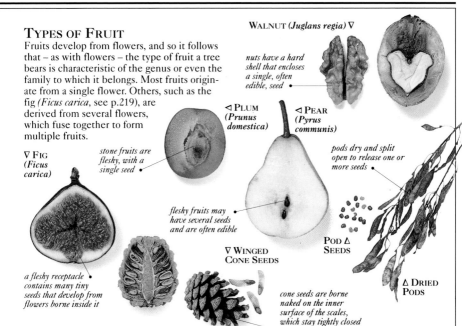

nuts have a hard shell that encloses a single, often edible, seed

◁ PLUM
(Prunus domestica)

◁ PEAR
(Pyrus communis)

▽ FIG
(Ficus carica)

stone fruits are fleshy, with a single seed

pods dry and split open to release one or more seeds

fleshy fruits may have several seeds and are often edible

▽ WINGED
CONE SEEDS

POD △
SEEDS

△ DRIED
PODS

a fleshy receptacle contains many tiny seeds that develop from flowers borne inside it

cone seeds are borne naked on the inner surface of the scales, which stay tightly closed until the seeds are ripe

TYPES OF BARK

Trees develop their characteristic bark patterns and textures as a means of dealing with the increasing circumference of the trunk as they grow. Because the outer bark is composed of dead cells, it cannot grow and so, as the trunk expands, the bark cracks or peels in various ways. Bark is a useful feature in identification, since it can be used at any time of the year.

smooth bark is dotted with lenticels

Smooth bark is a feature of many young trees. It may crack or peel as they age.

bark of young tree was all white

Plates are irregular areas of bark, often flaking, with fissures or cracks in between.

younger bark can be seen at base of ridges and fissures

Ridges and fissures may develop as thick bark cracks. They can be raised and prominent or deep.

freshly exposed bark is distinctively colored

Vertically peeling bark often hangs and falls from the tree in long strips and ribbons.

peeling bark by hand harms the tree

Horizontally peeling bark may unwind from the tree in paper-thin strips and wide sheets.

flaking bark shows many ages and colors

Irregularly flaking bark reveals different age layers and gives the trunk a shaggy appearance.

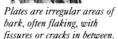

CONIFER OR BROADLEAF?

I N ORDER TO DISCOVER all there is to know about a specific tree, scientists often use microscopic characters that are not visible to the naked eye. These provide vital, yet hidden, clues toward the positive identification of a species (although even scientists can, and do, make mistakes). But for most people, careful, detailed observation of what is immediately visible must do. If you can recognize the distinctive features that categorize the two major groups, it is easy to distinguish conifers and their allies from broadleaves, and vice versa. The main characteristics are described and illustrated on these two pages.

CONIFERS AND THEIR ALLIES

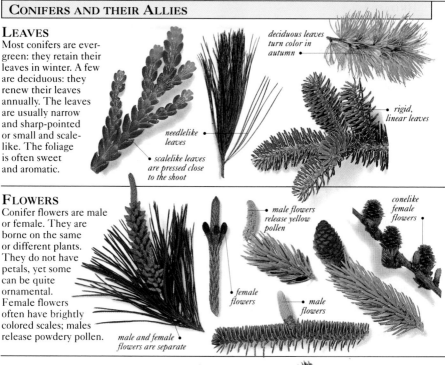

LEAVES
Most conifers are evergreen: they retain their leaves in winter. A few are deciduous: they renew their leaves annually. The leaves are usually narrow and sharp-pointed or small and scale-like. The foliage is often sweet and aromatic.

deciduous leaves turn color in autumn •

• rigid, linear leaves

needlelike leaves •

• scalelike leaves are pressed close to the shoot

FLOWERS
Conifer flowers are male or female. They are borne on the same or different plants. They do not have petals, yet some can be quite ornamental. Female flowers often have brightly colored scales; males release powdery pollen.

• male flowers release yellow pollen

conelike female flowers •

• female flowers

• male flowers

male and female • flowers are separate

FRUIT
The fruit of most conifers is a cone, composed of often woody scales, and colored brown when ripe. Juniper species have fleshy scales, so the fruit resembles a berry. Conifer allies, such as yews, are not true conifers but are related to them. Their fruit is a seed with a fleshy outer coat.

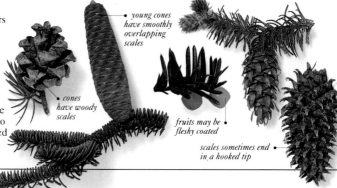

• young cones have smoothly overlapping scales

• cones have woody scales

fruits may be • fleshy coated

scales sometimes end • in a hooked tip

THE BOTANICAL DIFFERENCE

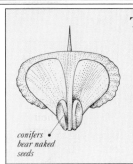

conifers bear naked seeds

CONIFERS
Conifers and their allies are classed as gymnosperms: plants with naked seeds not enclosed in an ovary. They are considered to be more primitive than broadleaves.

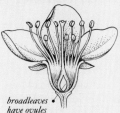

broadleaves have ovules inside an ovary

BROADLEAVES
Broadleaves are classed as angiosperms: plants with ovules enclosed for protection in an ovary. Following successful fertilization, the ovules develop into seeds.

BROADLEAVES

LEAVES
Broadleaves are evergreen or deciduous. The leaves are simple or compound, usually flattened and have a distinct network of fine veins. They vary greatly in shape. The foliage may have an aromatic scent, but lacks the resinous quality of conifers.

deciduous leaves turn color

compound leaves have leaflets

evergreen leaves stay green

veins are easy to see

leaf margin often has teeth or spines

FLOWERS
Broadleaf flowers are usually bisexual: male and female parts are in the same flower. Separate males and females are borne on the same or on different plants. Both types usually have petals, and are often fragrant. They can be small or large.

small flowers are often borne in clusters

sexes may be separate

bisexual flowers are usual

broadleaf flowers usually have petals

FRUIT
The fruit of broadleaves has much more diversity than that of most conifers, and comes in many forms. It may be a berry, acorn, capsule, nut, or pod; woody, fleshy-coated, or dry; spiny, rough, or smooth; inedible or edible; and any color when ripe.

winged fruits

fleshy-coated fruit

woody fruits resemble cones

berry fruits can be brightly colored

TREE IDENTIFICATION KEY

THE KEY on pages 18 to 33 uses leaf characteristics to help you to identify the trees that are described in this book. **Stage 1** (see right) establishes whether your tree is a conifer, broadleaf, or palm. **Stage 2** divides conifers and broadleaves into groups, according to leaf type. **Stage 3** divides each of these groups into more detailed groups that each contain two or more genera.

STAGE 1: WHICH GROUP?

The trees are divided into two major groups: Conifers, and Broadleaves (including Palms). Conifer features are described on page 16. Broadleaf features are described on page 17. Palm features are described on page 19.

CONIFER

BROADLEAF

PALM

STAGE 2: CONIFERS – DECIDUOUS OR EVERGREEN?

Only a few conifer species in this book are deciduous; most are evergreen. Deciduous species lose their leaves in autumn. In spring, their pale young leaves are clearly visible. Evergreens keep their leaves in winter, so they are easy to distinguish. In spring, look for pale young leaves together with dark old leaves. If your tree is deciduous, turn to pages 20–21. If it is evergreen, decide whether your leaf is not scalelike or is scalelike, then turn to pages 20–21 or 22–23.

LEAVES NOT SCALELIKE

- *Clustered or in whorls* 20–21
- *Single, shoots hidden* 20–21
- *Single, shoots not hidden, one-year stems green* 20–21
- *Single, shoots not hidden, one-year stems not green* 20–21

DECIDUOUS

EVERGREEN

- *Ginkgo* 20
- *Larix* 20
- *Pseudolarix* 20
- *Glyptostrobus* 21
- *Metasequoia* 21
- *Taxodium* 21

CONIFERS

AT LEAST SOME LEAVES SCALELIKE

- *Foliage in flattened sprays* 22–23
- *Foliage in irregular sprays* 22–23

STAGE 2: BROADLEAVES – OPPOSITE OR ALTERNATE LEAVES?

All broadleaves have their leaves arranged in one of two ways: either opposite or alternate. Opposite leaves are borne in pairs or threes, one directly opposite the other, on either side of the stem. Alternate leaves are borne singly, staggered on alternate sides of the stem. Leaflets are opposite or alternate, too. If your leaf is opposite, turn to pages 22–25. If it is alternate, turn to pages 24–33.

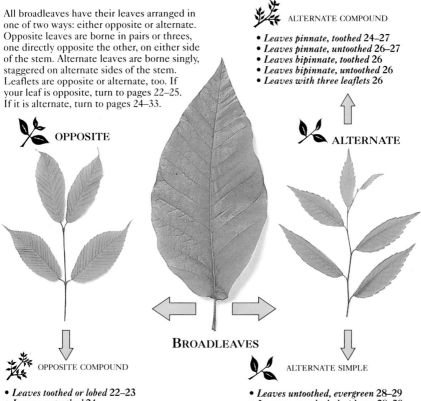

BROADLEAVES

ALTERNATE COMPOUND

- *Leaves pinnate, toothed 24–27*
- *Leaves pinnate, untoothed 26–27*
- *Leaves bipinnate, toothed 26*
- *Leaves bipinnate, untoothed 26*
- *Leaves with three leaflets 26*

OPPOSITE

ALTERNATE

OPPOSITE COMPOUND

- *Leaves toothed or lobed 22–23*
- *Leaves untoothed 24*

OPPOSITE SIMPLE

- *Leaves toothed 24–25*
- *Leaves untoothed 24–25*
- *Leaves lobed 24*

ALTERNATE SIMPLE

- *Leaves untoothed, evergreen 28–29*
- *Leaves untoothed, deciduous 28–29*
- *Leaves lobed, toothed 30–31*
- *Leaves lobed, untoothed 30–31*
- *Leaves unlobed, toothed, evergreen 30–31*
- *Leaves unlobed, toothed, deciduous 32–33*

STAGE 2: PALMS

Palms are often tree-like in habit but are not true trees. They have a single, unbranched stem that does not increase in girth with age, and distinctively divided leaves. Most palms are native to warm regions, but some species grow in warm temperate regions, such as the Mediterranean and the southern United States. Chusan palm *(Trachycarpus fortunei)*, included in this book of largely temperate plants as an example of palms, is the hardiest species. If your leaf belongs to this palm, turn to page 31.

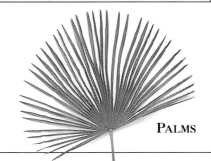

PALMS

STAGE 3: CONIFERS

This final stage in the identification key will guide you quickly to the correct section of the book. If you have turned straight to this part of the key, go back to pages 16 and 17, where the main characteristics that distinguish conifers and their allies, and broadleaves, from each other are illustrated and described. Having noted these features, move on to pages 18 and 19 and read through Stages 1 and 2 of the key. Now you are all set to start Stage 3.

Each individual leaf in the key represents a genus. You have already decided which type of conifer leaf you have – whether it is deciduous or evergreen, not scalelike or scalelike. You will

CONIFERS	LEAVES DECIDUOUS	Leaf type: not scalelike

Leaves renewed annually

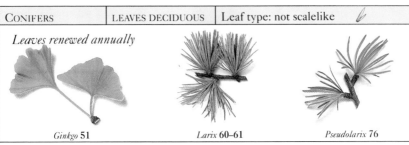

Ginkgo **51**   Larix **60–61**   Pseudolarix **76**

CONIFERS	LEAVES EVERGREEN	Leaf type: not scalelike

Leaves clustered or in whorls

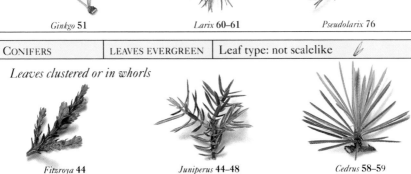

Fitzroya **44**   Juniperus **44–48**   Cedrus **58–59**

Leaves single, young shoots hidden by leaves or leaf bases

Araucaria **34**   Athrotaxis **80**   Cryptomeria **80**

Leaves single, young shoots not hidden, one-year stems green

Cephalotaxus **34–35**   Podocarpus **78**   Saxegothaea **78**

see that each large group has been further divided into several smaller groups. These give you an additional layer of information, which points you to finer detail, for example, whether the leaves are borne in clusters or whorls, or singly. Compare your leaf carefully with the leaves shown in the bands of each section, and decide to which group your leaf belongs. Compare your leaf with those in the final group, and find the individual leaf that it most closely resembles. The genus to which it belongs is written below the photograph of the leaf. Turn to the page(s) indicated beside the genus name to find the relevant species entry or entries.

Glyptostrobus **81**

Metasequoia **81**

Taxodium **83**

Pinus **66–75**

Sciadopitys **82**

Sequoia **82**

Sequoiadendron **82**

Taiwania **83**

Taxus **79**

Torreya **79**

Cunninghamia **81**

Leaves single, young shoots not hidden, one-year stems not green

Abies **52–57**   *Picea* **62–65**   *Pinus monophylla* **70**

| CONIFERS | LEAVES EVERGREEN | Leaf type: at least some leaves scalelike |

Foliage in flattened sprays

Austrocedrus **35**   *Calocedrus* **36**   *Chamaecyparis* **37–39**

Foliage in irregular sprays

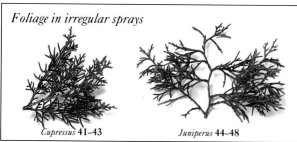

Cupressus **41–43**   *Juniperus* **44–48**

STAGE 3: BROADLEAVES

This final stage in the identification key will guide you quickly to the correct section of the book. If you have turned straight to this part of the key, go back to pages 16 and 17, where the main characteristics that distinguish conifers and their allies, and broadleaves, from each other are illustrated and described. Having noted these features, move on to pages 18 and 19 and read through Stages 1 and 2 of the key. Now you are all set to start Stage 3.

Each individual leaf in the key represents a genus. You have already decided which type of broadleaf leaf you have – whether it is opposite or alternate, compound or simple. You will see

| BROADLEAVES | LEAVES OPPOSITE | Leaf type: compound |

Leaves toothed or lobed

Acer **84–104**   *Eucryphia* **146–148**   *Aesculus* **178–181**

Pseudotsuga 76

Tsuga 77

x *Cupressocyparis* 40

Cupressus cashmeriana 41

Thuja 49–50

Thujopsis 51

that each large group has been further divided into several smaller groups. These give you an additional layer of information, which points you to finer detail, for example, whether the leaves are toothed, untoothed, or lobed, ever-green or deciduous. Compare your leaf carefully with the leaves shown in the bands of each section, and decide to which group your leaf belongs. Compare your leaf with those in the final group, and find the individual leaf that it most resembles. The genus to which it belongs is written below the leaf photograph. Turn to the page(s) indicated beside the genus name to find the relevant entry or entries.

Fraxinus 228–230

Leaves untoothed

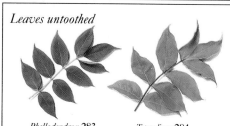

Phellodendron 283   *Tetradium* 284

BROADLEAVES	LEAVES OPPOSITE	Leaf type: simple

Leaves toothed

Acer 84–104   *Euonymus* 132   *Cercidiphyllum* 133   *Eucryphia* 146–148

Leaves untoothed

Catalpa 129–131   *Buxus* 131   *Cornus* 133–138   *Eucryphia* 146–148

Leaves lobed

Acer 84–104   *Catalpa* 129–131   *Paulownia* 296

BROADLEAVES	LEAVES ALTERNATE	Leaf type: compound

Leaves pinnate, toothed

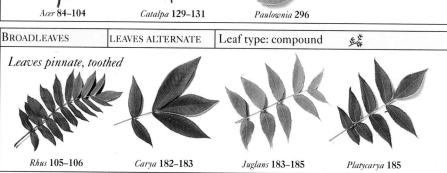

Rhus 105–106   *Carya* 182–183   *Juglans* 183–185   *Platycarya* 185

Chionanthus 227–228   *Phillyrea* 231   *Rhamnus cathartica* 237

Eucalyptus 222–225   *Myrtus* 225   *Chionanthus* 227–228   *Ligustrum* 231

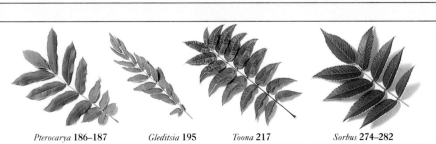

Pterocarya 186–187   *Gleditsia* 195   *Toona* 217   *Sorbus* 274–282

Zanthoxylum 285

Koelreuteria 295

Xanthoceras 295

Leaves pinnate, untoothed

Rhus trichocarpa 106

Juglans regia 185

Cladrastis 194

Leaves bipinnate, toothed

Aralia 114

Gleditsia 195

Leaves bipinnate, untoothed

Acacia 190–191

Albizia 192

Gymnocladus 195

Leaves with three leaflets

+ *Laburnocytisus* 196

Laburnum 197–198

Ptelea 28

Ailanthus 296

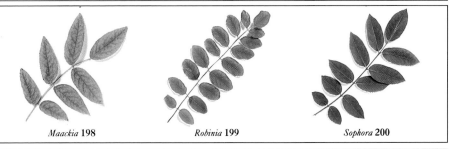

Maackia 198   *Robinia* 199   *Sophora* 200

BROADLEAVES	LEAVES ALTERNATE	Leaf type: simple

Leaves untoothed, evergreen

Ilex **108–113**

Arbutus **141–143**

Rhododendron **144**

Chrysolepis **150**

Acacia **191**

Magnolia **202–251**

Callistemon **221**

Eucalyptus **222–225**

Leaves untoothed, deciduous

Cotinus **105**

Asimina **107**

Cornus alternifolia **133**

Diospyros **138–139**

Sassafras **189**

Cercis **192–193**

Genista **194**

Magnolia **202–215**

Cotoneaster **240**

Cydonia **244**

Mespilus **255**

Pyrus salicifolia **273**

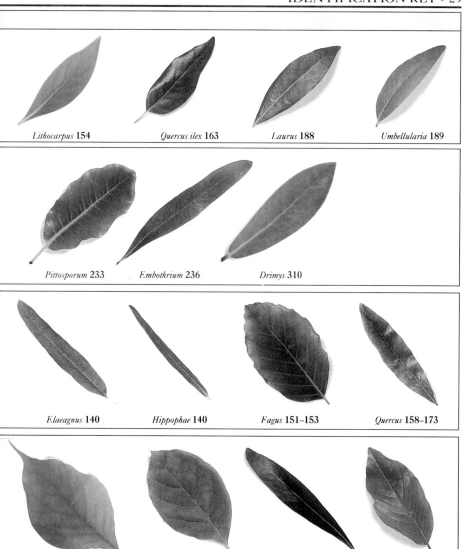

Lithocarpus 154

Quercus ilex 163

Laurus 188

Umbellularia 189

Pittosporum 233

Embothrium 236

Drimys 310

Elaeagnus 140

Hippophae 140

Fagus 151–153

Quercus 158–173

Maclura 220

Nyssa 226–227

Embothrium 236

Rhamnus frangula 237

Leaves lobed, toothed

Kalopanax 115   Quercus 158–173   Liquidambar 175–176   Broussonetia 218

x Crataemespilus 244   Malus 245–254   Sorbus 274–282   Populus alba 286

Leaves lobed, untoothed

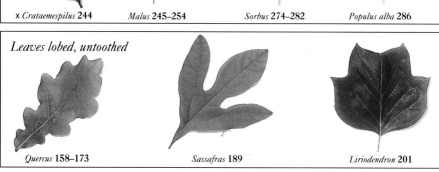

Quercus 158–173   Sassafras 189   Liriodendron 201

Leaves unlobed, toothed, evergreen

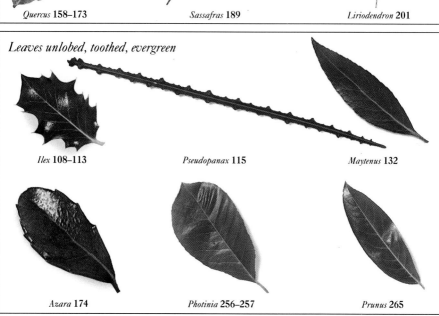

Ilex 108–113   Pseudopanax 115   Maytenus 132

Azara 174   Photinia 256–257   Prunus 265

Ficus 219

Morus 220

Platanus 234–235

Crataegus 240–243

Tilia mongolica 304

Trachycarpus 232

Arbutus 141–143

Nothofagus 155–157

Quercus 158–173

Trochodendron 306

Leaves unlobed, toothed, deciduous

Alnus 116–117

Betula 118–125

Carpinus 126–127

Corylus 127

Fagus 151–153

Nothofagus 155–157

Quercus 158–173

Idesia 174

Morus 220

Davidia 226

Amelanchier 238–239

Crataegus 240–243

Pyrus 273

Sorbus 274–282

Populus 286–290

Salix 291–294

Tilia 302–305

Celtis 306–307

Ulmus 308–309

Zelkova 309–310

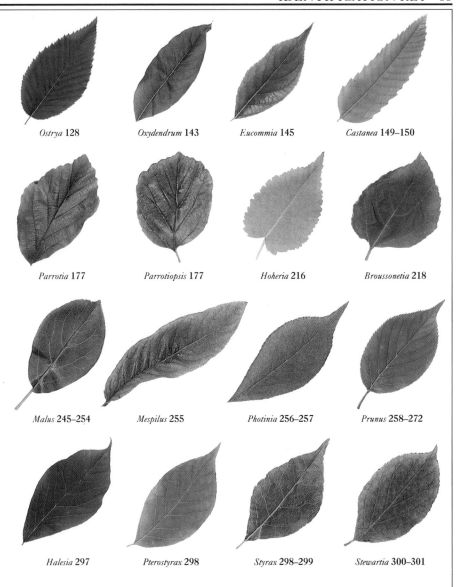

Ostrya 128

Oxydendrum 143

Eucommia 145

Castanea 149–150

Parrotia 177

Parrotiopsis 177

Hoheria 216

Broussonetia 218

Malus 245–254

Mespilus 255

Photinia 256–257

Prunus 258–272

Halesia 297

Pterostyrax 298

Styrax 298–299

Stewartia 300–301

CONIFERS
AND THEIR ALLIES

ARAUCARIACEAE

TWO GENERA AND ABOUT 30 species of large, evergreen trees belong to this family. They are mainly native to the southern hemisphere, but extend into Southeast Asia. Many are important timber trees. The monkey puzzle *(Araucaria araucana)* is the best-known member of the family.

Family ARAUCARIACEAE	Species *Araucaria araucana*	Author (Molina) K. Koch

MONKEY PUZZLE

Leaves Ovate, to 2 in (5 cm) long and ¾ in (2 cm) wide, broad at the base, with a spiny tip, glossy dark green, overlapping, all around the shoot. **Bark** Gray, wrinkled. **Flowers** 4 in (10 cm) long, males brown, clustered, females green-brown, singly, on separate plants in summer. **Fruit** An ovoid, brown cone, to 6 in (15 cm) long.
• **NATIVE REGION** Argentina, Chile.
• **HABITAT** Mountains.

brown male flowers borne in clusters

rigid leaves end in sharp point

long, pointed cone scales

Height 164 ft (50 m)	Shape Unique	Leaf persistence Evergreen	Leaf type

CEPHALOTAXACEAE

ALTHOUGH FOSSIL EVIDENCE shows that this family was once widely distributed, it is now restricted in the wild to the Far East. The species in the only genus are small trees or large shrubs, with linear leaves and plum-like fruits. Male and female flowers are borne in clusters on separate plants.

Family CEPHALOTAXACEAE	Species *Cephalotaxus fortunei*	Author W.J. Hooker

CHINESE PLUM YEW

Leaves Linear, to 4 in (10 cm) long and ⅛ in (3 mm) across, pointed, glossy green above, with two whitish bands beneath, spreading either side of the shoot. **Bark** Red-brown and flaking. **Flowers** Males and females creamy yellow, on separate plants in spring. **Fruit** Oval, fleshy-coated, purple-brown, 1 in (2.5 cm) long.
• **NATIVE REGION** C. and E. China.
• **HABITAT** Mountain forests.

male flowers in leaf axils

each fleshy fruit contains a single seed

female flowers at shoot tip

Height 30 ft (9 m)	Shape Broadly spreading	Leaf persistence Evergreen	Leaf type

Family CEPHALOTAXACEAE	Species *Cephalotaxus harringtonia*	Author (Forbes) K. Koch

HARRINGTON PLUM-YEW

Leaves Linear, to 2 in (5 cm) long and ⅛ in (3 mm) across, pointed, glossy dark green above, with two bands beneath, spreading either side of shoot. *Bark* Brown, flaking. *Flowers* Creamy white, males in the leaf axils, females at the tips of the shoots, on separate plants in spring. *Fruit* An oval seed, 1 in (2.5 cm) long, blue-green ripening to purple-brown
• NATIVE REGION Japan.
• HABITAT Known only in cultivation.
• REMARK This species was originally described from a Japanese garden plant.

VAR. DRUPACEA ▷
This Japanese form has shorter leaves.

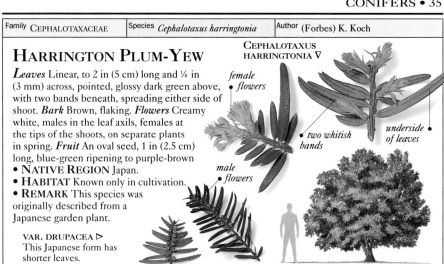

CEPHALOTAXUS HARRINGTONIA ▽

female flowers

two whitish bands

underside of leaves

male flowers

Height 20 ft (6 m)	Shape Broadly spreading	Leaf persistence Evergreen	Leaf type

CUPRESSACEAE

THIS FAMILY HAS ABOUT 20 genera, with more than 100 species of evergreen trees and shrubs, including the cypresses *(Cupressus,* see pp.41–43) and junipers *(Juniperus,* see pp.44–48), found worldwide. The small leaves are usually needlelike in young plants, but scalelike in mature trees; some juniper species bear both types. Male and female flowers are separate, on the same or different plants. The fruit is a cone, but is berrylike in junipers.

Family CUPRESSACEAE	Species *Austrocedrus chilensis*	Author (D. Don) Florin & Boutelje

CHILEAN CEDAR

Leaves Scalelike, to 3⁄16 in (5 mm) long, flattened, with a blunt point, glossy dark green sometimes marked with white above, with a conspicuous white band beneath, borne in flattened sprays; on upper and lower sides of shoot much smaller. *Bark* Gray-brown, scaly. *Flowers* Males and females both very small, males yellowish, females green, in small clusters at the tips of the shoots in early spring. *Fruit* An oblong cone, ⅜ in (1 cm) long, green ripening to brown, with four overlapping scales.
• NATIVE REGION Argentina, Chile.
• HABITAT Mountains.
• REMARK Also known as *Libocedrus chilensis.* It is closely related to the incense cedar *(Calocedrus decurrens,* see p.36).

flattened leaves spread out at tip

leaves banded with white on underside

Height 80 ft (25 m)	Shape Narrowly conical	Leaf persistence Evergreen	Leaf type

Family CUPRESSACEAE	Species *Calocedrus decurrens*	Author (Torrey) Florin

CALIFORNIA INCENSE CEDAR

Leaves Scalelike, to about ⅛ in (3 mm) long, in sets of two pairs together, with a triangular, sharp-pointed tip, glossy dark green, borne in flattened, aromatic sprays; upper and lower leaves largest. ***Bark*** Red-brown and scaly. ***Flowers*** Males and females both very small, males yellow, females green, in small clusters at the tips of the shoots in winter. ***Fruit*** An oblong, yellow-brown cone, 1 in (2.5 cm) long, with six overlapping scales.
• **NATIVE REGION** W. North America.
• **HABITAT** Forests on mountain slopes.
• **REMARK** Also known as *Libocedrus decurrens*. In the wild, old plants eventually become more open in shape. It produces a useful, very aromatic wood.

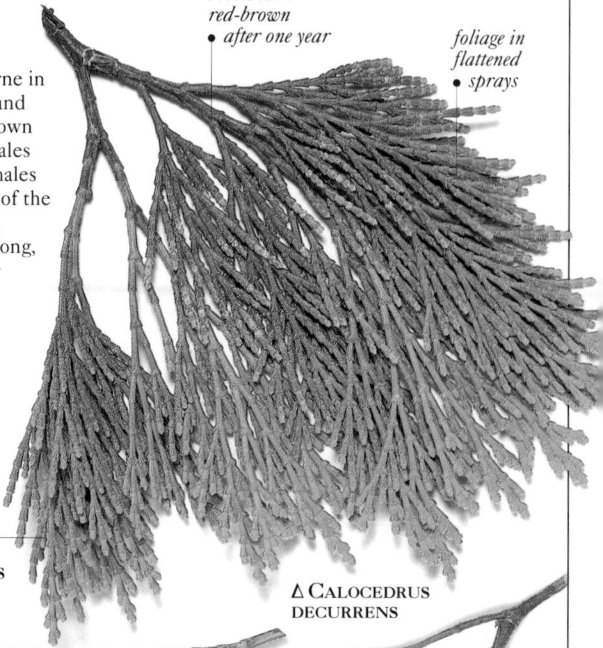

shoots turn red-brown after one year

foliage in flattened sprays

tiny leaves pressed close to shoot

∇ **CALOCEDRUS DECURRENS**

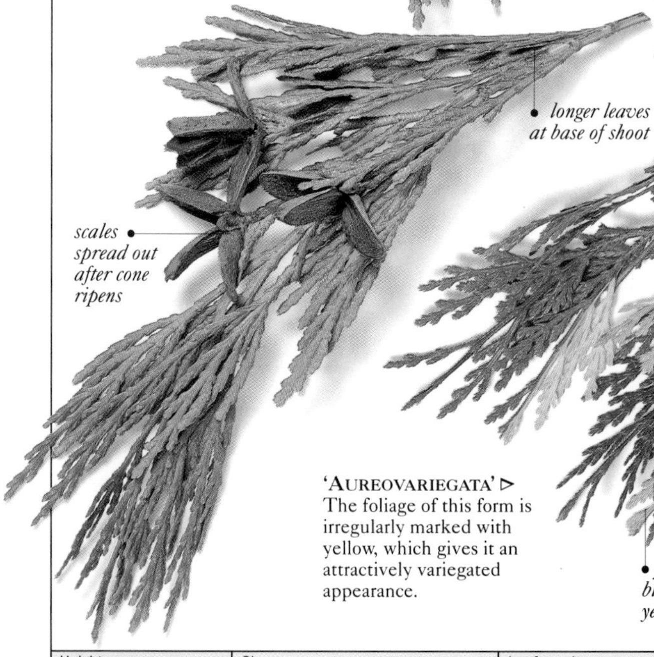

△ **CALOCEDRUS DECURRENS**

longer leaves at base of shoot

scales spread out after cone ripens

shoots may be colored half green, half cream

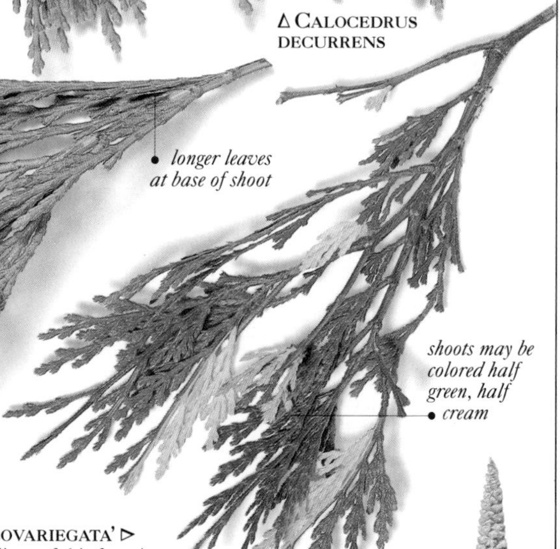

'AUREOVARIEGATA' ▷
The foliage of this form is irregularly marked with yellow, which gives it an attractively variegated appearance.

foliage irregularly blotched creamy yellow

Height 130 ft (40 m)	Shape Narrowly columnar	Leaf persistence Evergreen	Leaf type

Family CUPRESSACEAE	Species *Chamaecyparis lawsoniana*	Author (Murray) Parlatore

LAWSON CYPRESS

Leaves Scalelike, very small, pointed, the tip often slightly free from the shoot, dark green above, paler with white X-shaped marks where the leaves meet beneath, borne in flattened sprays. **Bark** Purple-brown and flaking. **Flowers** Males red, females bluish, in clusters at the tips of the shoots in early spring. **Fruit** A rounded cone, ⁵⁄₁₆ in (8 mm) across, with eight scales.
• **NATIVE REGION**
USA: N.W. California, S.W. Oregon.
• **HABITAT** Mountain slopes and canyons.

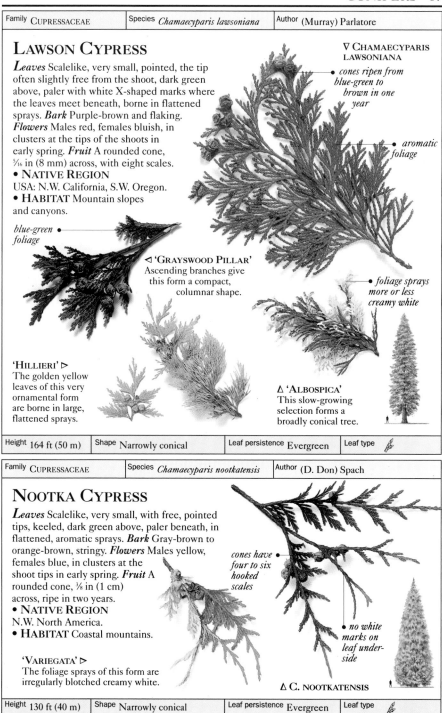

▽ CHAMAECYPARIS LAWSONIANA

cones ripen from blue-green to brown in one year

aromatic foliage

blue-green foliage

◁ 'GRAYSWOOD PILLAR'
Ascending branches give this form a compact, columnar shape.

foliage sprays more or less creamy white

'HILLIERI' ▷
The golden yellow leaves of this very ornamental form are borne in large, flattened sprays.

△ 'ALBOSPICA'
This slow-growing selection forms a broadly conical tree.

Height 164 ft (50 m)	Shape Narrowly conical	Leaf persistence Evergreen	Leaf type

Family CUPRESSACEAE	Species *Chamaecyparis nootkatensis*	Author (D. Don) Spach

NOOTKA CYPRESS

Leaves Scalelike, very small, with free, pointed tips, keeled, dark green above, paler beneath, in flattened, aromatic sprays. **Bark** Gray-brown to orange-brown, stringy. **Flowers** Males yellow, females blue, in clusters at the shoot tips in early spring. **Fruit** A rounded cone, ⅜ in (1 cm) across, ripe in two years.
• **NATIVE REGION**
N.W. North America.
• **HABITAT** Coastal mountains.

cones have four to six hooked scales

no white marks on leaf under-side

'VARIEGATA' ▷
The foliage sprays of this form are irregularly blotched creamy white.

△ C. NOOTKATENSIS

Height 130 ft (40 m)	Shape Narrowly conical	Leaf persistence Evergreen	Leaf type

| Family CUPRESSACEAE | Species *Chamaecyparis obtusa* | Author (Siebold & Zuccarini) Endlicher |

HINOKI CYPRESS

Leaves Scalelike, very small, blunt at the tip, dark green above, with bright white X- or Y-shaped marks where the leaves meet beneath, in flattened, aromatic sprays. *Bark* Red-brown and soft, peeling in thin strips. *Flowers* Males reddish yellow, females pale brown, in small clusters at the tips of the shoots in spring. *Fruit* A rounded cone, to ½ in (1.2 cm) across, green ripening to brown.
• NATIVE REGION Japan.
• HABITAT Usually mountain slopes.
• REMARK The cultivated forms include some of dwarf habit.

'CRIPPSII' ▷
The bright golden-yellow coloration of this ornamental form appears only on the outermost branches.

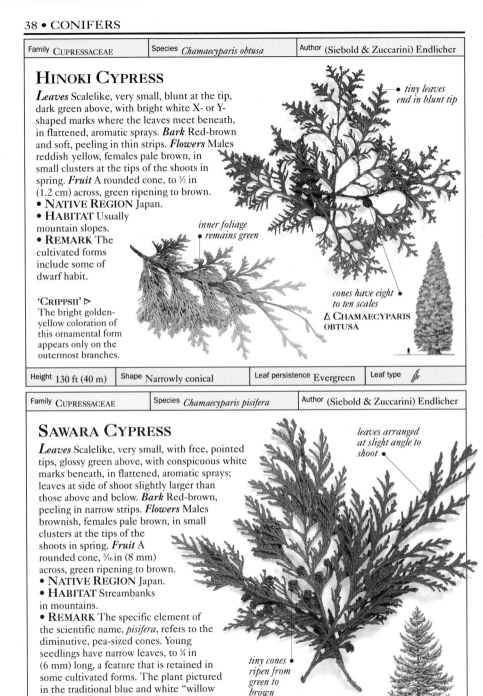

tiny leaves end in blunt tip

inner foliage remains green

cones have eight to ten scales
△ CHAMAECYPARIS OBTUSA

| Height 130 ft (40 m) | Shape Narrowly conical | Leaf persistence Evergreen | Leaf type |

| Family CUPRESSACEAE | Species *Chamaecyparis pisifera* | Author (Siebold & Zuccarini) Endlicher |

SAWARA CYPRESS

Leaves Scalelike, very small, with free, pointed tips, glossy green above, with conspicuous white marks beneath, in flattened, aromatic sprays; leaves at side of shoot slightly larger than those above and below. *Bark* Red-brown, peeling in narrow strips. *Flowers* Males brownish, females pale brown, in small clusters at the tips of the shoots in spring. *Fruit* A rounded cone, ⁵⁄₁₆ in (8 mm) across, green ripening to brown.
• NATIVE REGION Japan.
• HABITAT Streambanks in mountains.
• REMARK The specific element of the scientific name, *pisifera*, refers to the diminutive, pea-sized cones. Young seedlings have narrow leaves, to ¼ in (6 mm) long, a feature that is retained in some cultivated forms. The plant pictured in the traditional blue and white "willow" pattern" design on pottery and porcelain represents this species.

leaves arranged at slight angle to shoot

tiny cones ripen from green to brown

| Height 164 ft (50 m) | Shape Broadly conical | Leaf persistence Evergreen | Leaf type |

Family CUPRESSACEAE	Species *Chamaecyparis thyoides*	Author (L.) Britton, Sterns, Poggenberg

WHITE CYPRESS

Leaves Scalelike and very small, pointed at the tip, green to gray-green above, often with a tiny speck of resin, with bright white marks beneath, on slender shoots, in small, flattened, aromatic sprays; leaves at side of shoot slightly larger than those above. *Bark* Gray to brown, fibrous, peeling in strips. *Flowers* Males brownish, females green, in small clusters at the tips of the shoots in spring. *Fruit* A rounded cone, ¼ in (6 mm) across, glaucous ripening to brown, with six pointed scales.

• **NATIVE REGION**
E. United States.

• **HABITAT** Usually swamps, wet ground, and moist places.

• **REMARK** Also known as Atlantic white cedar, swamp cedar.

very small, pointed leaves

semi-ripe cone still whitish brown

typical coloration most striking on young foliage

very bloomy young cone

△ CHAMAECYPARIS THYOIDES

▽ 'VARIEGATA'
As the cultivar name indicates, this plant is a variegated form of the species. Its foliage sprays are blotched more or less pale yellow.

occasional shoots have yellow foliage

△ 'GLAUCA'
This form is distinguished by its foliage, which is noticeably bluish white to blue-gray. The cones are also more bloomy.

some foliage sprays may be colored bright green

Height 80 ft (25 m)	Shape Narrowly columnar	Leaf persistence Evergreen	Leaf type

Family CUPRESSACEAE	Species x *Cupressocyparis leylandii*	Author (Dallimore & Jackson) Dallimore

LEYLAND CYPRESS

Leaves Scalelike and very small, with pointed tips, dark green above, paler beneath, arranged at various angles to the shoot, borne in flattened sprays; leaves at side of and above shoot similar in size. *Bark* Red-brown, with shallow ridges. *Flowers* Males yellow, females green, in small clusters at the tips of the shoots in early spring. *Fruit* A rounded cone, to ¾ in (2 cm) across, blue-green ripening to glossy brown.

• **NATIVE REGION** Of garden origin.

• **REMARK** A hybrid between Nootka cypress *(Chamaecyparis nootkatensis*, see p.37) and Monterey cypress *(Cupressus macrocarpa*, see p.42). 'Haggerston Gray,' which has dull green foliage, is the form most commonly grown.

irregularly arranged leaves borne in sprays

dark green inner foliage

yellow-green outer foliage

△ 'HAGGERSTON GRAY'

yellow male flower clusters

cones ripen from blue-green to brown

△ 'CASTLEWELLAN GOLD'
Young specimens of this form exhibit bright yellow foliage. On older, mature plants, the color deepens to reddish bronze-yellow.

△ 'NAYLOR'S BLUE'
This form has foliage colored blue-gray to grayish green. It grows into a very narrowly columnar tree.

creamy white leaves borne on some shoots

some foliage sprays may remain almost entirely green

'SILVER DUST' ▷
This form originated in the United States, at the National Arboretum, Washington D.C.

Height 100 ft (30 m)	Shape Narrowly columnar	Leaf persistence Evergreen	Leaf type

| Family CUPRESSACEAE | Species *Cupressus cashmeriana* | Author Royle ex Carrière |

KASHMIR CYPRESS

Leaves Scalelike and very small, but with free, spreading tips making the foliage rough to the touch, borne in glaucous, drooping, flattened sprays. *Bark* Red-brown, peeling in vertical strips. *Flowers* Males and females both inconspicuous, in separate clusters on the same plant in early to midwinter. *Fruit* A rounded cone, ½ in (1.2 cm) across, blue-green becoming greenish-yellow ripening to brown, the scales each with a hooked point.
• **NATIVE REGION** Not known; probably Himalayas.
• **HABITAT** Now known only in cultivation.
• **REMARK** A particularly elegant tree of small to medium height. The habit becomes more spreading as it ages.

lax foliage appears noticeably blue-gray

greenish-yellow young cones become brown when ripe

branches carry long, weeping branchlets

| Height 65 ft (20 m) | Shape Narrowly weeping | Leaf persistence Evergreen | Leaf type |

| Family CUPRESSACEAE | Species *Cupressus glabra* | Author Sudworth |

SMOOTH ARIZONA CYPRESS

Leaves Scalelike and very small, with a pointed tip, blue-gray, with a minute fleck of white resin in the center on the underside, closely pressed to the stem, borne in irregular, aromatic sprays on reddish shoots. *Bark* Red-brown and red-purple, flaking in round patches. *Flowers* Males yellow and conspicuous, females green, in small clusters at the tips of the shoots, on the same plant in mid- to late winter. *Fruit* A rounded, gray-brown cone, to 1 in (2.5 cm) across, persisting on the branches for several years.
• **NATIVE REGION** Arizona.
• **HABITAT** Rocky mountain slopes.
• **REMARK** This species is commonly cultivated, and is usually found in the form 'Pyramidalis' with silvery-blue foliage and a dense habit. It is often found under the name of the similar, but much rarer, species *Cupressus arizonica*.

scales of cone closed over seeds

male flowers easily visible

| Height 65 ft (20 m) | Shape Narrowly conical | Leaf persistence Evergreen | Leaf type |

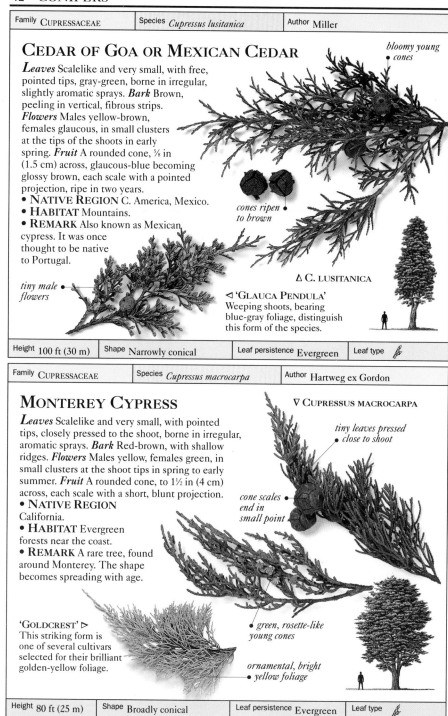

| Family CUPRESSACEAE | Species *Cupressus lusitanica* | Author Miller |

CEDAR OF GOA OR MEXICAN CEDAR

Leaves Scalelike and very small, with free, pointed tips, gray-green, borne in irregular, slightly aromatic sprays. *Bark* Brown, peeling in vertical, fibrous strips. *Flowers* Males yellow-brown, females glaucous, in small clusters at the tips of the shoots in early spring. *Fruit* A rounded cone, ⅗ in (1.5 cm) across, glaucous-blue becoming glossy brown, each scale with a pointed projection, ripe in two years.
• **NATIVE REGION** C. America, Mexico.
• **HABITAT** Mountains.
• **REMARK** Also known as Mexican cypress. It was once thought to be native to Portugal.

bloomy young cones

cones ripen to brown

△ **C. LUSITANICA**

tiny male flowers

◁ **'GLAUCA PENDULA'**
Weeping shoots, bearing blue-gray foliage, distinguish this form of the species.

| Height 100 ft (30 m) | Shape Narrowly conical | Leaf persistence Evergreen | Leaf type |

| Family CUPRESSACEAE | Species *Cupressus macrocarpa* | Author Hartweg ex Gordon |

MONTEREY CYPRESS

Leaves Scalelike and very small, with pointed tips, closely pressed to the shoot, borne in irregular, aromatic sprays. *Bark* Red-brown, with shallow ridges. *Flowers* Males yellow, females green, in small clusters at the shoot tips in spring to early summer. *Fruit* A rounded cone, to 1½ in (4 cm) across, each scale with a short, blunt projection.
• **NATIVE REGION** California.
• **HABITAT** Evergreen forests near the coast.
• **REMARK** A rare tree, found around Monterey. The shape becomes spreading with age.

▽ **CUPRESSUS MACROCARPA**

tiny leaves pressed close to shoot

cone scales end in small point

green, rosette-like young cones

'GOLDCREST' ▷
This striking form is one of several cultivars selected for their brilliant golden-yellow foliage.

ornamental, bright yellow foliage

| Height 80 ft (25 m) | Shape Broadly conical | Leaf persistence Evergreen | Leaf type |

| Family CUPRESSACEAE | Species *Cupressus sempervirens* | Author Linnaeus |

ITALIAN CYPRESS

Leaves Scalelike and very small, with blunt tips, very dark green, with no white marks beneath, only slightly aromatic or with no scent, borne in irregular sprays, closely pressed to the shoots. *Bark* Gray-brown, with shallow, spiral ridges. *Flowers* Males yellow-brown, females green, in small clusters at the tips of the shoots in spring. *Fruit* An egg-shaped to rounded cone, to 1½ in (4 cm) long, green ripening to brown, the scales overlapping, each scale with a small projection.
• **NATIVE REGION** S.W. Asia, E. Mediterranean.
• **HABITAT** Rocky places in mountains.
• **REMARK** The narrow form known as 'Stricta' is so commonly planted along the Mediterranean that it forms a characteristic feature of the landscape.

small, blunt leaves carried on short branchlets

branchlets arranged all around shoot

△ **CUPRESSUS SEMPERVIRENS**

dense, bright green foliage sprays change to yellow at tip

green unripe cone covered in smooth scales

cones ripen from glossy green to brown

hooked point in center of cone scales

'SWANE'S GOLDEN' ▷
This form, which was raised in Australia, grows slowly, becoming a small, compact tree of very narrow habit. The yellow-tipped foliage sprays give the plant an overall golden appearance.

| Height 164 ft (50 m) | Shape Narrowly columnar | Leaf persistence Evergreen | Leaf type 🌿 |

Family CUPRESSACEAE	Species *Fitzroya cupressoides*	Author (Molina) Johnston

PATAGONIAN CYPRESS

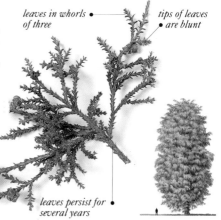

leaves in whorls
of three

tips of leaves
are blunt

Leaves Oblong and thick, to ⅛ in (3 mm) long, bluntly pointed, in whorls of three, dark green, with two white bands on each side, on slender, pendulous shoots. **Bark** Red-brown, peeling in long, vertical strips. **Flowers** Males yellow, females yellow-green, borne in small clusters at the tips of the shoots in spring. **Fruit** A rounded, brown cone, 5⁄16 in (8 mm) across.
• **NATIVE REGION** Argentina, Chile.
• **HABITAT** Mountains.
• **REMARK** Very rare. Also known as alerce, Fitzroy cypress. Scientifically named after the captain in whose ship Charles Darwin voyaged to South America.

leaves persist for
several years

Height 164 ft (50 m)	Shape Broadly columnar	Leaf persistence Evergreen	Leaf type

Family CUPRESSACEAE	Species *Juniperus chinensis*	Author Linnaeus

CHINESE JUNIPER

sharp-pointed
juvenile leaves

Leaves Adults scalelike and very small, with blunt tips, in irregular, aromatic sprays, closely pressed to the shoot; juveniles needlelike, to 5⁄16 in (8 mm) long, sharp-pointed, opposite or in whorls of three, green, with two glaucous bands on the upper surface, at the base of the shoots. **Bark** Red-brown, peeling in vertical strips. **Flowers** Males yellow, females small and purple-green, in small clusters at the tips of the shoots, on separate plants in spring. **Fruit** A berrylike glaucous cone, to 5⁄16 in (8 mm) long.
• **NATIVE REGION** China, Japan.
• **HABITAT** Hills and mountains.
• **REMARK** Although both adult and juvenile foliage are usually present on individual plants, some trees may have either one type or the other. The species can be shrubby. It has many cultivated forms.

J. CHINENSIS

'AUREA' ▷
This form, known as Young's golden juniper, has golden yellow foliage.

adult foliage
has scalelike
leaves

Height 80 ft (25 m)	Shape Narrowly conical	Leaf persistence Evergreen	Leaf type

Family CUPRESSACEAE	Species *Juniperus communis*	Author Linnaeus

COMMON JUNIPER

Leaves Needlelike and slender, to ½ in (1.2 cm) long, in whorls of three, sharp-pointed, glossy green, with a broad white band on the upper surface. *Bark* Red-brown, peeling in thin, vertical strips. *Flowers* Males yellow, females small and green, in small clusters in the leaf axils, on separate plants in spring. *Fruit* A berrylike cone, ¼ in (6 mm) long, green becoming glaucous-bloomed ripening to glossy black.
• **NATIVE REGION** Temperate zones of the northern hemisphere.
• **HABITAT** Open places, from coastal rocks to high mountains.
• **REMARK** The species is variable: it can be a prostrate and creeping plant, a bushy shrub, or sometimes a tree. The berries give gin its characteristic taste. They are also used as a culinary flavoring.

all leaves needlelike •

• *young green cones mature to black*

• *leaves banded with white above*

Height 20 ft (6 m)	Shape Narrowly conical	Leaf persistence Evergreen	Leaf type

Family CUPRESSACEAE	Species *Juniperus deppeana*	Author Steudel

ALLIGATOR JUNIPER

Leaves Scalelike and small, to ⅛ in (3 mm) long, bright green, with a conspicuous speck of white resin on the back and two white bands toward the base, pressed to the shoot at the base, free at the tip and ending in a sharp point, making the foliage rough to the touch, aromatic when crushed. *Bark* Dark gray, deeply cut into small, oblong plates. *Flowers* Inconspicuous. *Fruit* A berrylike, red-brown, bloomy cone, to ⅜ in (1.5 cm) across.
• **NATIVE REGION** Mexico, S.W. United States.
• **HABITAT** Rocky slopes in high mountains.
• **REMARK** Also known as *Juniperus deppeana* var. *pachyphlaea*. It is easily distinguished by its characteristically checkered bark.

tiny leaves have free tips •

• *foliage appears blue-gray*

leaves have white specks of resin •

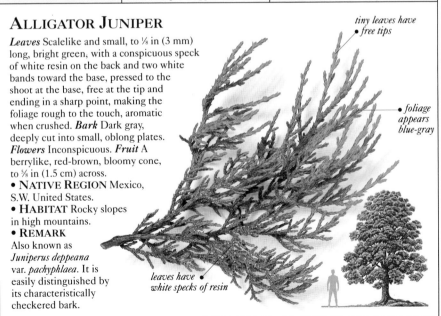

Height 50 ft (15 m)	Shape Broadly conical	Leaf persistence Evergreen	Leaf type

Family CUPRESSACEAE	Species *Juniperus drupacea*	Author Labillardière

SYRIAN JUNIPER

Leaves Needlelike, rigid, and slender, to 1 in (2.5 cm) long, in whorls of three, sharp-pointed, marked with two broad, whitish bands above with a green midrib and margin, glossy green and ridged beneath, spreading from three-angled shoots. *Bark* Orange-brown, peeling in thin, vertical strips. *Flowers* Males yellow, females very small and green, borne in small clusters at the tips of short, leafy shoots, on separate plants in spring. *Fruit* A very large, berrylike, bloomy cone, 1 in (2.5 cm) long, blue-green at first becoming brown ripening to blackish purple, the triangular scales ending in a pointed tip.
• **NATIVE REGION**
S.W. Asia, Greece.
• **HABITAT** Mountain forests.
• **REMARK** The species is easily distinguished by its leaves, which are broader than those of any other juniper. The large cones are seen only rarely in cultivated plants.

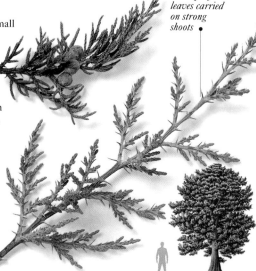

• *two whitish bands on upper surface of leaves*

distinctive, unusually • *large cones*

Height 33 ft (10 m)	Shape Narrowly columnar	Leaf persistence Evergreen	Leaf type

Family CUPRESSACEAE	Species *Juniperus occidentalis*	Author W.J. Hooker

WESTERN JUNIPER

Leaves Scalelike and small, in threes, minutely toothed, gray-green, with a small gland beneath, closely pressed to stout shoots; on vigorous shoots sharp-pointed and free. *Bark* Red-brown, furrowed, and flaking. *Flowers* Males yellow, females green, in small clusters at the tips of the shoots, usually on separate plants in spring. *Fruit* A rounded to egg-shaped, berrylike, bloomy, blue-black cone, to ⅜ in (1 cm) long, ripe in two years.
• **NATIVE REGION**
W. United States.
• **HABITAT** Rocky slopes and dry soil in mountains.
• **REMARK** The toothed leaf margin can be seen only under magnification. In the Sierra Nevada mountain range in California, specimens of this species that are more than 2,000 years old can be found growing out of solid rock.

some spiny leaves carried on strong shoots •

Height 65 ft (20 m)	Shape Broadly conical	Leaf persistence Evergreen	Leaf type

| Family CUPRESSACEAE | Species *Juniperus oxycedrus* | Author Linnaeus |

PRICKLY JUNIPER

Leaves Needlelike and slender, to 1 in (2.5 cm) long, spreading in whorls of three, sharp-pointed, green above, with two glaucous bands beneath. *Bark* Purple-brown, flaking in vertical strips. *Flowers* Males yellow, females green, borne in small clusters in the leaf axils, on separate plants in spring. *Fruit* A berrylike cone, ½ in (1.2 cm) across, bloomy ripening red to purple.
• NATIVE REGION S.W. Asia, S. Europe.
• HABITAT Dry hills and woods.
• REMARK Also known as cade. Oil of cade, traditionally used to treat skin ailments, is obtained from the wood. In the Balearic Islands, where the common juniper (*Juniperus communis*, see p.45) does not grow, prickly juniper berries are used instead as a substitute for flavoring gin.

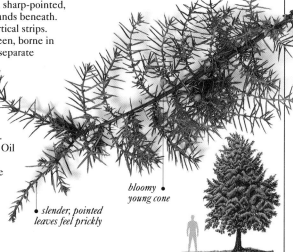

bloomy young cone

slender, pointed leaves feel prickly

| Height 33 ft (10 m) | Shape Broadly conical | Leaf persistence Evergreen | Leaf type |

| Family CUPRESSACEAE | Species *Juniperus recurva* | Author Buchanan-Hamilton ex D. Don |

DROOPING JUNIPER

Leaves Needlelike and slender, to ¼ in (6 mm) long, in whorls of three, sharp-pointed, matte gray-green above, with two white bands beneath, dry and papery to touch, pointing forward along drooping shoots. *Bark* Red-brown, peeling in vertical strips. *Flowers* Males yellow, females green, borne in small clusters at the tips of the shoots, on the same plant in spring. *Fruit* A berrylike, glossy, blue-black cone, to ⁵⁄₁₆ in (8 mm) long.
• NATIVE REGION S.W. China, Himalayas.
• HABITAT High mountains.
• REMARK Also known as Himalayan juniper. *Juniperus recurva* var. *coxii*, shown here, has slightly more spreading leaves, on drooping shoots.

needlelike leaves point forward

cones resemble black berries

shoots are slender and drooping

JUNIPERUS RECURVA VAR. COXII

| Height 50 ft (15 m) | Shape Narrowly conical | Leaf persistence Evergreen | Leaf type |

| Family CUPRESSACEAE | Species *Juniperus scopulorum* | Author Sargent |

ROCKY MOUNTAIN JUNIPER

Leaves Scalelike, very small, green to gray-blue, closely pressed to the shoot. **Bark** Red-brown, peeling in thin strips. **Flowers** Males yellow, females green, in small clusters at the tips of the shoots, usually on the same plant in spring. **Fruit** A berrylike cone, ¼ in (6 mm) across, blue-black with a glaucous bloom, ripe in two years.
• **NATIVE REGION** W. North America.
• **HABITAT** Woods and rocky soil in mountains.
• **REMARK** Also known as Colorado red cedar, river juniper, Rocky Mountain red cedar. 'Skyrocket,' shown here, is the best-known cultivated garden form. This species, which resembles a cypress, gives its name to Cypress Island in Washington State, where it grows abundantly.

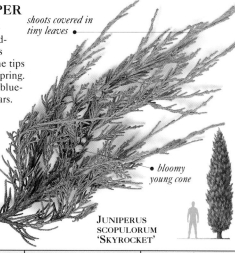

shoots covered in tiny leaves •

• *bloomy young cone*

JUNIPERUS
SCOPULORUM
'SKYROCKET'

| Height 40 ft (12 m) | Shape Narrowly conical | Leaf persistence Evergreen | Leaf type |

| Family CUPRESSACEAE | Species *Juniperus virginiana* | Author Linnaeus |

EASTERN RED CEDAR

Leaves Both juvenile and adult foliage usually present; adult leaves scalelike and very small, pointed, usually green to blue-green, closely pressed to the shoot; juvenile leaves needlelike, to ¼ in (6 mm) long, usually in pairs, sharp-pointed, gray-green above, glaucous beneath, at the tips of the shoots. **Bark** Red-brown, peeling in vertical strips.
Flowers Males yellow, females green, in small clusters at the tips of the shoots, usually on separate plants in spring.
Fruit A berrylike, glaucous, bloomy cone, ¼ in (6 mm) long, ripe in one year.
• **NATIVE REGION** E. North America.
• **HABITAT** Woods and rocky slopes.
• **REMARK** Also known as pencil cedar and red cedar. Widely distributed and planted. Its wood is used to make pencils.

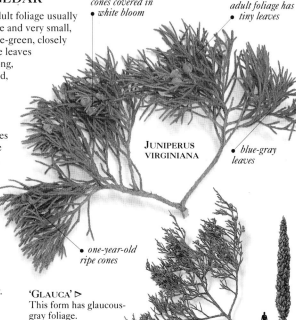

cones covered in • *white bloom*

adult foliage has • *tiny leaves*

JUNIPERUS
VIRGINIANA

• *blue-gray leaves*

• *one-year-old ripe cones*

'GLAUCA' ▷
This form has glaucous-gray foliage.

| Height 100 ft (30 m) | Shape Narrowly columnar | Leaf persistence Evergreen | Leaf type |

Family CUPRESSACEAE	Species *Thuja koraiensis*	Author Nakai

KOREAN ARBORVITAE

Leaves Scalelike and small, bright green above, with bright silvery marks beneath, in flattened sprays, aromatic when crushed. *Bark* Red-brown, peeling in thin scales. *Flowers* Males green, with black tips, females green, in separate clusters at the ends of the shoots, on the same plant in spring. *Fruit* An oblong, upright cone, ⅜ in (1 cm) long, yellow-green ripening to brown, with eight scales.
• **NATIVE REGION** N.E. China, Korea.
• **HABITAT** Mountain woods.
• **REMARK** This species can be either a small tree or a dense shrub.

bright green leaf upperside

bright white markings on leaf underside

small gland on leaf surface contains aromatic oil

Height 33 ft (10 m)	Shape Narrowly conical	Leaf persistence Evergreen	Leaf type

Family CUPRESSACEAE	Species *Thuja occidentalis*	Author Linnaeus

AMERICAN ARBORVITAE

Leaves Scalelike and very small, glossy yellowish green above, paler with no white marks beneath, borne in flattened, aromatic sprays, on flat shoots. *Bark* Orange-brown, peeling in vertical strips. *Flowers* Males red, females yellow-brown, in separate clusters at the ends of the shoots, on the same plant in spring. *Fruit* An oblong, upright cone, ⅜ in (1 cm) long, yellow-green ripening to brown, with eight to ten scales.
• **NATIVE REGION** E. North America.
• **HABITAT** Rocky mountain slopes, often on limestone, and swamps.
• **REMARK** Also known as white cedar. The species was one of the first North American trees to be grown in Europe. In cultivation, it has given rise to innumerable selections, including ornamental forms with colored foliage, and many of dwarf habit.

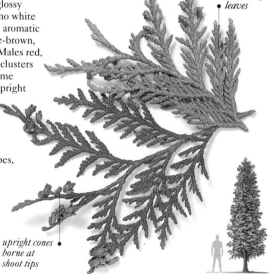

matte green underside of leaves

upright cones borne at shoot tips

Height 65 ft (20 m)	Shape Narrowly conical	Leaf persistence Evergreen	Leaf type

Family CUPRESSACEAE	Species *Thuja plicata*	Author D. Don

WESTERN RED CEDAR

Leaves Scalelike, very small, glossy green above, with white marks beneath, in flattened, aromatic sprays. **Bark** Purplish brown, peeling vertically. **Flowers** Males red-black opening yellow, females yellow-green, in separate clusters at the ends of the shoots, on the same plant in spring. **Fruit** An ovoid, upright cone, ½ in (1.2 cm) long, yellow-green ripening to brown.
• **NATIVE REGION** N.W. North America.
• **HABITAT** Mountains.

striped yellow and green foliage •

• white, X-shaped marks on underside of leaves

• larger branchlets have slightly longer leaves

each tiny • cone has about ten scales

△ THUJA PLICATA

◁ 'ZEBRINA'
Alternate bands of green and yellow foliage give this form a variegated appearance.

Height 164 ft (50 m)	Shape Narrowly conical	Leaf persistence Evergreen	Leaf type

Family CUPRESSACEAE	Species *Thuja standishii*	Author (Gordon) Carrière

JAPANESE ARBORVITAE

bright yellowish green upperside of leaves •

Leaves Scalelike and very small, bluntly pointed at the tip, yellow-green above, paler with small, whitish marks beneath, in flattened, drooping, aromatic sprays, on flat shoots. **Bark** Red-brown, peeling in strips and plates. **Flowers** Males blackish red opening yellow, females greenish, in separate clusters at the tips of the shoots, on the same plant in spring. **Fruit** An oblong, upright cone, ⅜ in (1 cm) long, green ripening to red-brown, with about ten scales.
• **NATIVE REGION** Japan.
• **HABITAT** Rocky mountain ridges and moors.
• **REMARK** When crushed, the foliage has a particularly sweet scent.

very small • brown cones at tip of shoots

paler green, whitish • underside of leaves

Height 65 ft (20 m)	Shape Broadly conical	Leaf persistence Evergreen	Leaf type

Family CUPRESSACEAE	Species *Thujopsis dolabrata*	Author (Linnaeus f.) Siebold & Zuccarini

HIBA (FALSE ARBORVITAE)

Leaves Scalelike, to ¼ in (6 mm) long, glossy dark green to yellow-green above, in flattened sprays, on broad, flat shoots. **Bark** Purple-brown, flaking in thin, vertical strips. **Flowers** Males blackish green, females blue-gray, in separate clusters at the ends of the shoots, on the same plant in spring. **Fruit** A brown, bloomy cone, ½ in (1.2 cm) long.
• NATIVE REGION Japan.
• HABITAT Moist mountain forests.

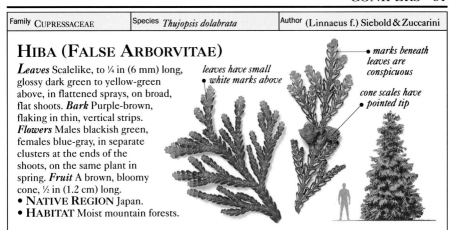

leaves have small white marks above

marks beneath leaves are conspicuous

cone scales have pointed tip

Height 65 ft (20 m)	Shape Broadly conical	Leaf persistence Evergreen	Leaf type

GINKGOACEAE

A LTHOUGH THIS FAMILY HAS only a single member with no closely related species, fossil records show that similar plants were at one time – between approximately 150 and 200 million years ago – widely distributed in all parts of the world. The species, usually classed as a conifer, is in fact the sole survivor of a group of plants more primitive than the true conifers.

Family GINKGOACEAE	Species *Ginkgo biloba*	Author Linnaeus

MAIDENHAIR TREE

Leaves Fan-shaped, about 3 in (7.5 cm) long, often variously notched and with numerous veins diverging from the base, matte green, turning bright yellow in autumn, carried singly on long shoots, clustered on short side shoots. **Bark** Gray-brown, ridged and fissured. **Flowers** Males and females both small and yellow-green, males in catkinlike clusters, females singly or in pairs on a short stalk, on separate plants in spring. **Fruit** A fleshy, plumlike seed, yellow-green ripening to orange-brown, the kernel edible.
• NATIVE REGION China.
• HABITAT Only in cultivation.
• REMARK The rotting fruit has a particularly unpleasant smell.

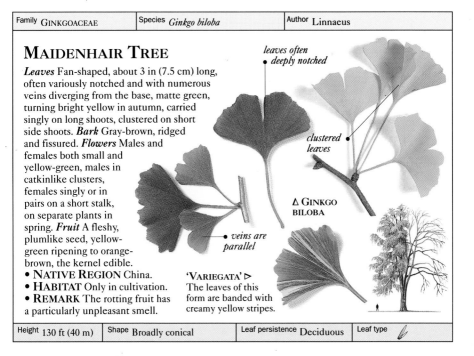

leaves often deeply notched

clustered leaves

△ GINKGO BILOBA

veins are parallel

'VARIEGATA' ▷
The leaves of this form are banded with creamy yellow stripes.

Height 130 ft (40 m)	Shape Broadly conical	Leaf persistence Deciduous	Leaf type

PINACEAE

THIS FAMILY INCLUDES THE silver firs *(Abies,* see pp.52–57), larches *(Larix,* see pp.60–61), and pines *(Pinus,* see pp.66–75). About 200 species of trees and shrubs, in ten genera, grow mainly in northern temperate regions. The species of larch and *Pseudolarix* (see p.76) are deciduous. The flowers are borne separately on the same plant; females develop into a woody cone.

Family PINACEAE	Species *Abies alba*	Author Miller

SILVER FIR

Leaves Linear, to 1¼ in (3 cm) long, with a notched tip, glossy dark green above, with two whitish bands beneath, spreading either side of the shoot, shorter and pointing forward above. *Bark* Gray and smooth, cracking into small plates with age. *Flowers* Males yellow, beneath the shoot, females green, upright, borne in separate clusters on the same plant in spring. *Fruit* A cylindrical, upright cone, to 6 in (15 cm) long, green at first ripening to brown, with protruding, down-turned bracts.
• **NATIVE REGION** Europe.
• **HABITAT** Mountain forests.
• **REMARK** Also known as European silver fir. Cones usually grow only high on the tree. This species is widely used as a Christmas tree in many parts of Europe.

notch at tip of leaves

male flowers open to yellow

cone bracts project outward

white bands on underside of leaves

Height 130 ft (40 m)	Shape Narrowly conical	Leaf persistence Evergreen	Leaf type

Family PINACEAE	Species *Abies bracteata*	Author (D. Don) Nuttall

BRISTLECONE FIR

Leaves Needlelike and rigid, to 2 in (5 cm) long, ending in a very sharp point, glossy dark green above, with two white bands beneath, spreading either side of the shoot. *Bark* Dark gray and smooth. *Flowers* Males yellowish, beneath the shoot, females green, upright, borne in separate clusters on the same plant in spring. *Fruit* An egg-shaped, upright cone, to 4 in (10 cm) long, green ripening to brown, with conspicuously long, bristly bracts.
• **NATIVE REGION** California.
• **HABITAT** Evergreen forests on mountain slopes.
• **REMARK** Also known as Santa Lucia fir. It is the rarest native North American fir.

two white bands on underside of leaves

pointed leaf bud

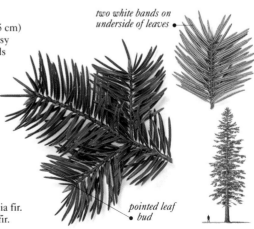

Height 115 ft (35 m)	Shape Narrowly conical	Leaf persistence Evergreen	Leaf type

Family PINACEAE	Species *Abies cephalonica*	Author Loudon

GREEK FIR

Leaves Linear and rigid, to 1¼ in (3 cm) long, sharp-pointed, glossy dark green above, with two white bands beneath, all around the shoot. *Bark* Dark gray, cracking into small, square plates. *Flowers* Males reddish opening yellow, beneath the shoot, females green, upright, in separate clusters on the same plant in spring. *Fruit* A brown, upright cone, to 6 in (15 cm) long, cylindrical narrowing at either end, with protruding, downturned bracts.
• **NATIVE REGION** S.E. Europe.
• **HABITAT** Mountains.

leaves end in sharp point

two white bands on underside of leaves

Height 100 ft (30 m)	Shape Narrowly conical	Leaf persistence Evergreen	Leaf type

Family PINACEAE	Species *Abies concolor*	Author (Gordon) Lindley

WHITE FIR

Leaves Linear, to 2½ in (6 cm) long, with a blunt tip, blue-gray or gray-green, spreading beneath the shoot, upswept above. *Bark* Gray, smooth, becoming scaly with age. *Flowers* Males yellow, beneath the shoot, females greenish-yellow, upright, in separate clusters on the same plant in spring. *Fruit* A cylindrical, upright cone, to 4 in (10 cm) long, green to purple ripening to brown.
• **NATIVE REGION** W. United States.
• **HABITAT** Mountain slopes.
• **REMARK** Also known as Colorado fir.

male flower clusters hang under shoot

same color on both sides of leaves

Height 130 ft (40 m)	Shape Narrowly conical	Leaf persistence Evergreen	Leaf type

Family PINACEAE	Species *Abies forrestii*	Author Rogers

ABIES FORRESTII

Leaves Linear, to 1½ in (4 cm) long, with a notched tip, very dark green above, spreading beneath the shoot, densely arranged above. *Bark* Gray, smooth. *Flowers* Males purple opening yellow, beneath the shoot, females purple, upright, in separate clusters on the same plant in spring. *Fruit* An upright cone, to 4 in (10 cm) long, broadly cylindrical with a flat top, deep purple ripening to purple-brown, with small, protruding, downturned bracts.
• **NATIVE REGION** W. China, S.E. Tibet.
• **HABITAT** High mountains.

purple female flower clusters

male flowers

bright bands on underside of leaves

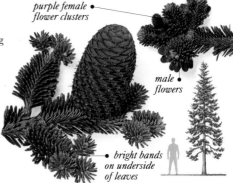

Height 65 ft (20 m)	Shape Narrowly conical	Leaf persistence Evergreen	Leaf type

Family PINACEAE	Species *Abies grandis*	Author (Douglas) Lindley

GIANT FIR

Leaves Linear and slender, to 2 in (5 cm) long, with a notched tip, bright green above, with two white bands beneath, spreading either side of the shoot. *Bark* Gray-brown, smooth, cracking with age. *Flowers* Males reddish opening yellow, females green, upright, in separate clusters on the same plant in spring. *Fruit* A cylindrical, upright cone, to 4 in (10 cm) long, green ripening to brown.
• **NATIVE REGION** W. North America.
• **HABITAT** Evergreen forests on low mountain slopes.

small leaf bud at end of shoot •

• *leaves spread either side of shoot*

Height 164 ft (50 m)	Shape Narrowly conical	Leaf persistence Evergreen	Leaf type

Family PINACEAE	Species *Abies homolepis*	Author Siebold & Zuccarini

NIKKO FIR

Leaves Linear, to 1¼ in (3 cm) long, with a notched tip, glossy dark green and bloomy at least when young above, with two broad white bands beneath, spreading either side of the shoot. *Bark* Gray tinged pink, scaly with age. *Flowers* Males reddish opening yellow-green, beneath the shoot, females purplish red, upright, in separate clusters on the same plant in spring. *Fruit* A cylindrical, upright cone, to 4 in (10 cm) long, purple-blue ripening to brown.
• **NATIVE REGION** Japan.
• **HABITAT** Mountain forests.

notch at tip of leaves •

underside of leaves

Height 100 ft (30 m)	Shape Narrowly conical	Leaf persistence Evergreen	Leaf type

Family PINACEAE	Species *Abies koreana*	Author Wilson

KOREAN FIR

Leaves Linear, to ¾ in (2 cm) long, rounded to notched at the tip, dark green above, with two white bands or all white beneath, densely arranged above the shoot, spreading beneath. *Bark* Dark gray-brown. *Flowers* Males yellow, beneath the shoot, females reddish purple, upright, borne in separate clusters on the same plant in spring. *Fruit* A cylindrical, upright cone, to 3 in (7.5 cm) long, with protruding, down-curved bracts.
• **NATIVE REGION** S. Korea.
• **HABITAT** Mountains.

• *underside of leaves often almost entirely white*

young plants bear purple cones

Height 50 ft (15 m)	Shape Narrowly conical	Leaf persistence Evergreen	Leaf type

Family PINACEAE	Species *Abies lasiocarpa*	Author (W.J. Hooker) Nuttall

ALPINE FIR

Leaves Linear, to 1½ in (4 cm) long, with a notched tip, gray-green above, with two white bands beneath, arranged upright above the shoot, the central leaves pointing forward, spreading beneath. *Bark* Gray-white, smooth, with resin blisters. *Flowers* Males tinged red opening yellow, beneath the shoot, females purple, upright, in separate clusters on the same plant in spring. *Fruit* A cylindrical, upright cone, to 4 in (10 cm) long, deep purple ripening to brown.
• **NATIVE REGION** W. North America.
• **HABITAT** From sea level to the mountains.

ABIES LASIOCARPA ▷

VAR. ARIZONICA ▷
This form, commonly known as the corkbark fir, comes from the south of the region. It is distinguished by its bluer leaves and corky bark.

two narrow, white bands on underside of leaves

Height 100 ft (30 m)	Shape Narrowly conical	Leaf persistence Evergreen	Leaf type

Family PINACEAE	Species *Abies magnifica*	Author Murray

CALIFORNIA RED FIR

Leaves Linear, to 1½ in (4 cm) long, bluntly pointed, gray-green, arranged upright above the shoot, spreading to upswept beneath. *Bark* Gray, rough, corky; red in very old plants. *Flowers* Males purple-red, beneath the shoot, females red, upright, in separate clusters on the same plant in spring. *Fruit* A broadly cylindrical, upright cone, 8 in (20 cm) or more long, purple at first becoming yellow-green ripening to brown.
• **NATIVE REGION** California, S. Oregon.
• **HABITAT** Dry mountain slopes and ridges.
• **REMARK** Also known as red fir.

leaves sweep upward from shoot •

Height 130 ft (40 m)	Shape Narrowly conical	Leaf persistence Evergreen	Leaf type

Family PINACEAE	Species *Abies nordmanniana*	Author (Steven) Spach

CAUCASIAN FIR

Leaves Linear, to 1½ in (4 cm) long, with a notched tip, glossy bright green above, with two white bands beneath, dense above the shoot, spreading beneath. **Bark** Gray and smooth, cracking into small, square plates with age. **Flowers** Males reddish, beneath the shoot, females green, upright, in separate clusters on the same plant in spring. **Fruit** A broadly cylindrical upright cone, to 6 in (15 cm) long, green ripening to purple-brown, with protruding, down-curved bracts.
• **NATIVE REGION** Caucasus, N.E. Turkey.
• **HABITAT** Mountain forests.

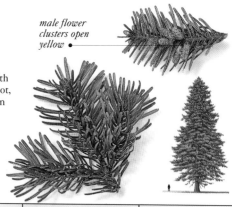

male flower clusters open yellow •

Height 164 ft (50 m)	Shape Broadly conical	Leaf persistence Evergreen	Leaf type

Family PINACEAE	Species *Abies numidica*	Author Carrière

ALGERIAN FIR

Leaves Linear and rigid, to ¾ in (2 cm) long, rounded or notched at the tip, dark gray-green above, with a small whitish patch toward the tip, with two white bands beneath, densely arranged all around the shoot, upright above, spreading beneath. **Bark** Gray-purple, smooth, flaking with age. **Flowers** Males tinged red opening yellow, beneath the shoot, females green, upright, in separate clusters on the same plant in spring. **Fruit** A cylindrical, upright cone, to 7¼ in (18 cm) long, purple-green ripening to brown, ending in an abrupt point.
• **NATIVE REGION** Algeria.
• **HABITAT** Mountains near the coast.
• **REMARK A** rare species in the wild. It is closely related to the Spanish fir *(Abies pinsapo, see p.57).*

• green female flower clusters

cones end in • blunt tip

purplish green • young cones ripen to brown

short, stubby, blunt-pointed leaves •

conspicuous white • bands on underside of leaves

• upper leaf surface is marked white toward tip

Height 80 ft (25 m)	Shape Narrowly conical	Leaf persistence Evergreen	Leaf type

Family PINACEAE	Species *Abies pinsapo*	Author Boissier

SPANISH FIR

Leaves Linear and rigid, to ¼ in (2 cm) long, bluntly pointed, gray-green to gray-blue, densely arranged and standing out all around the shoot. **Bark** Dark gray, cracking into small plates with age. **Flowers** Males red opening yellow, beneath the shoot, females green, upright, borne in separate clusters on the same plant in spring. **Fruit** A cylindrical upright cone, to 6 in (15 cm) long, green ripening to brown.
• **NATIVE REGION** S. Spain.
• **HABITAT** Dry mountain slopes.

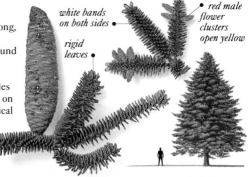

white bands on both sides •

rigid leaves •

• red male flower clusters open yellow

Height 80 ft (25 m)	Shape Broadly conical	Leaf persistence Evergreen	Leaf type

Family PINACEAE	Species *Abies procera*	Author Rehder

NOBLE FIR

Leaves Linear, to 1¼ in (3 cm) long, bluntly pointed, grooved above, gray-green to gray-blue. **Bark** Pale silvery gray or purplish, shallowly fissured with age. **Flowers** Males red tinged yellow, beneath the shoot, females reddish or green, upright, in separate clusters on the same plant in spring. **Fruit** A broadly cylindrical, purple-brown, upright cone, to 10 in (25 cm) long, with protruding, downcurved bracts.
• **NATIVE REGION** W. United States.
• **HABITAT** West-facing mountain slopes.

• whitish bands on both sides of leaves

Height 164 ft (50 m)	Shape Narrowly conical	Leaf persistence Evergreen	Leaf type

Family PINACEAE	Species *Abies veitchii*	Author Lindley

ABIES VEITCHII

Leaves Linear, to 1¼ in (3 cm) long, with a notched tip, glossy dark green above, with two blue-white bands beneath, dense and pointing forward along the shoot, spreading beneath. **Bark** Gray, smooth, scaly with age. **Flowers** Males reddish opening yellow, beneath the shoot, females red-purple, upright, in separate clusters on the same plant in late spring. **Fruit** A cylindrical, upright cone, to 3 in (7.5 cm) long, blue-purple ripening to brown.
• **NATIVE REGION** Japan.
• **HABITAT** Evergreen mountain forests.

bright bands on underside of leaves •

• bracts are paler brown at tip

Height 80 ft (25 m)	Shape Narrowly conical	Leaf persistence Evergreen	Leaf type

Family PINACEAE	Species *Cedrus atlantica*	Author Manetti

ATLAS CEDAR

Leaves Needlelike and slender, to ¾ in (2 cm) long, borne singly on long shoots, in dense whorls on very slow-growing, shorter side shoots, sharp-pointed, gray-green to dark green, on hairy shoots. *Bark* Dark gray on old trees fissured into scaly plates. *Flowers* Males yellow, females green, both carried upright, in separate clusters on the same plant in autumn. *Fruit* A barrel-shaped upright cone, to 3 in (7.5 cm) long, green-purple when young becoming purple-brown ripening to brown, ripe in two to three years, breaking up before falling.
• **NATIVE REGION** Algeria, Morocco.
• **HABITAT** Forests.
• **REMARK** The species is sometimes listed as a geographical subspecies of the cedar of Lebanon (*Cedrus libani*, see p.59), from which it is usually most easily distinguished by its habit. In the wild, it is found only in North Africa's Atlas Mountains, a mountain range that lies between the Mediterranean and the Sahara.

male flower clusters open • in autumn

• leaves borne singly on long shoots

CEDRUS ATLANTICA

cones break up • before falling

leaves whorled • on side shoots

△ **F. GLAUCA**
The blue cedar is the form most commonly seen in gardens. It has bright gray-blue foliage.

Height 130 ft (40 m)	Shape Broadly conical	Leaf persistence Evergreen	Leaf type

Family PINACEAE	Species *Cedrus brevifolia*	Author Henry

CYPRIAN CEDAR

Leaves Needlelike, to ¾ in (2 cm) long, borne singly on long shoots, in dense whorls on slow-growing side shoots, dark green. *Bark* Dark gray; cracking into vertical plates. *Flowers* Males blue-green, females green, both carried upright, in separate clusters on the same plant in autumn. *Fruit* A cylindrical upright cone, to 2¾ in (7 cm) long, purple-green at first ripening to brown.
• **NATIVE REGION** Cyprus.
• **HABITAT** Mountains.
• **REMARK** Short leaves distinguish this species from the closely related cedar of Lebanon (*Cedrus libani*, see p.59).

cones turn brown when • ripe

whorled leaves • are very short

Height 65 ft (20 m)	Shape Broadly conical	Leaf persistence Evergreen	Leaf type

Family PINACEAE	Species *Cedrus deodara*	Author G. Don

DEODAR

Leaves Needlelike, to 1½ in (4 cm) long, borne singly on long shoots, in dense whorls on slow-growing side shoots, green to gray-green, the shoots drooping conspicuously at the tip. **Bark** Dark gray, cracking vertically with age. **Flowers** Males purple opening yellow, upright, females green, upright, borne in separate clusters on the same plant in autumn. **Fruit** A barrel-shaped upright cone, to 4¾ in (12 cm) long, green ripening to purple-brown.
• **NATIVE REGION** W. Himalayas.
• **HABITAT** Mountain forests.
• **REMARK** Also known as Himalayan cedar.

longish leaves •

some leaves borne singly •

• *green unripe cones mature to brown*

male flower clusters open yellow •

whorled leaves on short side shoots •

Height 164 ft (50 m)	Shape Broadly conical	Leaf persistence Evergreen	Leaf type

Family PINACEAE	Species *Cedrus libani*	Author A. Richard

CEDAR OF LEBANON

Leaves Needlelike, to 1¼ in (3 cm) long, borne singly on long shoots, in dense whorls on slow-growing side shoots, dark green to gray-blue. **Bark** Dark gray, cracking into vertical plates. **Flowers** Males blue-green opening yellow, upright, females green, upright, borne in separate clusters on the same plant in autumn. **Fruit** A barrel-shaped upright cone, to 4¾ in (12 cm) long, purple-green ripening to brown.
• **NATIVE REGION** Lebanon, S.W. Turkey.
• **HABITAT** Mountain forests.
• **REMARK** Old plants of this species have a distinctive characteristic: the foliage is carried in broad, flattened sprays of branches, and is held on several massive stems.

shorter leaves borne in dense whorls •

leaf color varies from green to gray-blue •

• *open flowers release yellow pollen*

long shoots carry single leaves •

Height 130 ft (40 m)	Shape Broadly columnar	Leaf persistence Evergreen	Leaf type

Family PINACEAE	Species *Larix decidua*	Author Miller

EUROPEAN LARCH

Leaves Needlelike and soft, to 1½ in (4 cm) long, singly on long shoots, in dense whorls on side shoots, bright green, turning yellow in autumn. *Bark* Gray becoming red-brown, fissured, and scaly. *Flowers* Males yellow, drooping, females red, upright, in separate clusters on the same plant in spring. *Fruit* An egg-shaped, brown, upright cone, about 1½ in (4 cm) long.
• **NATIVE REGION** Europe.
• **HABITAT** Mountains.

cones develop from female flowers

yellow male flower clusters

cones have upright scales

Height 130 ft (40 m)	Shape Narrowly conical	Leaf persistence Deciduous	Leaf type

Family PINACEAE	Species *Larix* x *eurolepis*	Author Henry

DUNKELD LARCH

Leaves Needlelike, soft, gray-green to green. *Bark* Reddish brown, scaly. *Flowers* Males yellow, drooping, females red, upright, in separate clusters on the same plant in spring. *Fruit* An egg-shaped, brown, upright cone, to 1¼ in (3 cm) long.
• **NATIVE REGION** Of garden origin.
• **REMARK** A hybrid between the European larch *(Larix decidua,* see above) and the Japanese larch *(Larix kaempferi,* see below).

red female flower clusters

orange-brown shoots

cone scales spread slightly

Height 115 ft (35 m)	Shape Broadly conical	Leaf persistence Deciduous	Leaf type

Family PINACEAE	Species *Larix kaempferi*	Author (A.B. Lambert) Carrière

JAPANESE LARCH

Leaves Needlelike and soft, to 1½ in (4 cm) long, singly on long shoots, whorled on side shoots, gray-green to blue-green. *Bark* Reddish brown, scaly. *Flowers* Males yellow, drooping, females creamy or pinkish, upright, in separate clusters on the same plant in spring. *Fruit* An egg-shaped, upright cone, to 1¼ in (3 cm)
• **NATIVE REGION** C. Japan.
• **HABITAT** Mountains.

cone scales turn outward

female flowers borne in larger clusters

male flower clusters

variable leaves may be blue-green

Height 100 ft (30 m)	Shape Broadly conical	Leaf persistence Deciduous	Leaf type

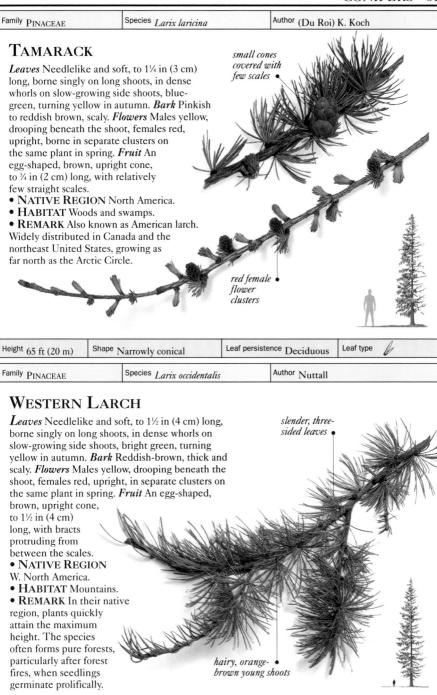

Family PINACEAE	Species *Larix laricina*	Author (Du Roi) K. Koch

TAMARACK

Leaves Needlelike and soft, to 1¼ in (3 cm) long, borne singly on long shoots, in dense whorls on slow-growing side shoots, blue-green, turning yellow in autumn. **Bark** Pinkish to reddish brown, scaly. **Flowers** Males yellow, drooping beneath the shoot, females red, upright, borne in separate clusters on the same plant in spring. **Fruit** An egg-shaped, brown, upright cone, to ¾ in (2 cm) long, with relatively few straight scales.
• **NATIVE REGION** North America.
• **HABITAT** Woods and swamps.
• **REMARK** Also known as American larch. Widely distributed in Canada and the northeast United States, growing as far north as the Arctic Circle.

small cones covered with few scales •

red female • flower clusters

Height 65 ft (20 m)	Shape Narrowly conical	Leaf persistence Deciduous	Leaf type

Family PINACEAE	Species *Larix occidentalis*	Author Nuttall

WESTERN LARCH

Leaves Needlelike and soft, to 1½ in (4 cm) long, borne singly on long shoots, in dense whorls on slow-growing side shoots, bright green, turning yellow in autumn. **Bark** Reddish-brown, thick and scaly. **Flowers** Males yellow, drooping beneath the shoot, females red, upright, in separate clusters on the same plant in spring. **Fruit** An egg-shaped, brown, upright cone, to 1½ in (4 cm) long, with bracts protruding from between the scales.
• **NATIVE REGION** W. North America.
• **HABITAT** Mountains.
• **REMARK** In their native region, plants quickly attain the maximum height. The species often forms pure forests, particularly after forest fires, when seedlings germinate prolifically.

slender, three-sided leaves •

hairy, orange-brown young shoots

Height 164 ft (50 m)	Shape Narrowly conical	Leaf persistence Deciduous	Leaf type

| Family PINACEAE | Species *Picea abies* | Author (Linnaeus) Karsten |

NORWAY SPRUCE

Leaves Needlelike, slender, and rigid, to ¾ in (2 cm) long, four-sided, with a sharp point at the tip, dark green, spreading beneath smooth, brown shoots. *Bark* Red-brown to gray, peeling in thin strips. *Flowers* Males red opening yellowish, females red, borne in separate, upright clusters on the same plant in spring. *Fruit* A cylindrical, brown, hanging cone, to 6 in (15 cm) long.
• **NATIVE REGION** Europe.
• **HABITAT** Mountain forests, on damp soil.
• **REMARK** This important species has many varieties and cultivars. It is widely planted for the commercial value of its timber.

• *pointed, four-sided leaves*

cone scales • have cut-off or toothed tip

female flowers develop into • cones

• underside of leaves

• male flower clusters fall after releasing pollen

| Height 164 ft (50 m) | Shape Narrowly conical | Leaf persistence Evergreen | Leaf type |

| Family PINACEAE | Species *Picea breweriana* | Author Watson |

BREWER SPRUCE

Leaves Needlelike, slender, often curved, to 1¼ in (3 cm) long, flattened, blunt, dark green, with two whitish bands beneath, arranged all around the shoot. *Bark* Gray-purple, scaly with age. *Flowers* Males red opening yellowish, females red or green, in separate clusters on the same plant in spring. *Fruit* A narrowly cylindrical, brown, hanging cone, to 4¾ in (12 cm) long.
• **NATIVE REGION** N. California, S. Oregon.
• **HABITAT** Mountains.

leaves borne • on vertically hanging shoots

• cones covered with broad, round-ended scales

| Height 115 ft (35 m) | Shape Narrowly weeping | Leaf persistence Evergreen | Leaf type |

Family PINACEAE	Species *Picea glauca*	Author (Moench) Voss

WHITE SPRUCE

Leaves Needlelike, slender, and rigid, to ⅗ in (1.5 cm) long, four-sided, blue-green, with white bands, densely arranged pointing forward above smooth, nearly white shoots. **Bark** Gray-brown and scaly. **Flowers** Males red opening yellow, females purple-red, borne in separate clusters on the same plant in spring. **Fruit** A cylindrical, pale brown, hanging cone, to 2½ in (6 cm) long.
• **NATIVE REGION** Canada, N.E. United States.
• **HABITAT** Woods.

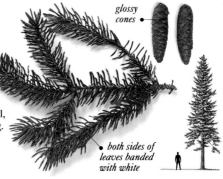

glossy cones •

• both sides of leaves banded with white

Height 100 ft (30 m)	Shape Narrowly conical	Leaf persistence Evergreen	Leaf type

Family PINACEAE	Species *Picea jezoensis*	Author (Siebold & Zuccarini) Carrière

YEZO SPRUCE

Leaves Needlelike and slender, to ⅗ in (1.5 cm) long, flattened, dark green above, with two broad, white bands beneath, pointing forward above smooth, pale shoots, spreading beneath. **Bark** Gray-brown, flaking and deeply fissured. **Flowers** Males reddish, females purple-red, in separate clusters on the same plant in spring. **Fruit** A cylindrical, red-brown, hanging cone, to 3 in (7.5 cm) long.
• **NATIVE REGION** N.E. Asia, Japan.
• **HABITAT** Subalpine forests on steep slopes and dry plateaus.

▽ VAR. HONDOENSIS

female flowers

• wavy-margined cone scales

green unripe cone

Height 164 ft (50 m)	Shape Narrowly conical	Leaf persistence Evergreen	Leaf type

Family PINACEAE	Species *Picea likiangensis*	Author (Franchet) Pritzel

PICEA LIKIANGENSIS

Leaves Needlelike and slender, to ⅗ in (1.5 cm) long, sharp at the tip, blue-green above, blue-white beneath, pointing forward above usually hairy, pale brown shoots, spreading beneath. **Bark** Pale gray and scaly, fissured with age. **Flowers** Males and females both profuse, males red opening yellowish, females bright red, in separate clusters on the same plant in spring. **Fruit** A cylindrical, hanging cone, to 4 in (10 cm) long, purple ripening to pale brown.
• **NATIVE REGION** W. China, Tibet.
• **HABITAT** Mountain woods.

female flower clusters •

toothed cone • scales

Height 100 ft (30 m)	Shape Broadly conical	Leaf persistence Evergreen	Leaf type

Family PINACEAE	Species *Picea mariana*	Author (Miller) B.S.P.

BLACK SPRUCE

Leaves Needlelike and slender, to ⅝ in (1.5 cm) long, four-sided, bluntly pointed, blue-green above, blue-white beneath, borne all around hairy, yellow-brown shoots. **Bark** Gray-brown and flaking. **Flowers** Males and females both red, in separate clusters on the same plant in spring. **Fruit** An egg-shaped, red-brown, hanging cone, to 1½ in (4 cm) long.
• **NATIVE REGION** Canada, N.E. United States.
HABITAT Mountain slopes and bogs.

rigid leaves are four-sided •

unusually short cones

Height 100 ft (30 m)	Shape Narrowly conical	Leaf persistence Evergreen	Leaf type

Family PINACEAE	Species *Picea omorika*	Author (Pančić) Purkyně

SERBIAN SPRUCE

Leaves Needlelike and slender, to ¾ in (2 cm) long, flattened, glossy dark green above, most lying above but some all around hairy, pale brown shoots. **Bark** Purple-brown, cracking into square plates. **Flowers** Males and females both red, borne in separate clusters on the same plant in spring. **Fruit** A narrowly egg-shaped, purple-brown, hanging cone, to 2½ in (6 cm) long.
• **NATIVE REGION** Bosnia-Herzegovina/Yugoslavia.
• **HABITAT** Near River Drina, on limestone.

leaves spread out from shoots •

bluish white bands on underside of • leaves

Height 100 ft (30 m)	Shape Narrowly conical	Leaf persistence Evergreen	Leaf type

Family PINACEAE	Species *Picea orientalis*	Author (Linnaeus) Link

ORIENTAL SPRUCE

Leaves Needlelike, to ⁵⁄₁₆ in (8 mm) long, four-sided, bluntly pointed at the tip, glossy dark green, pointing forward all around hairy, whitish to pale brown shoots. **Bark** Pinkish brown, flaking in small plates. **Flowers** Males red opening yellow, females red, in separate clusters on the same plant in spring. **Fruit** A cylindrical, hanging cone, to 4 in (10 cm) long, purple ripening to brown.
• **NATIVE REGION** Caucasus, N.E. Turkey.
• **HABITAT** Mountain forests.

rigid, blunt- • pointed leaves

PICEA ▷ ORIENTALIS

cone • marked with resin

◁ 'AUREA'
This form has bright yellow young foliage.

Height 164 ft (50 m)	Shape Narrowly conical	Leaf persistence Evergreen	Leaf type

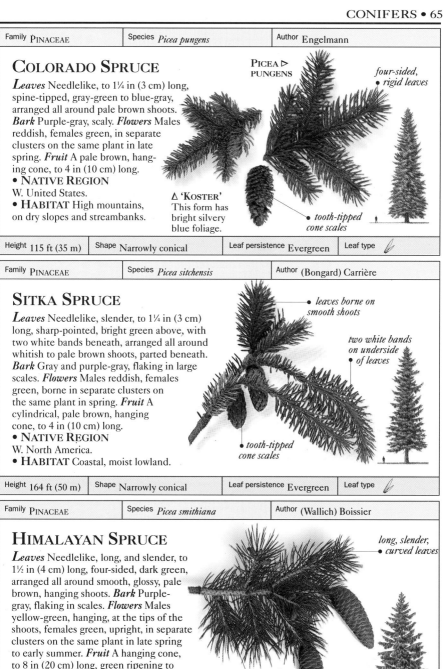

Family PINACEAE	Species *Picea pungens*	Author Engelmann

COLORADO SPRUCE

PICEA ▷
PUNGENS

four-sided,
• *rigid leaves*

Leaves Needlelike, to 1¼ in (3 cm) long, spine-tipped, gray-green to blue-gray, arranged all around pale brown shoots. **Bark** Purple-gray, scaly. **Flowers** Males reddish, females green, in separate clusters on the same plant in late spring. **Fruit** A pale brown, hanging cone, to 4 in (10 cm) long.
• **NATIVE REGION**
W. United States.
• **HABITAT** High mountains, on dry slopes and streambanks.

△ 'KOSTER'
This form has
bright silvery
blue foliage.

• *tooth-tipped*
cone scales

Height 115 ft (35 m)	Shape Narrowly conical	Leaf persistence Evergreen	Leaf type

Family PINACEAE	Species *Picea sitchensis*	Author (Bongard) Carrière

SITKA SPRUCE

• *leaves borne on*
smooth shoots

Leaves Needlelike, slender, to 1¼ in (3 cm) long, sharp-pointed, bright green above, with two white bands beneath, arranged all around whitish to pale brown shoots, parted beneath. **Bark** Gray and purple-gray, flaking in large scales. **Flowers** Males reddish, females green, borne in separate clusters on the same plant in spring. **Fruit** A cylindrical, pale brown, hanging cone, to 4 in (10 cm) long.
• **NATIVE REGION**
W. North America.
• **HABITAT** Coastal, moist lowland.

two white bands
on underside
• *of leaves*

• *tooth-tipped*
cone scales

Height 164 ft (50 m)	Shape Narrowly conical	Leaf persistence Evergreen	Leaf type

Family PINACEAE	Species *Picea smithiana*	Author (Wallich) Boissier

HIMALAYAN SPRUCE

long, slender,
• *curved leaves*

Leaves Needlelike, long, and slender, to 1½ in (4 cm) long, four-sided, dark green, arranged all around smooth, glossy, pale brown, hanging shoots. **Bark** Purple-gray, flaking in scales. **Flowers** Males yellow-green, hanging, at the tips of the shoots, females green, upright, in separate clusters on the same plant in late spring to early summer. **Fruit** A hanging cone, to 8 in (20 cm) long, green ripening to glossy brown.
• **NATIVE REGION** W. Himalayas.
• **HABITAT** High evergreen forests.

• *very pale-*
colored
shoots

Height 130 ft (40 m)	Shape Narrowly weeping	Leaf persistence Evergreen	Leaf type

Family PINACEAE	Species *Pinus ayacahuite*	Author Ehrenberg

MEXICAN WHITE PINE

Leaves Needlelike and slender, to 6 in (15 cm) long, in clusters of five, blue-green, borne on finely hairy, yellow-brown shoots. **Bark** Gray, rough and coarsely fissured. **Flowers** Males yellow, females red, in separate clusters on the shoots in early summer. **Fruit** A cylindrical, yellow-brown, resinous, hanging cone, to 18 in (45 cm) long, with purple-tipped scales.
• **NATIVE REGION** N. Guatemala, Mexico.
• **HABITAT** Mountain slopes.

long, often curved leaves droop on shoots

◁ VAR. VEITCHII

Height 115 ft (35 m)	Shape Broadly conical	Leaf persistence Evergreen	Leaf type

Family PINACEAE	Species *Pinus bungeana*	Author Zuccarini

LACE-BARK PINE

Leaves Needlelike and rigid, to 3 in (7.5 cm) long, in clusters of three, with a sharp point at the tip, yellow-green, borne on smooth, gray-green shoots. **Bark** Gray-green and creamy white, flaking in small patches. **Flowers** Males yellow, females green, borne in separate clusters on the young shoots in early summer. **Fruit** An egg-shaped, yellow-brown cone, to 2¾ in (7 cm) long, with spine-tipped scales.
• **NATIVE REGION** N. China.
• **HABITAT** Mainly steep mountain slopes, on shale.

sparsely arranged clusters of three leaves

small, squat cones

Height 65 ft (20 m)	Shape Broadly conical	Leaf persistence Evergreen	Leaf type

Family PINACEAE	Species *Pinus cembra*	Author Linnaeus

SWISS STONE PINE

Leaves Needlelike, to 3½ in (9 cm) long, in clusters of three, glossy green on the outer surface, blue-gray on the inner, on greenish shoots, the shoots covered in orange-brown hairs. **Bark** Gray-brown and scaly. **Flowers** Males purple opening yellow, females red, in separate clusters on the young shoots in late spring. **Fruit** An egg-shaped cone, to 3 in (7.5 cm) long, blue-purple ripening to red-brown, never opening fully.
• **NATIVE REGION** N. Asia, Europe.
• **HABITAT** Mountains.
• **REMARK** Also known as Arolla pine.

densely bunched leaf clusters

Height 65 ft (20 m)	Shape Narrowly columnar	Leaf persistence Evergreen	Leaf type

Family PINACEAE	Species *Pinus contorta*	Author Loudon

BEACH PINE

Leaves Needlelike and twisted, to 2 in (5 cm) long, in pairs, densely arranged, dark green or yellow-green, on smooth, green-brown shoots. *Bark* Red-brown, fissured into small squares. *Flowers* Males yellow, females red, in separate clusters on the young shoots in late spring. *Fruit* An egg-shaped, pale brown cone, pointing backward along the shoot, to 2 in (5 cm) long, the scales with slender spines.
• **NATIVE REGION** W. North America.
• **HABITAT** Coastal dunes and bogs.
• **REMARK** Also known as shore pine. Widely distributed from Alaska to Mexico. The lodgepole pine, var. *latifolia*, can reach 100 ft (30 m) in mountain habitats.

cone scales tipped with spines •

P. CONTORTA

female • flower clusters
∇ PINUS CONTORTA

male flower • clusters

shorter • cone

one-year cones still green •

longer leaves •

◁ VAR. LATIFOLIA

Height 33 ft (10 m)	Shape Broadly conical	Leaf persistence Evergreen	Leaf type

Family PINACEAE	Species *Pinus coulteri*	Author D. Don

BIG-CONE PINE

Leaves Needlelike and stiff, to 12 in (30 cm) long, in clusters of three, gray-green, on very stout, bloomy shoots. *Bark* Purple-brown, scaly, deeply fissured. *Flowers* Males purple opening yellow, females red, borne in separate clusters on the young shoots in late spring to early summer. *Fruit* An egg-shaped, yellow-brown, resinous cone, to 12 in (30 cm) long, the scales ending in hooked spines, usually remaining closed for many years.
• **NATIVE REGION** California.
• **HABITAT** Dry, rocky slopes in the mountains.

cone scales end in stout, hooked point •

long stiff needles in clusters of • three

Height 80 ft (25 m)	Shape Broadly spreading	Leaf persistence Evergreen	Leaf type

Family PINACEAE	Species *Pinus densiflora*	Author Siebold & Zuccarini

JAPANESE RED PINE

Leaves Needlelike and slender, to 4 in (10 cm) long, in pairs, bright green, pointing forward, on smooth, green shoots. **Bark** Reddish-brown becoming gray-red, cracking into irregular plates with age. **Flowers** Males yellow-brown, females red, in separate clusters on the young shoots in late spring. **Fruit** A conical, pale brown cone, to 2 in (5 cm) long, ripe in two years.
• **NATIVE REGION**
N.E. China, Japan, Korea.
• **HABITAT** Sea level to mountains.

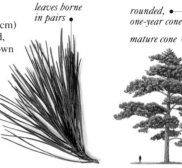

leaves borne in pairs

rounded, one-year cone

mature cone

Height 115 ft (35 m)	Shape Broadly spreading	Leaf persistence Evergreen	Leaf type

Family PINACEAE	Species *Pinus x holfordiana*	Author Jackson

PINUS X HOLFORDIANA

Leaves Needlelike, slender, to 7¼ in (18 cm) long, in clusters of five, the outer surface bright green, the inner surface blue-gray, borne on hairy, green shoots. **Bark** Gray and fissured. **Flowers** Males yellow, females red, in separate clusters on the young shoots in early summer. **Fruit** A resinous, orange-brown, hanging cone, to 12 in (30 cm) long.
• **NATIVE REGION** Of garden origin.
• **REMARK** A hybrid between Mexican white pine *(Pinus ayacahuite* var. *veitchii*, see p.66) and Himalayan pine *(Pinus wallichiana*, see p.75).

resinous cone scales darken toward tip

leaves borne five together

Height 80 ft (25 m)	Shape Broadly conical	Leaf persistence Evergreen	Leaf type

Family PINACEAE	Species *Pinus jeffreyi*	Author Murray

JEFFREY PINE

Leaves Needlelike, rigid, to 10 in (25 cm) long, in clusters of three, blue-green, on stout, smooth, bloomy shoots. **Bark** Dark gray-brown, with deep, narrow fissures. **Flowers** Males red opening yellow, females red-purple, in separate clusters on the young shoots in early summer. **Fruit** A conical, yellow-brown cone, to 12 in (30 cm) long, the scales each with a slender, curved spine.
• **NATIVE REGION** W. United States.
• **HABITAT** Dry slopes on high mountains.
• **REMARK** Closely related to western yellow pine *(Pinus ponderosa*, see p.73).

sharp-pointed leaves borne in clusters of three

bloomy young shoot

Height 130 ft (40 m)	Shape Broadly conical	Leaf persistence Evergreen	Leaf type

Family PINACEAE	Species *Pinus koraiensis*	Author Siebold & Zuccarini

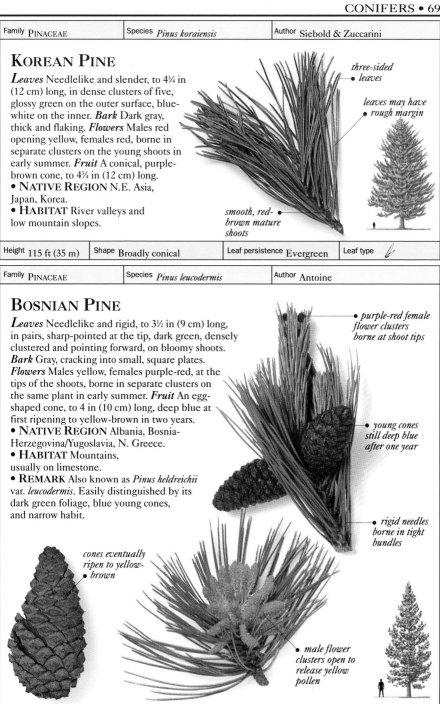

KOREAN PINE

Leaves Needlelike and slender, to 4¾ in (12 cm) long, in dense clusters of five, glossy green on the outer surface, blue-white on the inner. **Bark** Dark gray, thick and flaking. **Flowers** Males red opening yellow, females red, borne in separate clusters on the young shoots in early summer. **Fruit** A conical, purple-brown cone, to 4¾ in (12 cm) long.
• **NATIVE REGION** N.E. Asia, Japan, Korea.
• **HABITAT** River valleys and low mountain slopes.

three-sided leaves

leaves may have rough margin

smooth, red-brown mature shoots

Height 115 ft (35 m)	Shape Broadly conical	Leaf persistence Evergreen	Leaf type

Family PINACEAE	Species *Pinus leucodermis*	Author Antoine

BOSNIAN PINE

Leaves Needlelike and rigid, to 3½ in (9 cm) long, in pairs, sharp-pointed at the tip, dark green, densely clustered and pointing forward, on bloomy shoots. **Bark** Gray, cracking into small, square plates. **Flowers** Males yellow, females purple-red, at the tips of the shoots, borne in separate clusters on the same plant in early summer. **Fruit** An egg-shaped cone, to 4 in (10 cm) long, deep blue at first ripening to yellow-brown in two years.
• **NATIVE REGION** Albania, Bosnia-Herzegovina/Yugoslavia, N. Greece.
• **HABITAT** Mountains, usually on limestone.
• **REMARK** Also known as *Pinus heldreichii* var. *leucodermis*. Easily distinguished by its dark green foliage, blue young cones, and narrow habit.

purple-red female flower clusters borne at shoot tips

young cones still deep blue after one year

rigid needles borne in tight bundles

cones eventually ripen to yellow-brown

male flower clusters open to release yellow pollen

Height 80 ft (25 m)	Shape Narrowly conical	Leaf persistence Evergreen	Leaf type

| Family PINACEAE | Species *Pinus monophylla* | Author Torrey & Frémont |

ONE-LEAVED NUT PINE

Leaves Needlelike, curved, and rigid, to 2 in (5 cm) long, tapered to a sharp point, borne singly, gray-green to blue-green, on stout, orange shoots. **Bark** Gray, with narrow ridges. **Flowers** Males yellow, females red, in separate clusters on the young shoots in early summer. **Fruit** A cone, to 2¼ in (5.5 cm) long, green ripening to gray-brown.
• **NATIVE REGION** N. Mexico, S.W. United States.
• **HABITAT** Dry, rocky, mountain slopes and ridges.
• **REMARK** Also known as *P. cembroides* var. *monophylla.* Easily distinguished by its singly borne needles; most pines bear their needles in clusters of two or more.

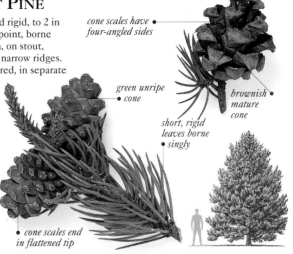

cone scales have four-angled sides

green unripe cone

brownish mature cone

short, rigid leaves borne singly

• cone scales end in flattened tip

| Height 50 ft (15 m) | Shape Broadly conical | Leaf persistence Evergreen | Leaf type |

| Family PINACEAE | Species *Pinus montezumae* | Author A.B. Lambert |

MONTEZUMA PINE

Leaves Needlelike, to 12 in (30 cm) long, borne usually in clusters of five, minutely toothed and slightly rough at the margin, gray-green, spreading in brushlike clusters, on stout, smooth, red-brown shoots. **Bark** Gray, thick and deeply furrowed. **Flowers** Males purple opening yellow, females red, in separate clusters on the young shoots in early summer. **Fruit** A conical to egg-shaped cone, to 6 in (15 cm) long, blue-purple ripening to yellow-brown or red-brown, with prickle-tipped scales, borne singly or in clusters.
• **NATIVE REGION** Guatemala, Mexico.
• **HABITAT** Mountains.
• **REMARK** Named after Montezuma II, the early sixteenth-century Aztec emperor of Mexico.

• foliage borne in dense bunches at end of shoots

• bluish unripe cone

leaves borne • usually five together

| Height 65 ft (20 m) | Shape Broadly spreading | Leaf persistence Evergreen | Leaf type |

Family PINACEAE	Species *Pinus muricata*	Author D. Don

BISHOP PINE

Leaves Needlelike and stiff, to 6 in (15 cm) long, in pairs, gray-green or blue-green, on orange-brown shoots. *Bark* Purple-brown, thick, furrowed and ridged. *Flowers* Males yellow, females red, in separate clusters on the young shoots in early summer. *Fruit* An egg-shaped red-brown cone, to 3¼ in (8 cm) long, oblique at the base, borne in whorls, persisting for many years.
• **NATIVE REGION** California.
• **HABITAT** Low hills in coastal areas.

• *paired leaves spread in untidy clusters*

prickle-tipped cone scales

Height 80 ft (25 m)	Shape Broadly columnar	Leaf persistence Evergreen	Leaf type

Family PINACEAE	Species *Pinus nigra*	Author Arnold

AUSTRIAN PINE

Leaves Needlelike and stiff, to 6 in (15 cm) long, in pairs, sharp-pointed, dark green, on stout, glossy brown shoots. *Bark* Nearly black, scaly. *Flowers* Males yellow, females red, borne in separate clusters on the young shoots in late spring to early summer. *Fruit* An egg-shaped brown cone, to 3¼ in (8 cm) long.
• **NATIVE REGION** C. and S.E. Europe.
• **HABITAT** Mountains and hills, often on limestone.

cones may be borne singly or in clusters

△ PINUS NIGRA

◁ SUBSP. LARICIO
Also known as var. *maritima*, the Corsican pine has gray-green leaves.

Height 130 ft (40 m)	Shape Broadly columnar	Leaf persistence Evergreen	Leaf type

Family PINACEAE	Species *Pinus parviflora*	Author Siebold & Zuccarini

JAPANESE WHITE PINE

Leaves Needlelike, slightly twisted, to 2½ in (6 cm) long, in clusters of five, the outer surface green or blue-green, the inner surface blue-white, on greenish shoots. *Bark* Gray, scaly, with deep fissures. *Flowers* Males purple-red opening yellow, females red, in separate clusters on the young shoots in early summer. *Fruit* An egg-shaped cone, to 2¾ in (7 cm) long, green ripening to red-brown, with leathery scales.
• **NATIVE REGION** Japan.
• **HABITAT** Mountains, on stony soil.

leathery cone scales

male flowers open from purple-red to yellow

leaves borne five together

Height 80 ft (25 m)	Shape Broadly columnar	Leaf persistence Evergreen	Leaf type

Family PINACEAE	Species *Pinus peuce*	Author Grisebach

MACEDONIAN PINE

Leaves Needlelike and stiff, to 4 in (10 cm) long, in dense clusters of five, blue-green, pointing forward on smooth, bloomy, green shoots. *Bark* Purple-brown, fissured and cracked into plates. *Flowers* Males yellow, females red, in separate clusters on the young shoots in early summer. *Fruit* A cylindrical to conical, resinous, drooping cone, to 6 in (15 cm) long, green at first ripening to brown.
• **NATIVE REGION** S.E. Europe.
• **HABITAT** Mountains.

female flowers

slender leaves in clusters of five

Height 100 ft (30 m)	Shape Narrowly columnar	Leaf persistence Evergreen	Leaf type

Family PINACEAE	Species *Pinus pinaster*	Author Aiton

CLUSTER PINE

Leaves Needlelike and stiff, to 8 in (20 cm) long, in pairs, sharp-pointed, gray-green becoming dark green, on stout shoots. *Bark* Purple-brown and ridged, deeply fissured. *Flowers* Males yellow, females red, in separate clusters on the young shoots in early summer. *Fruit* A conical, glossy brown cone, to 8 in (20 cm) long, the scales with sharp prickles, persisting for many years.
• **NATIVE REGION** N. Africa, S.W. Europe.
• **HABITAT** Sandy soil.

all leaves point forward on shoot

Height 115 ft (35 m)	Shape Broadly columnar	Leaf persistence Evergreen	Leaf type

Family PINACEAE	Species *Pinus pinea*	Author Linnaeus

UMBRELLA PINE

Leaves Needlelike and stout, to 4¾ in (12 cm) long, in pairs, gray-green, on smooth, orange-brown shoots; on young plants, singly, bright blue-gray. *Bark* Orange-brown, deeply fissured. *Flowers* Males yellow, females green, borne in separate clusters on the young shoots in early summer. *Fruit* A nearly rounded, heavy, glossy brown cone, to 4¾ in (12 cm) long.
• **NATIVE REGION** Mediterranean.
• **HABITAT** Sandy soil near the coast.

cones contain edible seeds

thick leaves borne in pairs

Height 65 ft (20 m)	Shape Broadly spreading	Leaf persistence Evergreen	Leaf type

Family PINACEAE	Species *Pinus ponderosa*	Author Lawson

WESTERN YELLOW PINE

Leaves Needlelike and rigid, to 10 in (25 cm) long, in clusters of three, dark gray-green, pointing forward, on stout, smooth, yellow- to red-brown shoots. **Bark** Yellow-brown or reddish, thick, in large plates. **Flowers** Males deep purple, females red, borne in separate clusters on the young shoots in late spring. **Fruit** An egg-shaped cone, to 4 in (10 cm) or more long, purple ripening to glossy red-brown.
• **NATIVE REGION** W. North America.
• **HABITAT** Mountain slopes.

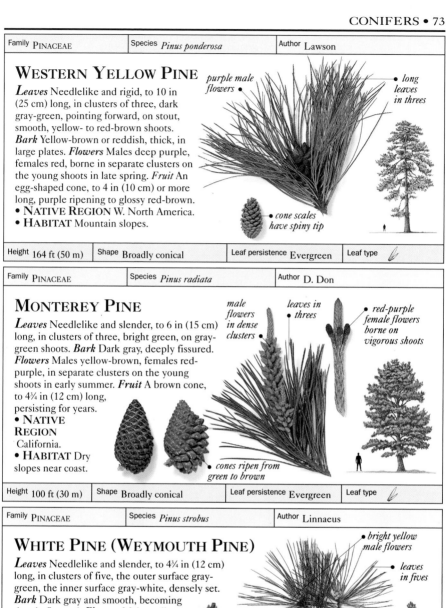

purple male flowers •

• long leaves in threes

• cone scales have spiny tip

Height 164 ft (50 m)	Shape Broadly conical	Leaf persistence Evergreen	Leaf type

Family PINACEAE	Species *Pinus radiata*	Author D. Don

MONTEREY PINE

Leaves Needlelike and slender, to 6 in (15 cm) long, in clusters of three, bright green, on gray-green shoots. **Bark** Dark gray, deeply fissured. **Flowers** Males yellow-brown, females red-purple, in separate clusters on the young shoots in early summer. **Fruit** A brown cone, to 4¾ in (12 cm) long, persisting for years.
• **NATIVE REGION** California.
• **HABITAT** Dry slopes near coast.

male flowers in dense clusters

leaves in • threes

• red-purple female flowers borne on vigorous shoots

• cones ripen from green to brown

Height 100 ft (30 m)	Shape Broadly conical	Leaf persistence Evergreen	Leaf type

Family PINACEAE	Species *Pinus strobus*	Author Linnaeus

WHITE PINE (WEYMOUTH PINE)

Leaves Needlelike and slender, to 4¾ in (12 cm) long, in clusters of five, the outer surface gray-green, the inner surface gray-white, densely set. **Bark** Dark gray and smooth, becoming deeply fissured. **Flowers** Males yellow, females pink, in separate clusters on the young shoots in early summer. **Fruit** A cylindrical, curved, hanging cone, to 6 in (15 cm) or more long, green ripening to pale brown.
• **NATIVE REGION** E. North America.
• **HABITAT** Woods at low altitudes.

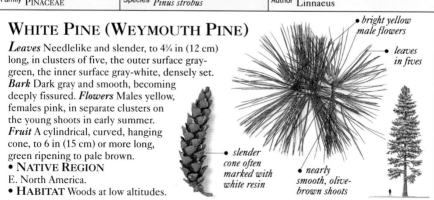

• bright yellow male flowers

• leaves in fives

• slender cone often marked with white resin

• nearly smooth, olive-brown shoots

Height 164 ft (50 m)	Shape Narrowly conical	Leaf persistence Evergreen	Leaf type

Family PINACEAE	Species *Pinus sylvestris*	Author Linnaeus

SCOTCH PINE

Leaves Needlelike, stout, and twisted, to 2¾ in (7 cm) long, in pairs, blue-green to blue-gray. **Bark** Purple-gray, peeling in irregular plates; orange and flaking toward the top of the plant. **Flowers** Males yellow, females red, in separate clusters on the young shoots in late spring to early summer. **Fruit** An egg-shaped cone, to 3 in (7.5 cm) long, green ripening to brown.
• **NATIVE REGION** Asia, Europe.
• **HABITAT** Mountains, on sandy or gravelly soil.
• **REMARK** This species makes a broadly spreading tree in open situations, but is narrow in confined places.

• *female flowers borne at end of shoots*

bluish green leaves have silvery tinge •

▽ **PINUS SYLVESTRIS**

male flowers borne at base of shoots

△ **'EDWIN HILLIER'**
This form is selected for its striking foliage and rust-colored bark.

paired, usually twisted leaves •

Height 115 ft (35 m)	Shape Broadly spreading	Leaf persistence Evergreen	Leaf type

Family PINACEAE	Species *Pinus tabuliformis*	Author Carrière

CHINESE PINE

Leaves Needlelike, to 6 in (15 cm) long, usually in pairs but sometimes in clusters of three, green to gray-green, on yellow-brown shoots; young shoots bloomy. **Bark** Gray and fissured; tinged with orange or pink toward the top of the plant. **Flowers** Males pale yellow, females red-purple, in separate clusters on the shoots in early summer. **Fruit** An egg-shaped, brown cone, to 2½ in (6 cm) long, the scales each with a small spine at the tip, long-persistent on the shoots.
• **NATIVE REGION** W., C., and N. China.
• **HABITAT** Mountains.
• **REMARK** Young plants are usually more conical in shape, developing the flat, spreading crown, typical of this species, as they mature.

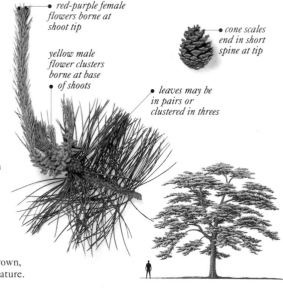

• *red-purple female flowers borne at shoot tip*

yellow male flower clusters borne at base of shoots •

• *cone scales end in short spine at tip*

• *leaves may be in pairs or clustered in threes*

Height 80 ft (25 m)	Shape Broadly spreading	Leaf persistence Evergreen	Leaf type

Family PINACEAE	Species *Pinus thunbergii*	Author Parlatore

JAPANESE BLACK PINE

Leaves Needlelike and rigid, to 4 in (10 cm) long, in pairs, sharp-pointed, densely set, pointing forward, on smooth, yellow-brown shoots. *Bark* Gray, cracking into irregular plates. *Flowers* Males yellowish, females purple-red, in separate clusters on the young shoots in early summer. *Fruit* An egg-shaped cone, to 2¾ in (7 cm) long, purple or green ripening to gray-brown.
• **NATIVE REGION** N.E. China, Japan, Korea.
• **HABITAT** Near coastline.
• **REMARK** This species is related to the Austrian pine *(Pinus nigra,* see p.71). In winter, it is easily distinguished by its white, hairy leaf buds.

thick, rigid leaves end in sharp point

young cones may be colored purple

pairs of leaves point toward shoot tip

cone scales have no prickles

Height 100 ft (30 m)	Shape Broadly conical	Leaf persistence Evergreen	Leaf type

Family PINACEAE	Species *Pinus wallichiana*	Author Jackson

HIMALAYAN PINE

Leaves Needlelike and slender, often kinked at first, flexible, to 8 in (20 cm) long, in clusters of five, the outer surface green, the inner surface blue-white, on smooth, green, bloomy shoots. *Bark* Gray and smooth, becoming dark gray and fissured. *Flowers* Males yellow, females blue-green and pink, in separate clusters on the young shoots in early summer. *Fruit* A curved, resinous, hanging cone, to 12 in (30 cm) long, green ripening to pale brown.
• **NATIVE REGION** The Himalayas.
• **HABITAT** Mountain forests.
• **REMARK** Also known as Bhutan pine, blue pine. The first name should be reserved for *P. bhutanica,* a recently described species from Bhutan, S. Asia.

very slender leaves borne in clusters of five

yellow male flower clusters

cones ripen from green to brown

bloomy young shoot

foliage appears overall blue-gray

Height 130 ft (40 m)	Shape Broadly conical	Leaf persistence Evergreen	Leaf type

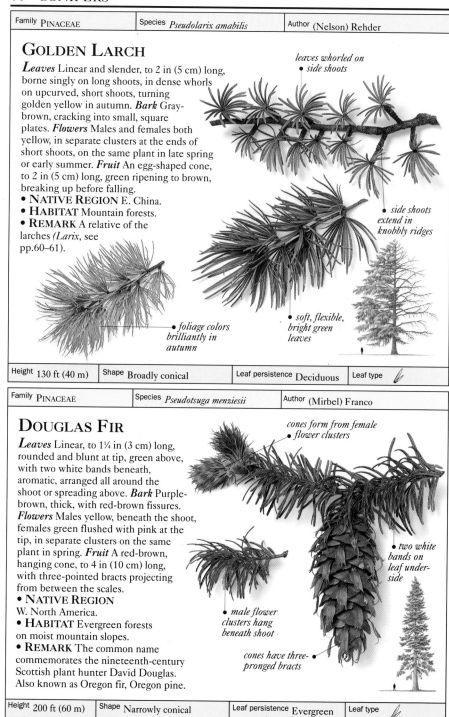

Family PINACEAE	Species *Pseudolarix amabilis*	Author (Nelson) Rehder

GOLDEN LARCH

Leaves Linear and slender, to 2 in (5 cm) long, borne singly on long shoots, in dense whorls on upcurved, short shoots, turning golden yellow in autumn. ***Bark*** Gray-brown, cracking into small, square plates. ***Flowers*** Males and females both yellow, in separate clusters at the ends of short shoots, on the same plant in late spring or early summer. ***Fruit*** An egg-shaped cone, to 2 in (5 cm) long, green ripening to brown, breaking up before falling.
• **NATIVE REGION** E. China.
• **HABITAT** Mountain forests.
• **REMARK** A relative of the larches *(Larix,* see pp.60–61).

leaves whorled on
• side shoots

• side shoots
extend in
knobbly ridges

• foliage colors
brilliantly in
autumn

• soft, flexible,
bright green
leaves

Height 130 ft (40 m)	Shape Broadly conical	Leaf persistence Deciduous	Leaf type

Family PINACEAE	Species *Pseudotsuga menziesii*	Author (Mirbel) Franco

DOUGLAS FIR

Leaves Linear, to 1¼ in (3 cm) long, rounded and blunt at tip, green above, with two white bands beneath, aromatic, arranged all around the shoot or spreading above. ***Bark*** Purple-brown, thick, with red-brown fissures. ***Flowers*** Males yellow, beneath the shoot, females green flushed with pink at the tip, in separate clusters on the same plant in spring. ***Fruit*** A red-brown, hanging cone, to 4 in (10 cm) long, with three-pointed bracts projecting from between the scales.
• **NATIVE REGION** W. North America.
• **HABITAT** Evergreen forests on moist mountain slopes.
• **REMARK** The common name commemorates the nineteenth-century Scottish plant hunter David Douglas. Also known as Oregon fir, Oregon pine.

cones form from female
• flower clusters

• two white
bands on
leaf under-
side

• male flower
clusters hang
beneath shoot

cones have three-
pronged bracts

Height 200 ft (60 m)	Shape Narrowly conical	Leaf persistence Evergreen	Leaf type

Family PINACEAE	Species *Tsuga canadensis*	Author (Linnaeus) Carrière

EASTERN HEMLOCK

Leaves Linear, to ½ in (1.2 cm) long, dark green above, with two white bands beneath.
Bark Purple-gray, with scaly ridges.
Flowers Males yellow, beneath the shoot, females resembling small, green cones, at the tip, in separate clusters in late spring.
Fruit An egg-shaped, pale brown, hanging cone, to ¾ in (2 cm) long.
• **NATIVE REGION**
E. North America.
• **HABITAT** Hilly or rocky woods.

leaves taper to rounded tip

cones persist after shedding seeds in autumn

leaves lie flat either side of shoot

Height 100 ft (30 m)	Shape Broadly conical	Leaf persistence Evergreen	Leaf type

Family PINACEAE	Species *Tsuga caroliniana*	Author Engelmann

CAROLINA HEMLOCK

Leaves Linear, to ¾ in (2 cm) long, dark green above, with two white bands beneath. **Bark** Red-brown, furrowed and ridged with age. **Flowers** Males and females both reddish, males below the shoot, females at the tip, borne in separate clusters in late spring.
Fruit An egg-shaped, pale brown, hanging cone, 1 in (2.5 cm) long.
• **NATIVE REGION**
S.E. United States.
• **HABITAT** Mountain slopes.

cones drop soon after shedding seeds

leaves spread from shoot at all angles

chunky leaves have parallel sides

Height 65 ft (20 m)	Shape Broadly conical	Leaf persistence Evergreen	Leaf type

Family PINACEAE	Species *Tsuga heterophylla*	Author (Rafinesque) Sargent

WESTERN HEMLOCK

Leaves Linear, to ¾ in (2 cm) long, with parallel sides, dark green above, with two white bands beneath. **Bark** Purple-brown, ridged, flaking. **Flowers** Both reddish, males beneath the shoot, females at the tip, in separate clusters on the same plant in spring. **Fruit** An egg-shaped, brown, hanging cone, ¾ in (2 cm) long.
• **NATIVE REGION**
W. North America.
• **HABITAT** Forests.

purplish red young cone

leaves spread either side of shoot

mature cone has slightly opened scales

Height 200 ft (60 m)	Shape Narrowly conical	Leaf persistence Evergreen	Leaf type

PODOCARPACEAE

OVER 100 SPECIES OF evergreen trees and shrubs, mainly in the genus *Podocarpus*, belong to this family; most grow in warm regions of the southern hemisphere. Male and female flowers are usually on separate plants, the males in catkinlike clusters. Females develop into a fleshy cone or seed.

Family PODOCARPACEAE	Species *Podocarpus andinus*	Author Endlicher

PLUM-FRUITED FIR

Leaves Linear, to 1 in (2.5 cm) long, abruptly short-pointed, deep blue-green above, with two whitish bands beneath, all around the shoot. *Bark* Dark gray and smooth. *Flowers* Males yellow, in branched clusters 1 in (2.5 cm) long, females small, green, on separate plants in early summer. *Fruit* Fleshy, plumlike, edible, green ripening to yellow, with a single seed.
• **NATIVE REGION**
Argentina, S. Chile.
• **HABITAT** Mountains.

• *flattened leaves*

• *two paler bands on underside of leaves*

fruit matures to pale yellow •

Height 50 ft (15 m)	Shape Broadly conical	Leaf persistence Evergreen	Leaf type

Family PODOCARPACEAE	Species *Saxegothaea conspicua*	Author Lindley

PRINCE ALBERT'S YEW

Leaves Linear, usually curved, to 1¼ in (3 cm) long, with a fine, sharp point at the tip, dark green above, with two whitish bands beneath, loosely arranged in two ranks either side of the shoot or spreading all around it. *Bark* Purple-brown, smooth, peeling in strips. *Flowers* Males purplish in the leaf axils beneath the shoot, females blue-green, at the tip of the shoot, in separate clusters on the same plant in late spring to early summer. *Fruit* A rounded, fleshy cone, to ¾ in (2 cm) across, with prickly, blue-green scales.
• **NATIVE REGION** Chile.
• **HABITAT** Forests.

• *tiny, purplish male flower clusters*

leaves end in small, sharp point at tip •

• *prickle-pointed cone scales*

Height 40 ft (12 m)	Shape Broadly conical	Leaf persistence Evergreen	Leaf type

TAXACEAE

T HIS FAMILY IS OFTEN classed apart from the true conifers because its members do not bear their seeds in cones. The six genera contain about 18 species of evergreen trees and shrubs. Male and female flowers are usually on separate plants. Females mature to a single seed surrounded by a fleshy aril.

Family TAXACEAE	Species *Taxus baccata*	Author Linnaeus

COMMON YEW

Leaves Linear, to 1¼ in (3 cm) long, pointed, dark green above, with two paler green bands beneath, mainly spreading in two ranks either side of the shoot. *Bark* Purple-brown, smooth and flaking. *Flowers* Males and females both small, males pale yellow, in clusters in the leaf axils, beneath the shoot, females singly, at the end of the young shoots, on separate plants in spring. *Fruit* A single seed, enclosed in a fleshy, usually red, aril, the whole ⅜ in (1 cm) long, open at the top, exposing the green seed.
• **NATIVE REGION** N. Africa, S.W. Asia, Europe.
• **HABITAT** Lime-rich soil.
• **REMARK** All parts are poisonous except the aril.

'LUTEA' ▷
The yellow-berried yew is named for the color of its fruits.

aril is green before expanding

very dark, blackish green leaves

△ TAXUS BACCATA

yellow aril

Height 65 ft (20 m)	Shape Broadly conical	Leaf persistence Evergreen	Leaf type

Family TAXACEAE	Species *Torreya californica*	Author Torrey

CALIFORNIA NUTMEG

Leaves Needlelike, to 2½ in (6 cm) long, sharp-pointed, glossy dark green above, with two whitish bands beneath. *Bark* Gray-brown, with vertical ridges. *Flowers* Males creamy white, in the leaf axils, females small and green, on separate plants in spring to early summer. *Fruit* A single large seed, enclosed in a green, purple-flushed aril, the whole about 1½ in (4 cm) long.
• **NATIVE REGION** California.
• **HABITAT** Cool slopes and canyons in coastal regions and mountains.

rigid leaves taper to sharp point

pale bands on underside of leaves

male flowers

Height 100 ft (30 m)	Shape Broadly conical	Leaf persistence Evergreen	Leaf type

TAXODIACEAE

T HE SWAMP CYPRESS family contains about ten genera and 15 species of deciduous and evergreen trees, found in North America, east Asia, and Tasmania. The leaves may be needle- or scalelike. Male and female flowers are borne separately on the same plant; females develop into woody cones.

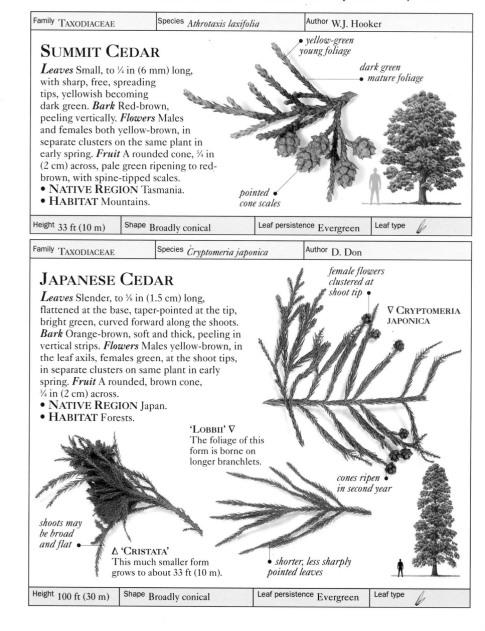

Family TAXODIACEAE	Species *Athrotaxis laxifolia*	Author W.J. Hooker

SUMMIT CEDAR

Leaves Small, to ¼ in (6 mm) long, with sharp, free, spreading tips, yellowish becoming dark green. **Bark** Red-brown, peeling vertically. **Flowers** Males and females both yellow-brown, in separate clusters on the same plant in early spring. **Fruit** A rounded cone, ¾ in (2 cm) across, pale green ripening to red-brown, with spine-tipped scales.
• **NATIVE REGION** Tasmania.
• **HABITAT** Mountains.

yellow-green young foliage

dark green mature foliage

pointed cone scales

Height 33 ft (10 m)	Shape Broadly conical	Leaf persistence Evergreen	Leaf type

Family TAXODIACEAE	Species *Cryptomeria japonica*	Author D. Don

JAPANESE CEDAR

Leaves Slender, to ⅝ in (1.5 cm) long, flattened at the base, taper-pointed at the tip, bright green, curved forward along the shoots. **Bark** Orange-brown, soft and thick, peeling in vertical strips. **Flowers** Males yellow-brown, in the leaf axils, females green, at the shoot tips, in separate clusters on same plant in early spring. **Fruit** A rounded, brown cone, ¾ in (2 cm) across.
• **NATIVE REGION** Japan.
• **HABITAT** Forests.

female flowers clustered at shoot tip

▽ CRYPTOMERIA JAPONICA

'LOBBII' ▽
The foliage of this form is borne on longer branchlets.

cones ripen in second year

shoots may be broad and flat

△ 'CRISTATA'
This much smaller form grows to about 33 ft (10 m).

shorter, less sharply pointed leaves

Height 100 ft (30 m)	Shape Broadly conical	Leaf persistence Evergreen	Leaf type

| Family TAXODIACEAE | Species *Cunninghamia lanceolata* | Author (A.B. Lambert) W.J. Hooker |

CHINESE FIR

Leaves Strap-shaped, to 2½ in (6 cm) long, glossy green, with two white bands beneath. *Bark* Red-brown, ridged. *Flowers* Males yellow-brown, in clusters, females yellow-green, in single clusters, at shoot tips. *Fruit* A rounded cone, to 1½ in (4 cm) across, green then brown.
• **NATIVE REGION** China.
• **HABITAT** Evergreen forests.

sharp-tipped leaves • taper at base

leaves arranged spirally around • shoot

| Height 80 ft (25 m) | Shape Broadly columnar | Leaf persistence Evergreen | Leaf type |

| Family TAXODIACEAE | Species *Glyptostrobus pensilis* | Author (Staunton) K. Koch |

CHINESE SWAMP CYPRESS

Leaves Linear, scalelike, to ⅝ in (1.5 cm) long, blue-green, spreading either side of deciduous side shoots, arranged spirally on persistent shoots, turning red in late autumn when they fall. *Bark* Gray-brown, with shallow fissures. *Flowers* Males and females inconspicuous. *Fruit* A rounded to egg-shaped rough, green cone, 1 in (2.5 cm) long.
• **NATIVE REGION** S.E. China.
• **HABITAT** Swamps and riverbanks.
• **REMARK** This species is now seen only rarely in the wild.

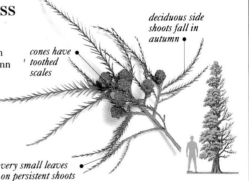

deciduous side shoots fall in autumn •

cones have • toothed scales

very small leaves on persistent shoots

| Height 33 ft (10 m) | Shape Narrowly conical | Leaf persistence Deciduous | Leaf type |

| Family TAXODIACEAE | Species *Metasequoia glyptostroboides* | Author Hu & Cheng |

DAWN REDWOOD

Leaves Linear, to 1 in (2.5 cm) long, soft, flattened, emerging early and pale green becoming dark green, arranged opposite on short, deciduous side shoots, spirally on persistent shoots, turning yellow, pink, or red in autumn. *Bark* Orange-brown to red-brown, peeling vertically in stringy flakes. *Flowers* Males yellow, females greenish, in separate clusters on young shoots, on the same plant in spring. *Fruit* A rounded cone, 1 in (2.5 cm) across, green ripening to brown.
• **NATIVE REGION** S.W. China.
• **HABITAT** Moist ground and riverbanks.

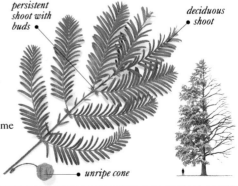

persistent shoot with buds •

deciduous • shoot

• unripe cone

| Height 130 ft (40 m) | Shape Narrowly conical | Leaf persistence Deciduous | Leaf type |

Family TAXODIACEAE	Species *Sciadopitys verticillata*	Author Siebold & Zuccarini

UMBRELLA PINE

Leaves Needlelike, to 4¾ in (12 cm) long, deeply grooved on both sides, deep green above, yellow-green beneath. **Bark** Red-brown, peeling in long, vertical strips. **Flowers** Males yellow, in many clusters, females green, at the ends of the shoots, on the same plant in spring. **Fruit** An egg-shaped cone, to 3 in (7.5 cm) long, green ripening to red-brown in two years.
• **NATIVE REGION** Japan.
• **HABITAT** Mountains.

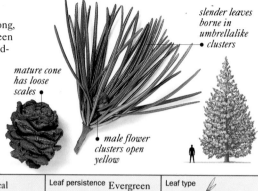

slender leaves borne in umbrellalike clusters

mature cone has loose scales

male flower clusters open yellow

Height 80 ft (25 m)	Shape Narrowly conical	Leaf persistence Evergreen	Leaf type

Family TAXODIACEAE	Species *Sequoia sempervirens*	Author (D. Don) Endlicher

CALIFORNIA REDWOOD

Leaves Linear, to ¾ in (2 cm) long, pointed at the tip, dark green above, with two white bands beneath, spreading either side of the shoot. **Bark** Red-brown, soft, fibrous, thick, with broad ridges. **Flowers** Males yellow-brown, females green, borne in separate clusters on the same plant in late winter to early spring. **Fruit** A barrel-shaped to rounded, red-brown cone, to 1¼ in (3 cm) long, ripe in one year.
• **NATIVE REGION** California, S. Oregon.
• **HABITAT** Low slopes in coastal regions.
• **REMARK** The tallest species of tree.

male flower buds

leaves are smaller on coning shoots

Height 330 ft (100 m)	Shape Narrowly conical	Leaf persistence Evergreen	Leaf type

Family TAXODIACEAE	Species *Sequoiadendron giganteum*	Author (Lindley) Buchholz

GIANT SEQUOIA

Leaves To ⁵⁄₁₆ in (8 mm) long, sharp-pointed, with spreading tips, deep blue-green, all around the shoot. **Bark** Red-brown, soft, fibrous, very thick. **Flowers** Males yellow, at the ends of the shoots, females green, in separate clusters in early spring. **Fruit** A barrel-shaped cone, to 3 in (7.5 cm) long, green ripening to brown in two years, often persisting for years.
• **NATIVE REGION** California.
• **HABITAT** West-facing mountain slopes.

year-old cone still green

tiny pointed leaves make foliage rough to the touch

male flower buds open in early spring

Height 260 ft (80 m)	Shape Narrowly conical	Leaf persistence Evergreen	Leaf type

| Family TAXODIACEAE | Species *Taiwania cryptomerioides* | Author Hayata |

TAIWANIA CRYPTOMERIOIDES

Leaves Slender, to ¾ in (2 cm) long, broad and flattened at the base, with a sharp, spiny point at the tip, blue-green, curved forward along the shoots; on coning shoots much smaller. **Bark** Red-brown, peeling in vertical strips. **Flowers** Males in several clusters together, females in single clusters, borne separately at the ends of the shoots, on the same plant in spring. **Fruit** A rounded cone, to ½ in (1.2 cm) across, green ripening to brown.
• **NATIVE REGION** Taiwan.
• **HABITAT** Mountain forests.

• sharp, taper-pointed leaf tip

• leaves are flat at base

| Height 200 ft (60 m) | Shape Broadly conical | Leaf persistence Evergreen | Leaf type |

| Family TAXODIACEAE | Species *Taxodium ascendens* | Author Brongniart |

POND CYPRESS

Leaves Linear, to ⅜ in (1 cm) long, closely pressed against and around upright, deciduous shoots, later spreading slightly. **Bark** Red-brown, thick, coarsely ridged. **Flowers** Males yellow-green, in hanging catkins to 8 in (20 cm) long, females green, in small clusters at the base of the male catkins, on the same plant, forming in autumn but opening in spring. **Fruit** A rounded cone, to 1¼ in (3 cm) long.
• **NATIVE REGION** S.E. United States.
• **HABITAT** Swamps and by lakes.

• deciduous shoots fall in autumn

persistent, branched shoots •

| Height 100 ft (30 m) | Shape Narrowly columnar | Leaf persistence Deciduous | Leaf type |

| Family TAXODIACEAE | Species *Taxodium distichum* | Author (Linnaeus) Richard |

BALD CYPRESS

Leaves Linear, to ¾ in (2 cm) long, soft and flattened, arranged spreading or spirally, emerging late. **Bark** Gray-brown, thin, rough, often fluted and buttressed at the base. **Flowers** Males yellow-green, in hanging catkins to 8 in (20 cm) long, females green, in clusters at the base of the male catkins, on the same plant, forming in autumn but opening in spring. **Fruit** A rounded cone, to 1¼ in (3 cm) across, green ripening to brown.
• **NATIVE REGION** S.E. United States.
• **HABITAT** Swamps, streambanks.
• **REMARK** Also known as swamp cypress.

• branches are alternate

persistent shoots have spiraled • leaves

• leaves spread either side of deciduous shoots

| Height 130 ft (40 m) | Shape Broadly conical | Leaf persistence Deciduous | Leaf type |

BROADLEAVES

ACERACEAE

T HE MAPLE FAMILY has two genera and over 100 species of evergreen and deciduous trees and shrubs. Some extend to the tropics, but most occur in northern temperate regions.

✍

The opposite leaves are often lobed, sometimes merely toothed, or may be divided into several leaflets. The small male and female flowers vary from cream to yellow, green, red, or purple. They are borne, sometimes separately, on the same or different plants, usually opening as the young foliage unfolds. The winged fruits are in two halves. In maples *(Acer)*, one side of each half has an elongated wing; in *Dipteronia*, each half is winged all the way around.

Family ACERACEAE	Species *Acer buergerianum*	Author Miquel

TRIDENT MAPLE

Leaves Palmate, to 4 in (10 cm) long and across, narrowed at the base, with three forward-pointing lobes, usually untoothed or sparsely toothed at the margin, dark green above, bluish beneath, becoming smooth on both sides, turning red in autumn. **Bark** Gray-brown, peeling in scaly plates with age. **Flowers** Small and yellow-green, in broadly conical upright clusters in spring with the young leaves. **Fruit** With parallel, upright wings, to 1 in (2.5 cm) long, green or reddish at first ripening to brown.
• **NATIVE REGION** China, Japan.
• **HABITAT** Mountain woods.

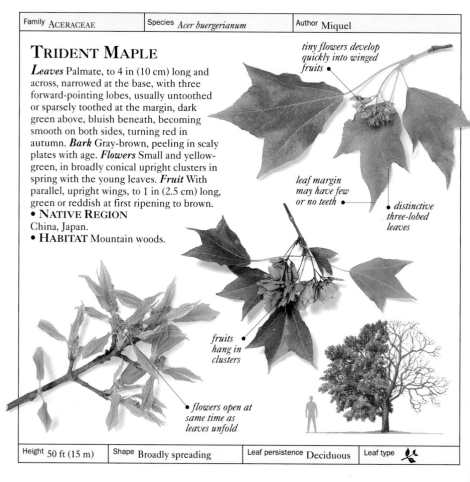

tiny flowers develop quickly into winged fruits

leaf margin may have few or no teeth

distinctive three-lobed leaves

fruits hang in clusters

flowers open at same time as leaves unfold

Height 50 ft (15 m)	Shape Broadly spreading	Leaf persistence Deciduous	Leaf type

Family ACERACEAE	Species *Acer campestre*	Author Linnaeus

HEDGE MAPLE

Leaves Palmately lobed, to 3 in (7.5 cm) long and 4 in (10 cm) across, with five lobes, heart-shaped at the base, dark green above, paler and downy beneath, turning yellow in autumn; leaf stalk with milky juice when cut. **Bark** Pale brown, corky, fissured with age. **Flowers** Small and green, borne in upright clusters in spring with the leaves. **Fruit** To 1 in (2.5 cm) long, sometimes red at first, in hanging clusters.
• **NATIVE REGION** N. Africa, S.W. Asia, Europe.
• **HABITAT** Woods, scrub, and hedgerows.

'PULVERULENTUM' ▷ The smaller leaves of this form are heavily mottled with white.

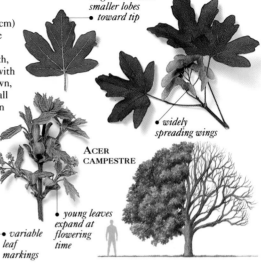

larger lobes have smaller lobes toward tip

• widely spreading wings

ACER CAMPESTRE

• young leaves expand at flowering time

• variable leaf markings

Height 50 ft (15 m)	Shape Broadly spreading	Leaf persistence Deciduous	Leaf type

Family ACERACEAE	Species *Acer capillipes*	Author Maximowicz

ACER CAPILLIPES

Leaves To 6 in (15 cm) long and 4 in (10 cm) across, with three lobes, the central lobe much the largest, the side lobes short, all tapering to a slender point, toothed, red when young becoming rich green above, paler and smooth beneath, usually red in autumn, on red stalks. **Bark** Green and gray, with vertical white stripes. **Flowers** Small and green, borne in drooping racemes in late spring at the same time as the young leaves emerge. **Fruit** With spreading wings, to ¾ in (2 cm) long, green ripening to red.
• **NATIVE REGION** Japan.
• **HABITAT** Woods by mountain streams, on moist soil.
• **REMARK** This species is one of the stripe-bark maples, which are easily distinguished by their characteristically striped bark.

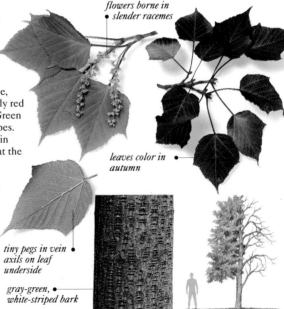

flowers borne in • slender racemes

leaves color in autumn

tiny pegs in vein • axils on leaf underside

gray-green, • white-striped bark

Height 65 ft (20 m)	Shape Broadly columnar	Leaf persistence Deciduous	Leaf type

Family ACERACEAE	Species *Acer cappadocicum*	Author Gleditsch

COLISEUM MAPLE

Leaves Palmately lobed, to 4 in (10 cm) long and 6 in (15 cm) across, with five to seven taper-pointed, untoothed lobes, heart-shaped at the base, bright green above, smooth on both sides except for tufts of hairs in the vein axils beneath, turning clear yellow in autumn; leaf stalk with milky juice when cut. **Bark** Gray and smooth. **Flowers** Small and yellow-green, borne in upright clusters in late spring with young leaves. **Fruit** With spreading wings, to 1½ in (4 cm) long.
• **NATIVE REGION** W. Asia to China.
• **HABITAT** Forests.
• **REMARK** In Tibet, burrs on the trunk of the tree are made into drinking cups.

leaf lobes taper to fine point

small flowers borne in rounded clusters

untoothed leaf margin

ripening fruits become pendulous

△ A. CAPPADOCICUM

◁ 'AUREUM'
The yellow leaves of this form turn green in late summer.

yellow leaves have bronze tips •

Height 65 ft (20 m)	Shape Broadly spreading	Leaf persistence Deciduous	Leaf type

Family ACERACEAE	Species *Acer carpinifolium*	Author Siebold & Zuccarini

HORNBEAM MAPLE

Leaves Oblong, to 6 in (15 cm) long and 2 in (5 cm) across, unlobed, taper-pointed at the tip, sharply toothed, with numerous parallel veins, dark green above, paler and downy on veins when young beneath, turning yellow and brown in autumn. **Bark** Gray and smooth, with conspicuous lenticels. **Flowers** Small and yellow-green, on slender stalks, borne in hanging clusters, late spring, with young leaves. **Fruit** With wings, to ¾ in (2 cm) long.
• **NATIVE REGION** Japan.
• **HABITAT** Deciduous woods by mountain streams.
• **REMARK** This unusual species is named for the resemblance of its leaves to those of the hornbeams *(Carpinus,* see pp.126–127), which distinguishes it from other maples.

conspicuously veined leaves •

leaves edged with sharp teeth

fruit wings arranged at right angles

tiny, slender-stalked flowers

Height 33 ft (10 m)	Shape Broadly conical	Leaf persistence Deciduous	Leaf type

Family ACERACEAE	Species *Acer circinatum*	Author Pursh

VINE MAPLE

Leaves To 4¾ in (12 cm) across, with seven to nine toothed lobes, pale green above, downy when young beneath, turning orange and red in autumn. ***Bark*** Gray-brown, smooth. ***Flowers*** Small, with white petals and reddish sepals, borne in drooping clusters in late spring. ***Fruit*** With spreading, reddish wings, to 1¼ in (3 cm) long.
• **NATIVE REGION** W. North America.
• **HABITAT** Evergreen forests.

• *lobes have pointed teeth*

• *wings turn red as fruits ripen*

Height 20 ft (6 m)	Shape Broadly spreading	Leaf persistence Deciduous	Leaf type

Family ACERACEAE	Species *Acer cissifolium*	Author (Siebold & Zuccarini) K. Koch

ACER CISSIFOLIUM

Leaves With three ovate to obovate leaflets, to 4 in (10 cm) long, dark green above, smooth, turning yellow or red in autumn. ***Bark*** Yellow-gray, rough, with raised lenticels. ***Flowers*** Males and females both tiny, yellow, numerous, in slender racemes to 4 in (10 cm) long, on separate plants in spring. ***Fruit*** With nearly parallel wings.
• **NATIVE REGION** Japan.
• **HABITAT** By streams.

• *deeply toothed leaflets*

• *green wings ripen to red*

• *slender, red stalks*

Height 50 ft (15 m)	Shape Broadly spreading	Leaf persistence Deciduous	Leaf type

Family ACERACEAE	Species *Acer crataegifolium*	Author Siebold & Zuccarini

HAWTHORN MAPLE

Leaves Ovate, to 3 in (7.5 cm) long and 2 in (5cm) across, with three toothed lobes, the central lobe long and taper-pointed, dark green above, paler beneath, smooth. ***Bark*** Green, with vertical stripes. ***Flowers*** Small and yellow-green, in upright or drooping racemes in spring with the leaves. ***Fruit*** With spreading, red-tinged wings, to 1¼ in (3 cm) long.
• **NATIVE REGION** C. and S. Japan.
• **HABITAT** Forests and sunny places on low mountains.

leaves expand at • *flowering time*

small flowers in • *dense racemes*

shallow lobes at • *base*

Height 23 ft (7 m)	Shape Broadly conical	Leaf persistence Deciduous	Leaf type

Family ACERACEAE	Species *Acer davidii*	Author Franchet

DAVID MAPLE

Leaves Ovate, to 6 in (15 cm) long and 4 in (10 cm) across, either with small lobes or unlobed, heart-shaped at the base, toothed, glossy dark green above, downy when young beneath, some forms turning orange in autumn. ***Bark*** Green, with vertical white stripes, becoming gray and cracking with age. ***Flowers*** Small, green, in drooping racemes in late spring with the young leaves. ***Fruit*** With spreading wings, to 1¼ in (3 cm) long.
• **NATIVE REGION** China.
• **HABITAT** Mountain thickets and woods.
• **REMARK** The species is one of the stripe-bark maples, and is variable in size and shape of leaf. Several cultivated forms are grown in gardens.

leaves often unlobed •

slender-pointed leaf • tip

wings turn red as • fruits ripen

△ ACER DAVIDII

leaves color in autumn •

• small, green flowers

striped bark •

△ 'GEORGE FORREST'
The dark leaves of this form scarcely color in autumn.

△ 'ERNEST WILSON'
The large leaves of this form turn orange in autumn.

Height 50 ft (15 m)	Shape Broadly conical	Leaf persistence Deciduous	Leaf type

Family ACERACEAE	Species *Acer ginnala*	Author Maximowicz

AMUR MAPLE

Leaves Ovate, to 3 in (7.5 cm) long and 2½ in (6 cm) across, with three deep lobes, the central lobe largest, toothed, glossy dark green above, smooth, turning bright red in early autumn. ***Bark*** Dark gray-brown, smooth. ***Flowers*** Creamy white, fragrant, in upright clusters in late spring after the young leaves. ***Fruit*** With nearly parallel, red-tinged wings, to 1 in (2.5 cm) long, in drooping clusters.
• **NATIVE REGION** China, Japan.
• **HABITAT** Thickets by riverbanks and exposed positions in mountain valleys.

sharply toothed lobes •

fruits have broad, red • wings

•small flowers open after leaves

• very glossy leaves

Height 33 ft (10 m)	Shape Broadly spreading	Leaf persistence Deciduous	Leaf type

Family ACERACEAE	Species *Acer griseum*	Author (Franchet) Pax

PAPERBARK MAPLE

Leaves With three elliptic leaflets, each with several large, blunt teeth on each side, the central leaflet to 4 in (10 cm) long and 2 in (5 cm) across, dark green above, blue-white and densely covered with soft hairs beneath, turning red in autumn. **Bark** Reddish to pale cinnamon-brown, peeling in thin, papery flakes. **Flowers** Small, yellow-green, on hairy stalks, in drooping clusters in late spring with the young leaves. **Fruit** With broad, pale green wings, to 1¼ in (3 cm) long.
• **NATIVE REGION**
C. China.
• **HABITAT**
Mountain woods.
• **REMARK** Easily distinguished by its peeling bark.

leaflets are blue-white on • underside

large fruits have broad • wings

distinctive • bark peels in wafer-thin flakes

green • flowers

Height 50 ft (15 m)	Shape Broadly columnar	Leaf persistence Deciduous	Leaf type

Family ACERACEAE ,	Species *Acer henryi*	Author Pax

HENRY MAPLE

Leaves With three elliptic, untoothed or few-toothed, taper-pointed leaflets, to 4 in (10 cm) long and 1½ in (4 cm) across, dark green above, usually hairy beneath, turning brilliant red in autumn. **Bark** Gray, with conspicuous raised lenticels. **Flowers** Tiny and yellowish, numerous, borne in slender racemes to 8 in (20 cm) long, in spring before or with the leaves. **Fruit** With nearly parallel wings, to 1 in (2.5 cm) long.
• **NATIVE REGION**
C. China.
• **HABITAT**
Mountain woods.

• tiny flowers borne in slender racemes

wings tinged red when • ripe

leaflets may be • untoothed

Height 50 ft (15 m)	Shape Broadly spreading	Leaf persistence Deciduous	Leaf type

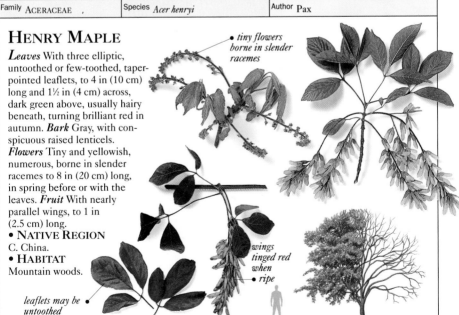

Family ACERACEAE	Species *Acer japonicum*	Author Thunberg

FULLMOON MAPLE

Leaves Rounded in outline, with 7 to 11 taper-pointed, sharply toothed, ovate to lanceolate lobes, to 5 in (13 cm) long and across, silky-hairy on both sides when young, becoming dark green above, nearly smooth on both sides, turning red in autumn, carried on downy stalks. **Bark** Gray-brown and smooth. **Flowers** Small and red-purple, with yellow anthers, borne in long-stalked, drooping clusters in spring as the young leaves emerge. **Fruit** With spreading wings, green or green tinged red, to 1 in (2.5 cm) long.
• **NATIVE REGION** Japan.
• **HABITAT** Mountain woods, usually in dry, sunny situations.
• **REMARK** The form shown, 'Vitifolium' has somewhat larger leaves, with 10 to 12 lobes, and bronzy young foliage.

'VITIFOLIUM' ▷

numerously
• lobed leaves

heart-shaped
• leaf base

leaves turn deep
• red in autumn

△ 'VITIFOLIUM'

◁ 'VITIFOLIUM'

• flower clusters droop on long stalks

red-purple •
flower petals

△ 'VITIFOLIUM'

◁ 'ACONITIFOLIUM'
The leaves of this form are deeply lobed and toothed.

◁ 'VITIFOLIUM'

• spreading fruit wings

leaves cut •
to base in
slender lobes

Height 33 ft (10 m)	Shape Broadly spreading	Leaf persistence Deciduous	Leaf type

| Family ACERACEAE | Species *Acer lobelii* | Author Tenore |

ACER LOBELII

Leaves Palmately lobed, to 6 in (15 cm) long
and slightly more across, with five usually
wavy-edged, untoothed, pointed lobes,
glossy deep green and smooth above,
with tufts of hairs in the vein axils
beneath, on blue-white, bloomy
shoots. **Bark** Pale gray and smooth,
with shallow, vertical fissures.
Flowers Small and yellow-green, in
upright clusters in late spring with
the leaves. **Fruit** With
spreading green wings, to
1¼ in (3 cm) long, in
upright clusters.
• **NATIVE REGION**
S. Italy.
• **HABITAT**
Mountain woods.

lobes end in tapered point

fruit has spreading wings

bloomy shoot

lobes have wavy margin

| Height 65 ft (20 m) | Shape Narrowly columnar | Leaf persistence Deciduous | Leaf type |

| Family ACERACEAE | Species *Acer macrophyllum* | Author Pursh |

OREGON MAPLE

Leaves Palmately lobed, to 10 in (25 cm) long and 12 in
(30 cm) across, with three to five lobes, each lobe with
few large teeth, dark green above, downy when young
beneath, turning deep yellow, orange to brown in
autumn, on long stalks. **Bark** Gray-brown,
shallowly fissured into vertical ridges.
Flowers Yellow, fragrant, in
hanging clusters to 10 in
(25 cm) long, in spring
as the leaves emerge.
Fruit Bristly, with large,
smooth wings set at right
angles, to 2 in (5 cm)
long, borne in large,
hanging clusters.
• **NATIVE REGION**
W. North America.
• **HABITAT** Streambanks,
moist woods, and canyons.
• **REMARK** Also known as big-leaf
maple, canyon maple. Size is a distinguishing feature of this handsome tree,
which is bold in leaf, flower, and fruit.

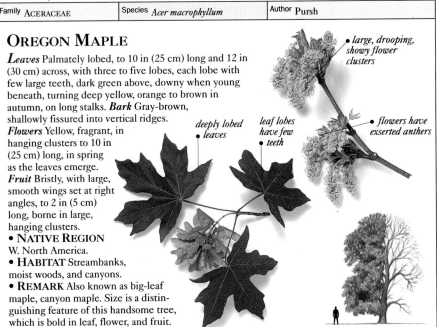

large, drooping, showy flower clusters

deeply lobed leaves

leaf lobes have few teeth

flowers have exserted anthers

| Height 80 ft (25 m) | Shape Broadly columnar | Leaf persistence Deciduous | Leaf type |

Family ACERACEAE	Species *Acer maximowiczianum*	Author Miquel

NIKKO MAPLE

Leaves With three untoothed or slightly toothed leaflets, the central leaflet to 4 in (10 cm) long and 2½ in (6 cm) across, the lateral leaflets smaller and unequal-sided at the base, dark green and smooth above, blue-white and softly hairy beneath, turning red in autumn. *Bark* Gray-brown and smooth. *Flowers* Small and yellow, borne drooping in clusters of three, on downy stalks, in late spring at the same time as the young leaves emerge. *Fruit* With broad, spreading, green wings, to 2 in (5 cm) long.
• NATIVE REGION Japan.
• HABITAT By streams.
• REMARK Also known as *Acer nikoense*. The most notable feature of this species is its autumn color. The fruits, though attractive, rarely contain good seed.

underside of leaflets covered in soft hairs

brilliant autumn color

leaflets edged with shallow teeth

Height 65 ft (20 m)	Shape Broadly spreading	Leaf persistence Deciduous	Leaf type

Family ACERACEAE	Species *Acer miyabei*	Author Maximowicz

ACER MIYABEI

Leaves Palmately lobed, to 5 in (13 cm) long, with three to five lobes, the larger lobes taper-pointed at the tip, each with few large, blunt teeth at the margin, heart-shaped at the base, bright green above, paler beneath, downy on both sides, more densely so beneath, turning yellow in autumn, carried on slender, red stalks; leaf stalk with milky juice when cut. *Bark* Gray-brown, corky, with shallow, orange-brown fissures, peeling in thin scales on old plants. *Flowers* Individually either male or male and female, small and yellow, borne drooping in slender-stalked clusters at the ends of short, leafy shoots, in spring at the same time as the young leaves emerge. *Fruit* With spreading or slightly curved wings, to 1 in (2.5 cm) long.
• NATIVE REGION Japan.
• HABITAT Woods.

green flowers borne in rounded clusters

deeply lobed leaves

fruit wings spread widely

leaf lobes have rounded teeth

Height 40 ft (12 m)	Shape Broadly columnar	Leaf persistence Deciduous	Leaf type

Family ACERACEAE	Species *Acer negundo*	Author Linnaeus

BOX ELDER

Leaves Pinnate, with three to five or seven
toothed, sometimes lobed leaflets, each borne
on a slender rachis and ending in a long, tapered
point, the terminal leaflet to 4 in (10 cm) long and
2½ in (6 cm) across, dark green and smooth
above, smooth or downy beneath.
Bark Gray-brown and smooth.
Flowers Males and females both small,
yellow-green, or pink in some forms,
without petals, the females soon
showing small, developing fruit wings,
in hanging, tassel-like clusters, on
separate plants in spring before or with
the leaves. **Fruit** With down-pointing,
curved wings, to 1½ in (4 cm) long,
persisting on the plant during winter.
• **NATIVE REGION** North America.
• **HABITAT** Riverbanks, on moist soil.
• **REMARK** Also known as ash-leaved
maple. The species
is variable, and has
several cultivated,
ornamental forms.

tassel-like male
flowers have long
filaments

ACER NEGUNDO

• red anthers

leaflet
margin is
• tinged pink

leaflets have
broad yellow
margin •

'ELEGANS' ▷
The leaflets of this form
have a distinctive yellow
variegation.

• leaflets
edged white

'FLAMINGO' ▷
The pink-tinged leaflets
of this form are later
margined with white.

deep pink •
leaf stalk

bronze •
young
leaves

◁ **VAR. VIOLACEUM**
The attractive, bloomy
shoots of this form later
become purplish. The
flowers are pink.

△ **'VARIEGATUM'**
This variegated form
has white-margined
leaflets.

• anthers hang
on long, pink
filaments

Height 65 ft (20 m)	Shape Broadly columnar	Leaf persistence Deciduous	Leaf type

| Family ACERACEAE | Species *Acer opalus* | Author Miller |

ITALIAN MAPLE

Leaves Palmately lobed, to 4 in (10 cm) long and across, with three to five bluntly toothed lobes, glossy green and smooth above, downy when young beneath, turning yellow in autumn. *Bark* Gray tinged pink, peeling in large, square plates. *Flowers* Small and bright yellow, opening on the bare shoots in early spring before the young leaves emerge. *Fruit* With wings, to 1½ in (4 cm) long.
• **NATIVE REGION** S. and W. Europe, from Italy to Spain.
• **HABITAT** Hills and mountains.
• **REMARK** This species is most beautiful when in flower.

flowers appear before leaves

shallow leaf lobes edged with blunt teeth

| Height 65 ft (20 m) | Shape Broadly spreading | Leaf persistence Deciduous | Leaf type |

| Family ACERACEAE | Species *Acer palmatum* | Author Thunberg |

JAPANESE MAPLE

Leaves Rounded in outline, with five to seven deep, taper-pointed, sharply toothed lobes, to 4 in (10 cm) long and across, bright green, smooth, with tufts of hairs in the vein axils beneath, turning red, orange, or yellow in autumn. *Bark* Gray-brown, smooth. *Flowers* Small, red-purple, in upright to drooping clusters in spring as the young leaves emerge. *Fruit* With green or red wings, to ⅜ in (1 cm) long.
• **NATIVE REGION** China, Japan, Korea.
• **HABITAT** Thickets.
• **REMARK** The numerous, mainly shrubby, garden forms include dwarfs, and those with cut-leaved, colored, or variegated foliage.

finely pointed leaf lobes

fruit wings may be tinged red

variable autumn leaf color

slender-stalked flowers

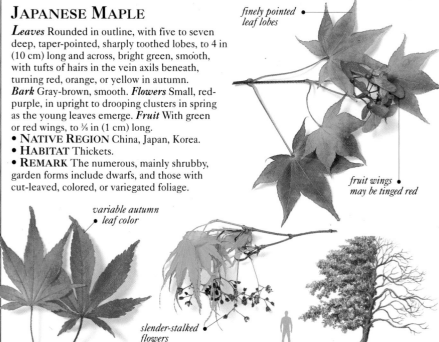

| Height 50 ft (15 m) | Shape Broadly spreading | Leaf persistence Deciduous | Leaf type |

| Family ACERACEAE | Species *Acer palmatum* | Author Thunberg |

leaf lobes taper to fine point

leaves unfold in spring from slender buds

bright pink winter shoots

△ 'ATROPURPUREUM'
This form is selected for its deep red-purple foliage, which turns brilliant red in autumn. It usually makes a smaller tree.

△ 'SENKAKI'

autumn coloration varies from yellow to shades of orange and brown

◁ 'SENKAKI'
Commonly known as coral-bark maple, this form has small leaves, which mature from orange-yellow to pale green, and turn bronze-yellow in autumn.

smaller, sharply lobed leaves crowded in dense masses

purplish leaves very deeply cut into long, slender lobes

△'RIBESIFOLIUM'
This smaller form makes a compact plant, reaching about 16 ft (5 m).

▷ 'LINEARILOBUM ATROPURPUREUM'
Spidery, red-purple leaves characterize this form. Its winged autumn fruits are tinged red, and hang in small clusters.

| Height 50 ft (15 m) | Shape Broadly spreading | Leaf persistence Deciduous | Leaf type |

Family ACERACEAE	Species *Acer pensylvanicum*	Author Linnaeus

MOOSEWOOD

Leaves To 6 in (15 cm) or more long and nearly the same across, with three triangular, taper-pointed, toothed, forward-pointing lobes toward the end, deep yellow-green and smooth above, with red-brown hairs when young beneath, turning yellow in autumn. **Bark** Green, vertically striped red-brown and white, becoming gray with age. **Flowers** Small, yellow-green, borne in drooping racemes in late spring at the same time as the young leaves. **Fruit** With green, down-curved wings, to 1 in (2.5 cm) long.
• **NATIVE REGION** E. North America.
• **HABITAT** Moist woods.
• **REMARK** Also known as striped maple. This species is the only North American stripe-bark maple. The common name, moosewood, is given because moose eat the bark in winter.

leaves cut into three pointed lobes

green flower petals

◁△ ACER PENSYLVANICUM

• *striking winter shoots*

short side lobes •

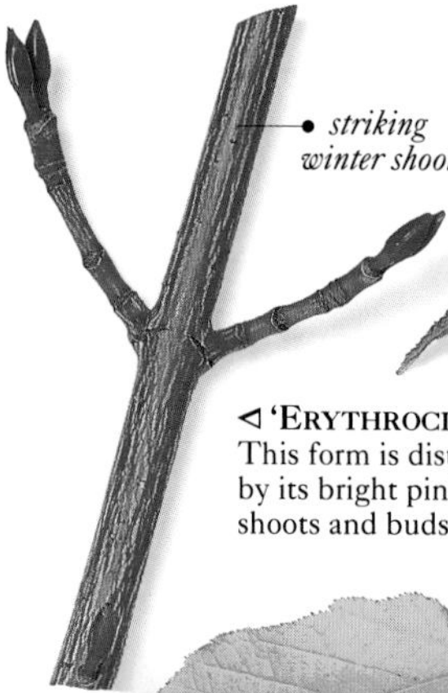

◁ 'ERYTHROCLADUM'
This form is distinguished by its bright pink young shoots and buds.

• *typically striped bark*

• *larger central lobe*

△ ACER PENSYLVANICUM

Height 26 ft (8 m)	Shape Broadly columnar	Leaf persistence Deciduous	Leaf type

Family ACERACEAE	Species *Acer platanoides*	Author Linnaeus

NORWAY MAPLE

Leaves Palmately lobed, to 6 in (15 cm) long
and 7 in (17.5 cm) across, with five lobes, each
lobe ending in several teeth with long, slender
points, bright green, smooth when mature on
both sides, turning yellow or sometimes red in
autumn; the long, slender leaf stalk exudes
milky juice when cut. *Bark* Gray and smooth.
Flowers Small and bright yellow-green, borne
in conspicuous clusters in spring before and
with the young leaves. *Fruit* With large,
spreading wings, to 2 in (5 cm) long.
• **NATIVE REGION** S.W. Asia, Europe.
• **HABITAT** Mountain woods.
• **REMARK** A fast-growing species that
quickly reaches its maximum height. In
cultivation, it has
many ornamental
forms, selected
for both foliage
and habit.

• *lobes end in
slender teeth*

*fruits have •
large wings*

◁ **ACER
PLATANOIDES**

△ **ACER
PLATANOIDES**

*flowers open •
before leaves*

▽ **'CRIMSON KING'**
This form has deep red-purple leaves
and red bud scales and flower stalks.

▽ **'CRIMSON SENTRY'**
The bright red young leaves
of this form mature to deep
purple-green. The tree has
an upright habit.

*red bud
• scales*

• *red
flower stalks*

• *leaf stalks
are deep purple*

*mature leaves •
are deep purple*

*young leaves •
are reddish*

Height 80 ft (25 m)	Shape Broadly columnar	Leaf persistence Deciduous	Leaf type

Family ACERACEAE	Species *Acer platanoides*	Author Linnaeus

∇ 'CUCULLATUM'
This form is selected for its unusual foliage. The leaves are fan-shaped, but end in downturned, twisted, clawlike lobes, which make the leaves appear almost distorted.

young leaves are purplish red •

lobe ends • turn under

mature leaves • are deep green

△ 'DEBORAH'
The leaves of this form are colored red as they emerge and unfold, and later mature to dark green.

• shallow leaf lobes

broad, creamy • leaf margin

∇ 'LORBERGII'
This smaller form reaches 50 ft (15 m). The pale green leaves are deeply cut into five lobes, which are smooth at the margin and long-pointed at the tip.

△ 'DRUMMONDII'
A strikingly variegated form in which the broad, creamy yellow leaf margin matures to creamy white. Reverting shoots with all green leaves are occasionally produced.

leaves are • divided to the base

Height 80 ft (25 m)	Shape Broadly columnar	Leaf persistence Deciduous	Leaf type

| Family ACERACEAE | Species *Acer pseudoplatanus* | Author Linnaeus |

SYCAMORE MAPLE

Leaves Palmately lobed, to 4¾ in (12 cm) long and 6 in (15 cm) across, with five coarsely toothed lobes, dark green and smooth above, blue-gray beneath. *Bark* Pinkish to yellowish gray, peeling in irregular plates. *Flowers* Small and yellow-green, without petals, in dense, hanging clusters in spring with the young leaves. *Fruit* With somewhat down-pointing wings, to 1 in (2.5 cm) long.
• **NATIVE REGION** S.W. Asia, Europe.
• **HABITAT** Deciduous mountain woods.
• **REMARK** In Scotland, also known as plane. The species is widely naturalized in North America and Great Britain. In open sites, it may tend toward a spreading shape.

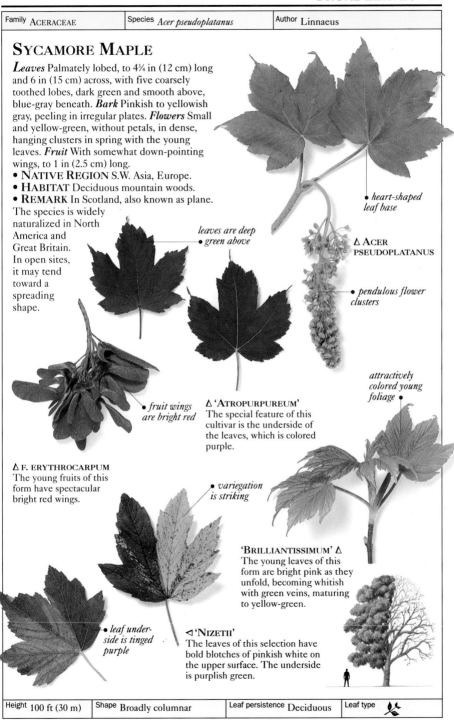

• *heart-shaped leaf base*

leaves are deep green above •

△ **ACER PSEUDOPLATANUS**

• *pendulous flower clusters*

attractively colored young foliage •

• *fruit wings are bright red*

△ **'ATROPURPUREUM'**
The special feature of this cultivar is the underside of the leaves, which is colored purple.

△ F. ERYTHROCARPUM
The young fruits of this form have spectacular bright red wings.

• *variegation is striking*

'BRILLIANTISSIMUM' △
The young leaves of this form are bright pink as they unfold, becoming whitish with green veins, maturing to yellow-green.

• *leaf underside is tinged purple*

◁ **'NIZETII'**
The leaves of this selection have bold blotches of pinkish white on the upper surface. The underside is purplish green.

| Height 100 ft (30 m) | Shape Broadly columnar | Leaf persistence Deciduous | Leaf type |

Family ACERACEAE	Species *Acer rubrum*	Author Linnaeus

RED MAPLE

Leaves To 4 in (10 cm) long and nearly the same across, with three or five toothed lobes, dark green and smooth above, blue-white with hairs on the veins beneath, turning red or yellow in autumn. **Bark** Dark gray and smooth. **Flowers** Small and red, on slender stalks, in dense clusters on the shoots in early spring. **Fruit** With red wings, about ¾ in (2 cm) long.
• **NATIVE REGION** E. North America.
• **HABITAT** Moist ground.

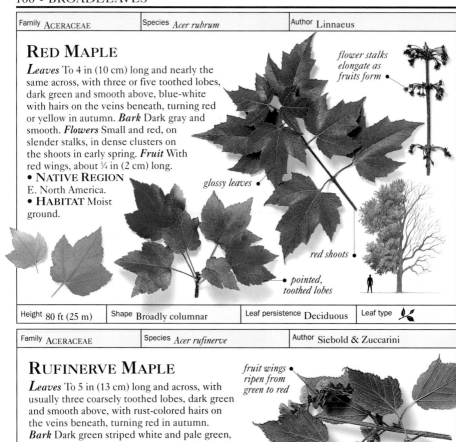

flower stalks elongate as fruits form

glossy leaves

red shoots

pointed, toothed lobes

Height 80 ft (25 m)	Shape Broadly columnar	Leaf persistence Deciduous	Leaf type

Family ACERACEAE	Species *Acer rufinerve*	Author Siebold & Zuccarini

RUFINERVE MAPLE

Leaves To 5 in (13 cm) long and across, with usually three coarsely toothed lobes, dark green and smooth above, with rust-colored hairs on the veins beneath, turning red in autumn. **Bark** Dark green striped white and pale green, with diamond-shaped marks, gray and fissured with age. **Flowers** Small and yellow-green, in upright racemes in spring. **Fruit** With spreading wings, to ¾ in (2 cm) long.
• **NATIVE REGION** Japan.
• **HABITAT** Mountain woods.

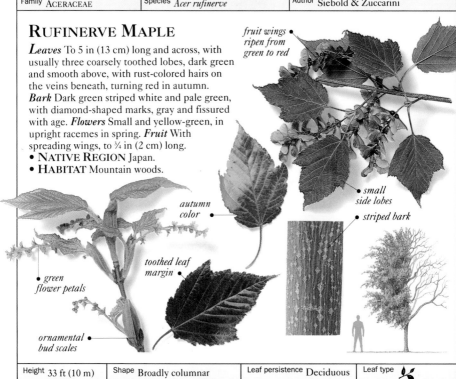

fruit wings ripen from green to red

autumn color

small side lobes

striped bark

toothed leaf margin

green flower petals

ornamental bud scales

Height 33 ft (10 m)	Shape Broadly columnar	Leaf persistence Deciduous	Leaf type

| Family ACERACEAE | Species *Acer saccharinum* | Author Linnaeus |

SILVER MAPLE

Leaves Palmately lobed, to 6 in (15 cm) long and across, with five lobes, each itself lobed and sharply toothed, light green and smooth above, blue-white and thinly hairy beneath, usually turning yellow in autumn. *Bark* Gray, smooth, flaking with age. *Flowers* Males and females both small and greenish yellow, without petals, in clusters on the shoots in early spring. *Fruit* With spreading wings, to ¾ in (2 cm) long.
• **NATIVE REGION**
E. North America.
• **HABITAT** Moist soil and riverbanks.

blue-white underside of leaf

leaves turn yellow in autumn

lobes narrow towards leaf base

| Height 100 ft (30 m) | Shape Broadly columnar | Leaf persistence Deciduous | Leaf type |

| Family ACERACEAE | Species *Acer saccharum* | Author Marshall |

SUGAR MAPLE

Leaves Palmately lobed, to 5 in (13 cm) long and slightly more across, with five lobes, the three largest with few prominent teeth, heart-shaped at the base, mid- to dark green above, with hairs in the vein axils beneath, turning yellow to orange or red in autumn. *Bark* Gray-brown, smooth, becoming furrowed and scaly with age. *Flowers* Small, yellow-green, without petals, drooping on slender stalks, in open clusters in spring with the young leaves. *Fruit* With nearly parallel wings, to 1 in (2.5 cm) long.
• **NATIVE REGION**
E. North America.
• **HABITAT** Rich woods.
• **REMARK** Also known as rock maple. The sap is processed into maple syrup.

tapered lobes edged with few teeth

variable autumn leaf color

| Height 100 ft (30 m) | Shape Broadly columnar | Leaf persistence Deciduous | Leaf type |

Family ACERACEAE	Species *Acer shirasawanum*	Author Koidzumi

ACER SHIRASAWANUM

Leaves Rounded in outline, to 4¾ in (12 cm) long and across, with about 11 sharply toothed lobes, bright green above, smooth on both sides, turning orange and red in autumn. **Bark** Gray-brown and smooth. **Flowers** Small, with a pink calyx and cream sepals, in spreading to upright clusters in spring with the leaves. **Fruit** With widely spreading wings, in upright clusters.
• **NATIVE REGION** Japan.
• **HABITAT** Mountain slopes and valleys.
• **REMARK** This species is often confused with the full-moon maple *(Acer japonicum,* see p.90), to which it is related.

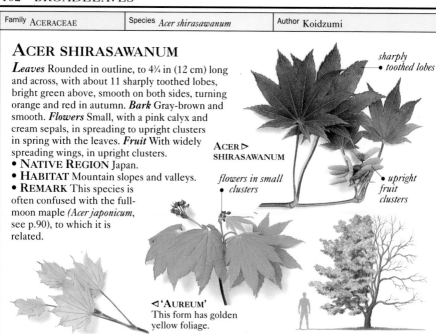

sharply • toothed lobes

ACER ▷
SHIRASAWANUM

flowers in small • clusters

• *upright fruit clusters*

◁ **'AUREUM'**
This form has golden yellow foliage.

Height 65 ft (20 m)	Shape Broadly spreading	Leaf persistence Deciduous	Leaf type

Family ACERACEAE	Species *Acer sieboldianum*	Author Miquel

ACER SIEBOLDIANUM

Leaves Rounded in outline, to 3 in (7.5 cm) long and the same across, with seven to nine or some-times eleven taper-pointed, sharply toothed lobes, cut nearly to the middle, pale green, covered in white hairs when young becoming dark green above, downy beneath, turning red in autumn, on downy stalks. **Bark** Dark gray-brown and smooth. **Flowers** Small, with yellow petals and purplish sepals, in long-stalked, drooping, downy clusters in spring at the same time as the young leaves emerge. **Fruit** With spreading wings, to ¾ in (2 cm) long.
• **NATIVE REGION** Japan.
• **HABITAT** Sunny ridges, streambanks in the mountains.

wings redden as fruits ripen

• *leaves color richly in autumn*

hairy leaf • stalks

shoots are hairy • when young

Height 33 ft (10 m)	Shape Broadly spreading	Leaf persistence Deciduous	Leaf type

Family ACERACEAE	Species *Acer spicatum*	Author Lamarck

MOUNTAIN MAPLE

Leaves Palmately lobed, to 4¾ in (12 cm) long, with three or five taper-pointed, coarsely toothed lobes, deep yellow-green and smooth with impressed veins above, downy beneath, turning yellow, orange, or red in autumn. *Bark* Gray-brown and smooth. *Flowers* Small and greenish white, numerous, borne in dense, slender, upright panicles to 6 in (15 cm) long, in early summer. *Fruit* With wings spreading at about a right angle, to 1 in (2.5 cm) long, green often becoming red.
• **NATIVE REGION** E. North America.
• **HABITAT** Cool, moist woods, usually in mountains.
• **REMARK** Can be either a small, bushy tree or a large shrub. It is widely distributed in its habitat. A number of related species are native to E. Asia.

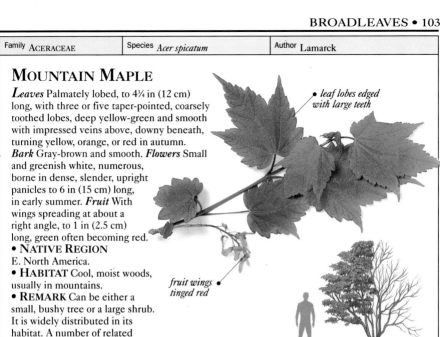

leaf lobes edged with large teeth

fruit wings tinged red

Height 26 ft (8 m)	Shape Broadly spreading	Leaf persistence Deciduous	Leaf type

Family ACERACEAE	Species *Acer trautvetteri*	Author Medwedew

RED-BUD MAPLE

Leaves Palmately lobed, to 6 in (15 cm) long and 8 in (20 cm) across, with five coarsely toothed lobes, cut more than halfway to the base, glossy dark green and smooth above, blue-green with tufts of hairs in the vein axils beneath, turning deep golden yellow in autumn, carried on long, red stalks. *Bark* Pale gray and smooth. *Flowers* Individually small and yellow, borne in upright clusters in spring at the same time as the young leaves emerge among bright red bud scales. *Fruit* With broad, bright red, nearly parallel wings, to 2 in (5 cm) long.
• **NATIVE REGION** S.W. Asia, Caucasus.
• **HABITAT** Mixed deciduous and evergreen forests.
• **REMARK** The fruits are an attractive feature.

young leaves emerge pale green

leaves are deeply lobed

bright red bud scales

leaf lobes edged with large teeth

fruits have broad, red wings

Height 50 ft (15 m)	Shape Broadly spreading	Leaf persistence Deciduous	Leaf type

Family ACERACEAE	Species *Acer triflorum*	Author Komarov

ACER TRIFLORUM

Leaves With three few-toothed leaflets, the central leaflet to 4 in (10 cm) long and 1½ in (4 cm) across, pale green above, with bristly hairs on both sides, turning bright orange or red in autumn. ***Bark*** Pale brown to gray-brown, peeling vertically. ***Flowers*** Small and yellow, in drooping clusters of three in spring with the young leaves. ***Fruit*** With nearly parallel wings, to 1½ in (4 cm) long.
• **NATIVE REGION** N.E. China, Korea.
• **HABITAT** Mountain woods and ravines.

leaflets edged with sparse teeth

very hairy flower stalks

bluish underside of leaflets

bronze young leaves

bright autumn foliage

Height 40 ft (12 m)	Shape Broadly spreading	Leaf persistence Deciduous	Leaf type

Family ACERACEAE	Species *Acer velutinum*	Author Boissier

PERSIAN MAPLE

Leaves Palmately lobed, to 6 in (15 cm) long and across, usually with five coarsely toothed lobes, yellow-green above, very downy beneath, on long stalks. ***Bark*** Gray-brown and smooth. ***Flowers*** Small and green, in large, upright clusters in late spring just after the young leaves emerge. ***Fruit*** With large wings set at right angles, to 1½ in (4 cm) long.
• **NATIVE REGION** Caucasus, N. Iran.
• **HABITAT** Mountain woods.
• **REMARK** Leaves are similar to, but larger than, those of sycamore *(Acer pseudoplatanus, see p.99).*

yellow-green upper surface of leaves

small lobes at leaf base

green flowers borne in upright clusters

leaf lobes edged with coarse teeth

Height 50 ft (15 m)	Shape Broadly spreading	Leaf persistence Deciduous	Leaf type

ANACARDIACEAE

WITH A WIDE DISTRIBUTION in the warm regions of the world, this family contains over 800 species of evergreen and deciduous trees, shrubs, and climbing plants, collected in 80 genera. The leaves are nearly always alternate and are pinnate or simple.

Small male and female flowers are sometimes borne on separate plants. The foliage often contains a skin-irritating resin. Other family members include the cashew nut *(Anacardium occidentale)*, mango *(Mangifera indica)*, and poison ivy *(Rhus radicans)*.

Family ANACARDIACEAE	Species *Cotinus obovatus*	Author Rafinesque

AMERICAN SMOKE TREE

Leaves Obovate, to 6 in (15 cm) long and 3 in (7.5 cm) across, thin, untoothed, bronze when young becoming blue-green, smooth above, hairy beneath, turning brilliant yellow to orange and red in autumn. **Bark** Gray-brown, becoming scaly with age. **Flowers** Males and females both small and yellow, in long, conical clusters at the ends of the shoots, usually on separate plants in early summer. **Fruit** Individually small, clustered together, with numerous, slender, feathery flower stalks.
• **NATIVE REGION** C. and S. United States.
• **HABITAT** Rocky hills.

tiny flowers borne in large panicles

bronze young leaves

brilliant autumn color

leaves have untoothed margin

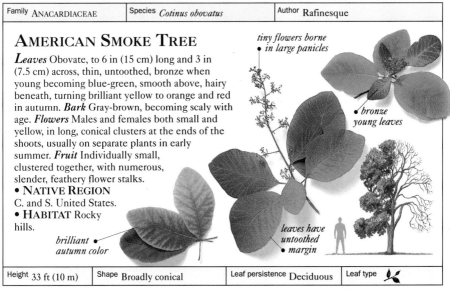

Height 33 ft (10 m)	Shape Broadly conical	Leaf persistence Deciduous	Leaf type

Family ANACARDIACEAE	Species *Rhus copallina*	Author Linnaeus

SHINY SUMAC

Leaves Pinnate, to 14 in (35 cm) long, with up to 23 oblong, narrow, usually untoothed leaflets, to 4 in (10 cm) long and ¾ in (2 cm) across, downy becoming glossy dark green above, paler and hairy beneath, turning bright red in autumn. **Bark** Dark gray, thinly scaly. **Flowers** Small, yellowish, in dense, conical clusters at the ends of the shoots in summer. **Fruit** Small, densely packed into a conical, bright red cluster, to 8 in (20 cm) long.
• **NATIVE REGION** E. North America.
• **HABITAT** Mountains, woods, and scrub, on dry soil.

leaf rachis has broad wings

Height 33 ft (10 m)	Shape Broadly spreading	Leaf persistence Deciduous	Leaf type

Family ANACARDIACEAE	Species *Rhus trichocarpa*	Author Miquel

RHUS TRICHOCARPA

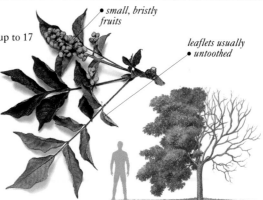

• *small, bristly fruits*

leaflets usually • untoothed

Leaves To 20 in (50 cm) long, with up to 17 ovate, taper-pointed leaflets, to 4 in (10 cm) long and 1½ in (4 cm) across, reddish becoming matte dark green, downy, turning orange-red in autumn. *Bark* Pale gray-brown, with conspicuous lenticels. *Flowers* Tiny, yellowish, in conical panicles in the leaf axils in summer. *Fruit* Small, brownish yellow.
• **NATIVE REGION** China, Japan, Korea.
• **HABITAT** Mountain and roadside thickets.

Height 26 ft (8 m)	Shape Broadly spreading	Leaf persistence Deciduous	Leaf type

Family ANACARDIACEAE	Species *Rhus typhina*	Author Linnaeus

STAGHORN SUMAC

◁ **RHUS TYPHINA**

Leaves To 24 in (60 cm) long, with up to 27 lanceolate to oblong, sharply toothed leaflets, to 4¾ in (12 cm) long and 2 in (5 cm) across, dark green above, blue-green beneath, downy on both sides when young becoming nearly smooth, turning bright orange and red in autumn, on stout, velvety shoots. *Bark* Dark brown and smooth. *Flowers* Males and females both small and green, in dense, conical clusters at the ends of the shoots, on the same plant or on separate plants in summer. *Fruit* Small, bright red, in a dense, conical cluster, to 8 in (20 cm) long.
• **NATIVE REGION** E. North America.
• **HABITAT** Meadows, scrub, and wood margins, often on dry, rocky soil.

• *leaves color brilliantly in autumn*

RHUS TYPHINA ▷

lobed leaflets •

flowers are green

◁ **'DISSECTA'**
This ornamental form has finely cut leaflets.

Height 33 ft (10 m)	Shape Broadly spreading	Leaf persistence Deciduous	Leaf type

ANNONACEAE

A MAINLY TROPICAL FAMILY, with more than 2,000 species, related to the magnolias *(Magnolia,* see pp.202–215). The trees typically have simple, alternate leaves, and flowers with the petals arranged in whorls of three. The custard apples *(Annona)* are well-known members of the family.

Family ANNONACEAE	Species *Asimina triloba*	Author (Linnaeus) Dunal

PAWPAW

Leaves Oblong to obovate, to 10 in (25 cm) long, taper-pointed at the tip, untoothed, rather pale green, downy when young becoming smooth beneath, turning yellow in autumn. **Bark** Gray-brown, becoming somewhat rough and scaly with age. **Flowers** To 1½ in (4 cm) across, green at first becoming purple-brown, with six petals, the inner three upright, the outer three larger and spreading, borne singly on short, stout stalks on the old shoots in late spring as the young leaves emerge. **Fruit** Fleshy and edible, to 6 in (15 cm) long, green at first becoming yellow-brown when ripe.
• **NATIVE REGION** E. North America.
• **HABITAT** Rich, moist woods.
• **REMARK** The flavor of the unusual fruits may be likened to that of bananas. This species is often confused with *Carica papaya,* a tropical tree grown for its edible fruits, and also known by the common name pawpaw.

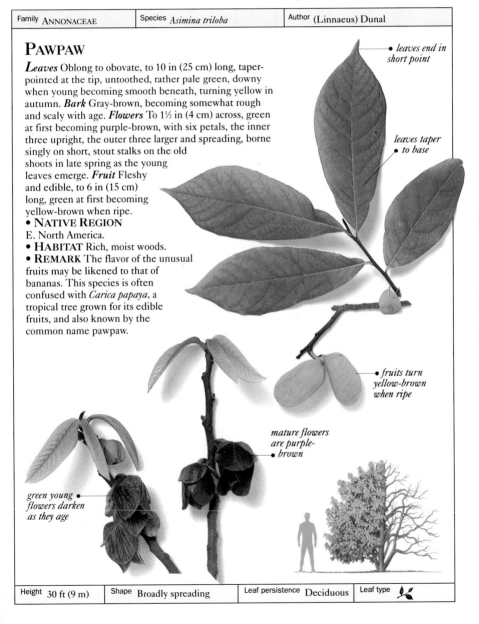

leaves end in short point

leaves taper to base

fruits turn yellow-brown when ripe

mature flowers are purple-brown

green young flowers darken as they age

Height 30 ft (9 m)	Shape Broadly spreading	Leaf persistence Deciduous	Leaf type

AQUIFOLIACEAE

A FAMILY OF WIDE DISTRIBUTION in temperate and tropical regions, comprising over 700 evergreen and deciduous species, almost all of which are hollies *(Ilex)*. The trees and shrubs usually have alternate leaves. Male and female flowers are small, white or pink, borne on separate plants; females develop in autumn into yellow, red, orange, or black berries. The leaves of *Ilex paraguariensis*, a South American species, are used for yerba maté tea.

Family AQUIFOLIACEAE	Species *Ilex* x *altaclerensis*	Author (hort. ex Loudon) Dallimore

HIGHCLERE HOLLY

Leaves Variable in size and shape, oblong to ovate or nearly rounded, to 5 in (13 cm) or more long and 3 in (7.5 cm) across, spine-tipped and often with a spiny margin, glossy dark green above. *Bark* Gray and smooth. *Flowers* Males and females both small and white, usually tinged purple, fragrant, in clusters in the leaf axils, borne on separate plants in spring.
Fruit A large, fleshy, red berry.
• NATIVE REGION Of garden origin.
• REMARK A hybrid between the common holly *(Ilex aquifolium,* see p.109) and *Ilex perado,* a species native to the Canary Islands, Madeira, and the Azores. This hybrid is recognized mainly as named cultivars and appears in many ornamental forms.

◁ 'BELGICA AUREA'
The long leaves of this female plant have few spines.

• *reddish purple leaf stalks*

• *creamy yellow leaf margin*

• *deeply veined leaves*

△ 'CAMELLIIFOLIA'
A female plant, with nearly spineless leaves, purple when young.

'GOLDEN KING' △
The broad, thick leaves of this female plant have a bold, yellow margin.

red-tinged buds open into white flowers •

'LAWSONIANA' ▷
The yellow-splashed leaves of this female plant have a nearly spineless margin.

glossy, dark leaves •

△ 'HODGINSII'
A male plant, with large, few-spined, dark green leaves and purple shoots.

◁ 'WILSONII'
This female plant has large leaves.

• *irregularly blotched yellow and green marks on leaves*

Height 65 ft (20 m)	Shape Broadly columnar	Leaf persistence Evergreen	Leaf type

Family AQUIFOLIACEAE	Species *Ilex aquifolium*	Author Linnaeus

ENGLISH HOLLY

Leaves Variable, elliptic to ovate, to 4 in (10 cm) long and 2 in (5 cm) across, spine-tipped, juveniles on lower part of plant with a very spiny margin, adults with a more or less spineless margin, glossy dark green above. *Bark* Pale gray and smooth. *Flowers* Males and females small and white or purple-tinged, fragrant, in clusters in the leaf axils, usually on separate plants in late spring. *Fruit* A usually red berry, to ⅜ in (1 cm) across.
• NATIVE REGION W. Asia, Europe.
• HABITAT Woods, particularly those of beech and oak.
• REMARK This species has given rise to numerous variations in both leaf and fruit.

▽ ILEX AQUIFOLIUM

• *female flowers have prominent green ovary*

• *male flowers*

◁ ILEX AQUIFOLIUM

• *leaves both with and without spines*

◁ ILEX AQUIFOLIUM

• *red, densely clustered berries*

'CRISPA AUREA PICTA' ▷
The thick, often twisted, leaves of this male form are spineless, except at the tip, and have a central yellow and pale green blotch.

• *spine emerges from indented leaf tip*

▽ 'ARGENTEA MARGINATA'
This female plant has pink young leaves, green shoots, and red berries.

spiny leaves have creamy white • *margin*

berries borne • *abundantly*

◁ 'FEROX'
The spines on the upper surface of the leaves give this male plant its common name, hedgehog holly.

'BACCIFLAVA' △
This handsome cultivar bears yellow berries and has spiny leaves.

• *pale spines on upper leaf surface*

Height 65 ft (20 m)	Shape Broadly columnar	Leaf persistence Evergreen	Leaf type

Family AQUIFOLIACEAE	Species *Ilex aquifolium*	Author Linnaeus

▽ 'FLAVESCENS'
The moonlight holly, a female plant, has leaves flushed yellow. The leaf stalk and midrib are also yellow.

creamy spines on leaf surface and
• at margin

• leaves may be irregularly spined

• glossy green surface either side of leaf midrib

△ 'FEROX ARGENTEA'
The leaves of this male cultivar have a creamy yellow to white margin. The tree is commonly known as silver hedgehog holly.

• leaves may have smooth margin

leaf margin may be tinged pink •

• red berries borne in abundance

◁ 'J.C. VAN TOL'
This is a female plant. Its thick leaves are glossy dark green and smooth above and have few spines or none at all.

△ 'HANDSWORTH NEW SILVER'
Purple stems, white-margined leaves, and small red berries characterize this female form.

• deeply impressed leaf veins

Height 65 ft (20 m)	Shape Broadly columnar	Leaf persistence Evergreen	Leaf type

Family AQUIFOLIACEAE	Species *Ilex aquifolium*	Author Linnaeus

'MADAME BRIOT' ▷
The leaves of this bushy
female form are broad
and have a dark
yellow margin. The
tree bears scarlet
berries in autumn.

*stems and
leaf stalks
flushed
purple* •

*older stems
become
• green*

• *large, strongly
spined
leaves*

*berries grow •
in tight
clusters*

△ **'PYRAMIDALIS
FRUCTU LUTEO'**
The oval, glossy
green, often spineless,
leaves of this female
plant contrast well
with the abundant
yellow berries.

• *leaves may
be spined at
tip only*

*some spines •
point up,
some down*

*berries carried •
close to the stem
on short stalks*

*flower
buds in
• leaf axils*

△ **'SILVER MILKMAID'**
The leaves of this old cultivar
are dark green, with a creamy
white blotch in the center. It
has red berries. In spite of the
inappropriate name, plants
that were once called 'Silver
Milkboy' are also female.

• *faint gray-
green marbling
on leaves*

△ **'SILVER QUEEN'**
This male clone has
broad white-margined
leaves, which are pale
orange-pink when young.
The shoots are colored
deep purple.

Height 65 ft (20 m)	Shape Broadly columnar	Leaf persistence Evergreen	Leaf type

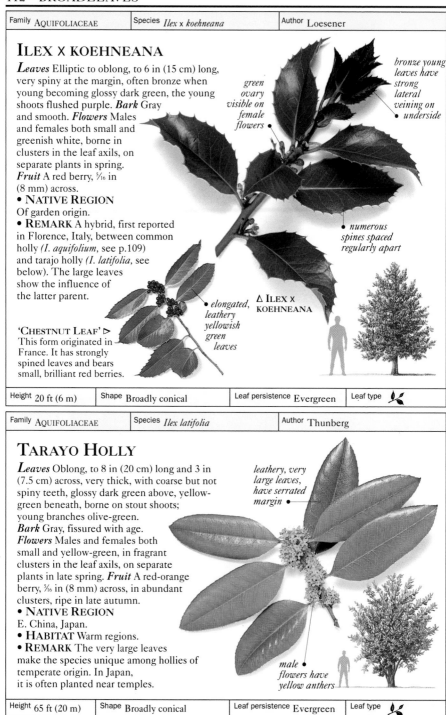

Family AQUIFOLIACEAE	Species *Ilex x koehneana*	Author Loesener

ILEX X KOEHNEANA

Leaves Elliptic to oblong, to 6 in (15 cm) long, very spiny at the margin, often bronze when young becoming glossy dark green, the young shoots flushed purple. **Bark** Gray and smooth. **Flowers** Males and females both small and greenish white, borne in clusters in the leaf axils, on separate plants in spring. **Fruit** A red berry, 5⁄16 in (8 mm) across.
• **NATIVE REGION**
Of garden origin.
• **REMARK** A hybrid, first reported in Florence, Italy, between common holly *(I. aquifolium, see p.109)* and tarajo holly *(I. latifolia, see below)*. The large leaves show the influence of the latter parent.

green ovary visible on female flowers

bronze young leaves have strong lateral veining on underside

numerous spines spaced regularly apart

△ ILEX X KOEHNEANA

elongated, leathery yellowish green leaves

'CHESTNUT LEAF' ▷
This form originated in France. It has strongly spined leaves and bears small, brilliant red berries.

Height 20 ft (6 m)	Shape Broadly conical	Leaf persistence Evergreen	Leaf type

Family AQUIFOLIACEAE	Species *Ilex latifolia*	Author Thunberg

TARAYO HOLLY

Leaves Oblong, to 8 in (20 cm) long and 3 in (7.5 cm) across, very thick, with coarse but not spiny teeth, glossy dark green above, yellow-green beneath, borne on stout shoots; young branches olive-green. **Bark** Gray, fissured with age. **Flowers** Males and females both small and yellow-green, in fragrant clusters in the leaf axils, on separate plants in late spring. **Fruit** A red-orange berry, 5⁄16 in (8 mm) across, in abundant clusters, ripe in late autumn.
• **NATIVE REGION**
E. China, Japan.
• **HABITAT** Warm regions.
• **REMARK** The very large leaves make the species unique among hollies of temperate origin. In Japan, it is often planted near temples.

leathery, very large leaves, have serrated margin

male flowers have yellow anthers

Height 65 ft (20 m)	Shape Broadly conical	Leaf persistence Evergreen	Leaf type

Family AQUIFOLIACEAE	Species *Ilex opaca*	Author Aiton

AMERICAN HOLLY

Leaves Elliptic, to 4 in (10 cm) long and 2 in (5 cm) across, spiny at the tip and margin, matte dark green or yellow-green above, yellow-green beneath. *Bark* Gray and smooth. *Flowers* Males and females small, dull white, in the leaf axils, usually on separate plants in late spring. *Fruit* A usually red berry, to ⅜ in (1 cm) across.
• **NATIVE REGION** E. United States.
• **HABITAT** Sandy soil near the coasts and moist woods.

smooth, matte upper leaf surface

female flowers

Height 50 ft (15 m)	Shape Broadly conical	Leaf persistence Evergreen	Leaf type

Family AQUIFOLIACEAE	Species *Ilex pedunculosa*	Author Miquel

ILEX PEDUNCULOSA

Leaves Ovate to elliptic, to 3 in (7.5 cm) long and 1¼ in (3 cm) across, taper-pointed, untoothed, glossy dark green above. *Bark* Gray-green, smooth. *Flowers* Males and females small, white, in the leaf axils and on the shoots, on separate plants in summer. *Fruit* A bright red berry, to 5/16 in (8 mm) across.
• **NATIVE REGION** China, Japan, Taiwan.
• **HABITAT** Woods and thickets.

leaf margin turns bronze

male flowers borne in clusters

long fruit stalks

Height 33 ft (10 m)	Shape Broadly conical	Leaf persistence Evergreen	Leaf type

Family AQUIFOLIACEAE	Species *Ilex purpurea*	Author Hasskarl

ILEX PURPUREA

Leaves Elliptic-lanceolate, to 4¾ in (12 cm) long and 1½ in (4 cm) across, tapered, toothed, glossy dark green above, paler beneath, smooth. *Bark* Gray, smooth. *Flowers* Males and females deep reddish lilac, the corona with four reflexed lobes, in the leaf axils and on the shoots, on separate plants in early to mid-summer. *Fruit* A red berry, 5/16 in (8 mm) long.
• **NATIVE REGION** China, Japan.
• **HABITAT** Mountain woods.

numerous male flowers clustered together

bronze young foliage

Height 42 ft (13 m)	Shape Broadly conical	Leaf persistence Evergreen	Leaf type

ARALIACEAE

WITH MORE THAN 50 GENERA and some 800 species, this family of evergreen and deciduous trees, shrubs, and herbaceous plants is found all over the world, particularly in the tropics. The leaves are usually compound or lobed, and the small, greenish white or white flowers are borne in clusters.

Family ARALIACEAE	Species *Aralia spinosa*	Author Linnaeus

DEVIL'S WALKING STICK

Leaves Bipinnate and very large, to 39 in (1 m) or more long, with numerous ovate, taper-pointed, toothed leaflets, to 3 in (7.5 cm) long and 1½ in (4 cm) across, bronze when young becoming dark green above, paler beneath, hairy on both sides, turning yellow to purple in autumn, with a prickly stalk, carried on very stout, spiny shoots. *Bark* Gray, with stout prickles. *Flowers* Small and white, in small, rounded clusters, the clusters forming large heads, borne on a single main axis in late summer. *Fruit* Rounded and purple-black, ¼ in (6 mm) long.
- **NATIVE REGION** E. United States.
- **HABITAT** Riverbanks and moist woods.
- **REMARK** Also known as angelica tree, Hercules' club.

small blackish fruits carried on red stalks

ARALIA △ ▽ SPINOSA

large leaves composed of numerous leaflets

▽ ARALIA ELATA
This similar species, from northeast Asia and Japan, flowers in autumn, when *Aralia spinosa* is in fruit.

flowers have exserted yellow anthers

flower clusters have one central stalk

flower clusters branch from base of stem

Height 33 ft (10 m)	Shape Broadly spreading	Leaf persistence Deciduous	Leaf type

Family ARALIACEAE	Species *Kalopanax pictus*	Author (Thunberg) Nakai

CASTOR ARALIA

Leaves Palmately lobed, with five to seven toothed lobes, to 10 in (25 cm) or more long and across, glossy dark green and smooth above, downy when young beneath. **Bark** Black-brown, spiny, deeply fissured. **Flowers** Individually small and white, numerous, with slender stalks, borne in large, rounded clusters in late summer. **Fruit** Rounded, blue-black, about ³⁄₁₆ in (5 mm) long.
• **NATIVE REGION** China, Eastern Russian Federation, Japan, Korea.
• **HABITAT** Riverbanks and other moist places in forests.
• **REMARK** The young leaves of this species are edible when cooked. The similar *Kalopanax pictus* var. *maximowiczii* has deeply lobed leaves, which are cut more than halfway to the base.

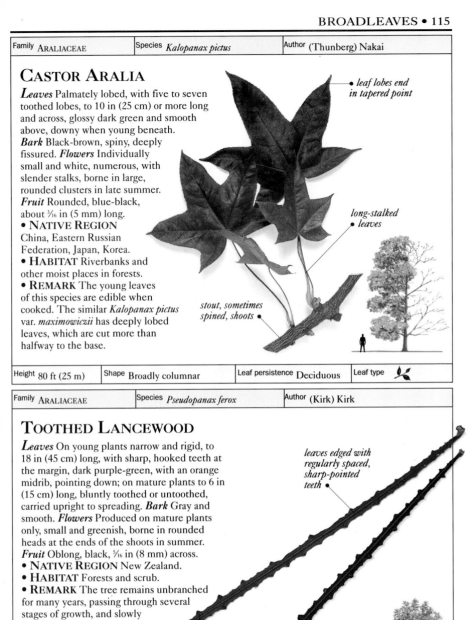

leaf lobes end in tapered point

long-stalked leaves

stout, sometimes spined, shoots

Height 80 ft (25 m)	Shape Broadly columnar	Leaf persistence Deciduous	Leaf type

Family ARALIACEAE	Species *Pseudopanax ferox*	Author (Kirk) Kirk

TOOTHED LANCEWOOD

Leaves On young plants narrow and rigid, to 18 in (45 cm) long, with sharp, hooked teeth at the margin, dark purple-green, with an orange midrib, pointing down; on mature plants to 6 in (15 cm) long, bluntly toothed or untoothed, carried upright to spreading. **Bark** Gray and smooth. **Flowers** Produced on mature plants only, small and greenish, borne in rounded heads at the ends of the shoots in summer. **Fruit** Oblong, black, ⁵⁄₁₆ in (8 mm) across.
• **NATIVE REGION** New Zealand.
• **HABITAT** Forests and scrub.
• **REMARK** The tree remains unbranched for many years, passing through several stages of growth, and slowly developing the small, rounded head of a mature plant. The related *P. crassifolius* is commoner in the wild. This New Zealand native has even longer juvenile leaves, which may reach 39 in (1 m) or more.

leaves edged with regularly spaced, sharp-pointed teeth

prominent central vein

Height 17 ft (5 m)	Shape Unique	Leaf persistence Evergreen	Leaf type

BETULACEAE

S OME OF THE best-known catkin-bearing plants belong to the birch family, which also includes the hazels *(Corylus,* see p.127). Its six genera and more than 150 species of deciduous trees and shrubs grow wild mainly in northern temperate regions; alders *(Alnus,* see pp.116–117) extend to the Andes. The leaves are alternate. Male and female flowers are borne in separate catkins on the same plant, but only the males are conspicuous.

Family BETULACEAE	Species *Alnus cordata*	Author Desfontaines

ITALIAN ALDER

Leaves Rounded, to 4 in (10 cm) long and across, toothed, glossy dark green and smooth above, paler with hairs in the vein axils beneath. **Bark** Gray, smooth, fissured with age. **Flowers** In catkins, males to 3 in (7.5 cm) long, yellow, females small, red, upright, borne on the same plant in early spring. **Fruit** Woody, 1¼ in (3 cm) long, green ripening to brown.
• **NATIVE REGION** Corsica, C. and S. Italy.
• **HABITAT** Deciduous woods in mountains.

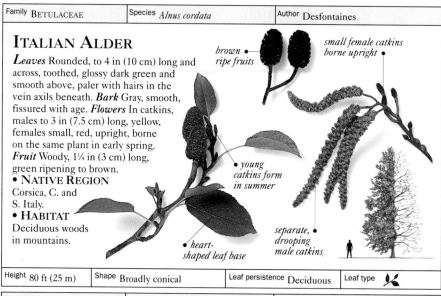

brown • ripe fruits

small female catkins borne upright •

• young catkins form in summer

separate, • drooping male catkins

• heart-shaped leaf base

Height 80 ft (25 m)	Shape Broadly conical	Leaf persistence Deciduous	Leaf type

Family BETULACEAE	Species *Alnus glutinosa*	Author (Linnaeus) Gaertner

COMMON ALDER

Leaves Obovate, to 4 in (10 cm) long and about 3 in (7.5 cm) across, toothed, dark green and smooth above, with tufts of hairs in the vein axils beneath. **Bark** Dark gray, fissured. **Flowers** In catkins, males to 4 in (10 cm) long, yellow-green, drooping, females small, red, upright, borne separately on the same plant in early spring. **Fruit** Woody, dark brown, ¾ in (2 cm) long.
• **NATIVE REGION** N. Africa, W. Asia, Europe.
• **HABITAT** By rivers.

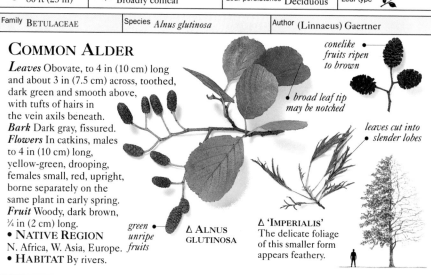

conelike • fruits ripen to brown

• broad leaf tip may be notched

leaves cut into • slender lobes

green • unripe fruits

△ ALNUS GLUTINOSA

△ 'IMPERIALIS'
The delicate foliage of this smaller form appears feathery.

Height 80 ft (25 m)	Shape Broadly conical	Leaf persistence Deciduous	Leaf type

Family BETULACEAE	Species *Alnus incana*	Author (Linnaeus) Moench

WHITE ALDER

Leaves Ovate, to 4 in (10 cm) long and 2 in (5 cm) across, pointed at the tip, double-toothed and sometimes shallowly lobed, dull dark green above and hairy at first, gray and downy beneath. *Bark* Dark gray and smooth. *Flowers* In catkins, males to 4 in (10 cm) long, reddish, drooping, females small, red, upright, borne separately on the same plant in late winter to early spring. *Fruit* Woody, to ¾ in (2 cm) long, green ripening to brown.
• **NATIVE REGION** Caucasus, Europe.
• **HABITAT** Mountains.

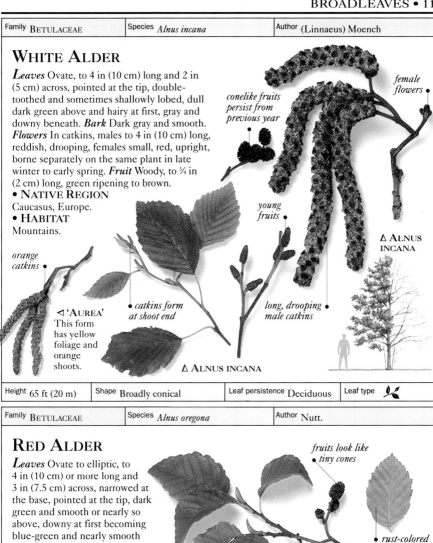

conelike fruits persist from previous year

female flowers

young fruits

△ **ALNUS INCANA**

orange catkins

◁ **'AUREA'** This form has yellow foliage and orange shoots.

• *catkins form at shoot end*

long, drooping male catkins

△ **ALNUS INCANA**

Height 65 ft (20 m)	Shape Broadly conical	Leaf persistence Deciduous	Leaf type

Family BETULACEAE	Species *Alnus oregona*	Author Nutt.

RED ALDER

Leaves Ovate to elliptic, to 4 in (10 cm) or more long and 3 in (7.5 cm) across, narrowed at the base, pointed at the tip, dark green and smooth or nearly so above, downy at first becoming blue-green and nearly smooth except for hairs along the veins beneath. *Bark* Light gray, rough. *Flowers* In catkins, males to 6 in (15 cm) long, yellow-orange, drooping, females small, red, upright, separately on the same plant in early spring. *Fruit* Cone-like, woody, to 1 in (2.5 cm) long.
• **NATIVE REGION** W. North America.
• **HABITAT** Riverbanks and canyons in mountains and along the coast.
• **REMARK** Resembles pale-barked birch species when seen from a distance.

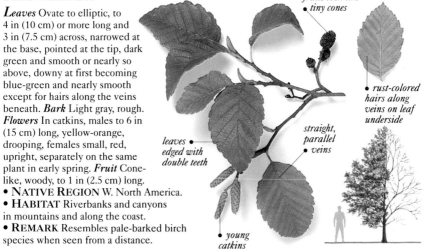

fruits look like tiny cones

rust-colored hairs along veins on leaf underside

straight, parallel veins

leaves edged with double teeth

young catkins

Height 50 ft (15 m)	Shape Broadly conical	Leaf persistence Deciduous	Leaf type

Family BETULACEAE	Species *Betula albosinensis*	Author Burkill

BETULA ALBOSINENSIS

Leaves Ovate, to 3 in (7.5 cm) long and 1½ in (4 cm) across, taper-pointed, toothed, downy when young becoming smooth and glossy green, turning yellow in autumn, carried on slightly rough shoots; young shoots sticky. *Bark* Orange-red to coppery red, peeling in thin, papery, horizontal strips; cream when freshly exposed. *Flowers* In catkins, males to 2½ in (6 cm), yellow, drooping, females green, upright, borne separately on the same plant in spring. *Fruit* A catkin, breaking up when ripe.
• NATIVE REGION W. China.
• HABITAT High woods in mountains.
• REMARK The colored, peeling bark makes this species one of the most striking of all the birches.

• *glossy, sharply toothed leaves*

catkins form in summer and open next spring

upright female • catkins

drooping male catkins

Δ BETULA ALBOSINENSIS

• *reddish bark marked with pale lenticels*

∇ VAR. SEPTENTRIONALIS
This form is distinguished by its matte, rather than glossy, green leaves, and coppery to gray-pink bark.

• *matte green leaves*

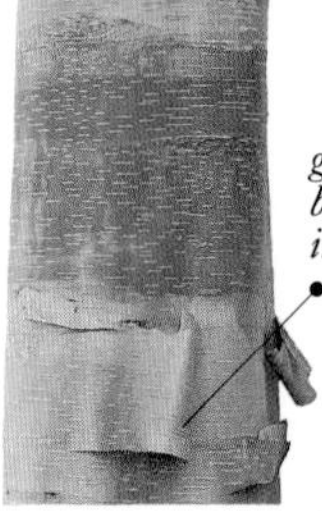

gray-pink bark peels in thin • strips

• *leaves carried on roughish shoots*

• *male catkins borne at end of shoots*

fruiting • female catkins borne upright

Height 80 ft (25 m)	Shape Broadly conical	Leaf persistence Deciduous	Leaf type

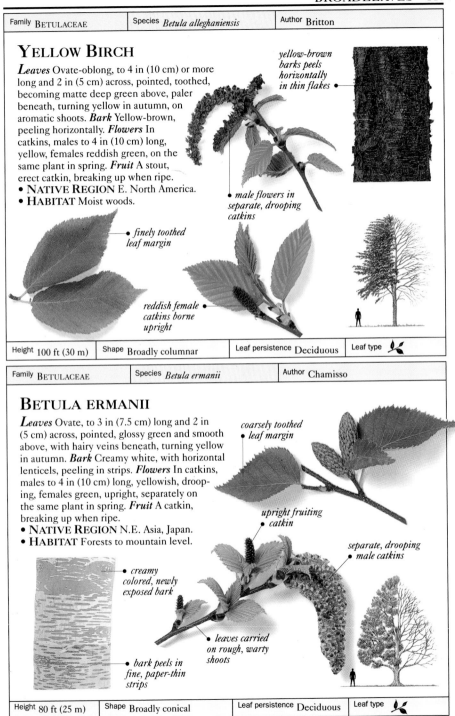

| Family BETULACEAE | Species *Betula alleghaniensis* | Author Britton |

YELLOW BIRCH

Leaves Ovate-oblong, to 4 in (10 cm) or more long and 2 in (5 cm) across, pointed, toothed, becoming matte deep green above, paler beneath, turning yellow in autumn, on aromatic shoots. *Bark* Yellow-brown, peeling horizontally. *Flowers* In catkins, males to 4 in (10 cm) long, yellow, females reddish green, on the same plant in spring. *Fruit* A stout, erect catkin, breaking up when ripe.
• **NATIVE REGION** E. North America.
• **HABITAT** Moist woods.

yellow-brown barks peels horizontally in thin flakes

male flowers in separate, drooping catkins

finely toothed leaf margin

reddish female catkins borne upright

| Height 100 ft (30 m) | Shape Broadly columnar | Leaf persistence Deciduous | Leaf type |

| Family BETULACEAE | Species *Betula ermanii* | Author Chamisso |

BETULA ERMANII

Leaves Ovate, to 3 in (7.5 cm) long and 2 in (5 cm) across, pointed, glossy green and smooth above, with hairy veins beneath, turning yellow in autumn. *Bark* Creamy white, with horizontal lenticels, peeling in strips. *Flowers* In catkins, males to 4 in (10 cm) long, yellowish, drooping, females green, upright, separately on the same plant in spring. *Fruit* A catkin, breaking up when ripe.
• **NATIVE REGION** N.E. Asia, Japan.
• **HABITAT** Forests to mountain level.

coarsely toothed leaf margin

upright fruiting catkin

separate, drooping male catkins

creamy colored, newly exposed bark

leaves carried on rough, warty shoots

bark peels in fine, paper-thin strips

| Height 80 ft (25 m) | Shape Broadly conical | Leaf persistence Deciduous | Leaf type |

Family BETULACEAE	Species *Betula grossa*	Author Siebold & Zuccarini

JAPANESE CHERRY BIRCH

Leaves Ovate, to 4 in (10 cm) long and 2 in (5 cm) across, taper-pointed, usually heart-shaped at the base, coarsely toothed, dark green above, silky-hairy on the veins beneath, turning yellow in autumn, carried on aromatic shoots. *Bark* Reddish, with horizontal bands, becoming dark gray with age. *Flowers* In catkins, males to 1 in (2.5 cm) long, yellow, drooping, females green, upright, separately on the same plant in spring. *Fruit* An erect catkin, breaking up when ripe.
• NATIVE REGION Japan.
• HABITAT Mountain forests.
• REMARK The species is closely related to the North American cherry birch *(Betula lenta,* see below), which has similar bark and aromatic shoots.

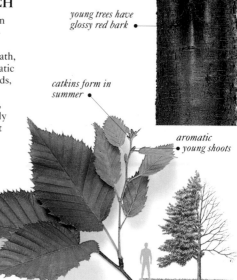

young trees have glossy red bark •

catkins form in summer •

aromatic • young shoots

• leaves edged with few coarse teeth between prominent veins

Height 65 ft (20 m)	Shape Broadly conical	Leaf persistence Deciduous	Leaf type

Family BETULACEAE	Species *Betula lenta*	Author Linnaeus

CHERRY BIRCH

Leaves Ovate, to 4¼ in (12 cm) long and 2½ in (6 cm) across, taper-pointed, sharply toothed, glossy dark green above, paler and silky-hairy at least when young beneath, turning yellow in autumn, carried on aromatic shoots. *Bark* Red-brown, with pale, horizontal lenticels, becoming dark and furrowed. *Flowers* In catkins, males to 3 in (7.5 cm) long, yellow, drooping, females green, upright, separately on the same plant in spring. *Fruit* An erect catkin, breaking up when ripe.
• NATIVE REGION E. North America.
• HABITAT Moist woods at low altitude in the north to mountains in the south of its native region.
• REMARK Also known as black birch, sweet birch.

leaves edged with small teeth between finely impressed veins •

• reddish, rough bark marked with paler lenticels

• leaves taper to short point

Height 80 ft (25 m)	Shape Broadly spreading	Leaf persistence Deciduous	Leaf type

Family BETULACEAE	Species *Betula maximowicziana*	Author Regel

MONARCH BIRCH

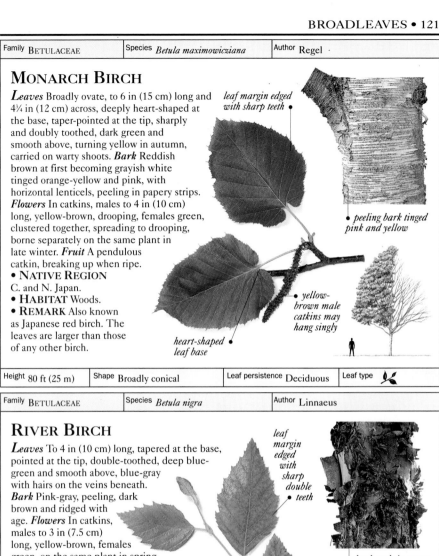

Leaves Broadly ovate, to 6 in (15 cm) long and 4¾ in (12 cm) across, deeply heart-shaped at the base, taper-pointed at the tip, sharply and doubly toothed, dark green and smooth above, turning yellow in autumn, carried on warty shoots. **Bark** Reddish brown at first becoming grayish white tinged orange-yellow and pink, with horizontal lenticels, peeling in papery strips. **Flowers** In catkins, males to 4 in (10 cm) long, yellow-brown, drooping, females green, clustered together, spreading to drooping, borne separately on the same plant in late winter. **Fruit** A pendulous catkin, breaking up when ripe.
• **NATIVE REGION** C. and N. Japan.
• **HABITAT** Woods.
• **REMARK** Also known as Japanese red birch. The leaves are larger than those of any other birch.

leaf margin edged with sharp teeth

peeling bark tinged pink and yellow

yellow-brown male catkins may hang singly

heart-shaped leaf base

Height 80 ft (25 m)	Shape Broadly conical	Leaf persistence Deciduous	Leaf type

Family BETULACEAE	Species *Betula nigra*	Author Linnaeus

RIVER BIRCH

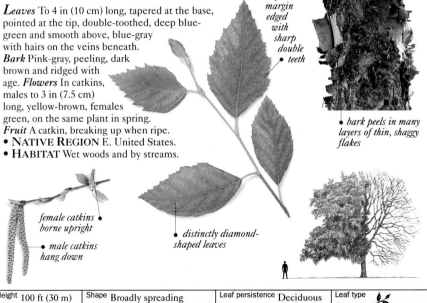

Leaves To 4 in (10 cm) long, tapered at the base, pointed at the tip, double-toothed, deep blue-green and smooth above, blue-gray with hairs on the veins beneath.
Bark Pink-gray, peeling, dark brown and ridged with age. **Flowers** In catkins, males to 3 in (7.5 cm) long, yellow-brown, females green, on the same plant in spring. **Fruit** A catkin, breaking up when ripe.
• **NATIVE REGION** E. United States.
• **HABITAT** Wet woods and by streams.

leaf margin edged with sharp double teeth

bark peels in many layers of thin, shaggy flakes

female catkins borne upright

male catkins hang down

distinctly diamond-shaped leaves

Height 100 ft (30 m)	Shape Broadly spreading	Leaf persistence Deciduous	Leaf type

Family BETULACEAE	Species *Betula papyrifera*	Author Marshall

PAPER BIRCH

Leaves Ovate, to 4 in (10 cm) long and 3 in
(7.5 cm) across, taper-pointed, toothed, dark
green above, paler and with hairs on the veins
at least when young beneath, turning yellow to
orange in autumn. *Bark* White, with conspicuous
dark lenticels, peeling in thin layers; pale pinkish
orange when freshly exposed. *Flowers* In catkins,
males to 4 in (10 cm) long, yellow, drooping,
females slender, green, spreading or drooping,
borne separately on the same plant in spring.
Fruit A catkin, breaking up when ripe.
• **NATIVE REGION** North America.
• **HABITAT** Woods in northerly latitudes
and on mountains.
• **REMARK** Also known as canoe birch.
The bark was used by Native Americans
to make canoes, which gives the
alternative common name. This most
widespread of the American birches
occurs from Labrador to Alaska and
in the northern United States.

smooth leaf
upperside

• green fruiting
catkins droop

leaf margin
edged with
• small teeth

• male catkins
hang down
from shoot tip

• leaves turn from
green to yellow
and orange in
autumn

bark spotted
with dark,
horizontal
lenticels •

• paler leaf
underside has
hairy veins

female catkins •
hang at an angle

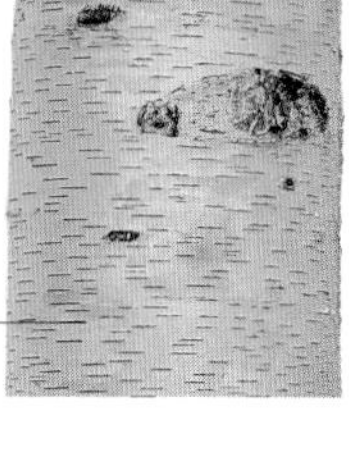

peeling bark reveals •
orange-pink layer
beneath

Height 100 ft (30 m)	Shape Broadly conical	Leaf persistence Deciduous	Leaf type 🌿

Family BETULACEAE	Species *Betula pendula*	Author Roth

SILVER BIRCH

Leaves Ovate to triangular, to 2½ in (6 cm) long and 1½ in (4 cm) across, taper-pointed, coarsely double-toothed, glossy dark green above, turning yellow in autumn, carried on slender, hairless, warty, pendulous shoots. *Bark* White, developing dark, rugged cracks at the base with age. *Flowers* In catkins, males to 2½ in (6 cm) long, yellow, drooping, females green, upright or drooping, borne separately on the same plant in early spring. *Fruit* A catkin, breaking up when ripe.
• NATIVE REGION N. Asia, Europe.
• HABITAT Light, especially sandy, soil.
• REMARK Also known as European white birch. Forms extensive woods in its habitat.

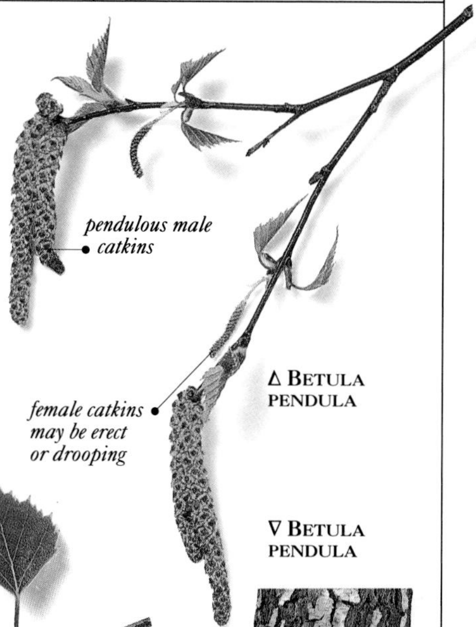

pendulous male catkins

female catkins may be erect or drooping

Δ **BETULA PENDULA**

∇ **BETULA PENDULA**

leaves edged with large, double teeth

BETULA ▷ **PENDULA**

bark at base of trunk develops dark cracks

fruiting catkins droop

'**DALECARLICA**' ▷
The small, slender leaves of the Swedish birch are cut into tapered, finely toothed lobes.

deeply cut leaves

leaves carried on red stalks

'**PURPUREA**' Δ
This ornamental form is selected for its deep purple foliage and red leaf stalks. The bark also develops a purple tinge.

Height 100 ft (30 m)	Shape Narrowly weeping	Leaf persistence Deciduous	Leaf type

Family BETULACEAE	Species *Betula populifolia*	Author Marshall

GRAY BIRCH

Leaves Ovate to triangular, to 3 in (7.5 cm) long, ending in a long, tapered point, sharply toothed, glossy dark green and slightly rough above, turning yellow in autumn. *Bark* White, with black marks under the branches, not peeling, becoming black at the base with age. *Flowers* In catkins, males to 3 in (7.5 cm) long, yellow-brown, drooping, females green, upright, borne separately on the same plant in spring. *Fruit* A catkin, breaking up when ripe.
• **NATIVE REGION**
E. North America.
• **HABITAT** Mountain woods.
• **REMARK** Also known as white birch. Grows in the wild from Nova Scotia in Canada to N. Carolina. The trees are often branched from the base, and are usually fast-growing, small, and short-lived.

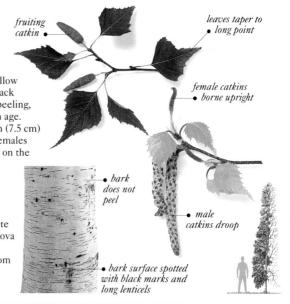

fruiting catkin

leaves taper to long point

female catkins borne upright

bark does not peel

male catkins droop

bark surface spotted with black marks and long lenticels

Height 33 ft (10 m)	Shape Narrowly conical	Leaf persistence Deciduous	Leaf type

Family BETULACEAE	Species *Betula pubescens*	Author Ehrhart

WHITE BIRCH

Leaves Rounded to ovate, to 2½ in (6 cm) long and 2 in (5 cm) across, pointed, with regular, single teeth, dark green and downy at least when young above and on the veins beneath, turning yellow in autumn, carried on downy shoots. *Bark* White to the base. *Flowers* In catkins, males to 2½ in (6 cm) long, yellow, drooping, females green, upright, borne separately on the same plant in spring. *Fruit* A catkin, breaking up when ripe.
• **NATIVE REGION** N. Asia, Europe.
• **HABITAT** Woods.
• **REMARK** Also known as downy birch. The species is related to the silver birch *(Betula pendula,* see p.123) but is easily distinguished by its shoots, which are hairy and not pendulous. In its habitat, it especially favors poor soil and wet ground.

fruiting catkin

leaves edged with small, single teeth

upright female catkins

young leaves carried on finely hairy shoots

pendulous male catkins hang from shoot tip

Height 80 ft (25 m)	Shape Broadly conical	Leaf persistence Deciduous	Leaf type

Family BETULACEAE	Species *Betula utilis*	Author D. Don

HIMALAYAN BIRCH

Leaves Ovate, to 4 in (10 cm) long and 2½ in (6 cm) across, taper-pointed, toothed, dark sometimes glossy green above, downy on the veins beneath, turning a rich, golden yellow in autumn, on downy shoots. *Bark* Very variable, glossy orange-brown or dark copper-brown to pinkish or pure white, paper-thin and peeling. *Flowers* In catkins, males yellow and drooping, to 4¾ in (12 cm) or more long, females green and upright, in spring. *Fruit* A catkin, green ripening to brown, breaking up when ripe.
• **NATIVE REGION** China, the Himalayas.
• **HABITAT** High mountain forests.
• **REMARK** This widely distributed species includes fine white-bark birches. The bark is used for roofing in the Himalayas.

• *fruits ripen from female catkins*

△ **BETULA UTILIS**

▽ **BETULA UTILIS**

• *female catkins borne upright*

• *raised brown lenticels clearly visible on smooth white bark*

• *male catkins may be as long as 7¼ in (18 cm)*

• *bark peels in horizontal strips*

△ VAR. JACQUEMONTII
This variety, characterized by its white bark, is variable in leaf. Three different forms are shown.

VAR. JACQUEMONTII ▽
'SILVER SHADOW'
A form with large and drooping dark green leaves.

VAR. JACQUEMONTII △
'GRAYSWOOD GHOST'
Very glossy leaves distinguish this attractive form.

◁ VAR. JACQUEMONTII
'JERMYNS'
This vigorous variety has broad leaves.

Height 80 ft (25 m)	Shape Broadly conical	Leaf persistence Deciduous	Leaf type

Family BETULACEAE	Species *Carpinus betulus*	Author Linnaeus

HORNBEAM

Leaves Ovate-oblong, to 4 in (10 cm) long and 2½ in (6 cm) across, pointed, double-toothed, with conspicuous veins, dark green and smooth above, downy on the veins beneath, turning yellow in autumn. **Bark** Pale gray, fluted, fissured with age. **Flowers** In catkins, males to 2 in (5 cm) long, yellowish, drooping, females small, green, at the tips of the shoots, borne separately on the same plant in spring. **Fruit** A nut, with three-lobed bracts, the bracts green turning yellowish brown, clustered in pendulous catkins, to 3 in (7.5 cm) long.
• **NATIVE REGION** S.W. Asia, Europe.
• **HABITAT** Hedgerows and broadleaf woods.
• **REMARK** A common hedging plant.

leaf margin edged with double teeth •

fruit bracts • colored green in summer

• three-lobed, usually untoothed, bract surrounds each fruit

female catkins • at shoot tip

male catkins hang down •

fruits ripen • in autumn

Height 100 ft (30 m)	Shape Broadly spreading	Leaf persistence Deciduous	Leaf type

Family BETULACEAE	Species *Carpinus caroliniana*	Author Walter

AMERICAN HORNBEAM

Leaves Ovate, to 4 in (10 cm) long, taper-pointed at the tip, double-toothed, dark green, turning orange to red in autumn, on slender shoots. **Bark** Gray, smooth, and fluted. **Flowers** In catkins, males to 1½ in (4 cm) long, yellowish, drooping, females small, green, at the tips of the shoots, borne separately on the same plant in spring. **Fruit** A nut, with two- or three-lobed, green bracts, clustered in pendulous catkins, to 3 in (7.5 cm) long.
• **NATIVE REGION** Mexico, E. North America.
• **HABITAT** Moist woods, riverbanks, and swamps.
• **REMARK** Also known as blue beech, water beech. Similar to beech *(Fagus*, see pp.151–153), but distinguished by its fruit.

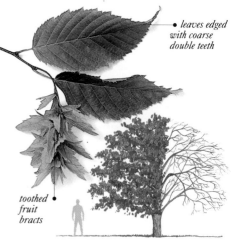

• leaves edged with coarse double teeth

toothed • fruit bracts

Height 33 ft (10 m)	Shape Broadly spreading	Leaf persistence Deciduous	Leaf type

Family BETULACEAE	Species *Carpinus cordata*	Author Blume

CARPINUS CORDATA

Leaves Oblong-ovate, to 4¾ in (12 cm) long and 3 in (7.5 cm) across, heart-shaped at the base, pointed, toothed, deep green above, smooth. *Bark* Gray-brown, smooth, furrowed with age. *Flowers* In catkins, males to 2 in (5 cm) long, yellowish, females small, green, at the tips of the shoots, separately on the same plant in spring. *Fruit* A nut, with green bracts, in hanging catkins, to 4 in (10 cm) long.
• **NATIVE REGION** Japan.
• **HABITAT** Mountain woods.

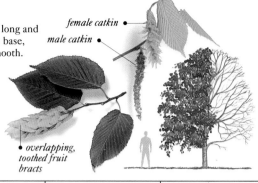

female catkin
male catkin

overlapping, toothed fruit bracts

Height 50 ft (15 m)	Shape Broadly columnar	Leaf persistence Deciduous	Leaf type

Family BETULACEAE	Species *Carpinus japonica*	Author Blume

CARPINUS JAPONICA

Leaves Ovate-oblong, to 4 in (10 cm) long and 1½ in (4 cm) across, pointed, toothed, dark green and smooth above, turning yellow in autumn. *Bark* Gray, smooth, dark brown and scaly with age. *Flowers* In catkins, males to 2 in (5 cm) long, yellowish, females small, green, at tips of the shoots, on the same plant in spring. *Fruit* A nut, with toothed bracts, in catkins, to 2½ in (6 cm) long.
• **NATIVE REGION** Japan.
• **HABITAT** Woods and thickets.

numerous parallel veins either side of midrib

hairy leaf underside

male catkins

unlobed, toothed fruit bracts

Height 50 ft (15 m)	Shape Broadly spreading	Leaf persistence Deciduous	Leaf type

Family BETULACEAE	Species *Corylus colurna*	Author Linnaeus

TURKISH HAZEL

Leaves Broadly oval, to 6 in (15 cm) long and 4 in (10 cm) across, heart-shaped at the base, coarsely double-toothed, dark green and nearly smooth above, downy on the veins beneath, turning yellow in autumn. *Bark* Gray and corky. *Flowers* In catkins, males to 3 in (7.5 cm) long, yellow, drooping, females very small, red, separately on the same plant in late winter to early spring. *Fruit* An edible nut, enclosed in a deeply lobed husk.
• **NATIVE REGION** S.W. Asia, S.E. Europe.
• **HABITAT** Shady mountain forests.

pendulous male catkins

broad leaves edged with coarse double teeth

Height 80 ft (25 m)	Shape Broadly conical	Leaf persistence Deciduous	Leaf type

Family BETULACEAE	Species *Ostrya carpinifolia*	Author Scopoli

HOP HORNBEAM

Leaves Ovate, to 4 in (10 cm) long and 2 in (5 cm) across, pointed, double-toothed, dark green above, sparsely hairy on both sides. *Bark* Gray and smooth, becoming brown and flaking with age. *Flowers* In catkins, males to 3 in (7.5 cm) long, yellow, drooping, females small, green, borne separately on the same plant in spring. *Fruit* A nut, enclosed in a bladderlike creamy husk, in pendulous clusters, to 2 in (5 cm) long.
• NATIVE REGION W. Asia, S. Europe.
• HABITAT Low forests in mountains.

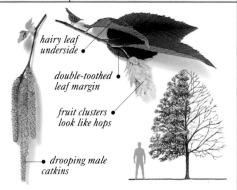

hairy leaf underside •

• double-toothed leaf margin

fruit clusters • look like hops

• drooping male catkins

Height 65 ft (20 m)	Shape Broadly conical	Leaf persistence Deciduous	Leaf type

Family BETULACEAE	Species *Ostrya japonica*	Author Sargent

JAPANESE HOP HORNBEAM

Leaves Ovate, to 4¾ in (12 cm) long and 2 in (5 cm) across, taper-pointed, sharply toothed, dark green above, softly hairy on both sides. *Bark* Gray-brown and scaly. *Flowers* In catkins, males to 3 in (7.5 cm) long, yellow, drooping, females very small, green, borne separately on the same plant in spring. *Fruit* A nut, enclosed in a bladderlike creamy husk, borne in pendulous clusters, to 2 in (5 cm) long.
• NATIVE REGION China, Japan, Korea.
• HABITAT Mountain woods.

fruit husk turns brown before falling •

male • catkins

• female catkins

Height 80 ft (25 m)	Shape Broadly conical	Leaf persistence Deciduous	Leaf type

Family BETULACEAE	Species *Ostrya virginiana*	Author (Miller) K. Koch

IRONWOOD

Leaves Ovate, to 4¾ in (12 cm) long and 2 in (5 cm) across, pointed, toothed, dark green and smooth above, with tufts of hairs in the vein axils beneath. *Bark* Gray-brown and scaly. *Flowers* In catkins, males to 2 in (5 cm) long, yellow, drooping, females small, green, borne separately on the same plant in spring. *Fruit* A nut, enclosed in a bladderlike creamy husk, borne in hanging clusters, to 2½ in (6 cm) long.
• NATIVE REGION E. North America.
• HABITAT Woods.
• REMARK Also known as American hop hornbeam.

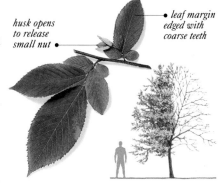

husk opens to release small nut •

• leaf margin edged with coarse teeth

Height 65 ft (20 m)	Shape Broadly conical	Leaf persistence Deciduous	Leaf type

BIGNONIACEAE

T HIS IS A LARGELY TROPICAL family, with evergreen and deciduous trees, shrubs, a few herbaceous plants, and many climbers. It comprises more than 100 genera and some 700 species, widely distributed, found particularly in South America. The leaves are often compound and are arranged in whorls or opposite. The tubular flowers end in an often frilly-petaled, flared bell.

Family BIGNONIACEAE	Species *Catalpa bignonioides*	Author Walter

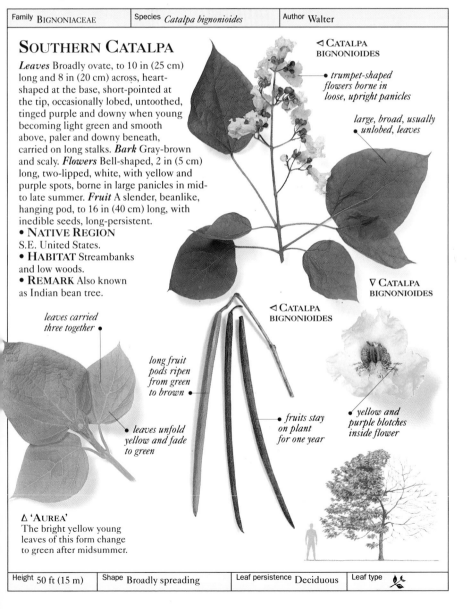

SOUTHERN CATALPA

Leaves Broadly ovate, to 10 in (25 cm) long and 8 in (20 cm) across, heart-shaped at the base, short-pointed at the tip, occasionally lobed, untoothed, tinged purple and downy when young becoming light green and smooth above, paler and downy beneath, carried on long stalks. **Bark** Gray-brown and scaly. **Flowers** Bell-shaped, 2 in (5 cm) long, two-lipped, white, with yellow and purple spots, borne in large panicles in mid- to late summer. **Fruit** A slender, beanlike, hanging pod, to 16 in (40 cm) long, with inedible seeds, long-persistent.
• **NATIVE REGION** S.E. United States.
• **HABITAT** Streambanks and low woods.
• **REMARK** Also known as Indian bean tree.

◁ CATALPA BIGNONIOIDES

• *trumpet-shaped flowers borne in loose, upright panicles*

large, broad, usually • unlobed, leaves

▽ CATALPA BIGNONIOIDES

◁ CATALPA BIGNONIOIDES

leaves carried three together •

long fruit pods ripen from green to brown •

• *leaves unfold yellow and fade to green*

• *fruits stay on plant for one year*

• *yellow and purple blotches inside flower*

△ 'AUREA'
The bright yellow young leaves of this form change to green after midsummer.

Height 50 ft (15 m)	Shape Broadly spreading	Leaf persistence Deciduous	Leaf type

Family BIGNONIACEAE	Species *Catalpa x erubescens*	Author Carrière

CATALPA X ERUBESCENS

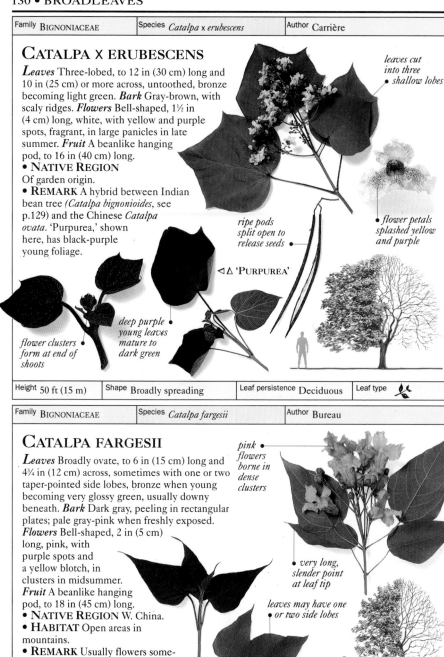

Leaves Three-lobed, to 12 in (30 cm) long and 10 in (25 cm) or more across, untoothed, bronze becoming light green. **Bark** Gray-brown, with scaly ridges. **Flowers** Bell-shaped, 1½ in (4 cm) long, white, with yellow and purple spots, fragrant, in large panicles in late summer. **Fruit** A beanlike hanging pod, to 16 in (40 cm) long.
• **NATIVE REGION**
Of garden origin.
• **REMARK** A hybrid between Indian bean tree *(Catalpa bignonioides,* see p.129) and the Chinese *Catalpa ovata.* 'Purpurea,' shown here, has black-purple young foliage.

leaves cut into three shallow lobes

ripe pods split open to release seeds

flower petals splashed yellow and purple

◁ △ 'PURPUREA'

deep purple young leaves mature to dark green

flower clusters form at end of shoots

Height 50 ft (15 m)	Shape Broadly spreading	Leaf persistence Deciduous	Leaf type

Family BIGNONIACEAE	Species *Catalpa fargesii*	Author Bureau

CATALPA FARGESII

Leaves Broadly ovate, to 6 in (15 cm) long and 4¾ in (12 cm) across, sometimes with one or two taper-pointed side lobes, bronze when young becoming very glossy green, usually downy beneath. **Bark** Dark gray, peeling in rectangular plates; pale gray-pink when freshly exposed.
Flowers Bell-shaped, 2 in (5 cm) long, pink, with purple spots and a yellow blotch, in clusters in midsummer.
Fruit A beanlike hanging pod, to 18 in (45 cm) long.
• **NATIVE REGION** W. China.
• **HABITAT** Open areas in mountains.
• **REMARK** Usually flowers somewhat earlier than other species of its genus. The most common form in cultivation is var. *duclouxii.*

pink flowers borne in dense clusters

very long, slender point at leaf tip

leaves may have one or two side lobes

Height 65 ft (20 m)	Shape Broadly columnar	Leaf persistence Deciduous	Leaf type

Family BIGNONIACEAE	Species *Catalpa speciosa*	Author (Warder ex Barney) Engelmann

WESTERN CATALPA

Leaves Broadly ovate, to 12 in (30 cm) long and 8 in (20 cm) across, with a long, tapering point at the tip, glossy dark green and downy when young becoming smooth above, downy beneath, carried on long stalks. **Bark** Gray, scaly and fissured. **Flowers** Bell-shaped, 2 in (5 cm) long, white, spotted with yellow and some purple, borne in large panicles in summer. **Fruit** Slender, beanlike, and hanging, to 18 in (45 cm) long, persisting until the following year.
• **NATIVE REGION** United States.
• **HABITAT** Riverbanks, damp woods, and swamps.

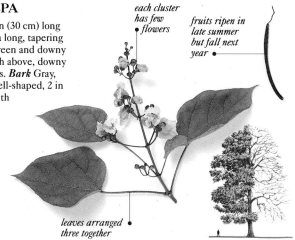

each cluster has few flowers

fruits ripen in late summer but fall next year

leaves arranged three together

Height 130 ft (40 m)	Shape Broadly columnar	Leaf persistence Deciduous	Leaf type

BUXACEAE

T HE PLANT KNOWN AS THE common box *(Buxus sempervirens)* is the most familiar tree in this family, which contains four or five genera, with some 60 species of evergreen trees, shrubs, and the occasional herbaceous plant. They usually have opposite leaves, and small flowers borne in clusters.

Family BUXACEAE	Species *Buxus sempervirens*	Author Linnaeus

COMMON BOX

Leaves Ovate to oblong, to 1 in (2.5 cm) long and ⅜ in (1 cm) across, notched at the tip, glossy dark green above, paler beneath, on four-angled shoots. **Bark** Gray and smooth, cracking into small squares with age. **Flowers** Males and females both small and green, males with conspicuous yellow anthers, separate but in the same cluster, in the leaf axils in early spring. **Fruit** A small, woody, green capsule, to 5/16 in (8 mm) long.
• **NATIVE REGION** N. Africa, S.W. Asia, Europe.
• **HABITAT** Usually alkaline soil.
• **REMARK** Can be either a small tree or a large shrub, producing a very hard, close-grained, yellow wood. In cultivation, it is traditionally used as a hedging plant and for topiary.

stigmas become horns on fruit

male flowers have yellow anthers

female flowers have three stigmas

Height 20 ft (6 m)	Shape Broadly conical	Leaf persistence Evergreen	Leaf type

CELASTRACEAE

T HIS WIDESPREAD FAMILY contains nearly 100 genera and over 1,000 species of evergreen and deciduous trees, shrubs, and climbing plants. The leaves are opposite or alternate, and the flowers usually small and greenish.

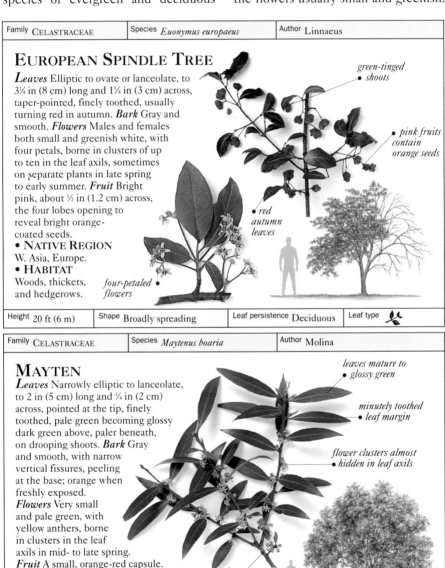

Family CELASTRACEAE	Species *Euonymus europaeus*	Author Linnaeus

EUROPEAN SPINDLE TREE

Leaves Elliptic to ovate or lanceolate, to 3¼ in (8 cm) long and 1¼ in (3 cm) across, taper-pointed, finely toothed, usually turning red in autumn. ***Bark*** Gray and smooth. ***Flowers*** Males and females both small and greenish white, with four petals, borne in clusters of up to ten in the leaf axils, sometimes on separate plants in late spring to early summer. ***Fruit*** Bright pink, about ½ in (1.2 cm) across, the four lobes opening to reveal bright orange-coated seeds.
• **NATIVE REGION**
W. Asia, Europe.
• **HABITAT**
Woods, thickets, and hedgerows.

green-tinged shoots

pink fruits contain orange seeds

red autumn leaves

four-petaled flowers

Height 20 ft (6 m)	Shape Broadly spreading	Leaf persistence Deciduous	Leaf type

Family CELASTRACEAE	Species *Maytenus boaria*	Author Molina

MAYTEN

Leaves Narrowly elliptic to lanceolate, to 2 in (5 cm) long and ¾ in (2 cm) across, pointed at the tip, finely toothed, pale green becoming glossy dark green above, paler beneath, on drooping shoots. ***Bark*** Gray and smooth, with narrow vertical fissures, peeling at the base; orange when freshly exposed. ***Flowers*** Very small and pale green, with yellow anthers, borne in clusters in the leaf axils in mid- to late spring. ***Fruit*** A small, orange-red capsule.
• **NATIVE REGION** South America.
• **HABITAT** Open areas in mountains.

leaves mature to glossy green

minutely toothed leaf margin

flower clusters almost hidden in leaf axils

tiny flowers

Height 65 ft (20 m)	Shape Broadly weeping	Leaf persistence Evergreen	Leaf type

CERCIDIPHYLLACEAE

THE SPECIES DESCRIBED here is the only member of this family. It was once thought to be related to the magnolias *(Magnolia,* see pp.202–215)

and was classified with them, but is now regarded as a plant of primitive origin, and more closely related to the planes *(Platanus,* see pp.234–235).

Family CERCIDIPHYLLACEAE	Species *Cercidiphyllum japonicum*	Author Siebold & Zuccarini

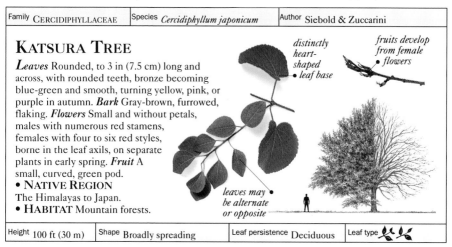

KATSURA TREE

Leaves Rounded, to 3 in (7.5 cm) long and across, with rounded teeth, bronze becoming blue-green and smooth, turning yellow, pink, or purple in autumn. **Bark** Gray-brown, furrowed, flaking. **Flowers** Small and without petals, males with numerous red stamens, females with four to six red styles, borne in the leaf axils, on separate plants in early spring. **Fruit** A small, curved, green pod.
• **NATIVE REGION**
The Himalayas to Japan.
• **HABITAT** Mountain forests.

distinctly heart-shaped • leaf base

fruits develop from female • flowers

leaves may • be alternate or opposite

Height 100 ft (30 m)	Shape Broadly spreading	Leaf persistence Deciduous	Leaf type

CORNACEAE

THIS FAMILY HAS about 12 genera and 100 species of evergreen and deciduous trees and shrubs, and includes the dogwoods *(Cornus,* see

pp.133–138); most grow in northern temperate regions. Leaves are usually opposite. The small flowers may be surrounded by conspicuous bracts.

Family CORNACEAE	Species *Cornus alternifolia*	Author Linnaeus f.

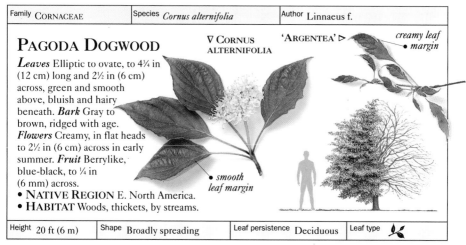

PAGODA DOGWOOD

Leaves Elliptic to ovate, to 4¾ in (12 cm) long and 2½ in (6 cm) across, green and smooth above, bluish and hairy beneath. **Bark** Gray to brown, ridged with age. **Flowers** Creamy, in flat heads to 2½ in (6 cm) across in early summer. **Fruit** Berrylike, blue-black, to ¼ in (6 mm) across.
• **NATIVE REGION** E. North America.
• **HABITAT** Woods, thickets, by streams.

▽ CORNUS ALTERNIFOLIA

'ARGENTEA' ▷

creamy leaf • margin

• smooth leaf margin

Height 20 ft (6 m)	Shape Broadly spreading	Leaf persistence Deciduous	Leaf type

Family CORNACEAE	Species *Cornus controversa*	Author Hemsley

GIANT DOGWOOD

Leaves Ovate to elliptic, to 6 in (15 cm) long
and 3 in (7.5 cm) across, taper-pointed,
untoothed, glossy dark green and smooth
above, blue-green beneath, turning purple
in autumn, carried on long, slender stalks,
clustered at the tips of the shoots.
Bark Smooth, gray, becoming fissured
with age. **Flowers** Small and creamy
white, with four petals, borne in
flattened heads to 6 in (15 cm) across,
along distinctly layered branches in
early to midsummer. **Fruit** A small,
rounded, blue-black berry.
• **NATIVE REGION** E. Asia.
• **HABITAT** Woods and thickets.
• **REMARK** This species and the much
smaller *Cornus alternifolia* (see p.133)
are the only two dogwoods that bear
their leaves alternately, rather than
opposite. In Japan, wooden dolls
are often made from the wood
of this tree.

small flowers clustered • in large heads

△ C. CONTROVERSA

• bluish leaf underside

broad, white • leaf margin

'VARIEGATA' △
The leaves of this
slower-growing form are
strikingly variegated.

Height 65 ft (20 m)	Shape Broadly spreading	Leaf persistence Deciduous	Leaf type

Family CORNACEAE	Species *C.* 'Eddie's White Wonder'	Author None

CORNUS 'EDDIE'S WHITE WONDER'

Leaves Broadly elliptic, to 4¾ in (12 cm) long,
with an abruptly pointed tip, slightly glossy
above, gray and hairy beneath, turning orange,
red, and purple in autumn. **Bark** Gray and
smooth, with few slender, pale stripes.
Flowers Individually small and
greenish, numerous, borne in dense,
hemispherical clusters, each cluster
surrounded by four white or slightly
pink-tinged bracts, the bracts not joined
at the tip at first, emerging in late spring
at the same time as the young leaves.
Fruit Individually small and red,
in hemispherical clusters, the fruits
separating when ripe.
• **NATIVE REGION** Of garden origin.
• **REMARK** A hybrid between the
flowering dogwood *(Cornus florida,*
see p.135) and the Pacific
dogwood *(Cornus nuttallii,*
see p.137). Individual
specimens do not
always produce fruit.

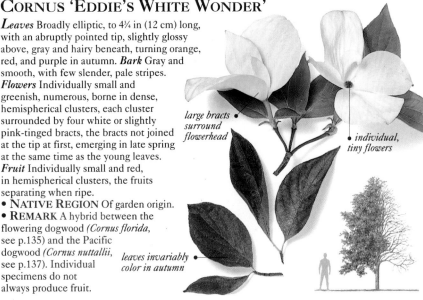

large bracts • surround flowerhead

• individual, tiny flowers

leaves invariably • color in autumn

Height 40 ft (12 m)	Shape Broadly conical	Leaf persistence Deciduous	Leaf type

Family CORNACEAE	Species *Cornus florida*	Author Linnaeus

FLOWERING DOGWOOD

Leaves Ovate to elliptic, to 4 in (10 cm) long
and 2½ in (6 cm) across, taper-pointed,
untoothed, dark green and smooth above,
whitish and softly hairy beneath, turning
red in autumn, carried on bloomy shoots.
Bark Red-brown to blackish, deeply cracked
into small, square plates. ***Flowers*** Small and
greenish, numerous, in dense, hemispherical
clusters, each cluster surrounded by four white
to deep pink bracts, each bract notched at the
tip, visible in bud during winter, opening in
late spring before or with the young leaves.
Fruit Individually small, red, in clusters,
the fruits separating when ripe.
• **NATIVE REGION**
E. North America.
• **HABITAT** Acid soil in woods.

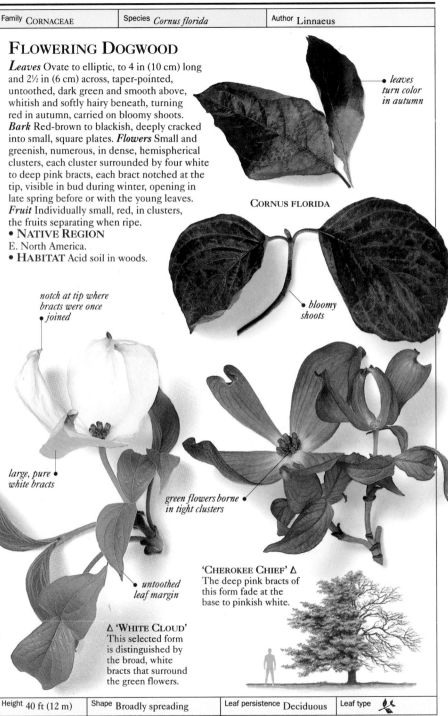

leaves
turn color
in autumn

CORNUS FLORIDA

bloomy
shoots

notch at tip where
bracts were once
• joined

large, pure •
white bracts

green flowers borne •
in tight clusters

untoothed
leaf margin

'CHEROKEE CHIEF' Δ
The deep pink bracts of
this form fade at the
base to pinkish white.

Δ 'WHITE CLOUD'
This selected form
is distinguished by
the broad, white
bracts that surround
the green flowers.

Height 40 ft (12 m)	Shape Broadly spreading	Leaf persistence Deciduous	Leaf type

Family CORNACEAE	Species *Cornus kousa*	Author Hance

JAPANESE STRAWBERRY TREE

Leaves Ovate, to 3 in (7.5 cm) long and 2 in (5 cm) across, taper-pointed, with a wavy margin, untoothed, dark green and smooth above, smooth with tufts of brown hairs in the vein axils beneath. **Bark** Red-brown, peeling in irregular plates with age. **Flowers** Tiny, yellow-white or greenish, numerous, in dense, hemispherical, long-stalked, upright clusters, each cluster surrounded by four creamy white or pink-tinged, taper-pointed bracts, in early summer. **Fruit** Individually small, clustered together in a fleshy, strawberrylike, edible, red, pendulous head.

- **NATIVE REGION** Japan.
- **HABITAT** Mountain woods.

many tiny flowers clustered together •

• showy bracts end in long point

CORNUS KOUSA ▷

smooth, • glossy leaf upperside

hairy vein axils on leaf underside •

VAR. CHINENSIS △

Height 50 ft (15 m)	Shape Broadly columnar	Leaf persistence Deciduous	Leaf type

Family CORNACEAE	Species *Cornus macrophylla*	Author Wallich

CORNUS MACROPHYLLA

small flowers borne in untidy clusters •

Leaves Ovate, to 6 in (15 cm) long and 3 in (7.5 cm) across, tapering to a slender tip, with a wavy margin, untoothed, glossy dark green and smooth above, with up to eight pairs of veins either side of the midrib, bluish green and thinly hairy beneath. **Bark** Dark gray, becoming fissured with age. **Flowers** Small and creamy white, with four petals, borne in loose, flattened heads to 6 in (15 cm) across, in mid- to late summer. **Fruit** Small, rounded, and berrylike, ripening from green to reddish purple and finally to blue-black, to ¼ in (6 mm) across.

- **NATIVE REGION** China, Himalayas, Japan.
- **HABITAT** Forests and thickets.
- **REMARK** A handsome tree, little known even in cultivation.

strong • veining on leaf underside

untoothed, wavy • leaf margin

Height 65 ft (20 m)	Shape Broadly spreading	Leaf persistence Deciduous	Leaf type

Family CORNACEAE	Species *Cornus nuttallii*	Author Audubon

PACIFIC DOGWOOD

Leaves Elliptic to obovate, to 6 in (15 cm) long and 3 in (7.5 cm) across, pointed, untoothed, dark green and nearly smooth above, hairy when young beneath, often turning yellow and occasionally red in autumn. ***Bark*** Gray and smooth, with few slender, pale stripes, slightly fluted at the base. ***Flowers*** Tiny and greenish, numerous, borne in dense, hemispherical, upright clusters, each cluster surrounded by four to seven large bracts to 3 in (7.5 cm) long, creamy white at first becoming white or white flushed pink, in late spring. ***Fruit*** Small, red, in hemispherical clusters, the fruits separating when ripe.

- **NATIVE REGION** W. North America.
- **HABITAT** Lowland forests, and on mountains in the south of its native region.

up to seven large bracts

many greenish flowers

leaves emerge at flowering time

leaves may turn red in autumn

Height 80 ft (25 m)	Shape Broadly conical	Leaf persistence Deciduous	Leaf type

Family CORNACEAE	Species *Cornus* 'Porlock'	Author None

CORNUS 'PORLOCK'

Leaves Elliptic, to 3 in (7.5 cm) long, bronze-green becoming pale green above, gray-green beneath, some turning pinkish in autumn, others persisting over winter. ***Bark*** Gray and smooth, with shallow orange fissures, flaking at the base, leaving pale brown and pale gray patches. ***Flowers*** Tiny, yellow-white, numerous, in dense, hemispherical, long-stalked, upright clusters, each cluster surrounded by four taper-pointed bracts, creamy white becoming deep pink, in early summer. ***Fruit*** Individually small, clustered in a fleshy, strawberrylike, edible, red, pendulous head.

- **NATIVE REGION** Of garden origin.
- **REMARK** A hybrid between *Cornus capitata* and *Cornus kousa* (see p.136).

taper-pointed leaves

flower heads carried at first on upright stalks

fruit clusters hang down

creamy bracts

Height 26 ft (8 m)	Shape Broadly spreading	Leaf persistence Deciduous	Leaf type

Family CORNACEAE	Species *Cornus walteri*	Author Wangerin

CORNUS WALTERI

Leaves Elliptic, to 4 in (10 cm) long and 2 in (5 cm) across, tapered at the tip, untoothed, slightly glossy dark green above, thinly hairy beneath. **Bark** Pale gray-brown, deeply fissured, with narrow, corky, ridges. **Flowers** Individually small and creamy white, with four petals, borne in flattened heads 3 in (7.5 cm) across, in midsummer. **Fruit** Small, rounded, and black.
• **NATIVE REGION** China.
• **HABITAT** Mountain woods.
• **REMARK** The species can be either a shrub or a small tree. It is uncommon in the wild and little known even in cultivation. In winter, the upperside of shoots exposed to the sun is purplish pink.

flowers have yellow anthers

leaves end in slender point

leaf margin often wavy-edged

Height 40 ft (12 m)	Shape Broadly conical	Leaf persistence Deciduous	Leaf type

EBENACEAE

ABOUT 500 SPECIES are collected in the two genera of this family; nearly all are in the genus *Diospyros*. These evergreen and deciduous trees and shrubs, mainly of tropical origin, normally have alternate, untoothed leaves. Small male and female flowers are usually borne on separate plants.

Family EBENACEAE	Species *Diospyros kaki*	Author Linnaeus f.

CHINESE PERSIMMON

Leaves Ovate to obovate, to 6 in (15 cm) or more long and 3 in (7.5 cm) across, pointed at the tip, untoothed, glossy dark green and smooth or nearly so above, paler and usually hairy beneath, turning red or orange in autumn. **Bark** Pale gray and scaly, peeling to furrowed. **Flowers** Males and females small and bell-shaped, about ⅝ in (1.5 cm) long, yellow, males in clusters together, females singly, on young shoots, on separate plants in midsummer. **Fruit** A large, juicy, yellow to orange or red berry, to 3 in (7.5 cm) across, edible when ripe.
• **NATIVE REGION** Unknown.
• **HABITAT** Known only in cultivation.
• **REMARK** Fruits are also known as kaki.

paper-thin calyx

flat, brown seed

large, glossy, leaves

Height 46 ft (14 m)	Shape Broadly spreading	Leaf persistence Deciduous	Leaf type

| Family EBENACEAE | Species *Diospyros lotus* | Author Linnaeus |

DATE PLUM

Leaves Ovate to lanceolate, to 6 in (15 cm) long, pointed, untoothed, glossy dark green above, gray-green beneath, smooth or hairy on both sides. *Bark* Gray, smooth, fissured into square plates with age. *Flowers* Males and females both bell-shaped, about ⅜ in (1 cm) long, deep pink or orange-yellow, males in clusters, females singly, on the underside of the young shoots, on separate plants in mid-summer. *Fruit* An edible berry, ¾ in (2 cm) across, green ripening to yellow-brown to blue-black, sometimes bloomy.
• **NATIVE REGION** S.W. Asia and N. Iran.
• **HABITAT** Woods.
• **REMARK** In its native region, the species is widely cultivated for its edible fruits.

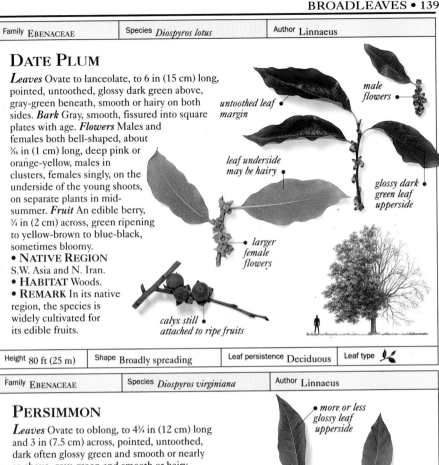

untoothed leaf margin

male flowers

leaf underside may be hairy

glossy dark green leaf upperside

larger female flowers

calyx still attached to ripe fruits

| Height 80 ft (25 m) | Shape Broadly spreading | Leaf persistence Deciduous | Leaf type |

| Family EBENACEAE | Species *Diospyros virginiana* | Author Linnaeus |

PERSIMMON

Leaves Ovate to oblong, to 4¾ in (12 cm) long and 3 in (7.5 cm) across, pointed, untoothed, dark often glossy green and smooth or nearly so above, gray-green and smooth or hairy beneath. *Bark* Dark brown to black, fissured into small, square plates. *Flowers* Males and females both bell-shaped, about ⅜ in (1 cm) long, yellow, males in clusters, females singly, along the young shoots, on separate plants in midsummer. *Fruit* An edible berry, to 1½ in (4 cm) across, green ripening to yellowish red or orange-red.
• **NATIVE REGION** E. United States.
• **HABITAT** Woods and dry soil.
• **REMARK** Also known as possumwood.

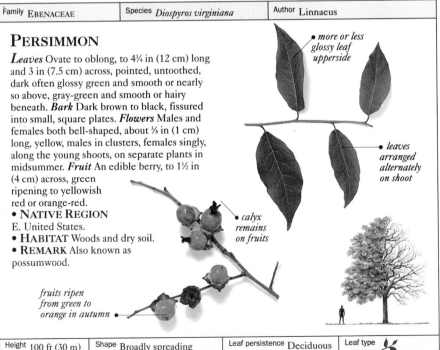

more or less glossy leaf upperside

leaves arranged alternately on shoot

calyx remains on fruits

fruits ripen from green to orange in autumn

| Height 100 ft (30 m) | Shape Broadly spreading | Leaf persistence Deciduous | Leaf type |

ELAEAGNACEAE

T HE OLEASTER FAMILY has three genera, with some 50 species of evergreen and deciduous small trees and shrubs spreading to all temperate northern regions. The plants are often spiny. The untoothed, usually scaly, leaves are opposite or alternate. Small, petalless male and female flowers may be borne on separate plants; in several species they develop into edible fruits.

Family ELAEAGNACEAE	Species *Elaeagnus angustifolia*	Author Linnaeus

OLEASTER

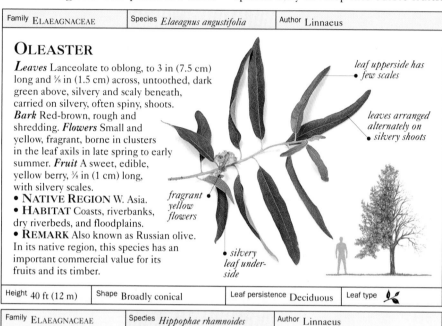

Leaves Lanceolate to oblong, to 3 in (7.5 cm) long and ⅝ in (1.5 cm) across, untoothed, dark green above, silvery and scaly beneath, carried on silvery, often spiny, shoots.
Bark Red-brown, rough and shredding. **Flowers** Small and yellow, fragrant, borne in clusters in the leaf axils in late spring to early summer. **Fruit** A sweet, edible, yellow berry, ⅜ in (1 cm) long, with silvery scales.
• **NATIVE REGION** W. Asia.
• **HABITAT** Coasts, riverbanks, dry riverbeds, and floodplains.
• **REMARK** Also known as Russian olive. In its native region, this species has an important commercial value for its fruits and its timber.

leaf upperside has few scales

leaves arranged alternately on silvery shoots

fragrant yellow flowers

silvery leaf underside

Height 40 ft (12 m)	Shape Broadly conical	Leaf persistence Deciduous	Leaf type

Family ELAEAGNACEAE	Species *Hippophae rhamnoides*	Author Linnaeus

SEA BUCKTHORN

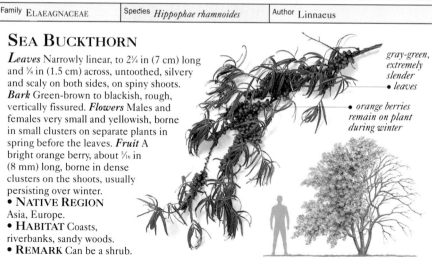

Leaves Narrowly linear, to 2¾ in (7 cm) long and ⅝ in (1.5 cm) across, untoothed, silvery and scaly on both sides, on spiny shoots.
Bark Green-brown to blackish, rough, vertically fissured. **Flowers** Males and females very small and yellowish, borne in small clusters on separate plants in spring before the leaves. **Fruit** A bright orange berry, about ⁵⁄₁₆ in (8 mm) long, borne in dense clusters on the shoots, usually persisting over winter.
• **NATIVE REGION** Asia, Europe.
• **HABITAT** Coasts, riverbanks, sandy woods.
• **REMARK** Can be a shrub.

gray-green, extremely slender leaves

orange berries remain on plant during winter

Height 10 ft (3 m)	Shape Broadly spreading	Leaf persistence Deciduous	Leaf type

ERICACEAE

T HE HEATHER FAMILY, with about 100 genera and some 3,000 species, occurs almost worldwide: it is of restricted distribution only in Australia. The plants are mostly evergreen and deciduous trees and shrubs, with usually alternate leaves. The flowers vary in shape and size, but normally have five petals, joined at least at the base. In all members of the family, a root-associated fungus assists the plant in absorbing nutrients.

Family ERICACEAE	Species *Arbutus andrachne*	Author Linnaeus

GREEK STRAWBERRY TREE

Leaves Elliptic to obovate, to 4 in (10 cm) long and 2 in (5 cm) across, usually entire but sometimes toothed, especially on vigorous shoots, glossy dark green above, paler beneath, smooth. *Bark* Red-brown, peeling in thin strips; orange-brown when freshly exposed. *Flowers* Urn-shaped and small, to about ¼ in (6 mm) long, greenish at first opening white, on a short stalk, borne in upright clusters to 4 in (10 cm) long and across, at the ends of the shoots in early spring. *Fruit* A nearly smooth, rounded, orange-red, berry, ⅜ in (1 cm) across.
• **NATIVE REGION** S.E. Europe to S.W. Asia.
• **HABITAT** Woods, thickets, and rocky slopes.
• **REMARK** Where it grows in the wild with the strawberry tree (*A. unedo*, see p.143), the two species can cross to produce the hybrid *A.* x *andrachnoides* (see p.142).

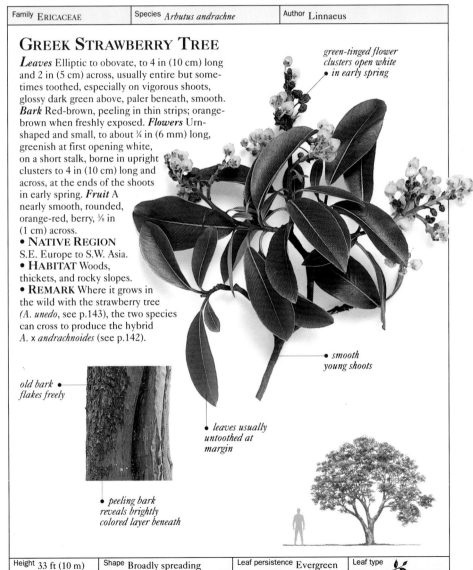

green-tinged flower clusters open white in early spring

smooth young shoots

old bark flakes freely

leaves usually untoothed at margin

peeling bark reveals brightly colored layer beneath

Height 33 ft (10 m)	Shape Broadly spreading	Leaf persistence Evergreen	Leaf type

| Family ERICACEAE | Species *Arbutus x andrachnoides* | Author Link |

ARBUTUS X ANDRACHNOIDES

Leaves Ovate to elliptic, to 4 in (10 cm) long and 2 in (5 cm) across, toothed, glossy dark green above, paler beneath, smooth on both sides. **Bark** Red-brown, peeling vertically in long, thin strips. **Flowers** Urn-shaped, small, and white, in drooping clusters at the ends of the shoots, over a long period between autumn and spring. **Fruit** A strawberrylike, warty, red berry, ⅝ in (1.5 cm) across.
• **NATIVE REGION** Greece.
• **HABITAT** Woods and thickets.
• **REMARK** A naturally occurring hybrid between the Greek strawberry tree *(Arbutus andrachne,* see p.141), whose rather beautiful, peeling bark it inherits, and the strawberry tree *(Arbutus unedo,* see p.143), found in the wild where the two parent plants grow together.

red-brown bark peels in strips

small flowers borne in nodding clusters

glossy, finely toothed leaves

| Height 33 ft (10 m) | Shape Broadly spreading | Leaf persistence Evergreen | Leaf type |

| Family ERICACEAE | Species *Arbutus menziesii* | Author Pursh |

MADROÑA

Leaves Elliptic, to 6 in (15 cm) long and 3 in (7.5 cm) across, usually untoothed, glossy dark green above, blue-white beneath, smooth. **Bark** Red-brown, smooth, peeling, becoming dark and fissured with age; green when freshly exposed. **Flowers** Urn-shaped, small, and white, or sometimes pink-tinged, borne upright, in large, upright clusters to 6 in (15 cm) long, at the ends of the shoots in late spring. **Fruit** A strawberrylike, rough, orange to red berry, ⅜ in (1 cm) across, covered in small warts.
• **NATIVE REGION** W. North America.
• **HABITAT** Moist, wooded slopes, canyons in forests of oak and redwood, and coastal rocks and cliffs.
• **REMARK** Also known as Pacific madrone. The fruits are edible in small quantities. During the fruiting season, trees attract many different bird species, which serve to distribute the seeds.

large flower clusters borne vertically

tiny, upright flowers

large, glossy, untoothed leaves

bark peels in papery flakes

| Height 130 ft (40 m) | Shape Broadly columnar | Leaf persistence Evergreen | Leaf type |

Family ERICACEAE	Species *Arbutus unedo*	Author Linnaeus

STRAWBERRY TREE

Leaves Elliptic to oblong or obovate, to 4 in (10 cm) long and 2 in (5 cm) across, toothed, very glossy dark green above, paler beneath, smooth on both sides. **Bark** Red-brown, rough and fissured, not peeling. **Flowers** Urn-shaped, small, and white, or sometimes pink, borne in drooping clusters about 2 in (5 cm) long, at the ends of the shoots in autumn. **Fruit** A strawberrylike, roughly warty red berry, ¾ in (2 cm) across, ripening in autumn from flowers borne the previous year.
• **NATIVE REGION** S.W. Ireland, Mediterranean.
• **HABITAT** Rocky places and thickets.
• **REMARK** This species is one of the few members of the family that grows on lime soil. With flowers and fruits borne at the same time, it is a particularly ornamental tree.

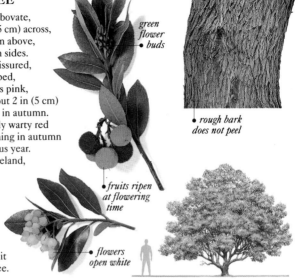

green flower buds

rough bark does not peel

fruits ripen at flowering time

flowers open white

Height 33 ft (10 m)	Shape Broadly spreading	Leaf persistence Evergreen	Leaf type

Family ERICACEAE	Species *Oxydendrum arboreum*	Author (Linnaeus) Candolle

SOURWOOD (SORREL) TREE

Leaves Elliptic to oblong, to 8 in (20 cm) long and 3 in (7.5 cm) across, taper-pointed, very finely toothed, glossy dark green and smooth above, slightly hairy beneath, turning red to yellow or purple in autumn. **Bark** Gray-brown, thick, deeply furrowed, with scaly ridges. **Flowers** Urn-shaped, small, white, and numerous, fragrant, borne in large, upright clusters at the ends of the shoots in autumn. **Fruit** A small, woody, brown capsule.
• **NATIVE REGION** E. North America.
• **HABITAT** Woods and along streams.
• **REMARK** The species can be either a tree or a shrub. The leaves have a sharp, acid taste, somewhat similar to that of the herbaceous plant sorrel, which gives the species one of its common names.

upright flower clusters arch with age

individual flowers are very small

leaves color in autumn

Height 65 ft (20 m)	Shape Broadly conical	Leaf persistence Deciduous	Leaf type

Family ERICACEAE	Species *Rhododendron arboreum*	Author W.W. Smith

RHODODENDRON ARBOREUM

Leaves Oblong to lanceolate, to 8 in (20 cm) long and 2 in (5 cm) across, with a pointed tip, glossy dark green and smooth with impressed midrib and veins above, variably hairy from silvery to rusty and often shining beneath. *Bark* Red-brown, rough and shredding. *Flowers* Bell-shaped, to 2 in (5 cm) long, red, pink, or sometimes white, borne in dense clusters of up to 20 in late winter to mid-spring. *Fruit* A woody, brown capsule, to ¼ in (2 cm), splitting open to release numerous tiny seeds.
• **NATIVE REGION** The Himalayas, with forms extending to S.W. China and Sri Lanka.
• **HABITAT** Forests and thickets in hills and mountains.
• **REMARK** In its native region and habitat, this species is a tree; in less favorable situations it may be only a large shrub. It was the first rhododendron to be introduced to Europe from the Himalayas. The young leaves are poisonous.

parallel veins run either side of prominent midrib

flowers vary in color from white through pink to deep red

thinly hairy, shining leaf underside

deep red anthers tipped with creamy pollen

flower petals marked with darker spots on inner surface

thick, leathery leaves have smooth, glossy upper surface

up to 20 flowers clustered together in each rounded head

Height 50 ft (15 m)	Shape Broadly columnar	Leaf persistence Evergreen	Leaf type

EUCOMMIACEAE

T HE ONLY MEMBER of this family, *Eucommia ulmoides* is a vigorous and decorative plant when mature. It is thought to be related most closely to the elms *(Ulmus,* see pp.308–309). If in doubt about its identity, the rubbery latex, which forms an integral part of the leaf structure, provides instant identification. However, the latex is present in quantities that are too small to make commercial extraction an economic proposition. This unique species is the only tree from temperate regions known to produce rubber.

Family EUCOMMIACEAE	Species *Eucommia ulmoides*	Author Oliver

EUCOMMIA ULMOIDES

Leaves Ovate to elliptic, to 8 in (20 cm) long and 3½ in (9 cm) across, leathery, taper-pointed at the tip, toothed, glossy dark green, with prominent lateral veining, drooping on thin shoots. **Bark** Pale dove-gray, deeply fissured. **Flowers** Males and females very small, without petals, opening on the old shoots, on separate plants in late spring just before or as the young leaves emerge. **Fruit** Winged, green keys, 1½ in (4 cm) long, in clusters, each key containing a seed.
• **NATIVE REGION** Not known; probably S.W. China.
• **HABITAT** Not established.
• **REMARK** This hardy tree was introduced to the West in about 1896, from plants propagated in China, and is now known only in cultivation. In China, the bark is used for medicinal purposes.

leaves just emerging at flowering time •

male flowers may each have up to ten stamens •

INVISIBLE RUBBER ▷
When a leaf is gently torn apart and held upside-down by its stalk, the two separate parts remain hanging together, connected almost invisibly by a network of gossamer-like latex fibers.

thin strands of rubber join two halves of a torn leaf •

deeply impressed • *leaf veins*

Height 65 ft (20 m)	Shape Broadly spreading	Leaf persistence Deciduous	Leaf type

EUCRYPHIACEAE

A FAMILY OF A SINGLE GENUS, with five species of evergreen trees or shrubs native to Chile and southeast Australia, including Tasmania. The leaves are opposite, and either simple or pinnate, toothed or untoothed. The white flowers usually have four petals and numerous stamens.

Family EUCRYPHIACEAE	Species *Eucryphia cordifolia*	Author Cavanilles

ULMO

Leaves Oblong, to 3 in (7.5 cm) long and 2 in (5 cm) across, heart-shaped at the base, toothed at the margin, dark green above, gray and hairy beneath. **Bark** Gray and smooth. **Flowers** 2 in (5 cm) across, white, with four petals, the numerous stamens turning from pink to orange, fragrant, singly in the leaf axils in late summer. **Fruit** A small, woody capsule.
- **NATIVE REGION** Chile.
- **HABITAT** Rain forests.
- **REMARK** At high altitudes, this species is a large shrub.

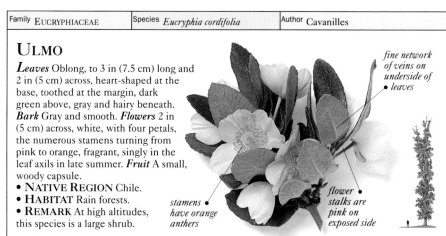

fine network of veins on underside of leaves

stamens have orange anthers

flower stalks are pink on exposed side

Height 130 ft (40 m)	Shape Narrowly columnar	Leaf persistence Evergreen	Leaf type

Family EUCRYPHIACEAE	Species *Eucryphia glutinosa*	Author (Poeppig & Endlicher) Baillon

EUCRYPHIA GLUTINOSA

Leaves Pinnate, with three to five leaflets, to 2½ in (6 cm) long and 1¼ in (3 cm) across, toothed, glossy dark green above, paler beneath, hairy at least when young on both sides. **Bark** Gray and smooth. **Flowers** 2 in (5 cm) across, white, with four petals and numerous pink-tipped stamens, fragrant, borne singly in the leaf axils in late summer. **Fruit** A small, woody capsule.
- **NATIVE REGION** Chile.
- **HABITAT** Forests and riverbanks.
- **REMARK** Cultivated plants of the species are semi-evergreen or deciduous, with most leaves turning orange-red in autumn before falling.

'PLENA' ▷
This selected form has double flowers.

▽ EUCRYPHIA GLUTINOSA

flowers have eight or more petals

prominently toothed glossy leaflets

anthers colored deep pink at first

Height 33 ft (10 m)	Shape Narrowly columnar	Leaf persistence Evergreen	Leaf type

Family EUCRYPHIACEAE	Species *Eucryphia x intermedia*	Author Bausch

EUCRYPHIA X INTERMEDIA

Leaves Variable, either simple and oblong, to
2½ in (6 cm) long and 1 in (2.5 cm) across, or
with three leaflets, the central leaflet largest,
both types either untoothed or with few teeth
towards the tip, glossy dark green above, gray-
green beneath. *Bark* Gray and smooth.
Flowers 2 in (5 cm) across,
white, with four petals and
numerous dark-tipped
stamens, fragrant, borne
singly in the leaf axils in
late summer to autumn.
Fruit A small, woody
capsule.
• **NATIVE REGION**
Of garden origin.
• **REMARK** A hybrid
between *Eucryphia glutinosa* (see
p.146) and *Eucryphia lucida* (see
below), first raised at Rostrevor in
Northern Ireland. The original and most
common form, 'Rostrevor,' is shown here.

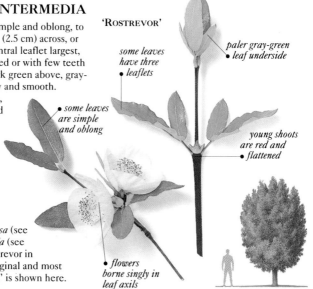

'ROSTREVOR'

*some leaves
have three
• leaflets*

*paler gray-green
• leaf underside*

*• some leaves
are simple
and oblong*

*young shoots
are red and
• flattened*

*• flowers
borne singly in
leaf axils*

Height 33 ft (10 m)	Shape Broadly columnar	Leaf persistence Evergreen	Leaf type

Family EUCRYPHIACEAE	Species *Eucryphia lucida*	Author (Labillardière) Baillon

EUCRYPHIA LUCIDA

Leaves Narrowly oblong, to 2 in (5 cm) long
and ⅗ in (1.5 cm) across, on short stalks,
untoothed, leathery, rounded to minutely
notched at the tip, glossy dark green and
thinly hairy above, blue-white and smooth
beneath with a distinct network of
veins; on vigorous shoots sometimes
with three leaflets. *Bark* Gray, smooth.
Flowers To 2 in (5 cm) across, white,
with four rounded petals and numerous
slender, dark-tipped stamens, fragrant,
borne singly in the leaf axils in late
summer, cup-shaped at first, opening
flat. *Fruit* A small, woody capsule,
splitting open when ripe.
• **NATIVE REGION** Tasmania.
• **HABITAT** Woods and riverbanks
in mountainous areas.
• **REMARK** In its native region, also
known as leatherwood. Cultivated plants
are smaller, usually reaching only about
50 ft (15 m). A pink-flowered form found in
Tasmania has been named 'Pink Cloud.'

*blue-white leaf •
underside*

*• anthers colored
pink before flowers
open fully*

*• fruits split
open to release
seed after one
year*

Height 65 ft (20 m)	Shape Narrowly columnar	Leaf persistence Evergreen	Leaf type

Family EUCRYPHIACEAE	Species *Eucryphia milliganii*	Author J.D. Hooker

EUCRYPHIA MILLIGANII

Leaves Oblong, to ¾ in (2 cm) long and ⁵⁄₁₆ in (8 mm) across, untoothed, glossy dark green above, blue-white beneath. *Bark* Gray and smooth. *Flowers* To ¾ in (2 cm) across, white, with four petals and numerous pink-tipped stamens, fragrant, borne singly in the leaf axils in late summer. *Fruit* A small, woody capsule.
• **NATIVE REGION** Tasmania.
• **HABITAT** Woods and riverbanks in mountainous areas.
• **REMARK** Can be a tree or a shrub.

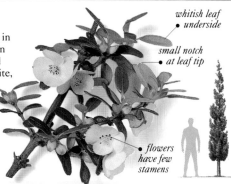

whitish leaf • underside

small notch • at leaf tip

flowers have few stamens

Height 20 ft (6 m)	Shape Narrowly columnar	Leaf persistence Evergreen	Leaf type

Family EUCRYPHIACEAE	Species *Eucryphia x nymansensis*	Author Bausch

EUCRYPHIA X NYMANSENSIS

Leaves Elliptic, to 2½ in (6 cm) long and 1¼ in (3 cm) across, or with three leaflets, toothed, glossy dark green above, paler beneath. *Bark* Gray and smooth. *Flowers* To 3 in (7.5 cm) across, white, with four petals and numerous pink-tipped stamens, in the leaf axils in late summer to autumn. *Fruit* A small, woody capsule.
• **NATIVE REGION** Of garden origin.
• **REMARK** A hybrid between ulmo (*Eucryphia cordifolia*, see p.146) and *Eucryphia glutinosa* (see p.146).

some leaves are • undivided

• *some leaves have three leaflets*

Height 50 ft (15 m)	Shape Narrowly columnar	Leaf persistence Evergreen	Leaf type

Family EUCRYPHIACEAE	Species *Eucryphia* 'Penwith'	Author None

EUCRYPHIA 'PENWITH'

Leaves Oblong, to 2¾ in (7 cm) long and 1¼ in (3 cm) across, slightly heart-shaped at the base, untoothed, dark green and smooth above, blue-white and nearly smooth beneath. *Bark* Dark gray and smooth. *Flowers* To 2 in (5 cm) across, white, with four petals and numerous pink-tipped stamens, fragrant, in the leaf axils in late summer to autumn. *Fruit* A small, woody capsule.
• **NATIVE REGION** Of garden origin.
• **REMARK** A hybrid between ulmo (*Eucryphia cordifolia*, see p.146) and *Eucryphia lucida* (see p.147).

few leaves have • three leaflets

wavy-edged • leaf margin

Height 50 ft (15 m)	Shape Narrowly columnar	Leaf persistence Evergreen	Leaf type

FAGACEAE

SOME VERY FAMILIAR deciduous and evergreen trees belong to this family, which includes the chestnuts *(Castanea, see pp.149–150)*, beeches *(Fagus, see pp.151–153)*, and oaks *(Quercus, see pp.158–173)*. Eight genera with over 1,000 species extend from northern temperate regions to parts of the southern hemisphere. The leaves are simple, lobed, or toothed. The small male or female flowers are often in separate catkins, on the same plant. The fruit is a nut, surrounded by or enclosed in a cupule.

Family FAGACEAE	Species *Castanea dentata*	Author (Marshall) Borkhausen

AMERICAN CHESTNUT

Leaves Oblong, to 10 in (25 cm) long and 2 in (5 cm) across, narrowed at the base, taper-pointed, sharply toothed, matte dark green above, paler beneath, smooth on both sides. **Bark** Dark brown, shallowly fissured, with broad, scaly ridges. **Flowers** Males and females both small and creamy yellow, in catkins to 8 in (20 cm) long, separate but usually on the same spike in summer. **Fruit** A spiny husk, to 2½ in (6 cm) across, enclosing one to three edible, sweet, glossy red-brown nuts.
• **NATIVE REGION** E. North America.
• **HABITAT** Woods.
• **REMARK** Increasingly rare due to disease.

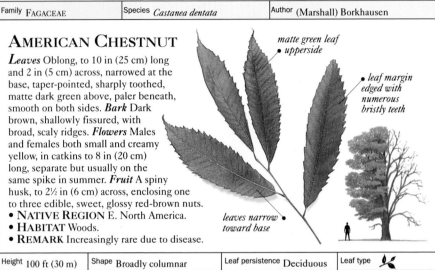

matte green leaf upperside

leaf margin edged with numerous bristly teeth

leaves narrow toward base

Height 100 ft (30 m)	Shape Broadly columnar	Leaf persistence Deciduous	Leaf type

Family FAGACEAE	Species *Castanea mollissima*	Author Blume

CHINESE CHESTNUT

Leaves Oblong to lanceolate, to 8 in (20 cm) long and 3 in (7.5 cm) across, usually rounded at the base, taper-pointed at the tip, coarsely toothed, glossy dark green and smooth above, softly hairy at least when young beneath. **Bark** Dark gray, smooth, becoming gray-brown and fissured with age. **Flowers** Males and females small and creamy yellow, in catkins to 8 in (20 cm) long, separate but usually on the same spike in summer. **Fruit** A spiny, downy husk, to 2 in (5 cm) across, enclosing two to three edible, glossy red-brown nuts.
• **NATIVE REGION** China.
• **HABITAT** Mountain woods.
• **REMARK** This species is grown in China for its nuts.

male flowers borne in slender, upright spikes

glossy leaf upperside

coarse teeth at leaf margin point forward

rounded leaf base

Height 80 ft (25 m)	Shape Broadly columnar	Leaf persistence Deciduous	Leaf type

Family FAGACEAE·	Species *Castanea sativa*	Author Miller

SWEET CHESTNUT

Leaves Oblong, to 8 in (20 cm) long and 3 in (7.5 cm) across, usually rounded or heart-shaped at the base, taper-pointed at the tip, toothed, glossy dark green and smooth above, paler becoming smooth beneath. *Bark* Gray and smooth, becoming brown and usually spirally ridged with age. *Flowers* Males and females both small and creamy yellow, in catkins to 10 in (25 cm) long, separate but usually on the same spike in summer. *Fruit* A spiny husk, to 2½ in (6 cm) across, enclosing one to three edible, glossy red-brown nuts.
• **NATIVE REGION** N. Africa, S.W. Asia, S. Europe.
• **HABITAT** Woods.

leaves edged • with coarse, bristly teeth

green fruit husks •

male and female • flowers clustered on same spike

• each prickly fruit husk contains up to three nuts

Height 100 ft (30 m)	Shape Broadly columnar	Leaf persistence Deciduous	Leaf type

Family FAGACEAE	Species *Chrysolepis chrysophylla*	Author (W.J. Hooker) Hjelmqvist

GOLDEN CHINKAPIN

Leaves Oblong to lanceolate, to 4 in (10 cm) or more long and 1 in (2.5 cm) across, leathery, untoothed, glossy dark green above, hairy beneath. *Bark* Gray, furrowed. *Flowers* Males and females both creamy white, fragrant, in catkins to 1½ in (4 cm) long, separate but usually on the same spike in summer. *Fruit* A spiny husk, to 1½ in (4 cm) across, enclosing one to three edible, glossy brown nuts.
• **NATIVE REGION** W. United States.
• **HABITAT** Woods and thickets in coastal mountains.

• leaves taper to very long, slender point

nuts inside densely prickly husk ripen • in two years

leaf underside covered in golden hairs •

Height 100 ft (30 m)	Shape Broadly conical	Leaf persistence Evergreen	Leaf type

Family FAGACEAE	Species *Fagus grandifolia*	Author Ehrhart

AMERICAN BEECH

Leaves Ovate to elliptic,
to 4¾ in (12 cm) long
and 2½ in (6 cm) across,
taper-pointed, toothed,
with 11 to 15 pairs of
veins, silky-hairy
becoming smooth or
nearly so, glossy dark
green above, paler beneath,
turning yellow in autumn.
Bark Gray and smooth.
Flowers Males and females both
small, males yellow, females green, in
separate clusters on the same plant in
mid-spring. **Fruit** A husk, to ¾ in (2 cm) long,
enclosing one to three small, edible nuts.
• **NATIVE REGION** E. North America.
• **HABITAT** Rich woods.

leaves edged with sharp teeth

up to 15 pairs of parallel veins

glossy dark green leaf upperside

bristly fruit husk matures from green to brown

Height 80 ft (25 m)	Shape Broadly spreading	Leaf persistence Deciduous	Leaf type

Family FAGACEAE	Species *Fagus orientalis*	Author Lipsky

ORIENTAL BEECH

Leaves Elliptic to obovate, to 4¾ in (12 cm) long
and 2½ in (6 cm) across, usually with a wavy
margin, untoothed or slightly toothed, with up
to 12 pairs of veins, dark green and smooth
above, silky-hairy on the veins beneath, turning
yellow in autumn. **Bark** Gray, smooth, sometimes furrowed. **Flowers** Males and females
small, males yellow, females green, borne in
separate clusters on the same plant in mid-
spring. **Fruit** A bristly husk, to 1 in (2.5 cm)
long, enclosing one to three small, edible nuts.
• **NATIVE REGION** S.W. Asia, S.E. Europe.
• **HABITAT** Hills and mountains.

fruit husk splits open into four lobes

leaves change color in autumn

up to 12 pairs of parallel veins

wavy leaf margin may be untoothed or sparsely toothed

Height 100 ft (30 m)	Shape Broadly spreading	Leaf persistence Deciduous	Leaf type

Family FAGACEAE	Species *Fagus sylvatica*	Author Linnaeus

COMMON BEECH

Leaves Ovate to obovate, to 4 in (10 cm) long and
2½ in (6 cm) across, abruptly short-pointed, with a
wavy margin, untoothed or edged with small teeth,
with fewer than ten pairs of veins, silky-hairy
when unfolding becoming smooth, glossy dark
green above, paler beneath, turning yellow in
autumn. **Bark** Gray, smooth. **Flowers** Small,
males yellow, females green, borne in
separate clusters on the same plant in
mid-spring as the young, pale green
leaves emerge. **Fruit** A bristly
husk, to 1 in (2.5 cm) long,
enclosing one to three
small, edible nuts.
• **NATIVE REGION**
Europe.
• **HABITAT** Woods,
particularly on chalk.

*fruit husk
covered in
dense bristles* •

◁ △ FAGUS SYLVATICA

• *wavy,
untoothed or
slightly toothed
leaf margin*

*no more than ten
pairs of parallel
veins* •

▽ 'ASPLENIIFOLIA'
The slender leaves of the
fern-leaved beech are
deeply cut into long,
narrow lobes.

• *leaves
taper to long,
fine point*

△ 'AUREA PENDULA'
This slender tree has hanging
branches, clothed from spring
to autumn with foliage that
matures from golden yellow
to green.

• *curiously
contorted
leaves*

'CRISTATA' ▷
Clustered and
seemingly misshapen
leaves are a feature of
this very unusual form.

Height 130 ft (40 m)	Shape Broadly spreading	Leaf persistence Deciduous	Leaf type

• *short-pointed, glossy dark green leaves*

▽ 'DAWYCK PURPLE'
The copper beeches are charaterized by their deep red-purple foliage. 'Dawyck Purple', one such form, grows into a narrowly columnar tree. It is a seedling of 'Dawyck', which is similar, but has green foliage.

broad, taper-pointed leaves colored very deep purple •

unequal-sided • *leaf base*

△ 'PRINCE GEORGE OF CRETE'
This form is selected for its particularly large, broad leaves. Other forms with large leaves also occur. This group is known as *Fagus sylvatica* f. *latifolia*.

▷ 'ROTUNDIFOLIA'
The cultivar name of this distinct form describes the small, rounded leaves that characterize this tree. They are carried on strongly upswept branches.

rounded • *leaves*

smaller leaves have fewer pairs of • *parallel veins*

deep red-purple • *leaves tinged green*

leaf margin cut into • *triangular teeth*

◁ 'ROHANII'
This cultivar resembles the fern-leaved beech *(Fagus sylvatica* 'Aspleniifolia,' see p.152). Its has somewhat broader leaves colored greenish purple.

red leaf veins • *and stalks*

Family FAGACEAE	Species *Lithocarpus edulis*	Author (Makino) Nakai

LITHOCARPUS EDULIS

Leaves Narrowly elliptic, to 6 in (15 cm) long and 2 in (5 cm) across, gradually tapered from the center of the leaf to the base, with a short, blunt point at the tip, untoothed, rigid and leathery, glossy pale green above, gray-green beneath, smooth. **Bark** Gray-brown, smooth. **Flowers** Males and females both very small and creamy white, in slender, upright catkins, males at the tip of the catkin, females at the base, in the leaf axils in late summer. **Fruit** A pointed acorn, to 1 in (2.5 cm) long, about one-third enclosed in a cup, in stalkless clusters, ripe in two years.
• **NATIVE REGION** Japan.
• **HABITAT** Woods.
• **REMARK** *Lithocarpus* species are closely related to the oaks *(Quercus,* see pp.158–173) but differ in their upright catkins.

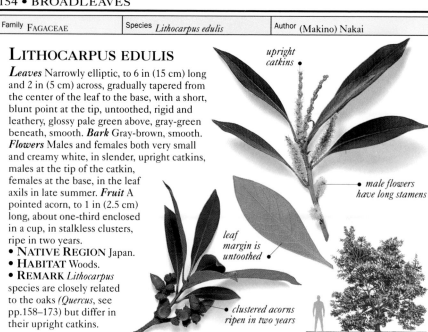

upright catkins

male flowers have long stamens

leaf margin is untoothed

clustered acorns ripen in two years

Height 50 ft (15 m)	Shape Broadly spreading	Leaf persistence Evergreen	Leaf type

Family FAGACEAE	Species *Lithocarpus henryi*	Author (Seemann) Rehder & Wilson

LITHOCARPUS HENRYI

Leaves Elliptic to oblong or lanceolate, to 10 in (25 cm) long and 3 in (7.5 cm) across, tapered to a slender point at the tip, untoothed, pale green becoming dark and slightly glossy, whitish when young beneath, thinly hairy becoming smooth on both sides. **Bark** Gray with pale gray lenticels, and shallow, orange-brown fissures at the base. **Flowers** Males and females both very small and creamy white, in slender, upright catkins, separately but on the same spike in late summer. **Fruit** A rounded acorn, about ¾ in (2 cm) long, enclosed in a shallow cup, borne in dense clusters.
• **NATIVE REGION** China.
• **HABITAT** Woods in hills and mountains.
• **REMARK** The bold, long-pointed leaves make the massed foliage a handsome sight.

leaves end in fine point

impressed veins on leaf upperside

leaves taper to slender stalk

Height 50 ft (15 m)	Shape Broadly conical	Leaf persistence Evergreen	Leaf type

Family FAGACEAE	Species *Nothofagus antarctica*	Author (J.G. Forster) Oersted

ANTARCTIC BEECH

Leaves Ovate, to 1¼ in (3 cm) long and ¾ in (2 cm) across, finely toothed, with usually four pairs of veins, glossy dark green above, more or less smooth on both sides. **Bark** Dark gray, cracking into plates and flaking with age. **Flowers** Males and females both very small, males with red anthers, in clusters of one to three, females with red stigmas, in clusters of two to three, in the leaf axils in late spring. **Fruit** A smooth husk, to ¼ in (6 mm) long, enclosing three small nuts.
• **NATIVE REGION** S. Argentina. S. Chile.
• **HABITAT** Deciduous woods and scrub in mountains.
• **REMARK** Also known as nirre. In its native region and habitat, the species is usually a medium-sized tree, but it can also form a large shrub.

• *usually four pairs of parallel veins*

leaf margin edged with numerous • *fine teeth*

husked • *fruits in short clusters*

Height 50 ft (15 m)	Shape Broadly columnar	Leaf persistence Deciduous	Leaf type

Family FAGACEAE	Species *Nothofagus betuloides*	Author (Mirbel) Blume

NOTHOFAGUS BETULOIDES

Leaves Ovate to elliptic, to 1 in (2.5 cm) long and ¾ in (2 cm) across, broadly tapered to the often unequal base, bluntly toothed, glossy dark blackish green above, paler and glossy with a fine network of veins beneath, smooth on both sides; older leaves often with small, dark spots beneath. **Bark** Very dark gray, cracking into plates and flaking with age. **Flowers** Males and females both very small, males with red anthers, singly, females with red stigmas, in clusters of three, in the leaf axils in late spring. **Fruit** A bristly husk, to ¼ in (6 mm) long, enclosing three small nuts.
• **NATIVE REGION** Argentina, Chile.
• **HABITAT** Evergreen forests.
• **REMARK** Sometimes shrubby.

• *fine network of veins on paler leaf underside*

leaf margin edged with many blunt teeth •

• *young shoots have small red stipules*

Height 80 ft (25 m)	Shape Broadly columnar	Leaf persistence Evergreen	Leaf type

Family FAGACEAE	Species *Nothofagus dombeyi*	Author (Mirbel) Blume

NOTHOFAGUS DOMBEYI

Leaves Narrowly ovate, to 1½ in (4 cm)
long and ⅜ in (1.5 cm) across, rounded
at the often unequal base, finely and
sharply toothed, glossy dark green above,
paler and glossy with a fine network of
veins beneath, smooth, with small, black
spots. **Bark** Dark gray, cracking into plates
and flaking with age. **Flowers** Males and
females both very small, males with red
anthers, in clusters of three, females
with red stigmas, in clusters of three,
in the leaf axils in late spring. **Fruit** A
bristly husk, to ¼ in (6 mm) long,
enclosing three small nuts.
• **NATIVE REGION**
Argentina, Chile.
• **HABITAT**
Mountain forests.
• **REMARK** This species is
similar to *Nothofagus betuloides*
(see p.155) but differs in its larger
leaves and taller growing habit.

*tiny fruit husks
split open when
ripe*

*lightly
impressed
veins*

*leaf margin
edged with fine,
sharp teeth*

Height 130 ft (40 m)	Shape Broadly columnar	Leaf persistence Evergreen	Leaf type

Family FAGACEAE	Species *Nothofagus nervosa*	Author (Poeppig & Endlicher) Oersted

RAULI

Leaves Oblong, to 4 in (10 cm) long and 1½ in
(4 cm) across, finely toothed, with 15 to 18 pairs
of veins, bronze becoming matte deep green
above, hairy on both sides, turning yellow in
autumn. **Bark** Dark gray, fissured with age.
Flowers Very small, greenish, males
singly, females in clusters of three,
in the leaf axils in late spring.
Fruit A bristly husk, to ⅜ in (1 cm)
long, enclosing three small nuts.
• **NATIVE REGION**
Argentina, Chile.
• **HABITAT** Forests.
• **REMARK** Also known as
Nothofagus procera.

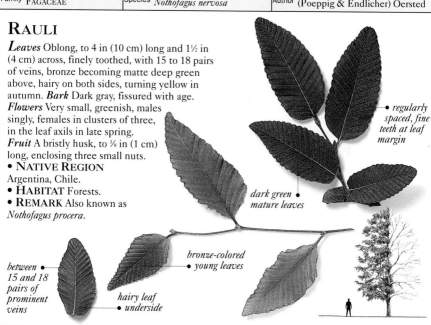

*regularly
spaced, fine
teeth at leaf
margin*

*dark green
mature leaves*

*bronze-colored
young leaves*

*between
15 and 18
pairs of
prominent
veins*

*hairy leaf
underside*

Height 80 ft (25 m)	Shape Broadly conical	Leaf persistence Deciduous	Leaf type

Family FAGACEAE	Species *Nothofagus obliqua*	Author (Mirbel) Blume

ROBLE BEECH

Leaves Ovate, to 3 in (7.5 cm) long and 1½ in (4 cm) across, toothed, dark green above, blue-green beneath, smooth on both sides, turning yellow in autumn. *Bark* Gray, smooth, cracking into plates with age. *Flowers* Tiny, greenish, males singly, females in threes, in late spring. *Fruit* A scaly husk, to ⅜ in (1 cm) long, with three nuts.
• **NATIVE REGION** Argentina, Chile.
• **HABITAT** Forests.

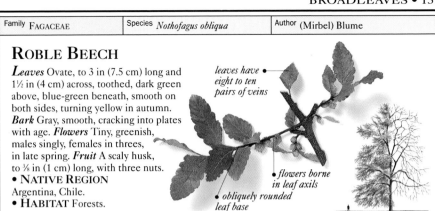

leaves have • eight to ten pairs of veins

• *flowers borne in leaf axils*

• *obliquely rounded leaf base*

Height 115 ft (35 m)	Shape Broadly columnar	Leaf persistence Deciduous	Leaf type

Family FAGACEAE	Species *Nothofagus pumilio*	Author (Poeppig & Endlicher) Krasser

LENGA

Leaves Elliptic to ovate, to 1¼ in (3 cm) long and ¾ in (2 cm) across, very dark green above, slightly hairy on both sides, turning yellow in autumn. *Bark* Purple-brown, with horizontal lenticels and wrinkles, fissured at the base. *Flowers* Very small, borne singly in the leaf axils in late spring. *Fruit* A scaly husk, to ⅜ in (1 cm) long, enclosing three small nuts.
• **NATIVE REGION** Argentina, Chile.
• **HABITAT** Forests.

leaves have • five to seven pairs of veins

two teeth between • each leaf vein

Height 80 ft (25 m)	Shape Broadly columnar	Leaf persistence Deciduous	Leaf type

Family FAGACEAE	Species *Nothofagus solandri*	Author (J.D. Hooker) Oersted

BLACK BEECH

Leaves Elliptic, to ⅝ in (1.5 cm) long and ⅜ in (1 cm) across, rounded at the tip, untoothed, dark green above, gray-hairy beneath. *Bark* Dark gray, rough, furrowed. *Flowers* Very small, males with red anthers, singly or in pairs, females in clusters of up to three, in the leaf axils in late spring. *Fruit* A scaly husk, enclosing three small nuts.
• **NATIVE REGION** New Zealand.
• **HABITAT** Lowland and mountain forests.

short point • at leaf tip

dull leaf • underside

Height 80 ft (25 m)	Shape Broadly conical	Leaf persistence Evergreen	Leaf type

Family FAGACEAE	Species *Quercus acutissima*	Author Carruthers

SAWTOOTH OAK

Leaves Oblong, to 8 in (20 cm) long and 2½ in (6 cm) across, with numerous veins ending in slender-tipped teeth, glossy green above, paler beneath, smooth on both sides. **Bark** Gray-brown, with deep fissures. **Flowers** Males in yellow-green, drooping catkins, females inconspicuous, separately on the same plant in late spring. **Fruit** A rounded acorn, to 1 in (2.5 cm) long, about two-thirds enclosed in a cup.
• **NATIVE REGION** Himalayas to Japan.
• **HABITAT** Woods.

acorn cup loosely covered with long, slender scales •

• *leaves edged with bristlelike teeth*

Height 50 ft (15 m)	Shape Broadly spreading	Leaf persistence Deciduous	Leaf type

Family FAGACEAE	Species *Quercus alba*	Author Linnaeus

WHITE OAK

Leaves Obovate, to 8 in (20 cm) long and 4 in (10 cm) across, tapered at the base, deeply cut into two to four lobes on each side, pink-tinged and white-hairy becoming bright green above, blue-green beneath, turning purple-red in autumn. **Bark** Pale gray and scaly, fissured with age. **Flowers** Males in yellow-green, drooping catkins, females inconspicuous, borne separately on the same plant in late spring. **Fruit** An acorn, to 1 in (2.5 cm) long, one-quarter enclosed in a roughened cup.
• **NATIVE REGION** E. North America.
• **HABITAT** Dry woods.
• **REMARK** The state tree of Connecticut, Illinois, and Maryland.

rough-textured, scaly acorn cup •

untoothed • *leaf lobes*

• *leaves color brilliantly in autumn*

Height 115 ft (35 m)	Shape Broadly spreading	Leaf persistence Deciduous	Leaf type

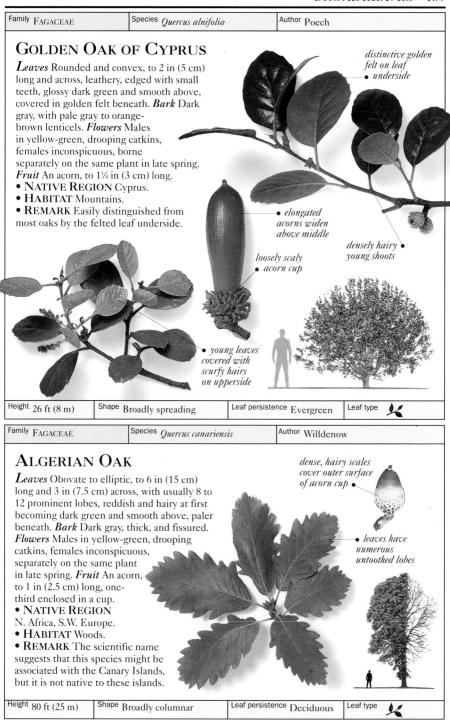

Family FAGACEAE	Species *Quercus alnifolia*	Author Poech

GOLDEN OAK OF CYPRUS

Leaves Rounded and convex, to 2 in (5 cm) long and across, leathery, edged with small teeth, glossy dark green and smooth above, covered in golden felt beneath. **Bark** Dark gray, with pale gray to orange-brown lenticels. **Flowers** Males in yellow-green, drooping catkins, females inconspicuous, borne separately on the same plant in late spring. **Fruit** An acorn, to 1¼ in (3 cm) long.
• **NATIVE REGION** Cyprus.
• **HABITAT** Mountains.
• **REMARK** Easily distinguished from most oaks by the felted leaf underside.

distinctive golden felt on leaf underside

elongated acorns widen above middle

loosely scaly acorn cup

densely hairy young shoots

young leaves covered with scurfy hairs on upperside

Height 26 ft (8 m)	Shape Broadly spreading	Leaf persistence Evergreen	Leaf type

Family FAGACEAE	Species *Quercus canariensis*	Author Willdenow

ALGERIAN OAK

Leaves Obovate to elliptic, to 6 in (15 cm) long and 3 in (7.5 cm) across, with usually 8 to 12 prominent lobes, reddish and hairy at first becoming dark green and smooth above, paler beneath. **Bark** Dark gray, thick, and fissured. **Flowers** Males in yellow-green, drooping catkins, females inconspicuous, separately on the same plant in late spring. **Fruit** An acorn, to 1 in (2.5 cm) long, one-third enclosed in a cup.
• **NATIVE REGION** N. Africa, S.W. Europe.
• **HABITAT** Woods.
• **REMARK** The scientific name suggests that this species might be associated with the Canary Islands, but it is not native to these islands.

dense, hairy scales cover outer surface of acorn cup

leaves have numerous untoothed lobes

Height 80 ft (25 m)	Shape Broadly columnar	Leaf persistence Deciduous	Leaf type

| Family FAGACEAE | Species *Quercus castaneifolia* | Author C.A. Meyer |

CHESTNUT-LEAVED OAK

Leaves Oblong, to 8 in (20 cm) long and 3 in (7.5 cm) across, with 10 to 12 teeth on each side, glossy dark green and smooth above, blue-gray and thinly hairy beneath. **Bark** Gray and smooth. **Flowers** Males in yellow-green, drooping catkins, females inconspicuous, borne separately on the same plant in late spring. **Fruit** An acorn, to 1 in (2.5 cm) long, one-half enclosed in a cup, the cup covered in long scales.
• **NATIVE REGION** Caucasus, N. Iran.
• **HABITAT** Forests.

veins end in triangular teeth

leaf underside

glossy upper leaf surface

| Height 100 ft (30 m) | Shape Broadly spreading | Leaf persistence Deciduous | Leaf type |

| Family FAGACEAE | Species *Quercus cerris* | Author Linnaeus |

TURKEY OAK

Leaves Elliptic to oblong, to 4¾ in (12 cm) long and 3 in (7.5 cm) across, deeply lobed, toothed, glossy dark green above, downy when young becoming smooth beneath. **Bark** Dark gray-brown, thick, rough, and deeply ridged. **Flowers** Males in yellow-green, drooping catkins, females inconspicuous, borne separately on the same plant in early summer. **Fruit** An acorn, to 1 in (2.5 cm) long, one-half enclosed in a cup, the cup covered in long, slender scales.
• **NATIVE REGION** C. and S. Europe.
• **HABITAT** Woods.

variable leaf lobing

slender stipules clustered around leaf bud

QUERCUS CERRIS

strikingly variegated ornamental foliage

'VARIEGATA' ▷
The leaves of this form are margined yellow when they unfold, and creamy white as they mature.

| Height 115 ft (35 m) | Shape Broadly spreading | Leaf persistence Deciduous | Leaf type |

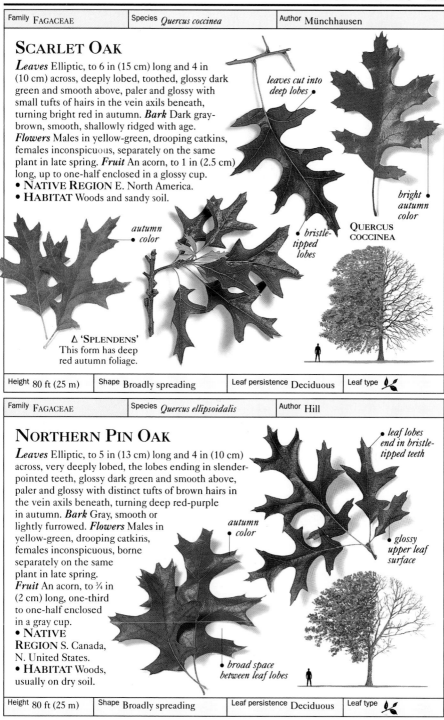

Family FAGACEAE	Species *Quercus coccinea*	Author Münchhausen

SCARLET OAK

Leaves Elliptic, to 6 in (15 cm) long and 4 in (10 cm) across, deeply lobed, toothed, glossy dark green and smooth above, paler and glossy with small tufts of hairs in the vein axils beneath, turning bright red in autumn. *Bark* Dark gray-brown, smooth, shallowly ridged with age. *Flowers* Males in yellow-green, drooping catkins, females inconspicuous, separately on the same plant in late spring. *Fruit* An acorn, to 1 in (2.5 cm) long, up to one-half enclosed in a glossy cup.
• **NATIVE REGION** E. North America.
• **HABITAT** Woods and sandy soil.

leaves cut into deep lobes •

bright • autumn color

QUERCUS COCCINEA

• bristle-tipped lobes

autumn • color

△ 'SPLENDENS'
This form has deep red autumn foliage.

Height 80 ft (25 m)	Shape Broadly spreading	Leaf persistence Deciduous	Leaf type

Family FAGACEAE	Species *Quercus ellipsoidalis*	Author Hill

NORTHERN PIN OAK

Leaves Elliptic, to 5 in (13 cm) long and 4 in (10 cm) across, very deeply lobed, the lobes ending in slender-pointed teeth, glossy dark green and smooth above, paler and glossy with distinct tufts of brown hairs in the vein axils beneath, turning deep red-purple in autumn. *Bark* Gray, smooth or lightly furrowed. *Flowers* Males in yellow-green, drooping catkins, females inconspicuous, borne separately on the same plant in late spring. *Fruit* An acorn, to ¾ in (2 cm) long, one-third to one-half enclosed in a gray cup.
• **NATIVE REGION** S. Canada, N. United States.
• **HABITAT** Woods, usually on dry soil.

• leaf lobes end in bristle-tipped teeth

autumn • color

• glossy upper leaf surface

• broad space between leaf lobes

Height 80 ft (25 m)	Shape Broadly spreading	Leaf persistence Deciduous	Leaf type

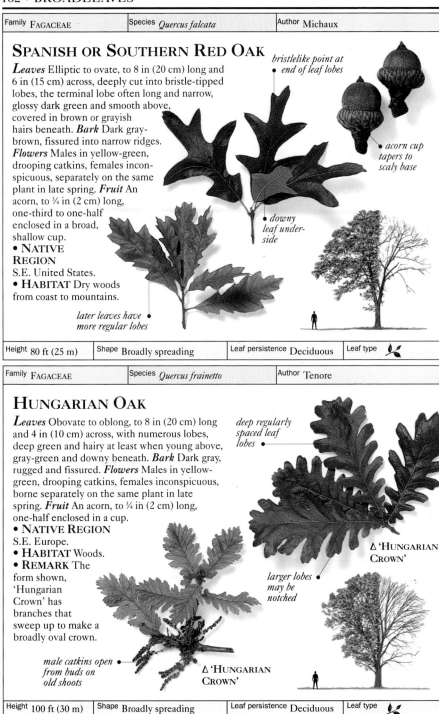

| Family FAGACEAE | Species *Quercus falcata* | Author Michaux |

SPANISH OR SOUTHERN RED OAK

bristlelike point at end of leaf lobes

Leaves Elliptic to ovate, to 8 in (20 cm) long and 6 in (15 cm) across, deeply cut into bristle-tipped lobes, the terminal lobe often long and narrow, glossy dark green and smooth above, covered in brown or grayish hairs beneath. **Bark** Dark gray-brown, fissured into narrow ridges. **Flowers** Males in yellow-green, drooping catkins, females inconspicuous, separately on the same plant in late spring. **Fruit** An acorn, to ¾ in (2 cm) long, one-third to one-half enclosed in a broad, shallow cup.
• **NATIVE REGION**
S.E. United States.
• **HABITAT** Dry woods from coast to mountains.

acorn cup tapers to scaly base

downy leaf under-side

later leaves have more regular lobes

| Height 80 ft (25 m) | Shape Broadly spreading | Leaf persistence Deciduous | Leaf type |

| Family FAGACEAE | Species *Quercus frainetto* | Author Tenore |

HUNGARIAN OAK

Leaves Obovate to oblong, to 8 in (20 cm) long and 4 in (10 cm) across, with numerous lobes, deep green and hairy at least when young above, gray-green and downy beneath. **Bark** Dark gray, rugged and fissured. **Flowers** Males in yellow-green, drooping catkins, females inconspicuous, borne separately on the same plant in late spring. **Fruit** An acorn, to ¾ in (2 cm) long, one-half enclosed in a cup.
• **NATIVE REGION**
S.E. Europe.
• **HABITAT** Woods.
• **REMARK** The form shown, 'Hungarian Crown' has branches that sweep up to make a broadly oval crown.

deep regularly spaced leaf lobes

△ 'HUNGARIAN CROWN'

larger lobes may be notched

male catkins open from buds on old shoots

△ 'HUNGARIAN CROWN'

| Height 100 ft (30 m) | Shape Broadly spreading | Leaf persistence Deciduous | Leaf type |

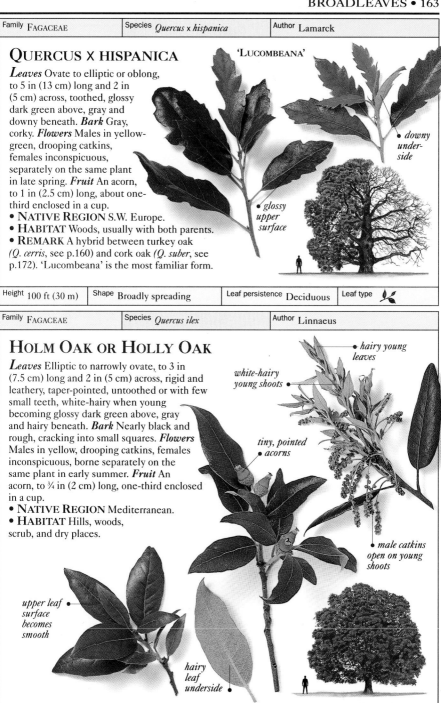

Family FAGACEAE	Species *Quercus* x *hispanica*	Author Lamarck

QUERCUS X HISPANICA

'LUCOMBEANA'

Leaves Ovate to elliptic or oblong, to 5 in (13 cm) long and 2 in (5 cm) across, toothed, glossy dark green above, gray and downy beneath. **Bark** Gray, corky. **Flowers** Males in yellow-green, drooping catkins, females inconspicuous, separately on the same plant in late spring. **Fruit** An acorn, to 1 in (2.5 cm) long, about one-third enclosed in a cup.
• **NATIVE REGION** S.W. Europe.
• **HABITAT** Woods, usually with both parents.
• **REMARK** A hybrid between turkey oak *(Q. cerris,* see p.160) and cork oak *(Q. suber,* see p.172). 'Lucombeana' is the most familiar form.

downy under-side

glossy upper surface

Height 100 ft (30 m)	Shape Broadly spreading	Leaf persistence Deciduous	Leaf type

Family FAGACEAE	Species *Quercus ilex*	Author Linnaeus

HOLM OAK OR HOLLY OAK

Leaves Elliptic to narrowly ovate, to 3 in (7.5 cm) long and 2 in (5 cm) across, rigid and leathery, taper-pointed, untoothed or with few small teeth, white-hairy when young becoming glossy dark green above, gray and hairy beneath. **Bark** Nearly black and rough, cracking into small squares. **Flowers** Males in yellow, drooping catkins, females inconspicuous, borne separately on the same plant in early summer. **Fruit** An acorn, to ¾ in (2 cm) long, one-third enclosed in a cup.
• **NATIVE REGION** Mediterranean.
• **HABITAT** Hills, woods, scrub, and dry places.

hairy young leaves

white-hairy young shoots

tiny, pointed acorns

male catkins open on young shoots

upper leaf surface becomes smooth

hairy leaf underside

Height 100 ft (30 m)	Shape Broadly spreading	Leaf persistence Evergreen	Leaf type

| Family FAGACEAE | Species *Quercus imbricaria* | Author A. Michaux |

SHINGLE OAK

Leaves Oblong to lanceolate, to 6 in (15 cm) long and 3 in (7.5 cm) across, ending in a fine point, untoothed, yellow when young becoming glossy dark green and smooth above, gray-hairy beneath, often persisting far into winter. **Bark** Gray-brown, smooth at first becoming fissured with age. **Flowers** Males in yellow-green, drooping catkins, females inconspicuous, borne separately on the same plant in early summer. **Fruit** An acorn, to ¼ in (2 cm) long, one-third to one-half enclosed in a cup, the cup covered in broad, hairy scales.
• **NATIVE REGION** C. and E. United States.
• **HABITAT** Rich woods and riverbanks.
• **REMARK** Early settlers made roof shingles from the wood, giving this species its common name.

untoothed leaves end in small, bristlelike tip

overlapping scales cover outer surface of acorn cup

| Height 80 ft (25 m) | Shape Broadly spreading | Leaf persistence Deciduous | Leaf type |

| Family FAGACEAE | Species *Quercus laurifolia* | Author A. Michaux |

LAUREL OAK

Leaves Oblanceolate to oblong, to 4 in (10 cm) long and 1½ in (4 cm) across, sometimes shallowly lobed, untoothed, glossy green, smooth on both sides. **Bark** Gray and scaly. **Flowers** Males in yellow-green, drooping catkins, females inconspicuous, borne separately on the same plant in early summer. **Fruit** An acorn, to ⅝ in (1.5 cm) long, one-third enclosed in a cup.
• **NATIVE REGION** S.E. United States.
• **HABITAT** Woods, sandy soil, and swamp margins on the coastal plain.
• **REMARK** A selected form is Darlington oak. The leaves look rather like those of the bay laurel *(Laurus nobilis, see p.188)*. They persist through autumn into winter, giving the tree a semi-evergreen appearance.

shallowly lobed leaves may appear almost unlobed

acorns are nearly rounded in shape

tapered leaf base

| Height 65 ft (20 m) | Shape Broadly conical | Leaf persistence Deciduous | Leaf type |

Family FAGACEAE	Species *Quercus macranthera*	Author Fischer & C.A. Meyer

QUERCUS MACRANTHERA

Leaves Obovate, to 6 in (15 cm) long and 4 in (10 cm) across, with 6 to 11 rounded lobes on each side, dark green above, paler and hairy beneath, carried on stout, densely hairy shoots. **Bark** Gray-brown, thick and fissured. **Flowers** Males in yellow-green, drooping catkins, females inconspicuous, borne separately on the same plant in early summer. **Fruit** An acorn, to 1 in (2.5 cm) long, one-half enclosed in a cup, the cup covered in hairy scales.
• **NATIVE REGION** Caucasus, N. Iran.
• **HABITAT** Forests on dry mountain slopes.

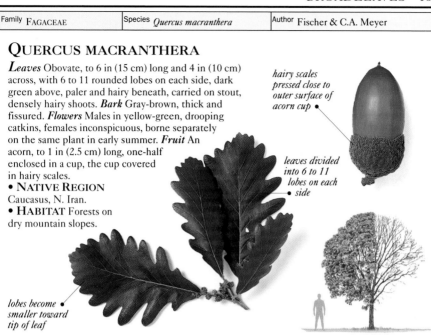

hairy scales pressed close to outer surface of acorn cup

leaves divided into 6 to 11 lobes on each side

lobes become smaller toward tip of leaf

Height 65 ft (20 m)	Shape Broadly spreading	Leaf persistence Deciduous	Leaf type

Family FAGACEAE	Species *Quercus macrocarpa*	Author A. Michaux

BURR OAK

Leaves Obovate, to 10 in (25 cm) long and 4¾ in (12 cm) across, deeply cut into round-ended lobes, with a distinct, broad sinus toward the base, glossy green and smooth above, paler and hairy beneath. **Bark** Gray, rough, deeply furrowed. **Flowers** Males in yellow, drooping catkins, females inconspicuous, borne separately on the same plant in early summer. **Fruit** An acorn, to 2 in (5 cm) long, one-half or more enclosed in a cup, the cup rimmed with a fringe of scales.
• **NATIVE REGION** E. North America.
• **HABITAT** Rich woods.
• **REMARK** Also known as blue oak, mossy cup oak. The acorns are larger than those of any other North American oak.

shallower lobes between middle and tip of leaf

wide space between lobes toward base of leaf

Height 130 ft (40 m)	Shape Broadly spreading	Leaf persistence Deciduous	Leaf type

| Family FAGACEAE | Species *Quercus marilandica* | Author Münchhausen |

BLACK JACK OAK

Leaves Triangular-obovate, to 10 in (25 cm) long and nearly the same across at the tip, tapered at the base, usually with three bristle-pointed lobes at the tip, glossy dark green above, paler beneath, thinly hairy becoming nearly smooth on both sides. **Bark** Blackish, cracking into small, square plates. **Flowers** Males in yellow-green, drooping catkins, females inconspicuous, borne separately on the same plant in early summer. **Fruit** An acorn, to ¾ in (2 cm) long, about one-half enclosed in a cup.
• **NATIVE REGION** E. United States.
• **HABITAT** Woods and poor, often sandy soil.

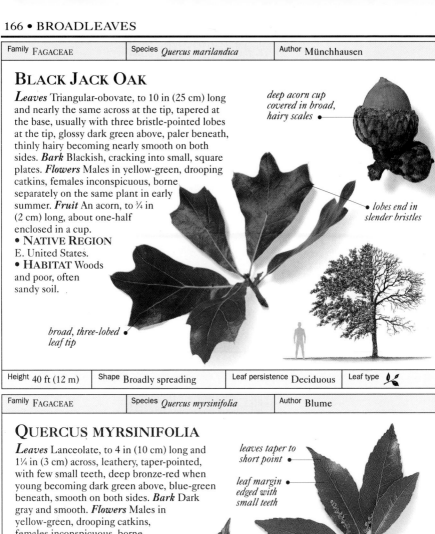

deep acorn cup covered in broad, hairy scales •

• lobes end in slender bristles

broad, three-lobed • leaf tip

| Height 40 ft (12 m) | Shape Broadly spreading | Leaf persistence Deciduous | Leaf type |

| Family FAGACEAE | Species *Quercus myrsinifolia* | Author Blume |

QUERCUS MYRSINIFOLIA

Leaves Lanceolate, to 4 in (10 cm) long and 1¼ in (3 cm) across, leathery, taper-pointed, with few small teeth, deep bronze-red when young becoming dark green above, blue-green beneath, smooth on both sides. **Bark** Dark gray and smooth. **Flowers** Males in yellow-green, drooping catkins, females inconspicuous, borne separately on the same plant in early summer. **Fruit** An acorn, to ¾ in (2 cm) long, one-third enclosed in a cup.
• **NATIVE REGION** China, Japan.
• **HABITAT** Forests.

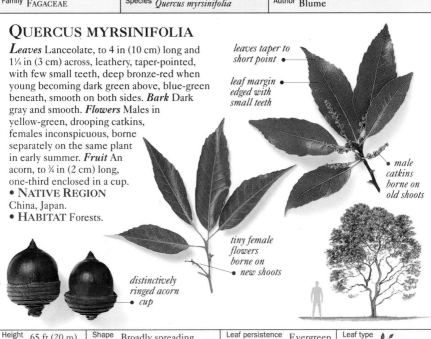

leaves taper to short point •

leaf margin • edged with small teeth

• male catkins borne on old shoots

tiny female flowers borne on • new shoots

distinctively ringed acorn • cup

| Height 65 ft (20 m) | Shape Broadly spreading | Leaf persistence Evergreen | Leaf type |

Family FAGACEAE	Species *Quercus palustris*	Author Münchhausen

Pin Oak

Leaves Elliptic to obovate, to 6 in (15 cm) long and 4¾ in (12 cm) across, deeply lobed, glossy green on both sides, paler with tufts of brown hairs in the vein axils beneath. *Bark* Gray-brown, smooth. *Flowers* Males in yellow-green, drooping catkins, females inconspicuous, separately on the same plant in late spring. *Fruit* An acorn, to ⅝ in (1.5 cm) long, one-quarter to one-third enclosed in a broad cup.
• **NATIVE REGION** S.E. Canada, E. United States.
• **HABITAT** Swampy woods.

hairy tufts in vein axils on underside of leaves

bristle-tipped teeth at end of leaf lobes

shallow, saucerlike acorn

Height 100 ft (30 m)	Shape Broadly conical	Leaf persistence Deciduous	Leaf type

Family FAGACEAE	Species *Quercus petraea*	Author (Mattuschka) Lieblein

Durmast Oak

Leaves Elliptic, to 4¾ in (12 cm) long and 3 in (7.5 cm) across, with rounded lobes, usually tapered at the base, without auricles, slightly glossy dark green and smooth above, paler and thinly hairy beneath, the stalk to ⅜ in (1 cm) or more long. *Bark* Gray, with vertical ridges. *Flowers* Males in yellow-green, drooping catkins, females inconspicuous, borne separately on the same plant in late spring. *Fruit* An acorn, to 1¼ in (3 cm) long, about one-third enclosed in a cup.
• **NATIVE REGION** Europe.
• **HABITAT** Woods.
• **REMARK** Also known as sessile oak.

rounded, untoothed leaf lobes

yellow-green leaf stalk

unstalked or very short-stalked acorns

small scales pressed close to acorn cup

Height 130 ft (40 m)	Shape Broadly spreading	Leaf persistence Deciduous	Leaf type

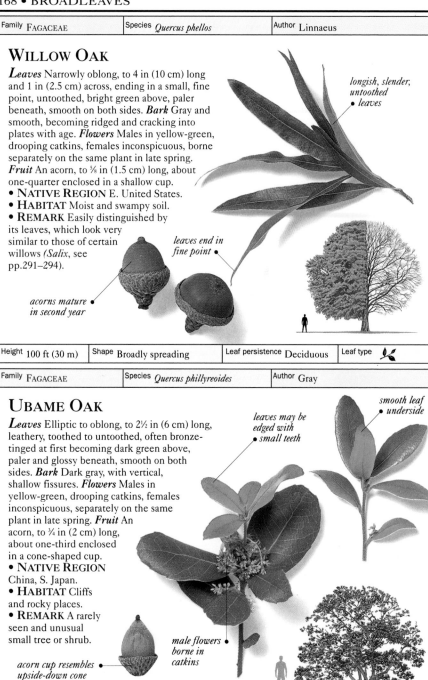

| Family FAGACEAE | Species *Quercus phellos* | Author Linnaeus |

WILLOW OAK

Leaves Narrowly oblong, to 4 in (10 cm) long
and 1 in (2.5 cm) across, ending in a small, fine
point, untoothed, bright green above, paler
beneath, smooth on both sides. ***Bark*** Gray and
smooth, becoming ridged and cracking into
plates with age. ***Flowers*** Males in yellow-green,
drooping catkins, females inconspicuous, borne
separately on the same plant in late spring.
Fruit An acorn, to ⅜ in (1.5 cm) long, about
one-quarter enclosed in a shallow cup.
• **NATIVE REGION** E. United States.
• **HABITAT** Moist and swampy soil.
• **REMARK** Easily distinguished by
its leaves, which look very
similar to those of certain
willows *(Salix*, see
pp.291–294).

*longish, slender,
untoothed
• leaves*

*leaves end in
fine point •*

*acorns mature
in second year*

| Height 100 ft (30 m) | Shape Broadly spreading | Leaf persistence Deciduous | Leaf type |

| Family FAGACEAE | Species *Quercus phillyreoides* | Author Gray |

UBAME OAK

Leaves Elliptic to oblong, to 2½ in (6 cm) long,
leathery, toothed to untoothed, often bronze-
tinged at first becoming dark green above,
paler and glossy beneath, smooth on both
sides. ***Bark*** Dark gray, with vertical,
shallow fissures. ***Flowers*** Males in
yellow-green, drooping catkins, females
inconspicuous, separately on the same
plant in late spring. ***Fruit*** An
acorn, to ¼ in (2 cm) long,
about one-third enclosed
in a cone-shaped cup.
• **NATIVE REGION**
China, S. Japan.
• **HABITAT** Cliffs
and rocky places.
• **REMARK** A rarely
seen and unusual
small tree or shrub.

*smooth leaf
• underside*

*leaves may be
edged with
• small teeth*

*acorn cup resembles •
upside-down cone*

*male flowers •
borne in
catkins*

| Height 50 ft (15 m) | Shape Broadly spreading | Leaf persistence Evergreen | Leaf type |

Family FAGACEAE	Species *Quercus pontica*	Author K. Koch

ARMENIAN OAK

Leaves Obovate to broadly elliptic, to 6 in (15 cm) long and 4 in (10 cm) across, tapered at the base, the numerous parallel veins ending in small, pointed teeth, hairy when young becoming bright green and smooth above, blue-green beneath, turning yellow-brown in autumn, carried on stout shoots. **Bark** Gray to purple-brown and thinly scaly, becoming rugged with age. **Flowers** Males in yellow-green, long, slender, drooping catkins, females inconspicuous, borne separately on the same plant in late spring. **Fruit** An acorn, to ¼ in (2 cm) long, one-half enclosed in a cup.
• **NATIVE REGION** Caucasus, N.E. Turkey.
• **HABITAT** Mountain woods.
• **REMARK** This species can be either a very small tree or a bushy shrub.

• *large, broad leaves edged with many pointed teeth*

male flowers in very long slender catkins

Height 20 ft (6 m)	Shape Broadly columnar	Leaf persistence Deciduous	Leaf type

Family FAGACEAE	Species *Quercus pubescens*	Author Willdenow

QUERCUS PUBESCENS

Leaves Elliptic to obovate, to 4 in (10 cm) long and 2 in (5 cm) across, with rounded lobes, the lobes ending in a small, sharp point, dark gray-green above, downy beneath, softly gray-hairy at least when young becoming nearly smooth on both sides. **Bark** Dark gray and deeply furrowed. **Flowers** Males in yellow-green, drooping catkins, females inconspicuous, borne separately on the same plant in late spring. **Fruit** An acorn, to 1½ in (4 cm) long, about one-third enclosed in a cup, the cup covered in hairy scales.
• **NATIVE REGION** W. Asia, C. and S. Europe.
• **HABITAT** Dry places in hills.

• *rounded leaf lobes tipped with sharp point*

• *downy leaf stalks*

acorn cup covered in dense, downy scales •

visibly hairy leaf under-side •

Height 65 ft (20 m)	Shape Broadly spreading	Leaf persistence Deciduous	Leaf type

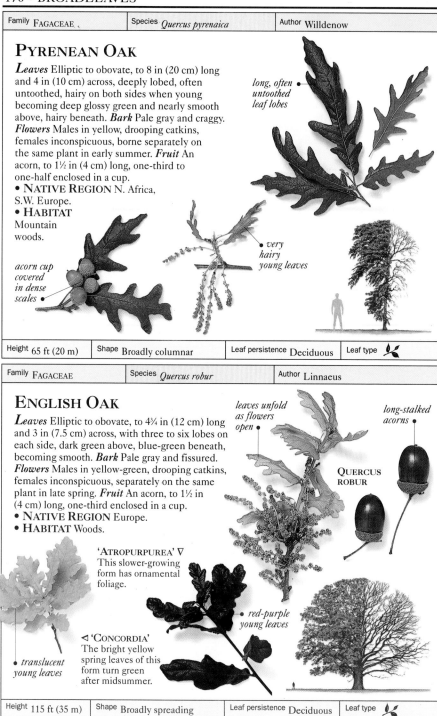

Family FAGACEAE	Species *Quercus pyrenaica*	Author Willdenow

PYRENEAN OAK

Leaves Elliptic to obovate, to 8 in (20 cm) long and 4 in (10 cm) across, deeply lobed, often untoothed, hairy on both sides when young becoming deep glossy green and nearly smooth above, hairy beneath. *Bark* Pale gray and craggy. *Flowers* Males in yellow, drooping catkins, females inconspicuous, borne separately on the same plant in early summer. *Fruit* An acorn, to 1½ in (4 cm) long, one-third to one-half enclosed in a cup.
• NATIVE REGION N. Africa, S.W. Europe.
• HABITAT Mountain woods.

long, often untoothed leaf lobes

very hairy young leaves

acorn cup covered in dense scales

Height 65 ft (20 m)	Shape Broadly columnar	Leaf persistence Deciduous	Leaf type

Family FAGACEAE	Species *Quercus robur*	Author Linnaeus

ENGLISH OAK

Leaves Elliptic to obovate, to 4¾ in (12 cm) long and 3 in (7.5 cm) across, with three to six lobes on each side, dark green above, blue-green beneath, becoming smooth. *Bark* Pale gray and fissured. *Flowers* Males in yellow-green, drooping catkins, females inconspicuous, separately on the same plant in late spring. *Fruit* An acorn, to 1½ in (4 cm) long, one-third enclosed in a cup.
• NATIVE REGION Europe.
• HABITAT Woods.

leaves unfold as flowers open

long-stalked acorns

QUERCUS ROBUR

'ATROPURPUREA' ▽
This slower-growing form has ornamental foliage.

red-purple young leaves

◁ 'CONCORDIA'
The bright yellow spring leaves of this form turn green after midsummer.

translucent young leaves

Height 115 ft (35 m)	Shape Broadly spreading	Leaf persistence Deciduous	Leaf type

Family FAGACEAE	Species *Quercus rubra*	Author Linnaeus

RED OR NORTHERN RED OAK

Leaves Elliptic, ovate, or obovate, to 8 in (20 cm) long and 6 in (15 cm) across, with slender-toothed lobes, matte dark green and smooth above, paler and smooth with small tufts of brown hairs in the vein axils beneath, turning red-brown in autumn. **Bark** Gray and smooth, becoming deeply furrowed. **Flowers** Males in yellowish green, drooping catkins, females inconspicuous, separately on the same plant in late spring. **Fruit** An acorn, to 1¼ in (3 cm) long, one-quarter enclosed in a shallow cup.
• **NATIVE REGION** E. North America.
• **HABITAT** Woods, and mountains in the south of its region.

acorns set in very shallow cup •

leaves cut into relatively shallow lobes •

• lobes end in bristlelike point

dull green upper leaf surface •

Height 80 ft (25 m)	Shape Broadly spreading	Leaf persistence Deciduous	Leaf type

Family FAGACEAE	Species *Quercus stellata*	Author Wangenheim

POST OAK

Leaves Obovate, to 8 in (20 cm) long and 4 in (10 cm) across, with two or three pairs of lobes, the central pair at least broad and often narrowed at the base, dark green and rough above, gray-hairy beneath. **Bark** Gray-brown, ridged, flaky. **Flowers** Males in yellow-green, drooping catkins, females inconspicuous, separately on the same plant in late spring. **Fruit** An acorn, to 1¼ in (3 cm) long, about one-third enclosed in a cup.
• **NATIVE REGION** C. and E. United States.
• **HABITAT** Dry soil.

broad, rounded • leaf lobes

• acorns ripen in first year

upper leaf surface roughened with hairs

hairy young • shoots

Height 65 ft (20 m)	Shape Broadly spreading	Leaf persistence Deciduous	Leaf type

Family FAGACEAE	Species *Quercus suber*	Author Linnaeus

CORK OAK

Leaves Ovate to oblong, to 2¾ in (7 cm) long and 1½ in (4 cm) across, rigid, usually toothed, glossy dark green above, gray-hairy beneath. **Bark** Pale gray, thick, corky, with prominent ridges; dark red when freshly exposed. **Flowers** Males in yellow-green, drooping catkins, females inconspicuous, borne separately on the same plant in late spring. **Fruit** An acorn, to 1¼ in (3 cm) long, about one-half enclosed in a cup.
• **NATIVE REGION** W. Mediterranean.
• **HABITAT** Woods in hills.
• **REMARK** Striping the bark, from which cork is produced in Portugal and Spain, does not damage the living tissue of the plant.

hairy, gray leaf underside

leaf margin edged with few small teeth

acorns ripen in first year

thick, but light corky bark

Height 65 ft (20 m)	Shape Broadly spreading	Leaf persistence Evergreen	Leaf type

Family FAGACEAE	Species *Quercus x turneri*	Author Willdenow

TURNER'S OAK

Leaves Oblong to obovate, to 4¾ in (12 cm) long and 2 in (5 cm) across, tapered at the base, with three to five triangular teeth on each side, glossy dark green above, paler beneath, some persisting until the following spring. **Bark** Dark gray, cracking into plates. **Flowers** Males in yellow-green, drooping catkins, females inconspicuous, separately on the same plant in late spring. **Fruit** An acorn, to ¾ in (2 cm) long, about one-half enclosed in a cup, usually several together on a long stalk.
• **NATIVE REGION**
Of garden origin.
• **REMARK** A hybrid between holm oak *(Quercus ilex, see p.163)* and English oak *(Quercus robur, see p.170).*

acorns may not develop into mature fruits

leaves persist far into winter

densely hairy shoots

small teeth at leaf margin point forward

Height 65 ft (20 m)	Shape Broadly spreading	Leaf persistence Deciduous	Leaf type

Family FAGACEAE	Species *Quercus variabilis*	Author Blume

QUERCUS VARIABILIS

Leaves Oblong, to 8 in (20 cm) long and 2 in (5 cm) across, pointed at the tip, with numerous parallel veins ending in bristle-tipped teeth, glossy dark green and smooth above, gray and thinly hairy beneath. **Bark** Pale gray-brown, thick and corky, deeply fissured. **Flowers** Males in yellow-green, drooping catkins, females inconspicuous, separately on the same plant in late spring. **Fruit** An acorn, to ¾ in (2 cm) long, almost enclosed in a cup, the cup covered in long, curly scales.
• **NATIVE REGION**
China, Japan, Korea.
• **HABITAT**
Mountain woods.

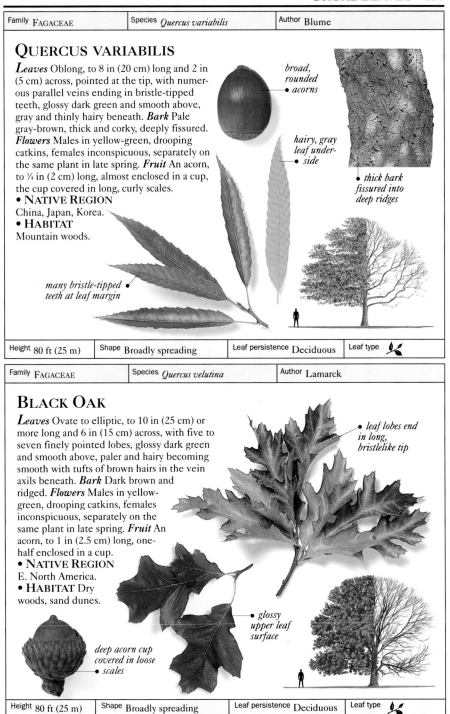

broad, rounded acorns

hairy, gray leaf under-side

thick bark fissured into deep ridges

many bristle-tipped teeth at leaf margin

Height 80 ft (25 m)	Shape Broadly spreading	Leaf persistence Deciduous	Leaf type

Family FAGACEAE	Species *Quercus velutina*	Author Lamarck

BLACK OAK

Leaves Ovate to elliptic, to 10 in (25 cm) or more long and 6 in (15 cm) across, with five to seven finely pointed lobes, glossy dark green and smooth above, paler and hairy becoming smooth with tufts of brown hairs in the vein axils beneath. **Bark** Dark brown and ridged. **Flowers** Males in yellow-green, drooping catkins, females inconspicuous, separately on the same plant in late spring. **Fruit** An acorn, to 1 in (2.5 cm) long, one-half enclosed in a cup.
• **NATIVE REGION**
E. North America.
• **HABITAT** Dry woods, sand dunes.

leaf lobes end in long, bristlelike tip

glossy upper leaf surface

deep acorn cup covered in loose scales

Height 80 ft (25 m)	Shape Broadly spreading	Leaf persistence Deciduous	Leaf type

FLACOURTIACEAE

T HIS LARGELY TROPICAL and sub-tropical family occurs in both hemispheres and contains about 90 genera and 900 species of evergreen and deciduous trees and shrubs. As well as the plants described here, the family includes species of the Southeast Asian genus, *Hydnocarpus*. These yield chaulmoogra oil, which is used to treat some skin diseases.

Family FLACOURTIACEAE	Species *Azara microphylla*	Author J.D. Hooker

AZARA MICROPHYLLA

Leaves Obovate to elliptic, to 1 in (2.5 cm) long, toothed, glossy dark green above, paler beneath, smooth, with a smaller, leaf-like stipule at the base. **Bark** Gray, with horizontal lenticels, cracking into thin flakes. **Flowers** Small, without petals, but with green sepals and conspicuous yellow stamens, in the leaf axils in late winter or early spring. **Fruit** A small, orange-red berry.
• **NATIVE REGION** Argentina, Chile.
• **HABITAT** Deciduous forests.

smaller stipule at leaf base

leaves edged with few small teeth

tiny, fragrant flowers clustered in leaf axils

Height 33 ft (10 m)	Shape Narrowly conical	Leaf persistence Evergreen	Leaf type

Family FLACOURTIACEAE	Species *Idesia polycarpa*	Author Maximowicz

IIGIRI TREE

Leaves Broadly heart-shaped, to 8 in (20 cm) long and nearly the same across, heart-shaped at the base, with a short, tapered tip, toothed, bronze-purple becoming dark green above, blue-white beneath, smooth, on long stalks. **Bark** Gray-white. **Flowers** Small and yellow-green, without petals, in large, drooping panicles at the ends of the shoots, on separate plants in early summer. **Fruit** A small, red berry, borne in hanging clusters.
• **NATIVE REGION** China, Japan.
• **HABITAT** Mountain slopes.
• **REMARK** Favors sunny situations.

red leaf stalks bear conspicuous glands

prominent veins on leaf under-side

Height 50 ft (15 m)	Shape Broadly spreading	Leaf persistence Deciduous	Leaf type

HAMAMELIDACEAE

A FAMILY OF ABOUT 25 genera and 100 species of deciduous and evergreen trees and shrubs, distributed widely in temperate and subtropical regions, yet unknown in the wild throughout Europe, most of South America, and Africa. In addition to the five species described here, this family contains genera of ornamental shrubs, such as the witch hazels *(Hamamelis)*, flowering in late winter, *Corylopsis*, and *Fothergilla*, flowering in early spring.

Family HAMAMELIDACEAE	Species *Liquidambar formosana*	Author Hance

LIQUIDAMBAR FORMOSANA

Leaves Palmately lobed, to 5 in (13 cm) long and 6 in (15 cm) across, heart-shaped at the base, usually with three taper-pointed, toothed lobes, purple when young becoming dark green, turning red to purple in autumn, carried on red-tinged stalks. **Bark** Gray-white, darker and fissured with age. **Flowers** Males and females small, yellow-green, without petals, borne in separate, rounded heads on the same plant in spring at the same time as the leaves emerge. **Fruit** Small, brown, in rounded, hanging clusters, 1½ in (4 cm) across.
• **NATIVE REGION** China, Taiwan.
• **HABITAT** Woods and thickets in mountainous areas.

• leaves are occasionally five-lobed

• reddish base of veins

Height 130 ft (40 m)	Shape Broadly conical	Leaf persistence Deciduous	Leaf type

Family HAMAMELIDACEAE	Species *Liquidambar orientalis*	Author Miller

LIQUIDAMBAR ORIENTALIS

Leaves Palmately lobed, to 3 in (7.5 cm) long and across, matte green above, smooth on both sides, turning orange in autumn. **Bark** Orange-brown and thick, cracking into small plates. **Flowers** Males and females both very small and yellow-green, without petals, borne in separate, rounded heads on the same plant in spring as the young leaves emerge. **Fruit** Small and brown, in rounded, hanging clusters, 1 in (2.5 cm) across.
• **NATIVE REGION** S.W. Turkey.
• **HABITAT** Moist woods, floodplains, and streamsides.

leaves deeply cut into three • to five lobes

oblong lobes have few teeth •

Height 80 ft (25 m)	Shape Broadly conical	Leaf persistence Deciduous	Leaf type

Family HAMAMELIDACEAE	Species *Liquidambar styraciflua*	Author Linnaeus

SWEET GUM

Leaves Palmately lobed, to 6 in (15 cm) long and across, with five or seven taper-pointed, finely toothed lobes, glossy green above, turning orange to red or purple in autumn, borne on often corky-winged shoots. **Bark** Dark gray-brown, deeply furrowed, with narrow ridges. **Flowers** Males and females both very small and yellow-green, without petals, in separate, rounded heads in late spring as the leaves emerge. **Fruit** Individually small and brown, borne in rounded, hanging clusters, 1½ in (4 cm) across.
• **NATIVE REGION** C. America, Mexico, E. United States.
• **HABITAT** Moist woods.
• **REMARK** Easily distinguished from the maples *(Acer*, see pp.84–104) by its alternate, rather than opposite, leaves.

leaves have five or seven tapering lobes •

• terminal lobe larger than side lobes

• heart-shaped leaf base

△ LIQUIDAMBAR STYRACIFLUA

leaves turn different colors in autumn •

▽ 'VARIEGATA'
Paler green and yellowish blotches and streaks mark the leaves of this variety. This distinct form has also been known as 'Aurea,' and has been confused with 'Silver King.'

△ 'LANE ROBERTS'
The leaves of this form invariably turn shades of orange to deep red-purple after midsummer.

colored leaf margin may be tinged pink •

'SILVER KING' ▷
This form is selected for its attractive foliage. The broad, creamy white to yellow leaf margin is often tinged pink in autumn.

random surface patterning of greenish yellow blotches •

Height 130 ft (40 m)	Shape Broadly conical	Leaf persistence Deciduous	Leaf type 🍃

| Family HAMAMELIDACEAE | Species *Parrotia persica* | Author (Candolle) C.A. Meyer |

PERSIAN IRONWOOD

Leaves Elliptic to obovate, to 4¾ in (12 cm) long and 2½ in (6 cm) across, wavy at margin, toothed above the middle, bright glossy green and smooth above, thinly hairy beneath. **Bark** Gray-brown, flaking. **Flowers** Small, without petals, but with red anthers in winter to early spring. **Fruit** Nutlike brown capsule, ⁵⁄₁₆ in (8 mm) long.

- **NATIVE REGION** E. Caucasus, N. Iran.
- **HABITAT** Forests.
- **REMARK** Can be either a tree of medium height or a large shrub.

colorful autumn foliage

leaves broaden above middle

rounded teeth edge upper half of leaf

| Height 65 ft (20 m) | Shape Broadly spreading | Leaf persistence Deciduous | Leaf type |

| Family HAMAMELIDACEAE | Species *Parrotiopsis jacquemontiana* | Author (Decaisne) Rehder |

PARROTIOPSIS JACQUEMONTIANA

Leaves Rounded, to 3 in (7.5 cm) long, toothed, glossy green becoming smooth or nearly so above, hairy beneath, carried on short stalks. **Bark** Gray and smooth. **Flowers** Small and without petals, with numerous stamens, the stamens with yellow anthers, borne in dense clusters, each cluster surrounded by up to six white bracts, the bracts dotted with numerous tiny brown scales beneath, forming a head to 2 in (5 cm) across, in mid- to late spring. **Fruit** A small bristly, brown capsule, borne in clusters.

- **NATIVE REGION** W. Himalayas.
- **HABITAT** Forests.
- **REMARK** This shrublike plant is the only species of *Parrotiopsis*. Flowers usually persist to early or midsummer.

rounded leaves

toothed leaf margin

tiny clustered flowers have yellow anthers

dark scales on underside of bracts

white bracts surround each flower

| Height 20 ft (6 m) | Shape Broadly conical | Leaf persistence Deciduous | Leaf type |

HIPPOCASTANACEAE

T HIS FAMILY HAS ONLY two genera. Its 15 species of deciduous trees and shrubs are native plants in North America, southeast Europe, and east Asia. They have palmately compound, opposite leaves, and conspicuous, four- or five-petaled flowers, borne in large clusters at the ends of the shoots.

Family HIPPOCASTANACEAE	Species *Aesculus californica*	Author (Spach) Nuttall

CALIFORNIA BUCKEYE

Leaves Palmately compound, with five to seven oblong, toothed leaflets, to 6 in (15 cm) long, deep blue-green above, gray-green beneath. **Bark** Pale gray, nearly smooth, thinly scaly. **Flowers** White or pale pink, with four petals, in dense, cylindrical, upright panicles to 8 in (20 cm) long, in summer. **Fruit** Smooth, pear-shaped, to 2¾ in (7 cm) long, with one glossy brown seed, on a long stalk.
• **NATIVE REGION**: California.
• **HABITAT** Dry slopes and canyons in hills.

leaflets have long, tapered • point

flowers borne in very dense • panicles

long, exserted flower stamens

Height 33 ft (10 m)	Shape Broadly spreading	Leaf persistence Deciduous	Leaf type

Family HIPPOCASTANACEAE	Species *Aesculus x carnea*	Author Hayne

RED HORSE CHESTNUT

Leaves Palmately compound, with five to seven obovate, sharply toothed, stalkless or short-stalked leaflets, to 10 in (25 cm) long, dark green, on long stalks. **Bark** Reddish brown. **Flowers** Creamy white blotched yellow becoming pink blotched red, with five petals, in conical, upright, or slightly spreading panicles to 8 in (20 cm) long, in late spring. **Fruit** Smooth or only slightly spiny, 1½ in (4 cm) across.
• **NATIVE REGION** Of garden origin.
• **REMARK** A hybrid between common horse chestnut *(Aesculus hippo-castanum,* see p.179) and red buckeye *(Aesculus pavia,* see p.181).

sharply toothed • leaflets

leaflets are often • twisted

AESCULUS x CARNEA

fruits contain up to three seeds

◁ 'BRIOTII'
Brighter red flowers distinguish this form.

Height 65 ft (20 m)	Shape Broadly columnar	Leaf persistence Deciduous	Leaf type

Family HIPPOCASTANACEAE	Species *Aesculus octandra*	Author Marsh

SWEET BUCKEYE

Leaves Palmately compound, usually with five sharply toothed, short-stalked leaflets, to 6 in (15 cm) long, dark green, turning orange-red in autumn. **Bark** Gray-brown, peeling in large, smooth scales. **Flowers** Yellow, with four petals, in conical, upright panicles to 6 in (15 cm) long, in late spring to early summer. **Fruit** Smooth, rounded, to 2½ in (6 cm) across, covered in brown scales, usually with two seeds.
• **NATIVE REGION** E. United States.
• **HABITAT** Moist, rich woods.
• **REMARK** Also known as *Aesculus flava*, yellow buckeye. The best buckeye for autumn color.

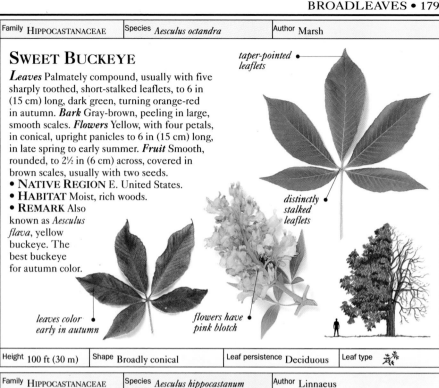

taper-pointed leaflets

distinctly stalked leaflets

leaves color early in autumn

flowers have pink blotch

Height 100 ft (30 m)	Shape Broadly conical	Leaf persistence Deciduous	Leaf type

Family HIPPOCASTANACEAE	Species *Aesculus hippocastanum*	Author Linnaeus

COMMON HORSE CHESTNUT

Leaves Palmately compound, with five to seven obovate, sharply toothed, unstalked leaflets, to 12 in (30 cm) long, dark green, usually turning yellow in autumn, on long stalks. **Bark** Red-brown or gray, scaly. **Flowers** Creamy yellow blotched yellow becoming white blotched red, with five petals, in large, conical, upright panicles to 12 in (30 cm) long, in late spring. **Fruit** Rounded, spiny, and green, with up to three glossy brown seeds.
• **NATIVE REGION** Albania, N. Greece.
• **HABITAT** Mountain woods.
• **REMARK** The native region of this species was unknown for many years, because of its introduction to European gardens via cultivation in Turkey.

AESCULUS ▷
HIPPOCASTANUM

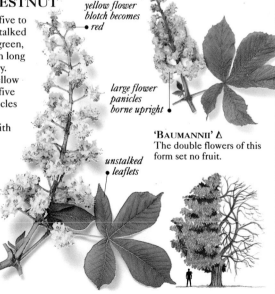

yellow flower blotch becomes red

large flower panicles borne upright

'BAUMANNII' ∆
The double flowers of this form set no fruit.

unstalked leaflets

Height 100 ft (30 m)	Shape Broadly columnar	Leaf persistence Deciduous	Leaf type

Family HIPPOCASTANACEAE	Species *Aesculus indica*	Author (Cambessèdes) J.D. Hooker

INDIAN HORSE CHESTNUT

Leaves Palmately compound, with usually seven but occasionally five obovate to lanceolate stalked and finely toothed leaflets, to 10 in (25 cm) long, bronze when young becoming glossy green above, turning orange or yellow in autumn. **Bark** Gray and smooth. **Flowers** White to pale pink blotched bright yellow, the blotch becoming red, with long, protruding stamens, in conical, upright panicles to 12 in (30 cm) long, in midsummer. **Fruit** Pear-shaped, scaly, and brown, with up to three seeds, on a stout stalk.
• **NATIVE REGION** N.W. Himalayas.
• **HABITAT** Forests and shady ravines.
• **REMARK** This species flowers much later than the common horse chestnut (*Aesculus hippocastanum*, see p.179).

scaly, spineless husk encloses seeds

some leaflets narrow toward tip

some leaflets have broader shape

leaflets edged with fine teeth

small point at leaflet tip

short stalk joins each leaflet to leaf stalk

yellow blotch turns red as flower ages

Height 100 ft (30 m)	Shape Broadly columnar	Leaf persistence Deciduous	Leaf type

Family HIPPOCASTANACEAE	Species *Aesculus x neglecta*	Author Lindley

AESCULUS X NEGLECTA

Leaves Palmately compound, with usually five elliptic, taper-pointed, finely toothed, stalked leaflets, to 8 in (20 cm) long and 3½ in (9 cm) across, smooth except for hairs on the veins above, thinly hairy beneath. **Bark** Gray-brown, shallowly fissured. **Flowers** 1 in (2.5 cm) long, whitish, borne in conical, upright panicles in late spring to early summer. **Fruit** Rounded and smooth, about 1½ in (4 cm) across.
• NATIVE REGION S.E. United States.
• HABITAT Mainly the coastal plain.
• REMARK A hybrid between sweet buckeye *(Aesculus flava,* see p.179) and *Aesculus sylvatica,* most well-known for the cultivar, 'Erythroblastos.'

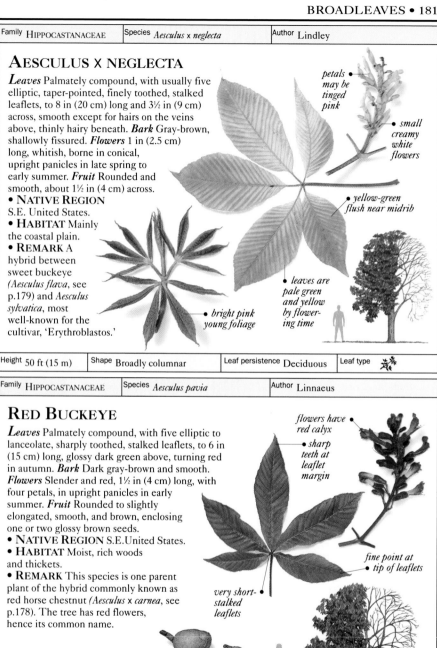

petals may be tinged pink

small creamy white flowers

yellow-green flush near midrib

leaves are pale green and yellow by flowering time

bright pink young foliage

Height 50 ft (15 m)	Shape Broadly columnar	Leaf persistence Deciduous	Leaf type

Family HIPPOCASTANACEAE	Species *Aesculus pavia*	Author Linnaeus

RED BUCKEYE

Leaves Palmately compound, with five elliptic to lanceolate, sharply toothed, stalked leaflets, to 6 in (15 cm) long, glossy dark green above, turning red in autumn. **Bark** Dark gray-brown and smooth. **Flowers** Slender and red, 1½ in (4 cm) long, with four petals, in upright panicles in early summer. **Fruit** Rounded to slightly elongated, smooth, and brown, enclosing one or two glossy brown seeds.
• NATIVE REGION S.E.United States.
• HABITAT Moist, rich woods and thickets.
• REMARK This species is one parent plant of the hybrid commonly known as red horse chestnut *(Aesculus x carnea,* see p.178). The tree has red flowers, hence its common name.

flowers have red calyx

sharp teeth at leaflet margin

fine point at tip of leaflets

very short-stalked leaflets

fruits resemble small, brown pears

Height 17 ft (5 m)	Shape Broadly spreading	Leaf persistence Deciduous	Leaf type

JUGLANDACEAE

MOST MEMBERS OF this family are deciduous plants. Seven genera with some 60 species grow wild in the Americas, and from southeast Europe to Japan and Southeast Asia. The leaves are usually alternate and pinnate. The small flowers lack petals and are clustered in catkins, males and females on the same plant. The fruit is either a large nut or small and winged.

Family JUGLANDACEAE	Species *Carya cordiformis*	Author (Wangenheim) K. Koch

BITTERNUT

Leaves Pinnate, with usually five to nine sharply toothed leaflets, to 6 in (15 cm) long, deep green above, turning golden yellow in autumn; winter buds with scurfy, yellow scales. *Bark* Gray, smooth, becoming thick, furrowed, and ridged. *Flowers* Small, without petals, clustered in catkins, male catkins with three hanging branches to 3 in (7.5 cm) long, females inconspicuous, separately on the same plant in late spring to early summer. *Fruit* A thin-shelled, bitter, inedible, gray nut, enclosed in a green husk, to 1½ in (4 cm) long, with four wings.
• **NATIVE REGION** E. North America.
• **HABITAT** Deciduous forests, in swamps, and on riverbanks.

middle leaflets are the largest

yellow-green male catkins

leaflets tapered at both ends

Height 100 ft (30 m)	Shape Broadly columnar	Leaf persistence Deciduous	Leaf type

Family JUGLANDACEAE	Species *Carya illinoensis*	Author (Wangenheim) K. Koch

PECAN

Leaves Pinnate, with 9 to 17 leaflets, to 6 in (15 cm) long, slender, taper-pointed, the tip curved backward, toothed at the margin, dark green. *Bark* Gray, thick, furrowed, and ridged. *Flowers* Males and females both small and without petals, clustered in catkins, male catkins yellow-green, with three hanging branches to 3 in (7.5 cm) long, females inconspicuous, separately on the same plant in late spring to early summer. *Fruit* A thin-shelled, sweet, edible, red-brown nut, in a green husk, to 2½ in (6 cm) long, with four wings.
• **NATIVE REGION** S. United States.
• **HABITAT** Moist forests and valleys.
• **REMARK** The nuts have an important commercial value.

variable number of leaflets

leaflets often slightly curved at tip

Height 100 ft (30 m)	Shape Broadly columnar	Leaf persistence Deciduous	Leaf type

Family JUGLANDACEAE	Species *Carya ovata*	Author (Miller) K. Koch

SHAGBARK HICKORY

Leaves Pinnate, with usually five taper-pointed leaflets, to 8 in (12 cm) long, toothed except at the base, deep yellow-green above, turning golden yellow and brown in autumn; winter buds with dark scales, the scales spreading at the tips. **Bark** Gray to brown, peeling in long, vertical plates with age. **Flowers** Males and females both small and without petals, clustered in catkins, male catkins yellow-green, with three hanging branches to 5 in (13 cm) long, females inconspicuous, borne separately on the same plant in late spring to early summer. **Fruit** A thick-shelled, sweet, edible, whitish nut, enclosed in a green husk, to 2½ in (6 cm) long, with four grooves.
• **NATIVE REGION** E. North America.
• **HABITAT** Rich woods and valleys.
• **REMARK** The distinctively peeling bark gives this species its common name.

female flowers at end of shoots

strips of bark hang free at either end

terminal leaflet largest

Height 100 ft (30 m)	Shape Broadly columnar	Leaf persistence Deciduous	Leaf type

Family JUGLANDACEAE	Species *Juglans ailantifolia*	Author Carrière

JAPANESE WALNUT

Leaves Pinnate, with 11 to 17 short-pointed, toothed leaflets, to 6 in (15 cm) long, dark green above, hairy on both sides, particularly so beneath, borne on stout, sticky, hairy shoots. **Bark** Gray-brown, fissured and separating into small plates with age. **Flowers** Males and females small and without petals, clustered in catkins, male catkins greenish, to 12 in (30 cm) long, hanging, on the old shoots, female catkins to 4 in (10 cm) long, with red stigmas, at the end of the young shoots, borne separately on the same plant in late spring to early summer. **Fruit** A shallowly pitted, brown nut, enclosed in a sticky, green husk, to 2 in (5 cm) long, in clusters of up to 20.
• **NATIVE REGION** Japan.
• **HABITAT** Wet areas and by streams.
• **REMARK** The fruit husk is poisonous. In Japan, it is traditionally used to catch fish. The nuts are also eaten, and the wood is used for building and other purposes.

female flowers have red stigmas

leaves at end of shoots unfold at flowering time

stout, very hairy leaf rachis

short, sticky hairs cover fruit husk

Height 80 ft (25 m)	Shape Broadly spreading	Leaf persistence Deciduous	Leaf type

Family JUGLANDACEAE	Species *Juglans cinerea*	Author Linnaeus

BUTTERNUT

Leaves Pinnate, with 7 to 17 pointed, toothed leaflets, to 5 in (13 cm) long, all unstalked except for the terminal one, dark green above, hairy on both sides, particularly so beneath. *Bark* Gray, furrowed, ridged. *Flowers* Males and females both small and without petals, clustered in catkins, male catkins greenish, to 4 in (10 cm) long, hanging, female catkins short, borne separately on the same plant in late spring to early summer. *Fruit* An elongated, rough, sweet, edible, oily nut, enclosed in a pointed, sticky, green husk, to 2½ in (6 cm) long, in clusters of up to five.
• **NATIVE REGION**
E. North America.
• **HABITAT** Rich woods or moist soil in valleys and on slopes.
• **REMARK** Also known as white walnut.

large leaves have numerous • leaflets

• leaf rachis covered with sticky hairs

Height 80 ft (25 m)	Shape Broadly spreading	Leaf persistence Deciduous	Leaf type

Family JUGLANDACEAE	Species *Juglans nigra*	Author Linnaeus

BLACK WALNUT

• terminal leaflet often missing

Leaves Pinnate, with 11 to 17 or more slender, taper-pointed, sharply toothed leaflets, to 4¾ in (12 cm) long, glossy dark green above, hairy at least beneath, aromatic. *Bark* Dark gray-brown to blackish, with narrow, rough ridges. *Flowers* Males and females both small and without petals, clustered in catkins, male catkins yellow-green, to 4 in (10 cm) long, hanging, female catkins short, borne separately on the same plant in late spring to early summer. *Fruit* A rounded, edible, brown nut, enclosed in a green husk, to 2 in (5 cm) long, borne singly or in pairs.
• **NATIVE REGION**
C. and E. United States.
• **HABITAT** Rich woods.
• **REMARK** Both the wood and the nuts are valuable commodities.

male catkins borne on old • wood

fruits contain a single, • edible nut

Height 100 ft (30 m)	Shape Broadly spreading	Leaf persistence Deciduous	Leaf type

Family JUGLANDACEAE	Species *Juglans regia*	Author Linnaeus

ENGLISH WALNUT

Leaves Pinnate, with five to nine short-pointed leaflets, to 6 in (15 cm) long, the terminal leaflet largest, bronze when young becoming dark green, smooth, aromatic when bruised. *Bark* Pale gray, smooth, fissured on old plants. *Flowers* Males and females both small, without petals, clustered in catkins, male catkins yellow-green, to 4 in (10 cm) long, hanging, females short, borne separately on the same plant in late spring to early summer. *Fruit* An edible nut, creamy white becoming brown, enclosed in a green husk, to 2 in (5 cm) long.
• **NATIVE REGION** China to S.E. Europe.
• **HABITAT** Valleys and streambanks.

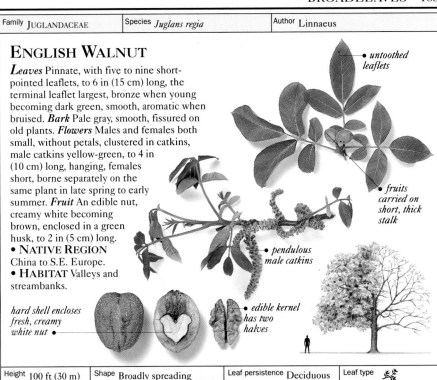

untoothed leaflets

fruits carried on short, thick stalk

pendulous male catkins

hard shell encloses fresh, creamy white nut •

• edible kernel has two halves

Height 100 ft (30 m)	Shape Broadly spreading	Leaf persistence Deciduous	Leaf type

Family JUGLANDACEAE	Species *Platycarya strobilacea*	Author Siebold & Zuccarini

PLATYCARYA STROBILACEA

Leaves Pinnate, with up to 15 taper-pointed, sharply toothed, unstalked leaflets, to 4 in (10 cm) long and 1¼ in (3 cm) across, hairy becoming smooth on both sides, turning yellow in autumn. *Bark* Yellow-brown, with vertical fissures. *Flowers* Males and females both small, without petals, in upright catkins, male catkins to 4 in (10 cm) long, clustered together around a single, green female catkin, borne separately on the same plant in summer. *Fruit* Conelike, brown, 1½ in (4 cm) long, long-persistent.
• **NATIVE REGION** E. Asia.
• **HABITAT** Forests in dry, sunny situations.
• **REMARK** An unusual relative of the wingnuts *(Pterocarya,* see pp.186–187), easily distinguished by its conelike fruit clusters.

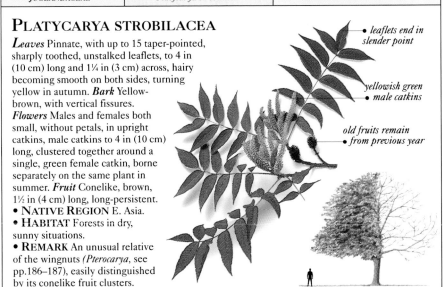

leaflets end in slender point

yellowish green • male catkins

old fruits remain • from previous year

Height 80 ft (25 m)	Shape Broadly spreading	Leaf persistence Deciduous	Leaf type

Family JUGLANDACEAE	Species *Pterocarya fraxinifolia*	Author (Lamarck) Spach

CAUCASIAN WINGNUT

Leaves Pinnate, with 11 to 23 or more toothed, unstalked leaflets, to 6 in (15 cm) long and 1½ in (4 cm) across, glossy dark green and smooth above, turning yellow in autumn, carried on an unwinged rachis; leaf buds covered in brown hairs during winter. **Bark** Whitish-gray, smooth, becoming furrowed with age. **Flowers** Small and without petals, with pink stigmas, in green, pendulous catkins, males stout, to 4¼ in (12 cm) long, females slender, to 6 in (15 cm) long, borne separately on the same plant in spring; flower stigmas elongate as fruits ripen. **Fruit** A small nut, surrounded by two semi-circular, green wings, borne in slender, hanging catkins, to 20 in (50 cm) long.
• **NATIVE REGION**
E. Caucasus, N. Iran.
• **HABITAT** Woods, near rivers, and in boggy places.

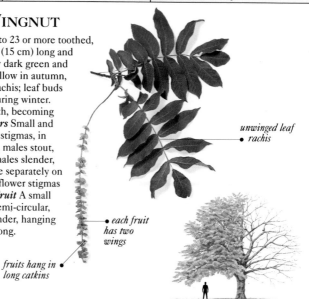

unwinged leaf rachis

each fruit has two wings

fruits hang in long catkins

Height 100 ft (30 m)	Shape Broadly spreading	Leaf persistence Deciduous	Leaf type

Family JUGLANDACEAE	Species *Pterocarya x rehderiana*	Author Schneider

PTEROCARYA X REHDERIANA

Leaves Pinnate, with 11 to 21 toothed, unstalked leaflets, to 4¼ in (12 cm) long, glossy dark green and smooth above, turning yellow in autumn, the rachis with small, untoothed, upright wings. **Bark** Purple-brown, cracked into diagonal, interlacing ridges; pale orange in the fissures. **Flowers** Males and females both small, without petals, in green, pendulous catkins, males to 4¼ in (12 cm) long, separately on the same plant in spring. **Fruit** A small nut, with two elongated, green wings, borne in slender, hanging catkins, to 18 in (45 cm) long.
• **NATIVE REGION**
Of garden origin.
• **REMARK** A hybrid between Caucasian wingnut *(P. fraxinifolia,* see above) and *P. stenoptera* (see p.187), raised at the Arnold Arboretum of Harvard University, Boston.

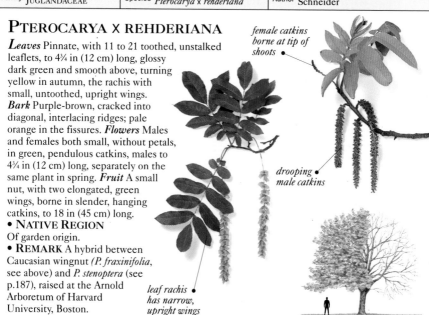

female catkins borne at tip of shoots

drooping male catkins

leaf rachis has narrow, upright wings

Height 80 ft (25 m)	Shape Broadly spreading	Leaf persistence Deciduous	Leaf type

Family JUGLANDACEAE	Species *Pterocarya rhoifolia*	Author Siebold & Zuccarini

JAPANESE WINGNUT

Leaves Pinnate, with 11 to 21
taper-pointed, toothed, unstalked
leaflets, to 4¾ in (12 cm) long,
glossy green above, turning
yellow in autumn, carried on an
unwinged rachis; leaf buds covered
with scales in winter. ***Bark*** Dark
gray, becoming vertically fissured
with age. ***Flowers*** Males and
females small and without petals, in
green, pendulous catkins, males to 3 in
(7.5 cm) long, at the base of the young
shoots, females at tip, separately on the
same plant in spring. ***Fruit*** A small nut,
with green wings, in clusters on slender,
hanging catkins, to 12 in (30 cm) long.
• **NATIVE REGION** Japan.
• **HABITAT** Near mountain
streams.
• **REMARK** In winter, it is easily
distinguished by the scaly leaf buds.

*leaflets
taper to long,
fine point*

*shoots end
in distinct
buds*

*unwinged
leaf rachis*

Height 80 ft (25 m)	Shape Broadly spreading	Leaf persistence Deciduous	Leaf type

Family JUGLANDACEAE	Species *Pterocarya stenoptera*	Author C. de Candolle

PTEROCARYA STENOPTERA

Leaves Pinnate, with 11 to 21
toothed, unstalked leaflets,
bright green and smooth
above, turning yellow in
autumn, the rachis with
narrow, often toothed, wings.
Bark Gray-brown, with deep
fissures. ***Flowers*** Males and
females both small and without
petals, in separate, green,
pendulous catkins, males to
2½ in (6 cm) long, on the same
plant in spring. ***Fruit*** A small
nut, with two narrow wings, in
clusters on slender, hanging
catkins, to 12 in (30 cm) long.
• **NATIVE REGION** China.
• **HABITAT** Moist woods
and streambanks.
• **REMARK** This species is
easily distinguished by the
characteristically angled
wings on the leaf rachis.

*leaf rachis has
spreading
wings*

*short-pointed
leaflets*

*green-winged
fruits*

Height 80 ft (25 m)	Shape Broadly spreading	Leaf persistence Deciduous	Leaf type

LAURACEAE

SOME 40 GENERA and more than 2,000 species belong to this widespread family; many grow wild in tropical South America and Southeast Asia. These deciduous and evergreen, usually aromatic trees and shrubs have either opposite, or alternate untoothed leaves. Flower petals and sepals, which resemble each other, are arranged in threes. The fruit is usually fleshy.

Family LAURACEAE	Species *Laurus nobilis*	Author Linnaeus

BAY LAUREL

Leaves Elliptic to ovate, to 4 in (10 cm) long and 1½ in (4 cm) across, pointed at the tip, with a wavy margin, glossy dark green above, paler beneath, smooth, leathery, aromatic when crushed.
Bark Dark gray, smooth.
Flowers About ⅜ in (1 cm) across, yellow-green, males with numerous yellow stamens, in clusters in the leaf axils, on separate plants in spring.
Fruit A rounded berry, about ⅜ in (1 cm) long, green ripening to black.
• **NATIVE REGION** Mediterranean.
• **HABITAT** Evergreen woods, thickets and rocky places.
• **REMARK** Also known as sweet bay. This species and the related Canary Island laurel *(Laurus azorica)* are the only members of the family native to Europe.

leaves taper gradually toward base

male flowers have many yellow anthers

small female flowers

wavy, untoothed leaf margin

berries ripen from green to black

flower buds form in autumn

Height 50 ft (15 m)	Shape Broadly conical	Leaf persistence Evergreen	Leaf type

Family LAURACEAE	Species *Sassafras albidum*	Author (Nuttall) Nees

SASSAFRAS

Leaves Elliptic to ovate, to 6 in (15 cm) or more long and 4 in (10 cm) across, untoothed but sometimes with a lobe on one or both sides, bright green above, blue-green and smooth beneath, turning yellow to orange or purple in autumn, aromatic. *Bark* Red-brown, thick, furrowed, aromatic. *Flowers* Males and females very small, yellow or greenish yellow, without petals, in small clusters or short racemes on separate plants in spring. *Fruit* An egg-shaped deep blue berry, ⅜ in (1 cm) long.
• NATIVE REGION E. North America.
• HABITAT Woods and thickets.
• REMARK Also known as *S. officinale.* Leaves may appear similar in outline to those of the common fig *(Ficus carica,* see p.219). The root bark is traditionally used to make tea and root beer.

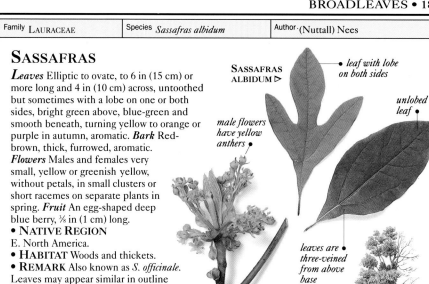

SASSAFRAS ALBIDUM ▷

leaf with lobe on both sides

unlobed leaf

male flowers have yellow anthers

leaves are three-veined from above base

△ VAR. MOLLE
This form has visibly downy young shoots and leaves.

Height 65 ft (20 m)	Shape Broadly columnar	Leaf persistence Deciduous	Leaf type

Family LAURACEAE	Species *Umbellularia californica*	Author (W.J. Hooker & Arnott) Nuttall

CALIFORNIA LAUREL

Leaves Elliptic to oblong, to 4 in (10 cm) long and 1 in (2.5 cm) across, untoothed, bright green or deep yellow-green. *Bark* Dark gray, cracking into rectangular plates with age. *Flowers* ⅜ in (1 cm) across, without petals, with six yellow-green sepals, in clusters of up to ten, in the leaf axils in late winter to spring. *Fruit* A rounded to egg-shaped berry, about 1 in (2.5 cm) long, green ripening to deep purple.
• NATIVE REGION S.W. Oregon, California.
• HABITAT Evergreen forests and scrub in canyons and valleys.
• REMARK Also known as California bay, California olive, Oregon myrtle. Forms a large tree in moist, sheltered situations, but can be reduced to the size of a small shrub in dry, exposed conditions. When crushed, the leaves emit an acrid smell. This poisonous vapor may induce nausea and headaches.

glossy green, leathery leaves

smooth, untoothed margin

flowers have six yellow-green sepals instead of petals

prominent, fine network of veins

Height 100 ft (30 m)	Shape Broadly spreading	Leaf persistence Evergreen	Leaf type

LEGUMINOSAE

T HE PEA FAMILY contains about 700 genera and over 15,000 species of trees, shrubs, and herbaceous plants, found worldwide. The leaves are often compound, and frequently pinnate or with three leaflets. Species that grow in cool temperate regions have pealike flowers. The fruit, usually a pod, splits open along both sides or breaks into portions to release its seeds.

Family LEGUMINOSAE	Species *Acacia dealbata*	Author Link

SILVER WATTLE

Leaves Bipinnate, to 4¾ in (12 cm) long, with numerous linear leaflets, to ³⁄₁₆ in (5 mm) long, the leaflets untoothed, blue-green, and finely hairy. **Bark** Smooth and green or blue-green, becoming nearly black with age. **Flowers** Very small, with bright yellow petals and numerous conspicuous stamens, fragrant, in panicles of small, rounded clusters in late winter to early spring. **Fruit** A flattened pod, to 3 in (7.5 cm) long, green becoming blue-white ripening to brown.
• **NATIVE REGION** S.E. Australia, Tasmania.
• **HABITAT** Mainly mountain gullies and streambanks.

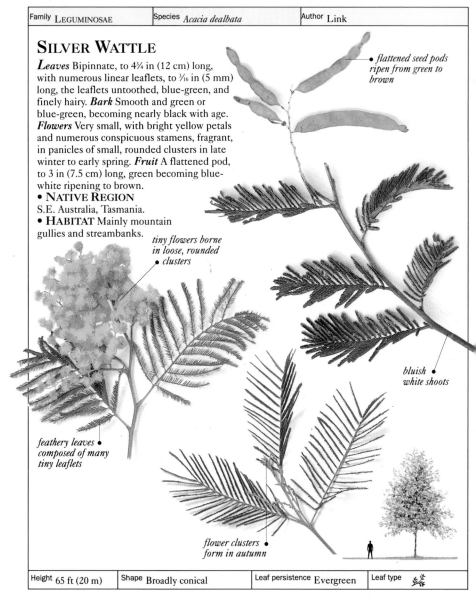

• *flattened seed pods ripen from green to brown*

tiny flowers borne in loose, rounded
• *clusters*

bluish •
white shoots

feathery leaves •
composed of many tiny leaflets

flower clusters •
form in autumn

Height 65 ft (20 m)	Shape Broadly conical	Leaf persistence Evergreen	Leaf type

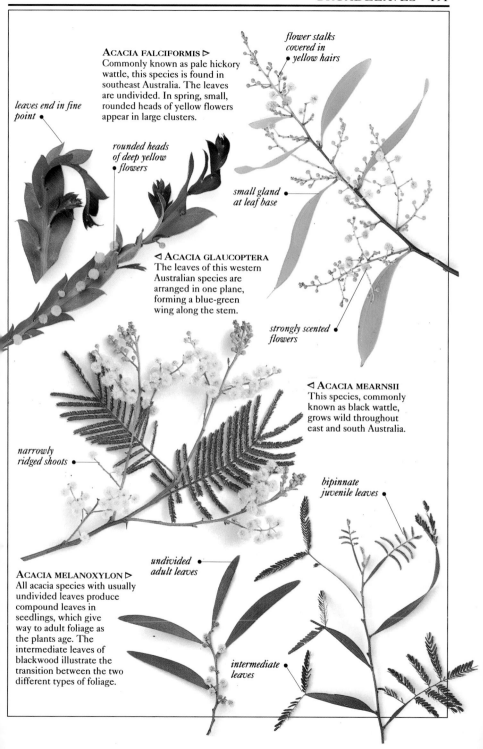

leaves end in fine point •

ACACIA FALCIFORMIS ▷
Commonly known as pale hickory wattle, this species is found in southeast Australia. The leaves are undivided. In spring, small, rounded heads of yellow flowers appear in large clusters.

flower stalks covered in • yellow hairs

rounded heads of deep yellow • flowers

small gland at leaf base

◁ **ACACIA GLAUCOPTERA**
The leaves of this western Australian species are arranged in one plane, forming a blue-green wing along the stem.

strongly scented • flowers

◁ **ACACIA MEARNSII**
This species, commonly known as black wattle, grows wild throughout east and south Australia.

narrowly ridged shoots •

bipinnate juvenile leaves •

undivided • adult leaves

ACACIA MELANOXYLON ▷
All acacia species with usually undivided leaves produce compound leaves in seedlings, which give way to adult foliage as the plants age. The intermediate leaves of blackwood illustrate the transition between the two different types of foliage.

intermediate • leaves

Family LEGUMINOSAE	Species *Albizia julibrissin*	Author (Willdenow) Durazzini

MIMOSA (SILK TREE)

Leaves Bipinnate, to 20 in (50 cm) long, with numerous small, taper-pointed, untoothed leaflets, about ⅜ in (1 cm) long, dark green and smooth on both sides. *Bark* Dark brown and smooth. *Flowers* Individually small, conspicuous by the numerous long, pink stamens, borne in dense, fluffy clusters, opening in late summer to early autumn. *Fruit* A pod, to 6 in (15 cm) long.
• **NATIVE REGION** S.W. Asia.
• **HABITAT** Woods and river banks.
• **REMARK** Also known as Persian acacia, pink siris, silk tree.

feathery leaves have numerous • small leaflets

• flower clusters have conspicuous pink stamens

Height 40 ft (12 m)	Shape Broadly spreading	Leaf persistence Deciduous	Leaf type

Family LEGUMINOSAE	Species *Cercis canadensis*	Author Linnaeus

REDBUD

Leaves Rounded, to 4 in (10 cm) long and 4¼ in (12 cm) across, heart-shaped at the base, untoothed, bronze becoming bright green and smooth above, smooth or hairy beneath, sometimes turning yellow in autumn. *Bark* Dark gray-brown to black. *Flowers* Pealike, ⅜ in (1 cm) long, pink, borne in clusters along the old shoots, and often from the main branches and trunk, in spring to early summer before and as the young leaves emerge. *Fruit* A flattened pod, to 3 in (7.5 cm) long, green becoming pink ripening to brown.
• **NATIVE REGION** North America.
• **HABITAT** Moist woods.

young leaves • emerge at flowering time

bronze young • leaf

• small flowers have slender stalks

CERCIS CANADENSIS

leaves do • not turn green

◁ **'FOREST PANSY'** This form is selected for its gorgeous red-purple foliage.

Height 33 ft (10 m)	Shape Broadly spreading	Leaf persistence Deciduous	Leaf type

Family LEGUMINOSAE	Species *Cercis racemosa*	Author Oliver

CERCIS RACEMOSA

Leaves Rounded, to 5 in (13 cm) long and 4 in (10 cm) across, rounded at the base, dark green above, hairy beneath. **Bark** Pale gray, flaking with age. **Flowers** Pealike, ⅜ in (1 cm) long, pale pink, borne in racemes from the old shoots in mid- to late spring or early summer. **Fruit** A flattened pod, to 4 in (10 cm) long, green becoming pink-tinged ripening to brown.
• **NATIVE REGION** China.
• **HABITAT** Woods and stream-banks in mountains.
• **REMARK** A rarely seen species, distinguished by its flowers borne in racemes.

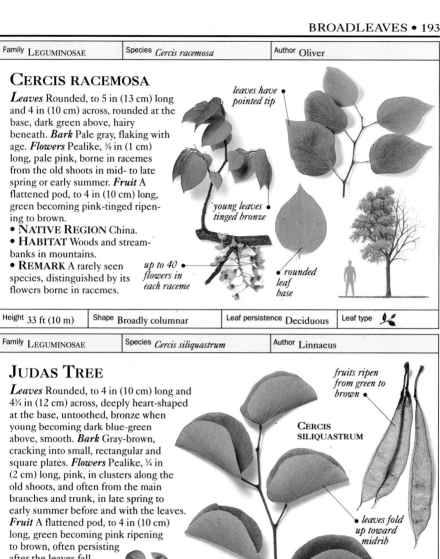

leaves have pointed tip

young leaves tinged bronze

up to 40 flowers in each raceme

rounded leaf base

Height 33 ft (10 m)	Shape Broadly columnar	Leaf persistence Deciduous	Leaf type

Family LEGUMINOSAE	Species *Cercis siliquastrum*	Author Linnaeus

JUDAS TREE

Leaves Rounded, to 4 in (10 cm) long and 4¾ in (12 cm) across, deeply heart-shaped at the base, untoothed, bronze when young becoming dark blue-green above, smooth. **Bark** Gray-brown, cracking into small, rectangular and square plates. **Flowers** Pealike, ¾ in (2 cm) long, pink, in clusters along the old shoots, and often from the main branches and trunk, in late spring to early summer before and with the leaves. **Fruit** A flattened pod, to 4 in (10 cm) long, green becoming pink ripening to brown, often persisting after the leaves fall.
• **NATIVE REGION** W. Asia, S.E. Europe.
• **HABITAT** Dry, rocky places.

fruits ripen from green to brown

CERCIS SILIQUASTRUM

leaves fold up toward midrib

◁ **'BODNANT'** A form raised at the National Trust garden at Bodnant, UK.

deep purple-pink flowers

flowers borne also from branches

Height 33 ft (10 m)	Shape Broadly spreading	Leaf persistence Deciduous	Leaf type

Family LEGUMINOSAE	Species *Cladrastis lutea*	Author K. Koch

YELLOW WOOD

Leaves Pinnate, with 7 to 11 elliptic to ovate, untoothed leaflets, to 4 in (10 cm) long, the terminal one largest, bright green above and smooth on both sides, turning bright yellow in autumn, the stalk swollen at the base and enclosing the bud. *Bark* Gray and smooth, often horizontally wrinkled. *Flowers* Pealike, 1¼ in (3 cm) long, white, slightly fragrant, in large, hanging panicles to 18 in (45 cm) long, at the ends of the shoots in early summer. *Fruit* A flattened brown pod, to 4 in (10 cm) long.

• **NATIVE REGION**
S.E. United States.
• **HABITAT** Rich woods and rocky bluffs.
• **REMARK** Also known as virgilia. This species is rare in the wild, with a restricted distribution in only a few States. The wood produces a yellow dye.

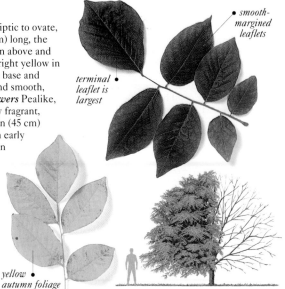

smooth-margined leaflets

terminal leaflet is largest

yellow autumn foliage

Height 50 ft (15 m)	Shape Broadly spreading	Leaf persistence Deciduous	Leaf type

Family LEGUMINOSAE	Species *Genista aetnensis*	Author (Bivona) Candolle

MOUNT ETNA BROOM

Leaves Linear and small, ⅜ in (1 cm) long, borne sparsely on slender, bright green shoots; on mature plants usually absent by flowering time. *Bark* Gray-brown, deeply fissured at the base. *Flowers* Pealike, ⅜ in (1.5 cm) long, bright golden yellow, fragrant, profuse, singly along the new shoots in mid- to late summer. *Fruit* A small, blackish brown pod, about ⅜ in (1 cm) long, ending in a short, slender, pointed tip, and containing two or three seeds.

• **NATIVE REGION** Sardinia, Sicily.
• **HABITAT** Rocky slopes.
• **REMARK** This species can be either a large shrub or a small tree. In the wild, it is found on the slopes of Mount Etna, in Sicily, where it grows on old volcanic lava. The rushlike shoots take over the role of photosynthesis from the leaves. They remain green even in the winter months, giving the tree an overall evergreen appearance.

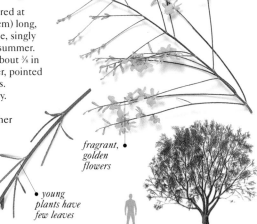

flowers borne on slender, leafless shoots

fragrant, golden flowers

• *young plants have few leaves*

Height 33 ft (10 m)	Shape Broadly spreading	Leaf persistence Deciduous	Leaf type

Family LEGUMINOSAE	Species *Gleditsia triacanthos*	Author Linnaeus

HONEY LOCUST

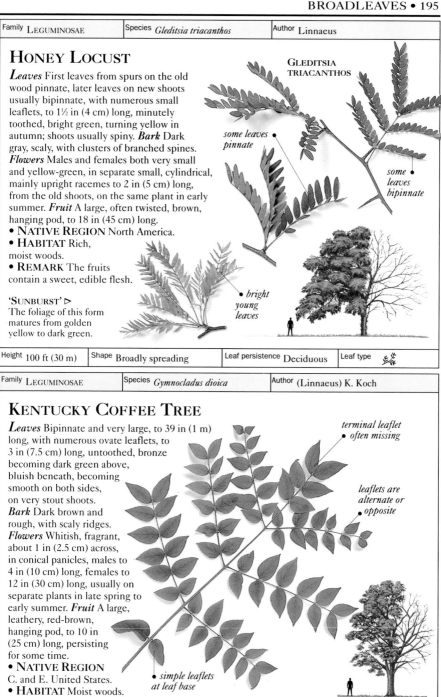

Leaves First leaves from spurs on the old wood pinnate, later leaves on new shoots usually bipinnate, with numerous small leaflets, to 1½ in (4 cm) long, minutely toothed, bright green, turning yellow in autumn; shoots usually spiny. **Bark** Dark gray, scaly, with clusters of branched spines. **Flowers** Males and females both very small and yellow-green, in separate small, cylindrical, mainly upright racemes to 2 in (5 cm) long, from the old shoots, on the same plant in early summer. **Fruit** A large, often twisted, brown, hanging pod, to 18 in (45 cm) long.
- **NATIVE REGION** North America.
- **HABITAT** Rich, moist woods.
- **REMARK** The fruits contain a sweet, edible flesh.

'SUNBURST' ▷
The foliage of this form matures from golden yellow to dark green.

GLEDITSIA
TRIACANTHOS

some leaves • pinnate

some • leaves bipinnate

• bright young leaves

Height 100 ft (30 m)	Shape Broadly spreading	Leaf persistence Deciduous	Leaf type

Family LEGUMINOSAE	Species *Gymnocladus dioica*	Author (Linnaeus) K. Koch

KENTUCKY COFFEE TREE

Leaves Bipinnate and very large, to 39 in (1 m) long, with numerous ovate leaflets, to 3 in (7.5 cm) long, untoothed, bronze becoming dark green above, bluish beneath, becoming smooth on both sides, on very stout shoots. **Bark** Dark brown and rough, with scaly ridges. **Flowers** Whitish, fragrant, about 1 in (2.5 cm) across, in conical panicles, males to 4 in (10 cm) long, females to 12 in (30 cm) long, usually on separate plants in late spring to early summer. **Fruit** A large, leathery, red-brown, hanging pod, to 10 in (25 cm) long, persisting for some time.
- **NATIVE REGION** C. and E. United States.
- **HABITAT** Moist woods.

terminal leaflet
• often missing

leaflets are
alternate or
• opposite

• simple leaflets
at leaf base

Height 80 ft (25 m)	Shape Broadly columnar	Leaf persistence Deciduous	Leaf type

Family LEGUMINOSAE	Species + *Laburnocytisus adamii*	Author (Poiteau) Schneider

+ LABURNOCYTISUS ADAMII

Leaves Variable, with three leaflets, resembling one parent or intermediate between both parents. *Bark* Dark gray, smooth, shallowly fissured with age. *Flowers* Pealike, of three types, either yellow laburnum or purple broom, resembling one parent, or between the two, the intermediate flowers pale purple-pink flushed yellow, borne in short, hanging racemes to 6 in (15 cm) long, in late spring to early summer. *Fruit* A brown pod, to 3 in (7.5 cm) long, hanging in clusters, with black seeds, produced from the yellow flowers.
• **NATIVE REGION**
Of garden origin.
• **REMARK** A chimera, or graft hybrid, between the common laburnum (*Laburnum anagyroides*, see p.197) and the shrubby purple broom (*Cytisus purpureus*). A graft hybrid is not a true hybrid, because it contains a mixture of the tissues of the two genetically distinct parents. All parts of this tree are poisonous.

intermediate leaves are dark green above, paler beneath •

△ + **LABURNOCYTISUS ADAMII**

• *intermediate flowers carried on most branches*

laburnum leaves are dull gray-green •

◁ **LABURNUM ANAGYROIDES** Common laburnum (*Laburnum anagyroides*) forms the inner core of the plant.

• *yellow laburnum flowers borne in drooping racemes*

dense • *clusters of purple broom flowers borne on some branches*

purple broom leaves have tiny leaflets •

△ **CYTISUS PURPUREUS** The outer envelope of the tree is formed by purple broom (*Cytisus purpureus*).

Height 20 ft (6 m)	Shape Broadly spreading	Leaf persistence Deciduous	Leaf type

Family LEGUMINOSAE	Species *Laburnum alpinum*	Author (Miller) Berchtold & Presl

SCOTCH LABURNUM

Leaves Each with three separate, elliptic leaflets, to 4 in (10 cm) long, slightly pointed at the tip, shining deep green above, smooth, glossy, and nearly hairless when young beneath. **Bark** Dark gray and smooth, becoming shallowly fissured with age. **Flowers** Pealike, ¾ in (2 cm) long, bright golden yellow, fragrant, borne in long, slender, hanging racemes to 18 in (45 cm) long, in early summer. **Fruit** A hairless brown pod, to 3 in (7.5 cm) long, the upper margin flattened to a narrow wing, containing brown seeds.
• **NATIVE REGION** C. and S. Europe, from the Alps to Czechoslovakia and the Balkans.
• **HABITAT** Mountains.
• **REMARK** This latest-flowering laburnum can be a either a small tree or a shrub. The very long, delicate racemes of flowers are a particular feature of the species. All parts of the plant are poisonous if consumed, the seeds especially so.

• *each leaf has three distinct leaflets*

• *pale green calyx encloses flower bud*

youngest flowers grow at tip of • *raceme*

Height 20 ft (6 m)	Shape Broadly spreading	Leaf persistence Deciduous	Leaf type

Family LEGUMINOSAE	Species *Laburnum anagyroides*	Author Medikus

COMMON LABURNUM

Leaves Each with three elliptic leaflets, to 3½ in (9 cm) long, rounded at the tip, dull deep green above, gray-green and silkyhairy when young beneath. **Bark** Dark gray and smooth, becoming shallowly fissured with age. **Flowers** Pealike, 1 in (2.5 cm) long, golden yellow, densely clustered, borne in hanging racemes to 10 in (25 cm) long, in late spring to early summer. **Fruit** A slightly rounded hairy brown pod, to 3 in (7.5 cm) long, the upper edge thickened, hanging in clusters, w̃ith black seeds.
• **NATIVE REGION** C. and S. Europe.
• **HABITAT** Mountainous areas, woods, and thickets.
• **REMARK** All parts of the plant contain a harmful alkaloid and are poisonous if consumed. The immature seeds look like small green peas.

• *grayish green, softly hairy leaf underside*

• *branches carry many simple leafless racemes crowded together*

Height 23 ft (7 m)	Shape Broadly spreading	Leaf persistence Deciduous	Leaf type

Family LEGUMINOSAE	Species *Laburnum x watereri*	Author (Wettstein) Dippel

LABURNUM X WATERERI

Leaves With three elliptic
leaflets, to 3 in (7.5 cm) long,
deep green above, hairy but
green when young beneath.
Bark Dark gray and smooth,
becoming shallowly fissured with
age. **Flowers** Pealike, 1 in (2.5 cm)
long, golden yellow, borne in dense,
hanging racemes to 12 in (30 cm)
long, in late spring to early summer.
Fruit A brown pod, to 2½ in (6 cm) long,
with few seeds, often sparsely produced.
• **NATIVE REGION** Austria, Switzerland.
• **HABITAT** Mountains, with the parents.
• **REMARK** A hybrid between the Scotch
laburnum *(L. alpinum,* see p.197) and the
common laburnum *(L. anagyroides,* see
p.197). It combines the long racemes of the
former with the large flowers of the latter.
The form shown, 'Vossii', is the most
familiar. It bears its flowers in very
long racemes, to 20 in (50 cm) or more.

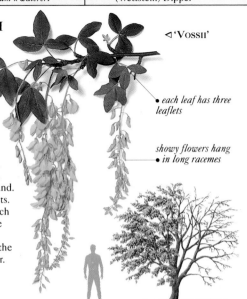

◁ 'VOSSII'

• *each leaf has three leaflets*

*showy flowers hang
in long racemes*

Height 23 ft (7 m)	Shape Broadly spreading	Leaf persistence Deciduous	Leaf type

Family LEGUMINOSAE	Species *Maackia chinensis*	Author Takeda

MAACKIA CHINENSIS

Leaves Pinnate, to 8 in (20 cm) long,
with 9 to 13 elliptic to ovate, untoothed
and shortly stalked leaflets, to 2½ in
(6 cm) long and ¾ in (2 cm) across,
silvery blue-gray when young
becoming green above, downy
beneath. **Bark** Gray-brown,
marked with con-
spicuous lenticels.
Flowers Pealike,
⅜ in (1 cm) long,
white, borne in dense,
upright racemes, clustered
at the ends of the shoots in
mid- to late summer. **Fruit** A
small pod, about 2 in (5 cm) long.
• **NATIVE REGION** S.W. China.
• **HABITAT** Woods and scrub
in mountains.
• **REMARK** This genus is related
to *Cladrastis* (see p.194), but is distinguished by its flowers, which are borne
in upright, rather than hanging, clusters.

*small flowers borne in
dense, upright clusters*

*long leaves
composed of up
to 13 untoothed
leaflets*

Height 50 ft (15 m)	Shape Broadly spreading	Leaf persistence Deciduous	Leaf type

Family LEGUMINOSAE	Species *Robinia x holdtii*	Author Beissner

ROBINIA X HOLDTII

Leaves Pinnate, to 18 in (45 cm) long, with up to 21 oblong leaflets, to 2 in (5 cm) long and 1 in (2.5 cm) across, often indented at the tip with a very fine point, deep green above, gray-green beneath, thinly hairy on both sides. **Bark** Gray-brown, deeply furrowed, with scaly ridges. **Flowers** Pealike, ¾ in (2 cm) long, white flushed purplish pink, faintly fragrant, in hanging clusters over a long period in summer. **Fruit** A slightly sticky, bristly, red pod, about 2½ in (6 cm) long.
• **NATIVE REGION** Of garden origin.
• **REMARK** This vigorous tree is a hybrid between the pink-flowered, often shrubby, *Robinia luxurians* and the black locust *(Robinia pseudoacacia*, see below). Of the two parent plants, it is most similar in appearance and habit to *R. pseudoacacia*, from which it is distinguished by the color of its flowers.

very long leaves have leaflets arranged opposite

flowers often produced into early autumn

very fine point at tip of leaflet

Height 65 ft (20 m)	Shape Broadly columnar	Leaf persistence Deciduous	Leaf type

Family LEGUMINOSAE	Species *Robinia pseudoacacia*	Author Linnaeus

BLACK LOCUST

Leaves Pinnate, to 12 in (30 cm) long, with 11 to 21 elliptic to ovate, untoothed leaflets, to 2 in (5 cm) long, often indented and ending in a slender point, blue-green above, gray-green and thinly hairy becoming smooth beneath, the shoot often with two spines at the base of each leaf. **Bark** Gray-brown, deeply furrowed, with scaly ridges. **Flowers** Pealike, ¾ in (2 cm) long, white, with a yellow-green blotch, fragrant, in dense, hanging racemes to 8 in (20 cm) long, in early to midsummer. **Fruit** A smooth, dark brown, hanging pod, to 4 in (10 cm) long.
• **NATIVE REGION** S.E. United States.
• **HABITAT** Woods and thickets.
• **REMARK** Widely planted and naturalized in North America.

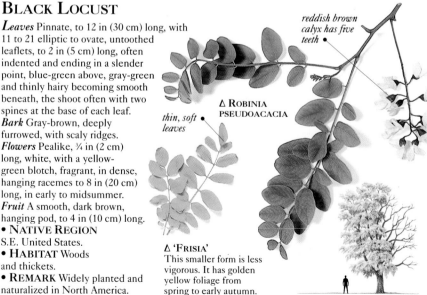

reddish brown calyx has five teeth

△ ROBINIA PSEUDOACACIA

thin, soft leaves

△ 'FRISIA'
This smaller form is less vigorous. It has golden yellow foliage from spring to early autumn.

Height 80 ft (25 m)	Shape Broadly columnar	Leaf persistence Deciduous	Leaf type

Family LEGUMINOSAE	Species *Sophora japonica*	Author Linnaeus

JAPANESE PAGODA TREE

Leaves Pinnate, to 10 in (25 cm) long, with
7 to 17 ovate, pointed leaflets, to 2 in (5 cm)
long, whitish becoming glossy dark green
above, blue-green and hairy beneath, sometimes turning yellow in autumn. **Bark** Gray-
brown, prominently ridged. **Flowers** Pealike,
⅝ in (1.5 cm) long, white, fragrant, in hanging
panicles to 12 in (30 cm) long, at the ends of
the shoots in late summer to early autumn.
Fruit A pod, to 3 in (7.5 cm) long,
constricted between the seeds.
• **NATIVE REGION** China, Korea.
• **HABITAT** Woods, thickets,
and dry valleys in
mountains.
• **REMARK**
Also known as
pagoda tree.

*short-pointed,
untoothed
leaflets*

*some leaves
turn yellow
before falling*

*swollen leaf base
encloses bud*

Height 65 ft (20 m)	Shape Broadly spreading	Leaf persistence Deciduous	Leaf type

Family LEGUMINOSAE	Species *Sophora microphylla*	Author Aiton

KOWHAI

Leaves Pinnate to nearly rounded, to
6 in (15 cm) long, with numerous oblong,
untoothed leaflets, to ⅜ in (1 cm) long,
rounded or notched at the tip, dark
green above, dull green beneath,
silky-hairy when young becoming
smooth, on silky-hairy shoots.
Bark Gray to gray-brown, smooth,
with small lenticels. **Flowers** Pealike, to
2 in (5 cm) long, golden yellow, borne in
hanging racemes in the leaf axils in late
winter to spring. **Fruit** A winged brown
pod, to 6 in (15 cm) or more long,
hairy when young.
• **NATIVE REGION** Chile, New Zealand.
• **HABITAT** Forests, open places, and
riverbanks from sea level to the mountains.
• **REMARK** Can be either a small tree or a
large shrub. It is closely related to the similar
Sophora tetraptera, which is also known by the
common name kowhai. Seedlings go through
an intricately branched juvenile phase, and
take many years to flower.

*many small,
paired
leaflets*

*slender
exserted
flower
stamens*

*dull green
underside
of leaflets*

Height 33 ft (10 m)	Shape Broadly spreading	Leaf persistence Deciduous	Leaf type

MAGNOLIACEAE

T HIS FAMILY of 12 genera and about 200 species is distributed in two main areas. Most species are found in east Asia, from the Himalayas through China to Japan, and in Southeast Asia to New Guinea; relatively few occur from the eastern United States through Mexico to tropical South America. The deciduous and evergreen trees and shrubs have alternate, untoothed, and (only occasionally) lobed leaves. The showy flowers are borne singly.

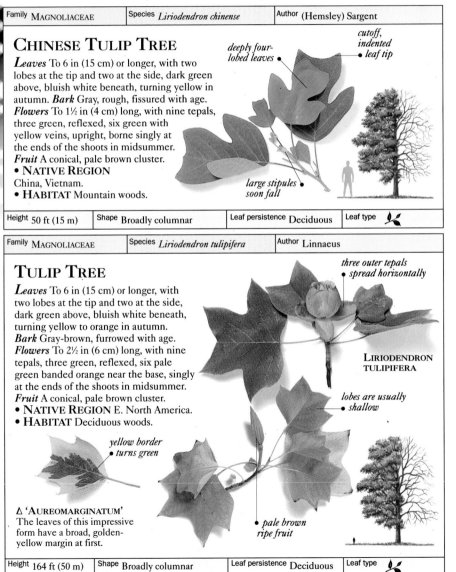

Family MAGNOLIACEAE	Species *Liriodendron chinense*	Author (Hemsley) Sargent

CHINESE TULIP TREE

Leaves To 6 in (15 cm) or longer, with two lobes at the tip and two at the side, dark green above, bluish white beneath, turning yellow in autumn. **Bark** Gray, rough, fissured with age. **Flowers** To 1½ in (4 cm) long, with nine tepals, three green, reflexed, six green with yellow veins, upright, borne singly at the ends of the shoots in midsummer. **Fruit** A conical, pale brown cluster.
• **NATIVE REGION** China, Vietnam.
• **HABITAT** Mountain woods.

deeply four-lobed leaves

cutoff, indented leaf tip

large stipules soon fall

Height 50 ft (15 m)	Shape Broadly columnar	Leaf persistence Deciduous	Leaf type

Family MAGNOLIACEAE	Species *Liriodendron tulipifera*	Author Linnaeus

TULIP TREE

Leaves To 6 in (15 cm) or longer, with two lobes at the tip and two at the side, dark green above, bluish white beneath, turning yellow to orange in autumn. **Bark** Gray-brown, furrowed with age. **Flowers** To 2½ in (6 cm) long, with nine tepals, three green, reflexed, six pale green banded orange near the base, singly at the ends of the shoots in midsummer. **Fruit** A conical, pale brown cluster.
• **NATIVE REGION** E. North America.
• **HABITAT** Deciduous woods.

three outer tepals spread horizontally

LIRIODENDRON TULIPIFERA

lobes are usually shallow

yellow border turns green

△ 'AUREOMARGINATUM'
The leaves of this impressive form have a broad, golden-yellow margin at first.

pale brown ripe fruit

Height 164 ft (50 m)	Shape Broadly columnar	Leaf persistence Deciduous	Leaf type

| Family MAGNOLIACEAE | Species *Magnolia acuminata* | Author Linnaeus |

CUCUMBER TREE

Leaves Elliptic to ovate, to 10 in (25 cm) long and 6 in (15 cm) across, taper-pointed, untoothed, light to dark green above, blue-green and usually hairy beneath. *Bark* Brown-gray, furrowed. *Flowers* Cup-shaped, to 3½ in (9 cm) long, with nine blue-green to yellow-green, upright tepals, borne singly at the ends of the shoots in early to mid-summer. *Fruit* A cylindrical cluster, to 3 in (7.5 cm) long, green becoming pink ripening to red.
• **NATIVE REGION**
E. North America.
• **HABITAT** Rich woods.
• **REMARK** The species gets its common name from the color and shape of the unripe fruit, which resembles a cucumber. The flowers are often hidden by the large leaves.

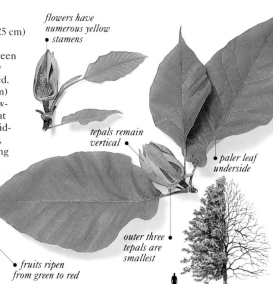

flowers have numerous yellow stamens

tepals remain vertical

paler leaf underside

outer three tepals are smallest

fruits ripen from green to red

| Height 100 ft (30 m) | Shape Broadly conical | Leaf persistence Deciduous | Leaf type |

| Family MAGNOLIACEAE | Species *Magnolia ashei* | Author Weatherby |

ASHEI MAGNOLIA

Leaves Broadly elliptic to oblong-obovate, to 12 in (30 cm) or more long and 8 in (20 cm) or more across, rather thin, usually auricled at the base, green and smooth above, blue-white and finely hairy beneath, carried in large whorls at the ends of the shoots. *Bark* Pale gray and smooth. *Flowers* Cup-shaped, 12 in (30 cm) across, white, fragrant, with nine tepals, the inner tepals usually marked with purple toward the base, borne at the ends of the shoots in early to midsummer before the leaves. *Fruit* A conical to egg-shaped pink cluster, about 3 in (7.5 cm) long.
• **NATIVE REGION**
N.W. Florida.
• **HABITAT** Moist woods.
• **REMARK** This species is closely related to *Magnolia macrophylla* (see p.209). It is rare and of very restricted distribution in the wild, where it can be either a small tree or a large shrub.

young leaves have large stipules

inner tepals blotched purple

whitish green outer tepals

| Height 33 ft (10 m) | Shape Broadly columnar | Leaf persistence Deciduous | Leaf type |

Family MAGNOLIACEAE	Species *Magnolia campbellii*	Author J.D. Hooker & Thomson

MAGNOLIA CAMPBELLII

Leaves Oblong to ovate or obovate, to 10 in (25 cm) or more long, usually abruptly pointed, untoothed, bronze when young becoming dark green and smooth above, paler and smooth or hairy beneath. **Bark** Gray and smooth. **Flowers** Very large, 12 in (30 cm) across, pale to deep pink to purplish pink or white, slightly fragrant, with up to 16 tepals, the outer tepals spreading, the inner tepals upright, giving the flower its characteristic cup-and-saucer shape, carried on smooth stalks, opening in late winter to early spring before the leaves. **Fruit** A cylindrical, conelike red cluster, to 6 in (15 cm) long.
• **NATIVE REGION** S.W. China, Himalayan mountains.
• **HABITAT** Forests in mountainous areas.
• **REMARK** A magnificent, large tree, much sought after in gardens for its huge flowers. On plants raised from seed, flowers are produced only after 20 years.

MAGNOLIA
CAMPBELLII

smooth flower stalks

inner tepals remain upright

large smooth leaves emerge after flowers

△ MAGNOLIA
CAMPBELLII

△ SUBSP. MOLLICOMATA
The flowers of this subspecies are produced slightly earlier in the year on younger plants.

outer tepals spread widely

Height 100 ft (30 m)	Shape Broadly conical	Leaf persistence Deciduous	Leaf type

Family MAGNOLIACEAE	Species *Magnolia dawsoniana*	Author Rehder & Wilson

MAGNOLIA DAWSONIANA

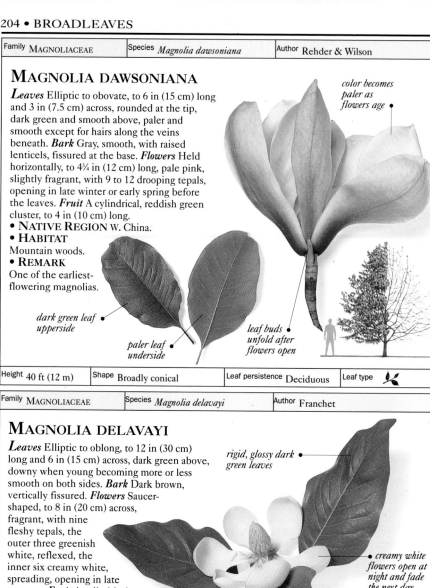

Leaves Elliptic to obovate, to 6 in (15 cm) long and 3 in (7.5 cm) across, rounded at the tip, dark green and smooth above, paler and smooth except for hairs along the veins beneath. *Bark* Gray, smooth, with raised lenticels, fissured at the base. *Flowers* Held horizontally, to 4¾ in (12 cm) long, pale pink, slightly fragrant, with 9 to 12 drooping tepals, opening in late winter or early spring before the leaves. *Fruit* A cylindrical, reddish green cluster, to 4 in (10 cm) long.
• NATIVE REGION W. China.
• HABITAT
Mountain woods.
• REMARK
One of the earliest-flowering magnolias.

color becomes paler as flowers age

dark green leaf upperside

paler leaf underside

leaf buds unfold after flowers open

Height 40 ft (12 m)	Shape Broadly conical	Leaf persistence Deciduous	Leaf type

Family MAGNOLIACEAE	Species *Magnolia delavayi*	Author Franchet

MAGNOLIA DELAVAYI

Leaves Elliptic to oblong, to 12 in (30 cm) long and 6 in (15 cm) across, dark green above, downy when young becoming more or less smooth on both sides. *Bark* Dark brown, vertically fissured. *Flowers* Saucer-shaped, to 8 in (20 cm) across, fragrant, with nine fleshy tepals, the outer three greenish white, reflexed, the inner six creamy white, spreading, opening in late summer. *Fruit* A cylindrical cluster, to 4 in (10 cm) long, green ripening to pale brown.
• NATIVE REGION
S.W. China.
• HABITAT Scrubland and open places.

rigid, glossy dark green leaves

creamy white flowers open at night and fade the next day

gray-green, hairy young leaves eventually become smooth on underside

Height 33 ft (10 m)	Shape Broadly spreading	Leaf persistence Evergreen	Leaf type

Family MAGNOLIACEAE	Species *Magnolia fraseri*	Author Walter

MAGNOLIA FRASERI

Leaves Obovate, to 16 in (40 cm) long and 8 in (20 cm) across, auricled at the base, pointed, bronze when young becoming pale green, smooth on both sides. **Bark** Brown or gray, smooth. **Flowers** Vase-shaped in bud, to 4¾ in (12 cm) long, opening saucer-shaped, the nine tepals creamy white flushed green on the outer surface, singly at the ends of the shoots in late spring to early summer. **Fruit** A cone-like, red cluster, to 4 in (10 cm) long.
• **NATIVE REGION** S.E. United States.
• **HABITAT** Rich mountain forests.

• creamy, yellowish white flowers open after leaves unfold

large, thin, soft • leaves whorled at shoot end

Height 46 ft (14 m)	Shape Broadly spreading	Leaf persistence Deciduous	Leaf type

Family MAGNOLIACEAE	Species *Magnolia grandiflora*	Author Linnaeus

BULL BAY

Leaves Elliptic to ovate or lanceolate, to 10 in (25 cm) long and 4 in (10 cm) across, rigid and leathery, glossy dark green and smooth above, paler or covered in rusty hairs beneath. **Bark** Gray, cracking into small plates. **Flowers** Cup-shaped, to 12 in (30 cm) across, creamy white, fragrant, with 9 to 12 thick tepals, borne singly at the ends of the shoots in early summer. **Fruit** An egg-shaped red cluster, to 4 in (10 cm) long.
• **NATIVE REGION** S.E. United States.
• **HABITAT** Riverbanks and moist places on coastal plain.
• **REMARK** Plants cultivated in areas that are cooler than the native region flower in late summer to autumn.

• very fragrant, large white flowers

leaf underside often covered in rust-colored hairs

• flowers have 9 to 12 or more tepals

• glossy dark green leaf upperside

Height 80 ft (25 m)	Shape Broadly conical	Leaf persistence Evergreen	Leaf type

| Family MAGNOLIACEAE | Species *Magnolia* 'Heaven Scent' | Author None |

MAGNOLIA 'HEAVEN SCENT'

Leaves Broadly elliptic, to 8 in (20 cm)
long, pointed at the tip, glossy green
above, paler beneath. **Bark** Gray and
smooth. **Flowers** Upright and vase-
shaped, 5 in (13 cm) long, narrow at
first later opening more widely,
strongly fragrant, the nine tepals pale
pink but more deeply shaded towards
the base, with a distinct, darker pink
band on the back, opening in spring to
early summer before and with the leaves.
Fruit Conelike, the ripe seeds protruding
and hanging for some time.
• **NATIVE REGION** Of garden origin.
• **REMARK** This hybrid between the shrubby
M. liliiflora 'Nigra' and *M. x veitchii* (see p.214)
is one of the Gresham Hybrids that resulted
from Drury Todd Gresham's program of
hybridization in California in the 1950s.
By careful selection of both parents and
offspring, he produced small trees that
combine attributes of some of the best
magnolias. 'Peppermint Stick' and
'Sayonara' belong also to this group.

pointed tepals spread slightly as flower ages

'HEAVEN SCENT'

◁ 'PEPPERMINT
STICK'
The buds of this
hybrid between
M. liliiflora and
M. x veitchii
are 4½ in
(11 cm) long.

tepals • eventually spread wider

• very faint pink flush at flower base

distinctively • narrow buds

△ 'SAYONARA'
This tree is a hybrid
between *Magnolia* x
soulangeana 'Lennei
Alba' and *Magnolia* x *veitchii*
'Rubra.' The abundant
flowers, which have fleshy
tepals, are 4 in (10 cm) long.

| Height 33 ft (10 m) | Shape Broadly spreading | Leaf persistence Deciduous | Leaf type |

Family MAGNOLIACEAE	Species *Magnolia hypoleuca*	Author Siebold & Zuccarini

MAGNOLIA HYPOLEUCA

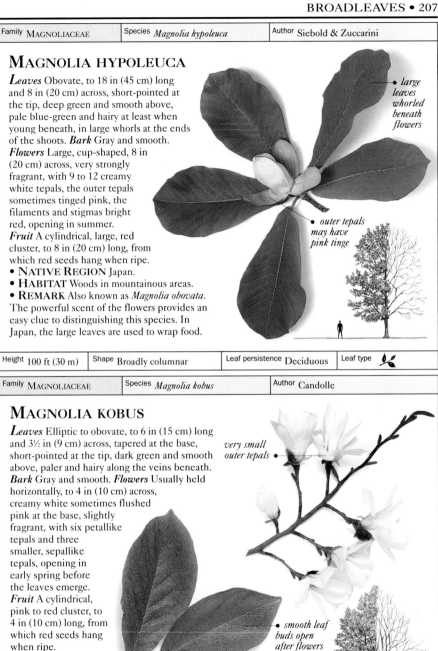

Leaves Obovate, to 18 in (45 cm) long and 8 in (20 cm) across, short-pointed at the tip, deep green and smooth above, pale blue-green and hairy at least when young beneath, in large whorls at the ends of the shoots. **Bark** Gray and smooth.
Flowers Large, cup-shaped, 8 in (20 cm) across, very strongly fragrant, with 9 to 12 creamy white tepals, the outer tepals sometimes tinged pink, the filaments and stigmas bright red, opening in summer.
Fruit A cylindrical, large, red cluster, to 8 in (20 cm) long, from which red seeds hang when ripe.
• **NATIVE REGION** Japan.
• **HABITAT** Woods in mountainous areas.
• **REMARK** Also known as *Magnolia obovata*. The powerful scent of the flowers provides an easy clue to distinguishing this species. In Japan, the large leaves are used to wrap food.

large leaves whorled beneath flowers

outer tepals may have pink tinge

Height 100 ft (30 m)	Shape Broadly columnar	Leaf persistence Deciduous	Leaf type

Family MAGNOLIACEAE	Species *Magnolia kobus*	Author Candolle

MAGNOLIA KOBUS

Leaves Elliptic to obovate, to 6 in (15 cm) long and 3½ in (9 cm) across, tapered at the base, short-pointed at the tip, dark green and smooth above, paler and hairy along the veins beneath. **Bark** Gray and smooth. **Flowers** Usually held horizontally, to 4 in (10 cm) across, creamy white sometimes flushed pink at the base, slightly fragrant, with six petallike tepals and three smaller, sepallike tepals, opening in early spring before the leaves emerge.
Fruit A cylindrical, pink to red cluster, to 4 in (10 cm) long, from which red seeds hang when ripe.
• **NATIVE REGION** Japan, S. Korea.
• **HABITAT** Mountain forests.

very small outer tepals

smooth leaf buds open after flowers

leaves taper toward base

Height 65 ft (20 m)	Shape Broadly conical	Leaf persistence Deciduous	Leaf type

Family MAGNOLIACEAE	Species *Magnolia x loebneri*	Author Kache

MAGNOLIA X LOEBNERI

Leaves Oblanceolate to elliptic, to 6 in (15 cm) long, glossy dark green to paler green, usually smooth.
Bark Gray, smooth. **Flowers** Variable, upright to horizontal, to 6 in (15 cm) across, white to pink, with up to 16 or more tepals and three small, sepallike tepals, opening in early to mid-spring. **Fruit** A cylindrical, pinkish red cluster, to 4 in (10 cm) long.

• NATIVE REGION
Of garden origin.

• REMARK A group of hybrids between *Magnolia kobus* (see p.207) and the usually shrubby *Magnolia stellata*, first raised in Germany, with many selected forms that combine the best qualities of both parents. The starry flowers are inherited from the aptly named *M. stellata*.

◁ 'LEONARD MESSEL'
Each lilac-pink flower of this form has about 12 drooping tepals.

slightly spreading flower buds
• *borne upright*

• *numerous narrow tepals*

'LEONARD MESSEL'

pink buds fade to white as flowers open •

broad, short-pointed leaves taper • *toward base*

◁ 'MERRILL'

• *relatively narrow leaves*

◁ 'MERRILL'

flowers open to • *entirely white*

flower buds • *enclosed in silky scales*

△ 'MERRILL'
This vigorous plant bears large, white flowers, flushed faint pink at first. Each flower has up to 15 tepals.

Height 33 ft (10 m)	Shape Broadly spreading	Leaf persistence Deciduous	Leaf type

Family MAGNOLIACEAE	Species *Magnolia macrophylla*	Author A. Michaux

LARGE-LEAVED MAGNOLIA

Leaves Very large and thin, broadly elliptic to oblong-ovate, to 24 in (60 cm) or longer and 12 in (30 cm) across, usually auricled at the base, green and smooth above, blue-green to blue-white and finely hairy beneath, in large whorls at the ends of stout shoots. ***Bark*** Pale gray and smooth. ***Flowers*** Very large and broadly cup-shaped, 12 in (30 cm) across, creamy white to yellowish, fragrant, with nine tepals, the inner tepals petal-like, usually marked with purple toward the base, the outer tepals sepallike, held upright, at the ends of the shoots in early to midsummer with the leaves. ***Fruit*** A rounded pink cluster, about 3 in (7.5 cm) long, from which red seeds hang when ripe.

• **NATIVE REGION** S.E. United States.
• **HABITAT** Rich, moist woods.
• **REMARK** The enormous leaves and flowers of this species are among the largest of those of all deciduous trees that are native to temperate regions.

distinctively large leaves

outer tepals streaked green

gray young shoot covered with soft hairs

bluish green leaf underside shows strong midrib

twin auricles at leaf base

Height 50 ft (15 m)	Shape Broadly columnar	Leaf persistence Deciduous	Leaf type

| Family MAGNOLIACEAE | Species *Magnolia officinalis* | Author Rehder & Wilson |

MAGNOLIA OFFICINALIS

Leaves Obovate, to 18 in (45 cm) long and 8 in (20 cm) across, tapered at the base, rounded to short-pointed at the tip, light green and smooth above, whitish and softly hairy when young beneath, carried in whorls at the ends of the shoots. *Bark* Pale gray and smooth. *Flowers* Cup- to saucer-shaped, 6 in (15 cm) across, creamy white, fragrant, the stamens with red filaments, at the ends of the shoots in late spring to early summer. *Fruit* An oblong, pinkish red cluster, to 6 in (15 cm) long, from which bright red seeds emerge and hang.
• **NATIVE REGION** C. China.
• **HABITAT** Now known only in cultivation.
• **REMARK** The form shown here, var. *biloba*, differs only in the large notch at the tip of the leaves. The bark was traditionally used for medicinal purposes. The practice of stripping it from the trees, thus killing them, may be responsible for the probable extinction of the species in the wild.

large fruits develop in autumn

△ VAR. BILOBA

VAR. BILOBA ▷

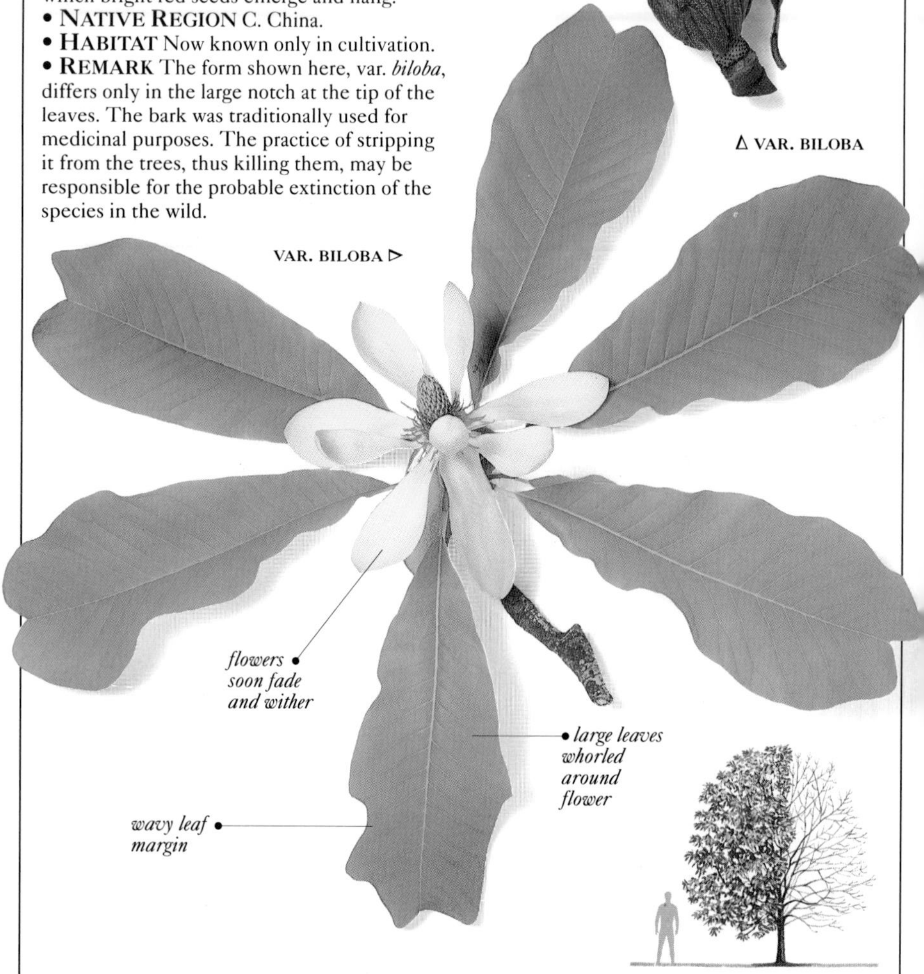

flowers soon fade and wither

large leaves whorled around flower

wavy leaf margin

| Height 65 ft (20 m) | Shape Broadly columnar | Leaf persistence Deciduous | Leaf type |

Family MAGNOLIACEAE	Species *Magnolia x soulangeana*	Author Soulange-Bodin

SAUCER MAGNOLIA

Leaves Elliptic to obovate, to 8 in (20 cm) long and 4¾ in (12 cm) across, tapered at the base, usually rounded at the tip, with a short point, dark green and nearly smooth above, paler and finely hairy beneath. *Bark* Gray and smooth. *Flowers* Variable, from goblet- to cup- or saucer-shaped, to 10 in (25 cm) across, with usually nine white to pink or deep purple-pink tepals, in spring to early summer from before to after the leaves emerge. *Fruit* A cylindrical cluster, to 4 in (10 cm) long, green ripening to pink.

• **NATIVE REGION** Of garden origin.

• **REMARK** A hybrid between *Magnolia heptapeta* and *Magnolia quinquepeta*.

leaves end in abruptly short-pointed tip

inner tepals spread more or less widely

leaves taper to narrowed base

three smaller outer tepals

deep pink flush at base of tepals fades to pale streak at tip

shoots marked with pale lenticels

flowers open from cylindrical buds

fruit clusters ripen from green to pink

silky-hairy flower buds

| Height 30 ft (9 m) | Shape Broadly spreading | Leaf persistence Deciduous | Leaf type |

Family MAGNOLIACEAE	Species *Magnolia x soulangeana*	Author Soulange-Bodin

▽ 'BROZZONII'
This conical tree has large, white flowers, faintly flushed pink at the base. They can reach 10 in (25 cm) across and are produced continuously over a long period from mid-spring to early summer.

• center of tepals colored rich purplish pink

large flowers have six tepals •

• edge of tepals colored nearly white

narrow • buds later open more widely

merest pink flush at base of tepals •

△ 'PICTURE'
The flowers of this form are strongly marked with purplish pink. The plant tends toward a compact and upright, rather than broadly spreading, habit.

silky bud scales • enclose new leaves

• richly colored tepals

goblet-shaped • flowers open from broad buds

'RUSTICA RUBRA' ▷
This form bears large, goblet-shaped flowers. The tepals are shaded deep purplish pink on the outer surface, particularly at the base. The color fades to cream flushed pink at the tip.

• first flowers open before leaves emerge

Height 30 ft (9 m)	Shape Broadly spreading	Leaf persistence Deciduous	Leaf type

Family MAGNOLIACEAE	Species *Magnolia salicifolia*	Author (Sieb. & Zucc.) Maximowicz

MAGNOLIA SALICIFOLIA

Leaves Ovate to lanceolate or elliptic, to 6 in (15 cm) long and 2½ in (6 cm) across, dark green above, blue-green and smooth beneath, aromatic when crushed. **Bark** Gray, smooth, lemon-scented when bruised. **Flowers** Usually held horizontally, to 5 in (13 cm) across, white, fragrant, with six narrow tepals, the inner three petal-like, the outer three smaller and sepal-like, opening in early spring before leaves. **Fruit** A cylindrical pink cluster, to 3 in (7.5 cm) long.
• **NATIVE REGION** Japan.
• **HABITAT** Oak and beech woods in mountains.

yellow stamens

dark green mature leaves

young leaves may be reddish

leaf buds

Height 33 ft (10 m)	Shape Broadly conical	Leaf persistence Deciduous	Leaf type

Family MAGNOLIACEAE	Species *Magnolia tripetala*	Author Linnaeus

UMBRELLA TREE

Leaves Obovate to elliptic, to 20 in (50 cm) long and 8 in (20 cm) across, tapered at the base, pointed at the tip, dark green above, gray-green and hairy beneath, in large whorls at the ends of the shoots. **Bark** Pale gray and smooth. **Flowers** To 8 in (20 cm) across, creamy white, pungently fragrant, with usually 12 narrow spreading tepals, the three outer tepals opening first from distinctive, slender buds at the ends of the shoots in late spring to early summer with the young leaves. **Fruit** A cylindrical to cone-shaped pinkish red cluster, to 4 in (10 cm) long.
• **NATIVE REGION** E. United States.
• **HABITAT** Rich woods.
• **REMARK** The scientific name, meaning "three-petaled" may seem inappropriate, but probably refers to the three outer sepallike tepals. The strong scent of the flowers is unpleasant to some people.

three outer tepals open first

tightly closed inner tepals eventually open more widely

Height 40 ft (12 m)	Shape Broadly spreading	Leaf persistence Deciduous	Leaf type

Family MAGNOLIACEAE	Species *Magnolia* x *veitchii*	Author Bean

MAGNOLIA X VEITCHII

Leaves Obovate to oblong, to 12 in (30 cm) long and 6 in (15 cm) across, short-pointed at the tip, bronze-purple at first becoming dark green and smooth above, downy at least on the veins beneath. **Bark** Gray and smooth. **Flowers** Vase-shaped, to 6 in (15 cm) long, white to pink, fragrant, with usually nine tepals, opening in mid-spring usually before the leaves. **Fruit** A cylindrical cluster to 4 in (10 cm) long, pinkish green ripening to purple-brown.

• **NATIVE REGION**
Of garden origin.

• **REMARK** One of a number of hybrids between the often shrubby yulan *(Magnolia denudata)* and *Magnolia campbellii* (see p.203). These vigorous trees owe their large size to the latter parent, which can reach 100 ft (30 m) in the wild. They are very attractive plants, usually producing abundant flowers and pretty young foliage.

• inner and outer tepals are upright

△ 'ISCA'
This cultivar flowers in mid-spring.

lustrous young leaves tinged bronze •

• flowers flushed slightly pink at base

• white flowers flushed deep pink appear pale pink from a distance

△ 'PETER VEITCH'
The goblet-shaped, soft pink blooms of this hardy magnolia appear in mid-spring before the leaves. Flowers are produced even on young plants.

mature leaves • are dark green and smooth on upper surface

Height 100 ft (30 m)	Shape Broadly columnar	Leaf persistence Deciduous	Leaf type

Family MAGNOLIACEAE	Species *Magnolia* 'Wada's Memory'	Author None

MAGNOLIA 'WADA'S MEMORY'

Leaves Obovate to narrowly ovate, to 7 in (17.5 cm) long, tapered at the base, abruptly pointed, red-purple becoming glossy dark green above, blue-green beneath, smooth on both sides. *Bark* Gray, smooth. *Flowers* Held horizontally, 6 in (15 cm) across, creamy white becoming white, fragrant, the tepals soon drooping, opening from felted buds. *Fruit* A cylindrical, pink to red cluster, to 4 in (10 cm) long, not usually produced.
• **NATIVE REGION** Of garden origin.
• **REMARK** Probably a hybrid between *Magnolia kobus* (see p.207) and *Magnolia salicifolia* (see p.213), which originated in Japan. It is named after the Japanese nurseryman, Koichiro Wada.

tepals soon flop as flower buds open

much smaller tepals at base of flower

young leaves colored reddish purple

silky scales enclose flower bud

young leaves emerge just after first flowers

leaves mature to olive green

Height 30 ft (9 m)	Shape Broadly conical	Leaf persistence Deciduous	Leaf type

MALVACEAE

WITH MORE THAN 100 GENERA and 1,500 species, the mallow family is found worldwide, except in the very coldest parts. The plants are deciduous and evergreen trees and shrubs, as well as herbaceous. The alternate leaves are often palmately lobed. Flowers vary from large and showy to very small.

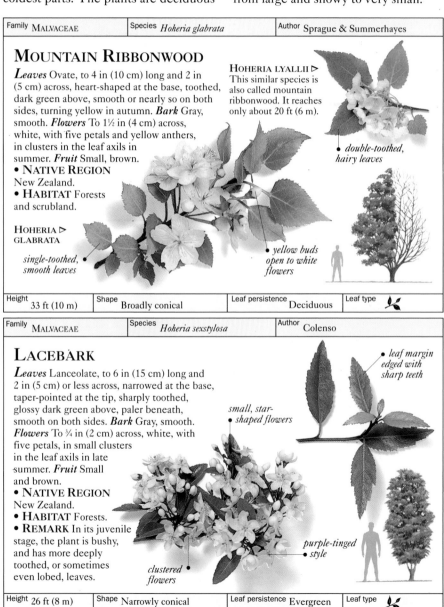

Family MALVACEAE	Species *Hoheria glabrata*	Author Sprague & Summerhayes

MOUNTAIN RIBBONWOOD

Leaves Ovate, to 4 in (10 cm) long and 2 in (5 cm) across, heart-shaped at the base, toothed, dark green above, smooth or nearly so on both sides, turning yellow in autumn. **Bark** Gray, smooth. **Flowers** To 1½ in (4 cm) across, white, with five petals and yellow anthers, in clusters in the leaf axils in summer. **Fruit** Small, brown.
• NATIVE REGION New Zealand.
• HABITAT Forests and scrubland.

HOHERIA ▷
GLABRATA

single-toothed, smooth leaves

HOHERIA LYALLII ▷
This similar species is also called mountain ribbonwood. It reaches only about 20 ft (6 m).

double-toothed, hairy leaves

yellow buds open to white flowers

Height 33 ft (10 m)	Shape Broadly conical	Leaf persistence Deciduous	Leaf type

Family MALVACEAE	Species *Hoheria sexstylosa*	Author Colenso

LACEBARK

Leaves Lanceolate, to 6 in (15 cm) long and 2 in (5 cm) or less across, narrowed at the base, taper-pointed at the tip, sharply toothed, glossy dark green above, paler beneath, smooth on both sides. **Bark** Gray, smooth. **Flowers** To ¾ in (2 cm) across, white, with five petals, in small clusters in the leaf axils in late summer. **Fruit** Small and brown.
• NATIVE REGION New Zealand.
• HABITAT Forests.
• REMARK In its juvenile stage, the plant is bushy, and has more deeply toothed, or sometimes even lobed, leaves.

leaf margin edged with sharp teeth

small, star-shaped flowers

purple-tinged style

clustered flowers

Height 26 ft (8 m)	Shape Narrowly conical	Leaf persistence Evergreen	Leaf type

MELIACEAE

OCCURRING IN TEMPERATE regions of east Asia, this largely tropical and subtropical family is composed of some 50 genera and nearly 600 species. The plants, which are evergreen and deciduous trees and shrubs, have leaves that are most often pinnate, arranged alternately. The flowers are usually small, frequently borne in large clusters. The fruit is a woody capsule. Many trees that belong to Meliaceae have an important commercial value for their timber: several of the species produce the hardwood mahogany.

Family MELIACEAE	Species *Cedrela sinensis*	Author Jussieu

CEDRELA SINENSIS

Leaves Pinnate, to 24 in (60 cm) long, with up to 26 oblong-lanceolate, taper-pointed, remotely toothed leaflets, to 6 in (15 cm) long, the terminal leaflet often missing, bronze to pinkish and downy when young becoming dark green and smooth or nearly so, tinged yellow in autumn, smelling of onions when crushed. *Bark* Brown, peeling in long strips. *Flowers* Small and white, fragrant, in large, drooping panicles 12 in (30 cm) or more long, from the ends of the shoots in midsummer. *Fruit* A woody, brown capsule, 1¼ in (3 cm) long.
• **NATIVE REGION** China.
• **HABITAT** Woods.
• **REMARK** Also known as *Toona sinensis*.

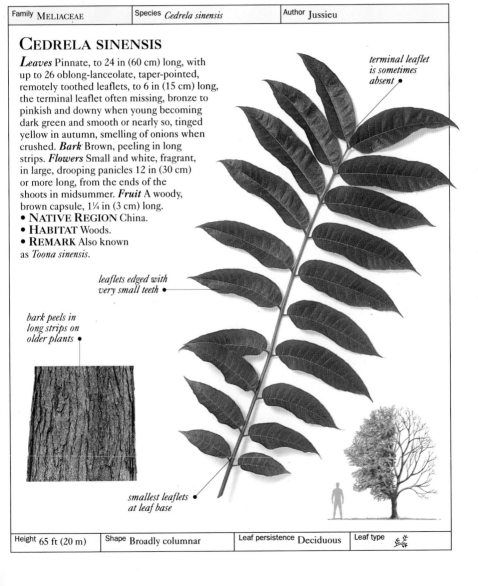

terminal leaflet is sometimes absent

leaflets edged with very small teeth

bark peels in long strips on older plants

smallest leaflets at leaf base

Height 65 ft (20 m)	Shape Broadly columnar	Leaf persistence Deciduous	Leaf type

MORACEAE

T HIS LARGE FAMILY includes the figs *(Ficus, see p.219)* and mulberries *(Morus, see p.220)*. Its 50 genera and some 1,200 species of deciduous and evergreen trees, shrubs, and climbing and herbaceous plants are distributed worldwide. The leaves are usually alternate and simple, and, occasionally, lobed. Male and female flowers are borne separately, in small clusters.

Family MORACEAE	Species *Broussonetia papyrifera*	Author (Linnaeus) Ventenat

PAPER MULBERRY

Leaves Ovate to broadly ovate, to 8 in (20 cm) long and 6 in (15 cm) across, sometimes lobed, coarsely toothed, purplish at first becoming matt dark green, roughly hairy above, softly hairy beneath. **Bark** Gray-brown, shallowly fissured. **Flowers** Males and females both small, males white, in stout, drooping catkins, females green, with slender, purple, protruding stigmas, borne in dense, rounded heads on separate plants in late spring to early summer. **Fruit** Red, protruding from a rounded cluster, ¾ in (2 cm) across.
• **NATIVE REGION** China, Japan.
• **HABITAT** Sunny, fertile situations.
• **REMARK** In Japan, the bark is traditionally used to make paper.

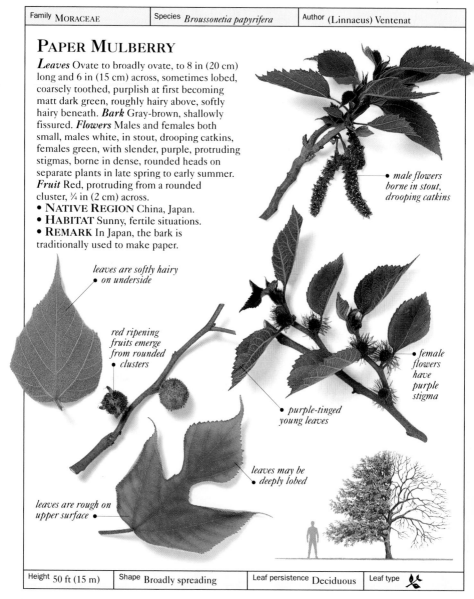

• *male flowers borne in stout, drooping catkins*

leaves are softly hairy on underside

red ripening fruits emerge from rounded clusters

• *female flowers have purple stigma*

• *purple-tinged young leaves*

leaves may be deeply lobed

leaves are rough on upper surface •

Height 50 ft (15 m)	Shape Broadly spreading	Leaf persistence Deciduous	Leaf type

Family MORACEAE	Species *Ficus carica*	Author Linnaeus

COMMON FIG

Leaves Rounded in outline, to 12 in (30 cm) long and across, deeply cut into three to five lobes, heart-shaped at the base, toothed, glossy green above, rough with hairs on both sides, turning yellow in autumn. *Bark* Gray and smooth. *Flowers* Males and females both very small, borne inconspicuously inside a fleshy green receptacle, on separate plants in late spring. *Fruit* Numerous small seeds borne inside a receptacle, the whole green ripening to brown or purple, forming the edible fig.
• **NATIVE REGION** S.W. Asia.
• **HABITAT** Broadleaf forests.
• **REMARK** This species is commonly naturalized in the Mediterranean. It favors rocky places, including old walls. Plants are fertilized by female wasps, which take pollen from the tree in which they hatched to one in which they lay their eggs. Most cultivated plants produce fruit without pollination.

fleshy receptacle contains many • tiny seeds

• fruits of some forms ripen to purple

green unripe • fruit

long • leaf stalk

leathery leaves have • visible ribs and network of veins

Height 33 ft (10 m)	Shape Broadly spreading	Leaf persistence Deciduous	Leaf type

Family MORACEAE	Species *Maclura pomifera*	Author (Rafinesque) Schneider

OSAGE ORANGE

Leaves Ovate, to 4 in (10 cm) long and 2 in (5 cm) across, untoothed, glossy bright green above, smooth, turning yellow in autumn. *Bark* Orange-brown, fissured. *Flowers* Males and females small, yellow-green, in clusters ⅜ in (1 cm) long, on separate plants in early summer. *Fruit* A yellow-green cluster, to 4 in (10 cm) across.
• **NATIVE REGION** C. and S. United States.
• **HABITAT** Rich, moist soil.

small fruits fuse to form heavy fruit mass

leaves taper to long, slender point

Height 50 ft (15 m)	Shape Broadly spreading	Leaf persistence Deciduous	Leaf type

Family MORACEAE	Species *Morus alba*	Author Linnaeus

WHITE MULBERRY

Leaves Ovate to rounded, to 8 in (20 cm) long and 4¾ in (12 cm) across, toothed, bright green above, turning yellow in autumn. *Bark* Orange-brown. *Flowers* Males and females green, in clusters about ⅜ in (1 cm) long, on the same or separate plants in early summer. *Fruit* A white to pink or red cluster, to 1 in (2.5 cm) long.
• **NATIVE REGION** N. China.
• **HABITAT** Hill slopes.

stalked, edible fruit clusters

heart-shaped leaf base

smooth leaf upperside

Height 50 ft (15 m)	Shape Broadly spreading	Leaf persistence Deciduous	Leaf type

Family MORACEAE	Species *Morus nigra*	Author Linnaeus

BLACK MULBERRY

Leaves Ovate, to 6 in (15 cm) long and 4¾ in (12 cm) across, heart-shaped at the base, toothed, green above, hairy beneath. *Bark* Orange-brown and ridged. *Flowers* Males and females tiny, green, in small clusters on the same or separate plants in early summer. *Fruit* A dark red cluster, 1 in (2.5 cm) long.
• **NATIVE REGION** Far East.
• **HABITAT** Not known.
• **REMARK** Extensive cultivation makes its precise origin uncertain.

rough, hairy leaves

male flowers

barely stalked, edible fruit clusters

Height 33 ft (10 m)	Shape Broadly spreading	Leaf persistence Deciduous	Leaf type

MYRTACEAE

T HIS LARGE FAMILY is distributed most widely in the southern hemisphere. Despite the fact that it extends to temperate regions of the northern hemisphere, it does not grow wild in North America, and is represented in Europe only by the myrtle *(Myrtus communis)*. It contains nearly 4,000 species of usually evergreen and frequently aromatic, trees and shrubs, in over 100 genera. The leaves are often opposite. The flowers usually have four or five petals and numerous stamens. In eucalyptus species, the petals form a cap over the flower, which falls as the flower opens.

Family MYRTACEAE	Species *Callistemon* species	Author None

CALLISTEMONS

The callistemons, or bottlebrushes, are all native to Australia, and can be found growing usually in moist habitats. Some make small trees, reaching about 33 ft (10 cm), for example *C. salignus* and *C. viminalis*, although most are shrubby. These evergreen plants have usually narrow, pointed leaves, often colored bronze or red when young. The flowers have very small petals, but their numerous long stamens, which range in color from creamy white or yellow to red, pink, or purplish, radiate around the stem, forming dense spikes, and giving the flower clusters their characteristic appearance.

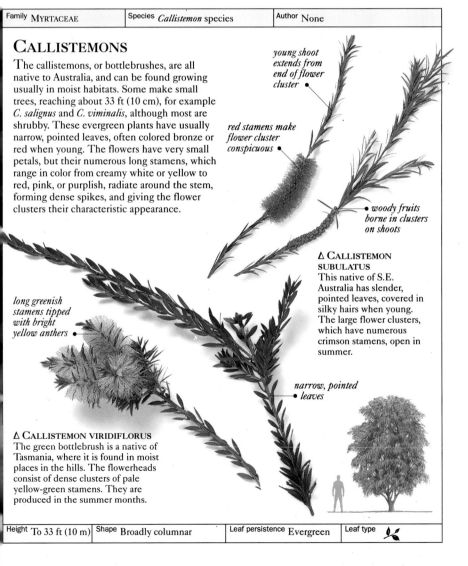

young shoot extends from end of flower cluster

red stamens make flower cluster conspicuous

woody fruits borne in clusters on shoots

△ CALLISTEMON SUBULATUS
This native of S.E. Australia has slender, pointed leaves, covered in silky hairs when young. The large flower clusters, which have numerous crimson stamens, open in summer.

long greenish stamens tipped with bright yellow anthers

narrow, pointed leaves

△ CALLISTEMON VIRIDIFLORUS
The green bottlebrush is a native of Tasmania, where it is found in moist places in the hills. The flowerheads consist of dense clusters of pale yellow-green stamens. They are produced in the summer months.

Height To 33 ft (10 m)	Shape Broadly columnar	Leaf persistence Evergreen	Leaf type

Family MYRTACEAE	Species *Eucalyptus coccifera*	Author J.D. Hooker

MOUNT WELLINGTON PEPPERMINT

Leaves Juvenile leaves rounded, usually glaucous, unstalked, adult leaves lanceolate, to 2 in (5 cm) long and ¾ in (2 cm), across, with a hooked tip, green to blue-green, smooth on both sides, aromatic, on often bloomy shoots. **Bark** Gray and white, smooth, peeling in long strips; creamy white when freshly exposed. **Flowers** White, with numerous stamens, borne in clusters of three to seven in the leaf axils in early summer. **Fruit** Resembling an inverted cone, small and woody, ⅜ in (1 cm) long.
• **NATIVE REGION** Tasmania.
• **HABITAT** Mountains.
• **REMARK** Also known as Tasmanian snow gum. Juvenile leaves are opposite, adult leaves alternate: plants often bear both stages together. On mature plants, juvenile foliage is produced on shoots from the base of the trunk.

three to seven flowers clustered together

woody fruits have flattened top

Height 80 ft (25 m)	Shape Broadly spreading	Leaf persistence Evergreen	Leaf type

Family MYRTACEAE	Species *Eucalyptus cordata*	Author Labillardière

SILVER GUM

Leaves Nearly rounded to ovate, to 4 in (10 cm) long and 2½ in (6 cm) across, with rounded, shallow teeth, blue-gray and bloomy on both sides, aromatic, unstalked, lying close to square, white-bloomed shoots. **Bark** Smooth and white, with gray and green patches, peeling in long ribbons. **Flowers** Creamy white, with numerous stamens, in clusters of three in the leaf axils, opening from bloomy buds on a flattened and bloomy common stalk in winter. **Fruit** A hemispherical, small, bloomy capsule, ⅜ in (1 cm) long.
• **NATIVE REGION** Tasmania.
• **HABITAT** Woods in hills and mountains.
• **REMARK** Juvenile and adult leaves are similar: the foliage does not change in shape or type as the tree matures, unlike that of most eucalyptus species.

flower buds clustered three together

leaves overlap each other at base

four-angled shoots

very small, bloomy fruits

Height 50 ft (15 m)	Shape Broadly columnar	Leaf persistence Evergreen	Leaf type

Family MYRTACEAE	Species *Eucalyptus dalrympleana*	Author Maiden

MOUNTAIN GUM

Leaves Juvenile leaves rounded, unstalked, adult leaves lanceolate, to 7 in (17.5 cm) long and 1¼ in (3 cm) across, tapered to a fine point, bronze when young becoming blue-green and smooth on both sides. *Bark* Gray-brown and smooth, peeling in large flakes; creamy white when freshly exposed. *Flowers* White, with numerous stamens, in clusters of three in the leaf axils in late summer. *Fruit* Hemispherical, small, woody, ⅜ in (1 cm) long.
• **NATIVE REGION**
S.E. Australia, Tasmania.
• **HABITAT**
Mountain slopes.
• **REMARK** Juvenile leaves are opposite, adult leaves alternate: plants often bear both stages together.

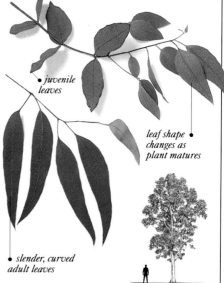

• *juvenile leaves*

leaf shape changes as plant matures •

peeling bark exposes creamy layer beneath •

• *slender, curved adult leaves*

Height 100 ft (30 m)	Shape Broadly columnar	Leaf persistence Evergreen	Leaf type

Family MYRTACEAE	Species *Eucalyptus gunnii*	Author J.D. Hooker

CIDER GUM

Leaves Juvenile leaves rounded, unstalked, to 1½ in (4 cm) long, gray-blue, adult leaves ovate to lanceolate, to 4 in (10 cm) long and 1½ in (4 cm) across, silvery becoming gray-green, smooth on both sides. *Bark* Gray, green, or orange, rough at the very base, peeling in large patches; creamy when freshly exposed. *Flowers* White, with numerous stamens, in clusters of three in the leaf axils in late spring to summer. *Fruit* Cup-shaped, green or bloomy, ¾₆ in (5 mm) long.
• **NATIVE REGION**
Tasmania.
• **HABITAT** Alpine woods.
• **REMARK** Juvenile leaves are opposite, adult leaves alternate: plants often bear both stages together.

silvery gray-blue young leaves •

rounded • *juvenile leaves*

cup-shaped fruits

bark peels in large patches •

• *long, pointed adult leaves*

Height 80 ft (25 m)	Shape Broadly columnar	Leaf persistence Evergreen	Leaf type

Family MYRTACEAE	Species *Eucalyptus pauciflora*	Author Siebold ex Sprengel

SNOW GUM

Leaves Juvenile leaves ovate to rounded, to
2½ in (6 cm) long, leathery, gray, adult leaves
lanceolate, to 6 in (15 cm) long and 1½ in (4 cm)
across, often curved, glossy green and smooth.
Bark Gray and white, peeling in large flakes.
Flowers White, with numerous stamens, in
clusters in the leaf axils in summer.
Fruit Rounded, woody, ¼ in (6 mm) long.
• **NATIVE REGION** S.E. Australia, Tasmania.
• **HABITAT** From sea level
to the tree line.

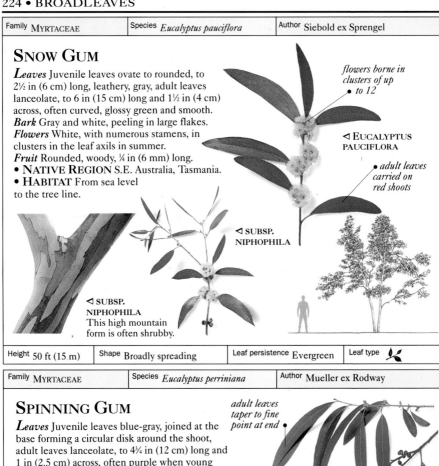

*flowers borne in
clusters of up
to 12*

◁ **EUCALYPTUS
PAUCIFLORA**

*adult leaves
carried on
red shoots*

◁ **SUBSP.
NIPHOPHILA**

◁ **SUBSP.
NIPHOPHILA**
This high mountain
form is often shrubby.

Height 50 ft (15 m)	Shape Broadly spreading	Leaf persistence Evergreen	Leaf type

Family MYRTACEAE	Species *Eucalyptus perriniana*	Author Mueller ex Rodway

SPINNING GUM

Leaves Juvenile leaves blue-gray, joined at the
base forming a circular disk around the shoot,
adult leaves lanceolate, to 4¾ in (12 cm) long and
1 in (2.5 cm) across, often purple when young
becoming deep blue-green and smooth on both
sides, pendulous. **Bark** Gray and brown, peeling.
Flowers White, with numerous stamens, in
clusters in the leaf axils in late summer.
Fruit Small, woody, ³⁄₁₆ in (5 mm) long.
• **NATIVE REGION** S.E. Australia, Tasmania.
• **HABITAT** Mountains, on moist soil.

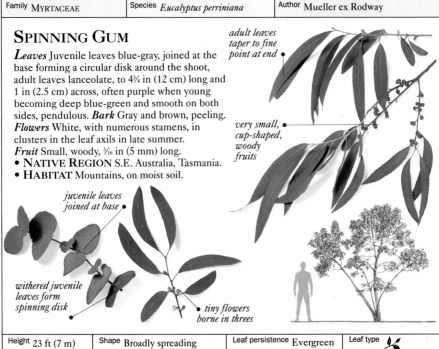

*adult leaves
taper to fine
point at end*

*very small,
cup-shaped,
woody
fruits*

*juvenile leaves
joined at base*

*withered juvenile
leaves form
spinning disk*

*tiny flowers
borne in threes*

Height 23 ft (7 m)	Shape Broadly spreading	Leaf persistence Evergreen	Leaf type

Family MYRTACEAE	Species *Eucalyptus urnigera*	Author J.D. Hooker

URN GUM

Leaves Juvenile leaves rounded, to 2 in (5 cm) long, with a blue-white bloom, adult leaves ovate to lanceolate, to 4¾ in (12 cm) long and 2 in (5 cm) across, glossy green to blue-green, smooth on both sides. **Bark** Pale gray to creamy white or orange-yellow, peeling vertically in long ribbons. **Flowers** White, with numerous stamens, in clusters of three in the leaf axils in spring. **Fruit** Urn-shaped, ¼ in (6 mm) long, distinctly constricted below the rim.
• **NATIVE REGION** S.E. Tasmania.
• **HABITAT** Rocky slopes in the mountains.
• **REMARK** Juvenile leaves are opposite, adult leaves alternate: plants bear both stages together. Similar to cider gum *(Eucalyptus gunnii*, see p.223), this species is distinguished by its fruits.

urn-shaped fruits

rounded juvenile leaves arranged opposite

flowers clustered in threes

elongated adult leaves arranged alternately

conspicuous white stamens

Height 40 ft (12 m)	Shape Broadly columnar	Leaf persistence Evergreen	Leaf type

Family MYRTACEAE	Species *Myrtus luma*	Author Molina

MYRTUS LUMA

Leaves Broadly elliptic, to 1 in (2.5 cm) long, short-pointed, untoothed, bronze-purple when young becoming glossy dark green and smooth above, paler beneath, aromatic. **Bark** Bright cinnamon-orange, flaking in patches; nearly white when freshly exposed. **Flowers** ¾ in (2 cm) across, white, with four petals, numerous stamens, and yellow anthers, borne singly in the leaf axils of young shoots in late summer to autumn. **Fruit** Rounded and fleshy, ⅜ in (1 cm) long, red ripening to purple-black.
• **NATIVE REGION** Argentina, Chile.
• **HABITAT** Forests.
• **REMARK** Also known as *Luma apiculata*, *Myrtus apiculata*.

four-petaled flowers have numerous stamens

leaves taper to fine point

leaves are arranged opposite

young leaves tinged bronze

Height 40 ft (12 m)	Shape Broadly spreading	Leaf persistence Evergreen	Leaf type

NYSSACEAE

T HE THREE GENERA and seven species of the tupelo family are native to North America and East Asia. The best-known genus is *Nyssa*, whose species display brilliant autumn color. The leaves are alternate, and the small flowers petalless, but those of *Davidia involucrata* have conspicuous bracts.

Family NYSSACEAE	Species *Davidia involucrata*	Author Baillon

HANDKERCHIEF TREE

Leaves Heart-shaped, to 6 in (15 cm) long and 4¾ in (12 cm) across, with a slender, pointed tip, sharply toothed, bright green above, densely hairy beneath. **Bark** Orange-brown, peeling vertically in small flakes. **Flowers** Individually small, in a rounded head ¾ in (2 cm) across, conspicuous by purple anthers, surrounded by two white bracts of unequal size, the larger to 8 in (20 cm) long, in late spring with leaves. **Fruit** Rounded, 1 in (2.5 cm) across, green ripening to purple-brown.
• **NATIVE REGION** China.
• **HABITAT** Moist mountain woods.

VAR. VILMORINIANA ▷
The leaves of this variety have smooth undersides.

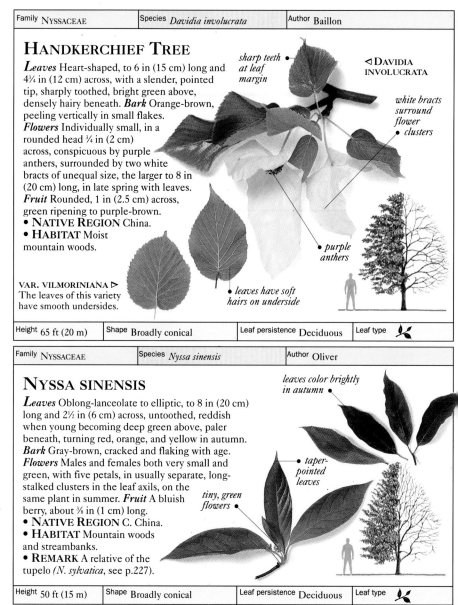

sharp teeth at leaf margin

◁ DAVIDIA INVOLUCRATA

white bracts surround flower clusters

purple anthers

leaves have soft hairs on underside

Height 65 ft (20 m)	Shape Broadly conical	Leaf persistence Deciduous	Leaf type

Family NYSSACEAE	Species *Nyssa sinensis*	Author Oliver

NYSSA SINENSIS

Leaves Oblong-lanceolate to elliptic, to 8 in (20 cm) long and 2½ in (6 cm) across, untoothed, reddish when young becoming deep green above, paler beneath, turning red, orange, and yellow in autumn. **Bark** Gray-brown, cracked and flaking with age. **Flowers** Males and females both very small and green, with five petals, in usually separate, long-stalked clusters in the leaf axils, on the same plant in summer. **Fruit** A bluish berry, about ⅜ in (1 cm) long.
• **NATIVE REGION** C. China.
• **HABITAT** Mountain woods and streambanks.
• **REMARK** A relative of the tupelo *(N. sylvatica*, see p.227).

leaves color brightly in autumn

taper-pointed leaves

tiny, green flowers

Height 50 ft (15 m)	Shape Broadly conical	Leaf persistence Deciduous	Leaf type

Family NYSSACEAE	Species *Nyssa sylvatica*	Author Marshall

TUPELO

Leaves Variable, ovate to elliptic or obovate, to 6 in (15 cm) long and 3 in (7.5 cm) across, tapering to a short, blunt point at the tip, untoothed, glossy dark green above, blue-green beneath, turning yellow to orange, red, or purple in autumn. **Bark** Dark gray, vertically ridged and breaking into square plates. **Flowers** Males and females both very small and green, with five petals, in usually separate, long-stalked clusters in the leaf axils, on the same plant in summer. **Fruit** A bluish berry, about ⅜ in (1 cm) long.
• **NATIVE REGION** E. North America.
• **HABITAT** Moist woods and swamps.
• **REMARK** Also known as black gum, pepperidge, sour gum.

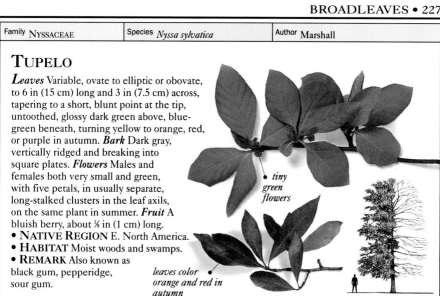

• *tiny green flowers*

leaves color orange and red in autumn

Height 80 ft (25 m)	Shape Broadly columnar	Leaf persistence Deciduous	Leaf type

OLEACEAE

A WIDELY DISTRIBUTED family of about 25 genera that contain nearly 1,000 species of deciduous and evergreen trees, shrubs, and climbers. The plants have opposite, sometimes compound, leaves. The small flowers are either with four petals, which are frequently joined, or without petals.

Family OLEACEAE	Species *Chionanthus retusus*	Author Lindley

CHINESE FRINGE TREE

Leaves Elliptic to ovate or obovate, to 4 in (10 cm) long and 2 in (5 cm) across, bluntly pointed or indented at the tip, very finely toothed or untoothed at the margin, glossy green above, paler and downy beneath. **Bark** Gray-brown, corky, deeply furrowed. **Flowers** Males and females both about ¼ in (2 cm) long, white, with four strap-shaped petals, borne in upright panicles at the ends of the young shoots, on separate plants in summer. **Fruit** An egg-shaped, deep blue berry, ⅝ in (1.5 cm) long.
• **NATIVE REGION** China, Japan.
• **HABITAT** Woods and on cliffs in sunny, moist places.

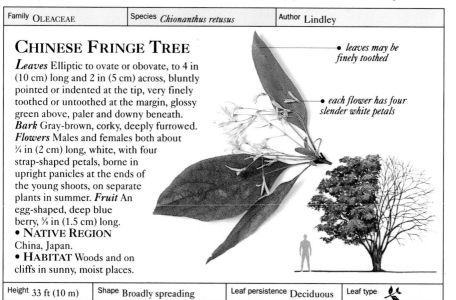

• *leaves may be finely toothed*

• *each flower has four slender white petals*

Height 33 ft (10 m)	Shape Broadly spreading	Leaf persistence Deciduous	Leaf type

Family OLEACEAE	Species *Chionanthus virginicus*	Author Linnaeus

FRINGE TREE

Leaves Elliptic, to 8 in (20 cm) long and 4 in (10 cm) across, tapered to a short point at the tip, untoothed, glossy green above, turning yellow in autumn. *Bark* Gray and smooth, furrowed with age. *Flowers* Males and females both to 1¼ in (3 cm) long, white, slightly fragrant, with four to six slender, strap-shaped petals, on slender, drooping stalks, borne in conical, upright panicles, male panicles to 8 in (20 cm) long, females shorter, usually on separate plants in summer. *Fruit* An egg-shaped, bloomy, deep blue berry, ¾ in (2 cm) long.
• **NATIVE REGION** E. United States.
• **HABITAT** Moist woods and riverbanks.
• **REMARK** Also known as old man's beard. This species can be either a shrub or a small tree.

• *taper-pointed leaves*

leaves have untoothed • *margin*

flowers have four • or six petals

Height 33 ft (10 m)	Shape Broadly spreading	Leaf persistence Deciduous	Leaf type

Family OLEACEAE	Species *Fraxinus americana*	Author Linnaeus

WHITE ASH

Leaves Pinnate, to 14 in (35 cm) long, with five to nine ovate to lanceolate, taper-pointed, sparsely toothed leaflets, to 4¾ in (12 cm) long and 3 in (7.5 cm) across, the lateral leaflets carried on short stalks, dark green and smooth above, blue-green to green and smooth or slightly hairy beneath, usually turning yellow or sometimes purple in autumn; winter leaf buds dark brown or nearly black. *Bark* Gray-brown, with narrow, interlacing ridges. *Flowers* Males and females both very small, green or purple, without petals, borne in clusters on separate plants in spring before the young leaves emerge. *Fruit* A key, to 2 in (5 cm) long, green ripening to pale brown, ending in a flattened wing, hanging in clusters.
• **NATIVE REGION** E. North America.
• **HABITAT** Rich woods.
• **REMARK** The trees produce a close-grained durable wood which is traditionally used for making tool handles.

• *leaflets edged with sparse teeth*

Height 100 ft (30 m)	Shape Broadly columnar	Leaf persistence Deciduous	Leaf type

| Family OLEACEAE | Species *Fraxinus angustifolia* | Author Vahl |

NARROW-LEAVED ASH

Leaves Pinnate, to 10 in (25 cm) long, with 7 to 13 lanceolate leaflets, to 3 in (7.5 cm) long and ¾ in (2 cm) across, with a slender, tapered point, sharply toothed, glossy bright green and smooth above, the lateral leaflets unstalked; winter buds dark brown. **Bark** Gray-brown, ridged. **Flowers** Very small, green or purple, without petals, borne in clusters in spring before the leaves. **Fruit** With a flattened wing at the end, to 1½ in (4 cm) long, green at first ripening to pale brown, in hanging clusters.
• **NATIVE REGION** N. Africa, S.W. Europe.
• **HABITAT** Woods and riversides.

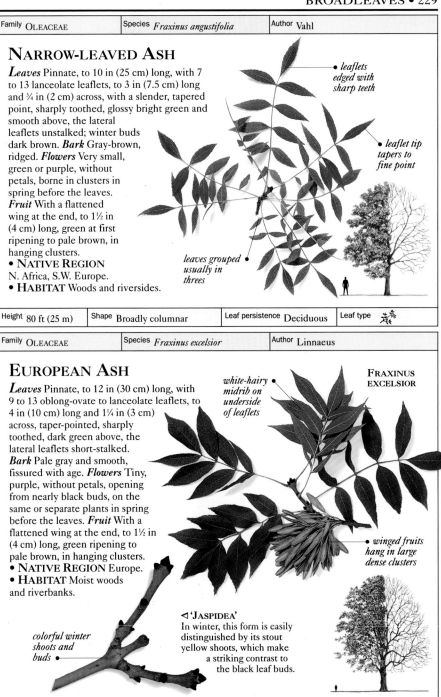

• *leaflets edged with sharp teeth*

• *leaflet tip tapers to fine point*

leaves grouped usually in threes •

| Height 80 ft (25 m) | Shape Broadly columnar | Leaf persistence Deciduous | Leaf type |

| Family OLEACEAE | Species *Fraxinus excelsior* | Author Linnaeus |

EUROPEAN ASH

Leaves Pinnate, to 12 in (30 cm) long, with 9 to 13 oblong-ovate to lanceolate leaflets, to 4 in (10 cm) long and 1¼ in (3 cm) across, taper-pointed, sharply toothed, dark green above, the lateral leaflets short-stalked. **Bark** Pale gray and smooth, fissured with age. **Flowers** Tiny, purple, without petals, opening from nearly black buds, on the same or separate plants in spring before the leaves. **Fruit** With a flattened wing at the end, to 1½ in (4 cm) long, green ripening to pale brown, in hanging clusters.
• **NATIVE REGION** Europe.
• **HABITAT** Moist woods and riverbanks.

white-hairy midrib on underside of leaflets •

FRAXINUS EXCELSIOR

• *winged fruits hang in large dense clusters*

colorful winter shoots and buds •

◁ '**JASPIDEA**'
In winter, this form is easily distinguished by its stout yellow shoots, which make a striking contrast to the black leaf buds.

| Height 130 ft (40 m) | Shape Broadly columnar | Leaf persistence Deciduous | Leaf type |

Family OLEACEAE	Species *Fraxinus ornus*	Author Linnaeus

FLOWERING ASH

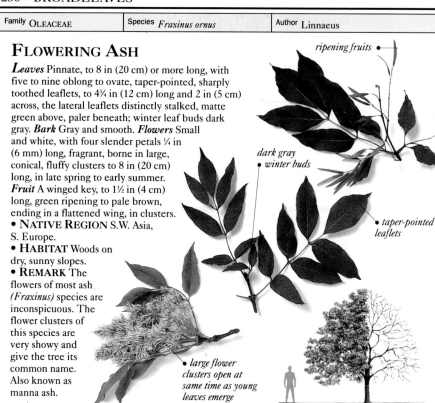

ripening fruits •

Leaves Pinnate, to 8 in (20 cm) or more long, with five to nine oblong to ovate, taper-pointed, sharply toothed leaflets, to 4¾ in (12 cm) long and 2 in (5 cm) across, the lateral leaflets distinctly stalked, matte green above, paler beneath; winter leaf buds dark gray. **Bark** Gray and smooth. **Flowers** Small and white, with four slender petals ¼ in (6 mm) long, fragrant, borne in large, conical, fluffy clusters to 8 in (20 cm) long, in late spring to early summer. **Fruit** A winged key, to 1½ in (4 cm) long, green ripening to pale brown, ending in a flattened wing, in clusters.
• **NATIVE REGION** S.W. Asia, S. Europe.
• **HABITAT** Woods on dry, sunny slopes.
• **REMARK** The flowers of most ash *(Fraxinus)* species are inconspicuous. The flower clusters of this species are very showy and give the tree its common name. Also known as manna ash.

dark gray
• winter buds

• taper-pointed
leaflets

• large flower
clusters open at
same time as young
leaves emerge

Height 65 ft (20 m)	Shape Broadly spreading	Leaf persistence Deciduous	Leaf type

Family OLEACEAE	Species *Fraxinus pennsylvanica*	Author Marshall

GREEN ASH

leaflets may
have sharply
toothed
• margin

Leaves Pinnate, to 12 in (30 cm) long, with five to nine ovate to lanceolate, taper-pointed, sharply toothed or sometimes smooth leaflets, to 4¾ in (12 cm) long and 2 in (5 cm) across, the lateral leaflets distinctly stalked, glossy dark green above, turning yellow in autumn; winter leaf buds with brown hairs. **Bark** Gray-brown, with narrow, interlacing ridges. **Flowers** Males and females very small, green or purple, with no petals, borne in clusters on separate plants in spring before the young leaves. **Fruit** A key, to 2 in (5 cm) long, green at first ripening to pale brown, ending in a flattened wing, hanging in clusters.
• **NATIVE REGION** North America.
• **HABITAT** Moist woods.

brown •
winter leaf
buds

Height 80 ft (25 m)	Shape Broadly columnar	Leaf persistence Deciduous	Leaf type

Family OLEACEAE	Species *Ligustrum lucidum*	Author Aiton f.

CHINESE PRIVET

Leaves Ovate, to 4 in (10 cm) long and 2 in (5 cm) across, tapering to a fine point at the tip, untoothed, bronze when young becoming glossy dark green above, paler and dull beneath, smooth on both sides. *Bark* Gray and smooth. *Flowers* Small and white, odd fragrance, with four joined petals, profusely borne in large, conical, upright panicles to 8 in (20 cm) long, over a long period in late summer and autumn. *Fruit* A blue-black berry, ⅜ in (1 cm) long.
• **NATIVE REGION** China.
• **HABITAT** Hillside woods and river valleys in mountains.
• **REMARK** This species, which can be either a large shrub or a small to medium-sized tree, is one of the evergreen privets. Its flowering season is unusually long.

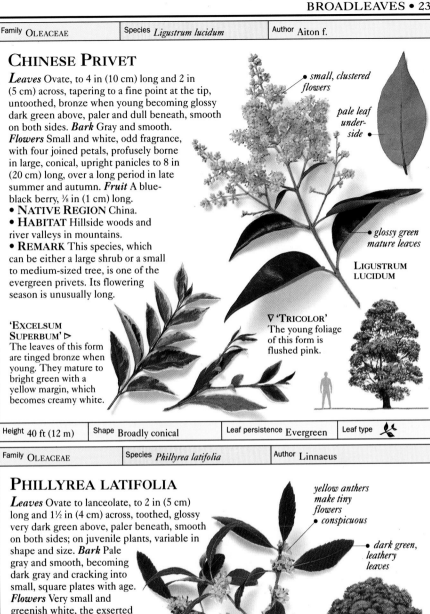

small, clustered flowers

pale leaf underside

glossy green mature leaves

LIGUSTRUM LUCIDUM

'EXCELSUM SUPERBUM' ▷
The leaves of this form are tinged bronze when young. They mature to bright green with a yellow margin, which becomes creamy white.

▽ 'TRICOLOR'
The young foliage of this form is flushed pink.

Height 40 ft (12 m)	Shape Broadly conical	Leaf persistence Evergreen	Leaf type

Family OLEACEAE	Species *Phillyrea latifolia*	Author Linnaeus

PHILLYREA LATIFOLIA

Leaves Ovate to lanceolate, to 2 in (5 cm) long and 1½ in (4 cm) across, toothed, glossy very dark green above, paler beneath, smooth on both sides; on juvenile plants, variable in shape and size. *Bark* Pale gray and smooth, becoming dark gray and cracking into small, square plates with age. *Flowers* Very small and greenish white, the exserted stamens with yellow anthers, borne in clusters in the leaf axils in late spring to early summer. *Fruit* A small, rounded, blue-black berry, about ⅜ in (1 cm) across.
• **NATIVE REGION** S. Europe.
• **HABITAT** Evergreen woods.

yellow anthers make tiny flowers conspicuous

dark green, leathery leaves

Height 33 ft (10 m)	Shape Broadly spreading	Leaf persistence Evergreen	Leaf type

PALMAE

T HE PALMS FORM A distinct group of more than 200 genera with over 2,500 species of mainly tropical distribution. In North America they are native to the southern States alone; Europe has two native species, in the western Mediterranean and in Crete.

Palms are trees or shrubs, sometimes climbing, that differ from other trees in several ways. With few exceptions, they have a single, unbranched stem which, once formed, does not increase in girth. The often very large leaves are mainly one of two types, either palmately divided, as in the fan palms (eg *Trachycarpus)*, or pinnately divided, as in the feather palms (eg *Phoenix)*. The small flowers have three sepals and three petals, and are often carried in very large, heavy clusters, males and females sometimes on separate plants.

Family PALMAE	Species *Trachycarpus fortunei*	Author (W.J. Hooker) Wendland

CHUSAN PALM

Leaves Fan-shaped, to 4 ft (120 cm) across, segmented, dark green above, blue-green beneath. *Bark* Densely covered with brown, fibrous remnants of old leaves. *Flowers* Very small and yellow, fragrant, in large, drooping panicles on separate plants in early summer. *Fruit* A rounded to kidney-shaped, three-lobed, blue-black berry, ½ in (1.2 cm) across.
• NATIVE REGION C. and S. China.
• HABITAT Mountain slopes.

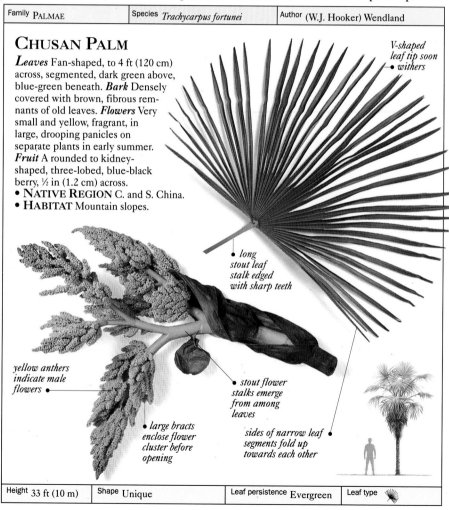

V-shaped
leaf tip soon
• withers

long
stout leaf
stalk edged
with sharp teeth

yellow anthers
indicate male
flowers •

• stout flower
stalks emerge
from among
leaves

• large bracts
enclose flower
cluster before
opening

sides of narrow leaf •
segments fold up
towards each other

Height 33 ft (10 m)	Shape Unique	Leaf persistence Evergreen	Leaf type

PITTOSPORACEAE

T HE NINE GENERA and more than 200 species in this family of evergreen trees, shrubs, and climbing plants are native to tropical regions, particularly Australasia. The leaves are alternate, most often untoothed. Small, usually tubular, five-lobed flowers develop into a dry or fleshy fruit.

Family PITTOSPORACEAE	Species *Pittosporum tenuifolium*	Author Gaertner

PITTOSPORUM TENUIFOLIUM

Leaves Oblong to elliptic, to 2½ in (6 cm) long and ¾ in (2 cm) across, with a wavy margin, light green, smooth, on deep purple-black shoots. **Bark** Dark gray and smooth. **Flowers** Small, tubular, about ⅜ in (1 cm) long, whitish, with five reflexed, deep red-purple lobes and yellow anthers, strongly fragrant, borne singly or in clusters in the leaf axils in late spring. **Fruit** A rounded capsule, about ½ in (1.2 cm) across, green ripening to nearly black.
• **NATIVE REGION** New Zealand.
• **HABITAT** Forests from coastline to mountain level.

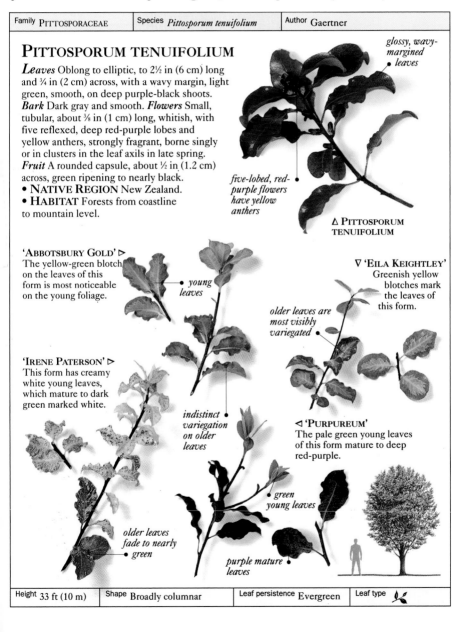

glossy, wavy-margined leaves

five-lobed, red-purple flowers have yellow anthers

△ PITTOSPORUM TENUIFOLIUM

'ABBOTSBURY GOLD' ▷
The yellow-green blotch on the leaves of this form is most noticeable on the young foliage.

young leaves

▽ **'EILA KEIGHTLEY'**
Greenish yellow blotches mark the leaves of this form.

older leaves are most visibly variegated

'IRENE PATERSON' ▷
This form has creamy white young leaves, which mature to dark green marked white.

indistinct variegation on older leaves

◁ **'PURPUREUM'**
The pale green young leaves of this form mature to deep red-purple.

green young leaves

older leaves fade to nearly green

purple mature leaves

Height 33 ft (10 m)	Shape Broadly columnar	Leaf persistence Evergreen	Leaf type

PLATANACEAE

T HE PLANE FAMILY CONSISTS of only one genus, *Platanus*, and seven species. The large, deciduous trees grow wild mainly in the United States and Mexico. The leaves are alternate and palmately lobed, except for those of the Southeast Asian *Platanus kerrii*, which are unlobed. The dense clusters of tiny flowers hang on slender stalks, either singly or in groups.

Family PLATANACEAE	Species *Platanus x acerifolia*	Author Willdenow

LONDON PLANE

Leaves Palmately lobed, to 8 in (20 cm) long and 10 in (25 cm) across, with three to five large toothed lobes, glossy bright green above, paler beneath, covered in scurfy brown hairs when young.
Bark Brown, gray, and cream, flaking in patches. *Flowers* Males and females both very small, males yellow, females reddish, borne in separate, small, rounded clusters on the same plant in late spring.
Fruit A rounded, dense cluster, 1 in (2.5 cm) across, green ripening to brown, covered in spiky brown bristles, hanging two to four together, persisting over winter.
• **NATIVE REGION**
Of garden origin.
• **REMARK** Also known as *Platanus x hispanica*. This species is probably a hybrid between the American sycamore *(Platanus occidentalis*, see p.235) and the oriental plane *(Platanus orientalis*, see p.235).

veins usually meet near leaf base

bright green leaf • upperside

paler green • leaf underside

leaf lobes • edged with sharp teeth

up to four fruits hang together on a single stalk

Height 115 ft (35 m)	Shape Broadly columnar	Leaf persistence Deciduous	Leaf type

| Family PLATANACEAE | Species *Platanus occidentalis* | Author Linnaeus |

AMERICAN SYCAMORE

Leaves Palmately lobed, to 8 in (20 cm) long and across, with three lobes, glossy green above, paler beneath. *Bark* Gray, brown, cream, flaking. *Flowers* Very small, males yellow, females reddish, in separate, rounded clusters on the same plant in late spring. *Fruit* A rounded, dense, brown cluster, 1 in (2.5 cm) across.
• **NATIVE REGION**
E. North America.
• **HABITAT** Rich, moist soil.

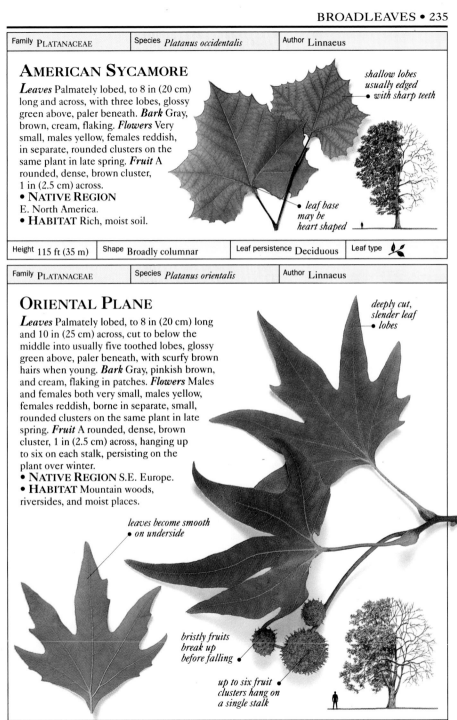

shallow lobes usually edged with sharp teeth

leaf base may be heart shaped

| Height 115 ft (35 m) | Shape Broadly columnar | Leaf persistence Deciduous | Leaf type |

| Family PLATANACEAE | Species *Platanus orientalis* | Author Linnaeus |

ORIENTAL PLANE

Leaves Palmately lobed, to 8 in (20 cm) long and 10 in (25 cm) across, cut to below the middle into usually five toothed lobes, glossy green above, paler beneath, with scurfy brown hairs when young. *Bark* Gray, pinkish brown, and cream, flaking in patches. *Flowers* Males and females both very small, males yellow, females reddish, borne in separate, small, rounded clusters on the same plant in late spring. *Fruit* A rounded, dense, brown cluster, 1 in (2.5 cm) across, hanging up to six on each stalk, persisting on the plant over winter.
• **NATIVE REGION** S.E. Europe.
• **HABITAT** Mountain woods, riversides, and moist places.

deeply cut, slender leaf lobes

leaves become smooth on underside

bristly fruits break up before falling

up to six fruit clusters hang on a single stalk

| Height 100 ft (30 m) | Shape Broadly columnar | Leaf persistence Deciduous | Leaf type |

PROTEACEAE

SOME 75 GENERA and over 1,000 species of evergreen trees and shrubs are included in this family. Native to the southern hemisphere, they grow wild throughout this part of the world. Some species extend also to warm regions of the northern hemisphere. The leaves are alternate, simple to pinnate; the flowers have a petal-like calyx divided into four lobes, although the petals themselves are very small and inconspicuous.

Proteaceae is best known for its ornamental plants (eg species of *Grevillea*, *Banksia*, *Protea*, and *Telopea)*, and for *Macadamia* species, cultivated in Australia and Hawaii for their edible nuts.

Family PROTEACEAE	Species *Embothrium coccineum*	Author J.R. & J.G. Forster

CHILEAN FIRE BUSH

Leaves Elliptic to oblong, variable, to 6 in (15 cm) long and 1¼ in (3 cm) across, untoothed, dark green to blue-green above, paler beneath, leathery, smooth on both sides. **Bark** Purple-brown, smooth, flaking with age. **Flowers** Tubular at first, to 2 in (5 cm) long, splitting into four lobes, the lobes curling backward leaving the style protruding, bright orange-red, borne in clusters in late spring to early summer. **Fruit** A woody capsule, to 1¼ in (3 cm) long, with a long beak.
• **NATIVE REGION** Argentina, Chile.
• **HABITAT** Open places, at all altitudes from the coast to the mountains.
• **REMARK** This species is one of the most striking representatives of its family.

open flowers have curled lobes

flower lobes closed over long style

leaves are evergreen only in mild climates

flowers borne in axillary racemes

young shoot in leaf axil

Height 30 ft (9 m)	Shape Broadly columnar	Leaf persistence Evergreen	Leaf type

RHAMNACEAE

T HE 60 GENERA AND around 900 species of deciduous and evergreen trees, shrubs, and climbing plants belonging to this family grow wild in all parts of the world. They are sometimes spiny, bearing alternate or opposite leaves, and small male and female flowers, found sometimes on separate plants. Several species of buckthorn *(Rhamnus)* yield dyes.

Family RHAMNACEAE	Species *Rhamnus cathartica*	Author Linnaeus

COMMON BUCKTHORN

Leaves Broadly ovate to nearly rounded, to 2½ in (6 cm) long and 1½ in (4 cm) across, with a short point at the tip, finely toothed, glossy green above, paler beneath, turning yellow in autumn, borne on sparsely spiny shoots. **Bark** Dark orange-brown and scaly. **Flowers** Small, with tiny petals and a green, four-lobed calyx, fragrant, in clusters in early to midsummer. **Fruit** Rounded, fleshy, berrylike, to ⅜ in (1 cm) across, green ripening to black.
• **NATIVE REGION** Asia, Europe.
• **HABITAT** Woods, thickets, and hedgerows, on chalky soil.

dense clusters of ripe fruits

rounded teeth at leaf margin

tiny, green flowers

Height 33 ft (10 m)	Shape Broadly spreading	Leaf persistence Deciduous	Leaf type

Family RHAMNACEAE	Species *Rhamnus frangula*	Author Linnaeus

ALDER BUCKTHORN

Leaves Obovate, to 2¾ in (7 cm) long and 1½ in (4 cm) across, with a short, blunt point, untoothed, glossy dark green above, paler beneath, turning red in autumn. **Bark** Gray, smooth, with vertical, shallow, pale cracks. **Flowers** Very small, with tiny petals and a green, five-lobed calyx, in clusters in early to late summer. **Fruit** Rounded, fleshy, and berrylike, to ⅜ in (1 cm) across, green becoming red ripening to black.
• **NATIVE REGION** N. Africa, W. Asia, Europe.
• **HABITAT** Woods and scrub, usually on wet soil.
• **REMARK** Also known as *Frangula alnus*.

glossy dark leaf surface

fruits ripen from red to black

untoothed leaves

tiny, pink-tinged flowers

Height 17 ft (5 m)	Shape Broadly spreading	Leaf persistence Deciduous	Leaf type

ROSACEAE

THIS FAMILY is a widely distributed and very important collection of deciduous and evergreen trees, shrubs, and herbaceous plants, containing over 100 genera and 3,000 species.

———— 🌿 ————

The leaves are usually alternate, and vary from simple and untoothed to pinnate. The flowers are usually five-petaled. Several different types of fruit are produced, and the family is divided into groups on the basis of their structure. The trees in this book fall into two of these groups. Both have fleshy, often edible, fruits, but whereas those of *Prunus* species contain only a single seed, those of *Amelanchier*, *Cotoneaster*, *Crataegus*, *Malus*, *Mespilus*, *Photinia*, *Pyrus*, and *Sorbus* contain two or more seeds.

Family ROSACEAE	Species *Amelanchier arborea*	Author (A. Michaux) Fernald

SERVICEBERRY

Leaves Ovate to obovate, to 3 in (7.5 cm) long and 1½ in (4 cm) across, rounded to heart-shaped at the base, usually short-pointed at the tip, finely toothed, becoming deep green above, folded and white with hairs when young becoming smooth beneath, turning orange to red in autumn. *Bark* Gray and smooth when young, becoming ridged and scaly with age. *Flowers* White, with five narrow petals, in upright racemes to 2 in (5 cm) long, in spring before the leaves are fully open. *Fruit* A rounded, dry or juicy, sweet, edible, reddish purple berry, to ⁵⁄₁₆ in (8 mm) across, ripening in summer.
• **NATIVE REGION** C. and E. United States.
• **HABITAT** Woods and thickets, on moist soil.
• **REMARK** Also known as downy serviceberry, shadblow.

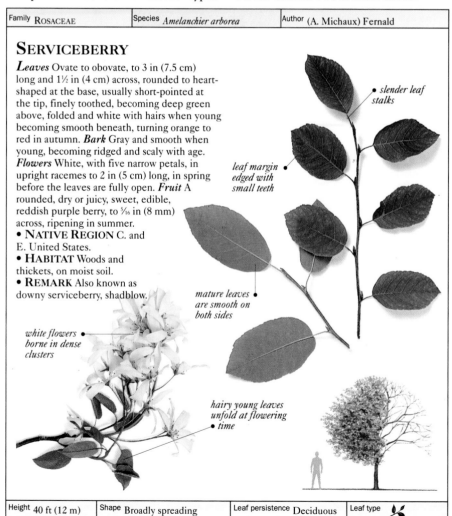

slender leaf stalks

leaf margin edged with small teeth

mature leaves are smooth on both sides

white flowers borne in dense clusters

hairy young leaves unfold at flowering time

Height 40 ft (12 m)	Shape Broadly spreading	Leaf persistence Deciduous	Leaf type

Family ROSACEAE	Species *Amelanchier asiatica*	Author (Siebold & Zuccarini) Walpers

AMELANCHIER ASIATICA

Leaves Ovate, to 3 in (7.5 cm) long and 1½ in (4 cm) across, rounded at the base, pointed, toothed, dark green above, hairy then smooth beneath, turning orange and red in autumn. **Bark** Gray-brown, fissured with age. **Flowers** White, in upright later spreading racemes to 2½ in (6 cm) long, in spring. **Fruit** Black-purple, to ⅜ in (1 cm) across.
• **NATIVE REGION** China, Japan, Korea.
• **HABITAT** Dry, sunny sites.

five narrow flower petals

finely toothed leaves

pointed leaf tip

Height 40 ft (12 m)	Shape Broadly spreading	Leaf persistence Deciduous	Leaf type

Family ROSACEAE	Species *Amelanchier laevis*	Author Wiegand

ALLEGHENY SERVICEBERRY

Leaves Elliptic to ovate or obovate, to 2½ in (6 cm) long and 1 in (2.5 cm) across, pointed, finely toothed, bronze-red becoming dark green above, smooth, turning red or orange in autumn. **Bark** Gray-brown and smooth. **Flowers** White, with five narrow petals, in upright to spreading racemes to 3 in (7.5 cm) long, in spring. **Fruit** Rounded, juicy, purple-black, 5/16 in (8 mm) across.
• **NATIVE REGION** E. North America.
• **HABITAT** Woods, thickets.

flowers borne in open clusters

smooth, bronze young leaves

Height 40 ft (12 m)	Shape Broadly spreading	Leaf persistence Deciduous	Leaf type

Family ROSACEAE	Species *Amelanchier lamarckii*	Author Schroeder

AMELANCHIER LAMARCKII

Leaves Ovate to elliptic, to 3 in (7.5 cm) long and 1½ in (4 cm) across, usually rounded at the base, pointed, finely toothed, bronze becoming dark green. **Bark** Gray, smooth, developing vertical, narrow cracks. **Flowers** White, with five narrow petals, borne in upright or spreading racemes to 3 in (7.5 cm) long, in spring. **Fruit** Rounded, juicy, and purple-black, ⅜ in (1 cm) across.
• **NATIVE REGION** Europe.
• **HABITAT** Sandy soil.

red autumn leaves

silky-hairy young leaves

Height 40 ft (12 m)	Shape Broadly spreading	Leaf persistence Deciduous	Leaf type

Family ROSACEAE	Species *Cotoneaster frigidus*	Author Wallich

COTONEASTER FRIGIDUS

Leaves Elliptic to ovate, to 4¾ in (12 cm) long and 2 in (5 cm) across, rounded at the tip, untoothed, often with a wavy margin, matte dark green and smooth above, gray and hairy at least when young beneath. **Bark** Gray, flaking with age. **Flowers** ⁵⁄₁₆ in (8 mm) across, white, in dense, flattened heads to 4 in (10 cm) across, in midsummer. **Fruit** Rounded, bright red, ³⁄₁₆ in (5 mm) across, borne in hanging clusters on thick stems.
• **NATIVE REGION**
The Himalayas.
• **HABITAT** Thickets and riverbanks.
• **REMARK** Can be either a small tree or a large shrub.

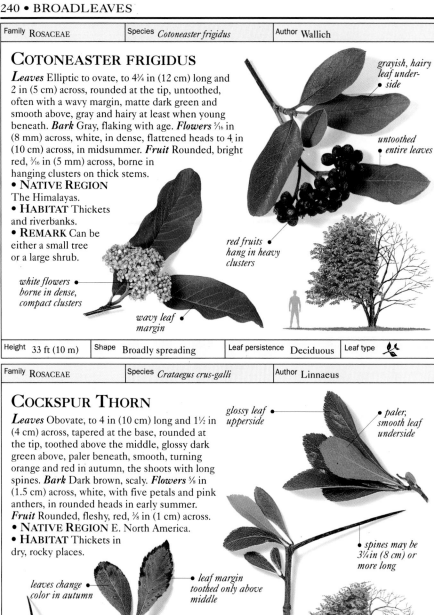

grayish, hairy leaf underside

untoothed entire leaves

red fruits hang in heavy clusters

white flowers borne in dense, compact clusters

wavy leaf margin

Height 33 ft (10 m)	Shape Broadly spreading	Leaf persistence Deciduous	Leaf type

Family ROSACEAE	Species *Crataegus crus-galli*	Author Linnaeus

COCKSPUR THORN

Leaves Obovate, to 4 in (10 cm) long and 1½ in (4 cm) across, tapered at the base, rounded at the tip, toothed above the middle, glossy dark green above, paler beneath, smooth, turning orange and red in autumn, the shoots with long spines. **Bark** Dark brown, scaly. **Flowers** ⁵⁄₈ in (1.5 cm) across, white, with five petals and pink anthers, in rounded heads in early summer. **Fruit** Rounded, fleshy, red, ³⁄₈ in (1 cm) across.
• **NATIVE REGION** E. North America.
• **HABITAT** Thickets in dry, rocky places.

glossy leaf upperside

paler, smooth leaf underside

spines may be 3¼ in (8 cm) or more long

leaves change color in autumn

leaf margin toothed only above middle

red fruits persist through winter to following spring

Height 26 ft (8 m)	Shape Broadly spreading	Leaf persistence Deciduous	Leaf type

Family ROSACEAE	Species *Crataegus laciniata*	Author Ucria

CRATAEGUS LACINIATA

Leaves Diamond-shaped, to 2 in (5 cm) long and across, lobed, the lobes often toothed at the tip, glossy dark green above, gray and hairy beneath. **Bark** Gray, flaking in thin plates. **Flowers** ¼ in (2 cm) across, white, with five petals and pink anthers, in dense clusters in early summer. **Fruit** Rounded or slightly oblong, red or red flushed yellow, ¾ in (2 cm) long, with a flattened top.
• NATIVE REGION S.W. Asia, S.E. Europe.
• HABITAT Wood margins and thickets.

sharply toothed stipules

three or four lobes each side of leaf

ornamental fruits

Height 20 ft (6 m)	Shape Broadly spreading	Leaf persistence Deciduous	Leaf type

Family ROSACEAE	Species *Crataegus laevigata*	Author (Poiret) Candolle

ENGLISH HAWTHORN

Leaves Ovate to obovate, to 2 in (5 cm) long and across, shallowly lobed, toothed, glossy dark green above, paler beneath, becoming smooth. **Bark** Gray, smooth, cracking with age. **Flowers** ¾ in (2 cm) across, usually white, with five petals, borne in small clusters in late spring. **Fruit** Rounded to oval, red, to ¾ in (2 cm) long.
• NATIVE REGION Europe.
• HABITAT Woods and hedgerows.

▽ 'GIREOUDII'
The green young leaves of this form are later followed by variegated foliage.

each fruit has two stones

vibrantly deep pink double flowers

◁ 'PAUL'S SCARLET'
This lovely cultivar is selected for its flowers, borne through late spring and early summer.

creamy-mottled leaves

Height 33 ft (10 m)	Shape Broadly spreading	Leaf persistence Deciduous	Leaf type

Family ROSACEAE	Species *Crataegus x lavallei*	Author Herincq ex Lavallée

CRATAEGUS X LAVALLEI

Leaves Obovate to elliptic, to 4 in (10 cm) long and 2 in (5 cm) across, tapered at the base, pointed at the tip, toothed, glossy dark green and smooth above, paler and hairy beneath. **Bark** Gray, flaking in plates. **Flowers** 1 in (2.5 cm) across, white, with five petals and pink anthers, in flattened heads on downy stalks in early to midsummer. **Fruit** Rounded, red, ¾ in (2 cm) across.
• **NATIVE REGION**
Of garden origin.
• **REMARK** A hybrid between cockspur thorn *(Crataegus crus-galli*, see p.240) and *Crataegus pubescens*, formerly known as *Crataegus carrierei*.

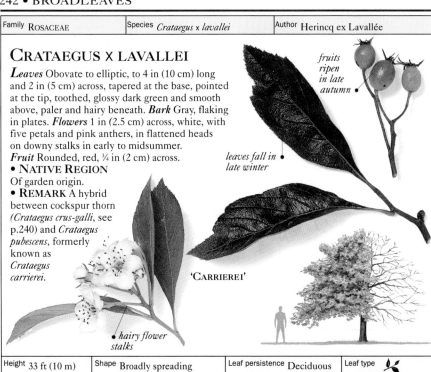

fruits ripen in late autumn

leaves fall in late winter

'CARRIEREI'

• hairy flower stalks

Height 33 ft (10 m)	Shape Broadly spreading	Leaf persistence Deciduous	Leaf type

Family ROSACEAE	Species *Crataegus mollis*	Author (Torrey & Gray) Scheele

DOWNY HAWTHORN

Leaves Broadly ovate, to 4 in (10 cm) long and across, with four or five shallow lobes on each side, sharply toothed, dark green and hairy above, hairy particularly when young beneath; shoots with glossy spines to 2 in (5 cm) long. **Bark** Red-brown becoming gray-brown, cracking vertically into scaly plates. **Flowers** 1 in (2.5 cm) across, white, with five petals and yellow anthers, in broad heads on downy stalks in late spring to early summer. **Fruit** Rounded, downy, red, to 1 in (2.5 cm) across.
• **NATIVE REGION**
C. United States.
• **HABITAT** Near streams in woods, often on limestone.

shallow, toothed leaf lobes •

large • stipules at leaf base

• fruits ripen from green to red

• spiny or nearly spineless shoots

Height 40 ft (12 m)	Shape Broadly columnar	Leaf persistence Deciduous	Leaf type

Family ROSACEAE	Species *Crataegus monogyna*	Author Jacquin

COMMON HAWTHORN

Leaves Ovate to obovate, to 2 in (5 cm) or more long and nearly the same across, deeply cut into pointed, toothed lobes, glossy dark green and smooth above, paler and smooth with hairs in the vein axils beneath. *Bark* Orange-brown, cracking. *Flowers* To ⅝ in (1.5 cm) across, white, in clusters in late spring. *Fruit* Oval, red, to ½ in (1.2 cm) across.
• **NATIVE REGION** Europe.
• **HABITAT** Woods and thickets.

flowers have pink anthers

red fruits contain a single stone

each leaf side has one to three lobes

Height 33 ft (10 m)	Shape Broadly spreading	Leaf persistence Deciduous	Leaf type

Family ROSACEAE	Species *Crataegus phaenopyrum*	Author Linnaeus f.

WASHINGTON THORN

Leaves Broadly ovate, with three or five pointed, sharply toothed lobes, glossy dark green and smooth above, paler and smooth or sparsely hairy beneath. *Bark* Red-brown to gray-brown, thin, scaly. *Flowers* ½ in (1.2 cm) across, with five petals, in clusters in early to midsummer. *Fruit* Rounded, small, red, ¼ in (6 mm) across.
• **NATIVE REGION** S.E. United States.
• **HABITAT** Woods and thickets.

shoots carry long spines

small glossy fruits ripen late

Height 40 ft (12 m)	Shape Broadly spreading	Leaf persistence Deciduous	Leaf type

Family ROSACEAE	Species *Crataegus prunifolia*	Author (Lamarck) Person

CRATAEGUS PRUNIFOLIA

Leaves Broadly elliptic to obovate, to 3 in (7.5 cm) long and 2½ in (6 cm) across, sharply toothed, glossy dark green and smooth above, hairy on the veins beneath. *Bark* Purple-brown and cracking. *Flowers* ⅝ in (1.5 cm) across, white, with five petals, in rounded clusters in early summer. *Fruit* Rounded, bright red, ⅝ in (1.5 cm) across.
• **NATIVE REGION** Of garden origin.
• **REMARK** Possibly a hybrid between cockspur thorn *(C. crus-galli,* see p.240) and *C. macracantha.*

fruits shrivel before falling

leaves change color in autumn

spiny shoots

Height 20 ft (6 m)	Shape Broadly spreading	Leaf persistence Deciduous	Leaf type

Family ROSACEAE	Species x *Crataemespilus grandiflora*	Author (W.W. Smith) E.G. Camus

x CRATAEMESPILUS GRANDIFLORA

Leaves Elliptic to obovate, to 3 in (7.5 cm) long
and 2 in (5 cm) across, glossy green above, turning bright orange in autumn; on vigorous shoots
deeply lobed. *Bark* Pale orange-brown, flaking
in thin plates. *Flowers* 1 in (2.5 cm) across,
white, with five petals, borne in
clusters of up to three in late spring.
Fruit Rounded, slightly hairy, glossy
orange-brown, ¾ in (2 cm) across.
• NATIVE REGION Of garden origin.
• REMARK Thought to be a hybrid
between the Midland hawthorn
(Crataegus laevigata, see p.241)
and the medlar *(Mespilus
germanica,* see p.255).

+ CRATAEGOMESPILUS ▽
DARDARII 'JULES
D'ASNIÈRES'
This graft hybrid
has rounded leaf
lobes, smaller flowers,
and small, brown fruits.

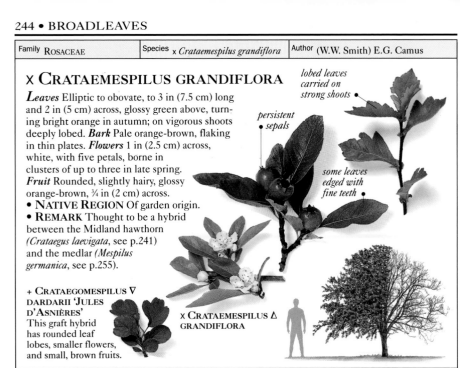

lobed leaves
carried on
strong shoots •

persistent
• sepals

some leaves
edged with
fine teeth •

x CRATAEMESPILUS △
GRANDIFLORA

Height 26 ft (8 m)	Shape Broadly spreading	Leaf persistence Deciduous	Leaf type

Family ROSACEAE	Species *Cydonia oblonga*	Author Miller

QUINCE

Leaves Broadly elliptic to ovate, to
4 in (10 cm) long and 2½ in (6 cm) across,
untoothed, grayish white and downy when
young becoming dark green above, gray and
downy beneath, on short stalks. *Bark* Purple-
brown, flaking; orange-brown when freshly
exposed. *Flowers* 2 in (5 cm) across, pale pink
or white, with five petals, borne singly in late
spring. *Fruit* Pear- or sometimes apple-shaped,
yellow, to 4 in (10 cm) long, downy at first
becoming oily to the touch, very fragrant;
on wild plants much smaller.
• NATIVE REGION C. and S.W. Asia.
• HABITAT Wood margins, forests, and
mountain slopes, often on limestone.

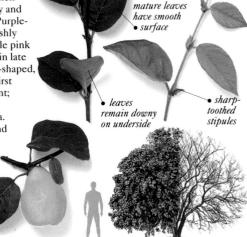

hairy young
leaves •

mature leaves
have smooth
• surface

• leaves
remain downy
on underside

• sharp-
toothed
stipules

thin-skinned
fruits have very
hard flesh •

Height 17 ft (5 m)	Shape Broadly spreading	Leaf persistence Deciduous	Leaf type

| Family ROSACEAE | Species *Malus baccata* | Author (Linnaeus) Borkhausen |

SIBERIAN CRAB APPLE

Leaves Elliptic to ovate, to 3 in (7.5 cm) long and 1½ in (4 cm) across, tapered to a pointed tip, finely toothed, dark green above, paler beneath, smooth on both sides. *Bark* Gray-brown, flaking in square plates; red-brown when freshly exposed. *Flowers* Individually to 1½ in (4 cm) across, white tinged pink opening white, with five petals and yellow anthers, fragrant, borne in clusters in mid-spring at the same time as the young leaves emerge. *Fruit* Rounded, small, red or yellow, ⅜ in (1 cm) across.
• **NATIVE REGION** E. Asia.
• **HABITAT** Woods and scrub.

pale green young leaves unfold as flowers open

small fruits carried on slender stalks

leaf margin edged with fine teeth

| Height 50 ft (15 m) | Shape Broadly spreading | Leaf persistence Deciduous | Leaf type |

| Family ROSACEAE | Species *Malus coronaria* | Author (Linnaeus) Miller |

WILD SWEET CRAB APPLE

Leaves Ovate, to 4 in (10 cm) long and 2½ in (6 cm) across, sharply often double-toothed, reddish and downy becoming deep green above, smooth; on vigorous shoots lobed towards the base. *Bark* Red-brown, scaly, vertically fissured. *Flowers* 2 in (5 cm) across, pink, borne in clusters in late spring. *Fruit* Rounded, green, 1½ in (4 cm) across, slightly broader than long.
• **NATIVE REGION** E. North America.
• **HABITAT** Woods and thickets.

fragrant flowers

leaves often color in autumn

MALUS CORONARIA

hairy underside of young leaf

hard fruits remain green

◁ **'CHARLOTTAE'**
This form has double, violet-scented flowers.

| Height 30 ft (9 m) | Shape Broadly spreading | Leaf persistence Deciduous | Leaf type |

Family ROSACEAE	Species *Malus domestica*	Author Borkhausen

COMMON APPLE

Leaves Ovate to broadly elliptic, to 4¾ in (12 cm) long and 3 in (7.5 cm) across, toothed, yellowish green becoming dark green above, usually hairy at least beneath. *Bark* Gray-brown to purple-brown, peeling in small, thin flakes. *Flowers* To 2 in (5 cm) across, white flushed pink, with five petals, borne in clusters in late spring. *Fruit* Very variable, rounded, sweet to sour, edible, to 4 in (10 cm) or more across, green to yellow or variously streaked with, to entirely, red.
• **NATIVE REGION**
Of garden origin.
• **REMARK** A hybrid involving several European and Asian species, long cultivated for its edible fruit, now widely grown in temperate regions of the world.

young leaves at tip • of woody shoot

deep pink • flower buds

• edible fruits contain many seeds

Height 33 ft (10 m)	Shape Broadly spreading	Leaf persistence Deciduous	Leaf type

Family ROSACEAE	Species *Malus florentina*	Author (Zuccagni) Schneider

MALUS FLORENTINA

Leaves Broadly ovate, to 2½ in (6 cm) long and 2 in (5 cm) across, lobed, toothed, deep green above, densely hairy beneath, turning purple and red in autumn. *Bark* Red- to purple-brown, flaking freely in small, thin, square plates; orange-brown when freshly exposed. *Flowers* ¾ in (2 cm) across, white, with five petals and yellow anthers, in clusters in late spring to early summer. *Fruit* Rounded to pear-shaped, reddish orange, about ⅜ in (1 cm) across.
• **NATIVE REGION** N. Italy to N. Turkey.
• **HABITAT** Scrub and rocky slopes.
• **REMARK** Possibly a hybrid between a crab apple *(Malus)* and the wild service tree *(Sorbus torminalis*, see p.282), rarely seen in the wild.

leaves turn purple as fruits ripen

• small fruits carried on long, slender stalks

• yellowish unripe fruit

sharply • pointed lobes

• flowers borne in open clusters

Height 26 ft (8 m)	Shape Broadly columnar	Leaf persistence Deciduous	Leaf type

Family ROSACEAE	Species *Malus floribunda*	Author Siebold ex van Houtte

JAPANESE CRAB APPLE

Leaves Elliptic, to 4 in (10 cm) long and 2 in
(5 cm) across, taper-pointed, sharply toothed,
dark green and smooth above, hairy when
young beneath; on vigorous shoots sometimes
lobed. *Bark* Purple-brown, flaking in thin
plates with age. *Flowers* 1 in (2.5 cm) across,
deep red in bud opening pale pink becoming
white, with five petals, very profuse, borne in
clusters in mid-spring. *Fruit* Rounded and
yellow, ¾ in (2 cm) across.
• **NATIVE REGION** Of garden origin.
• **REMARK** A hybrid of
unknown origin,
introduced to
the West from
Japan.

*sharp teeth at
edge of leaf
margin*

*flowers open
from deep
red buds*

*one or more
fruits clustered
together on long,
slender stalks*

Height 17 ft (5 m)	Shape Broadly spreading	Leaf persistence Deciduous	Leaf type

Family ROSACEAE	Species *Malus hupehensis*	Author (Pampanini) Rehder

MALUS HUPEHENSIS (CRAB APPLE)

Leaves Elliptic to ovate, to 4 in (10 cm) long
and 2¼ in (6 cm) across, taper-pointed, finely
toothed, becoming dark green and smooth
above. *Bark* Purple-brown, flaking in
rectangular plates; orange-brown when
freshly exposed. *Flowers* 2 in (5 cm)
across, pink in bud opening white, with
five broad, overlapping petals,
fragrant, usually very profuse,
borne in large clusters in mid-
spring. *Fruit* Rounded and
rather flattened, deep red, ⅜ in
(1 cm) across, hanging in clusters
on long, slender, red stalks, persisting
long after the leaves have fallen.
• **NATIVE REGION** China.
• **HABITAT** Mountain
woodlands.

*flowers
borne on very
long stalks*

*leaves edged
with small
teeth*

*glossy fruits
resemble tiny
cherries*

Height 40 ft (12 m)	Shape Broadly spreading	Leaf persistence Deciduous	Leaf type

Family ROSACEAE	Species *Malus ioensis*	Author (Wood) Britton

PRAIRIE CRAB APPLE

Leaves Broadly ovate, to 4 in (10 cm) long and 2 in (5 cm) across, shallowly lobed, toothed, glossy green above, downy beneath, turning bright orange-red in autumn. **Bark** Reddish to purplish brown, and flaking. **Flowers** Pink to white, with five petals, borne in clusters of up to six in spring. **Fruit** Rounded, smooth, hard, and acid, pale green or green flushed red, 1½ in (4 cm) across.
• **NATIVE REGION** C. United States.
• **HABITAT** Moist streambanks and wood margins.

very glossy mature leaves

flaking bark reveals orange-brown wood beneath

MALUS IOENSIS

▽ 'PLENA'
Known as Bechtel's crab, this form has semidouble flowers, which fade from pink to white.

hard fruits carried on short stalks

semidouble flowers borne in clusters

single flowers

Height 26 ft (8 m)	Shape Broadly spreading	Leaf persistence Deciduous	Leaf type

Family ROSACEAE	Species *Malus prunifolia*	Author (Willdenow) Borkhausen

MALUS PRUNIFOLIA

Leaves Elliptic to ovate, to 4 in (10 cm) long and 2½ in (6 cm) across, toothed, dark green. **Bark** Purple-brown to gray-brown, flaking in rectangular plates; red-brown when freshly exposed. **Flowers** 1½ in (4 cm) across, pink in bud opening white, with five petals, fragrant, in clusters of up to ten in mid-spring. **Fruit** Rounded to egg-shaped, bright red, 1 in (2.5 cm) across, with persistent, woolly sepals at the top.
• **NATIVE REGION** Of garden origin.
• **REMARK** Also known as plum-leaved crab apple. Although its precise origin is not established, this hybrid is thought to have been introduced to the West from N.E. Asia.

flowers borne in compact clusters

leaves vary in shape

persistent sepals at top of fruits

Height 33 ft (10 m)	Shape Broadly spreading	Leaf persistence Deciduous	Leaf type

Family ROSACEAE	Species *Malus x purpurea*	Author (Barbier) Rehder

MALUS X PURPUREA

Leaves Elliptic to narrowly ovate, to 3 in (7.5 cm) long, pointed, toothed, purplish green. *Bark* Purple-brown, cracked, flaking. *Flowers* 1½ in (4 cm) across, opening deep purple-pink, borne in clusters in spring. *Fruit* Rounded, deep reddish purple, 1 in (2.5 cm) across.
• **NATIVE REGION** Of garden origin.
• **REMARK** A hybrid between *M. x atrosanguinea* and *M. niedzwetzkyana*.

flowers have
• *five petals*

Height 26 ft (8 m)	Shape Broadly spreading	Leaf persistence Deciduous	Leaf type

Family ROSACEAE	Species *Malus sieboldii*	Author (Regel) Rehder

TORINGO CRAB APPLE

Leaves Elliptic to ovate, to 2½ in (6 cm) long and 1¼ in (3 cm) across, taper-pointed, toothed, matte deep green above, paler beneath, downy on both sides when young becoming nearly smooth; on vigorous shoots with three to five lobes. *Bark* Dark gray, cracking into small plates. *Flowers* ¾ in (2 cm) across, pink in bud opening white, with five petals, fragrant, in small clusters in mid-spring. *Fruit* Rounded, red or yellow, ⅜ in (1 cm) across, with no sepals when ripe, on slender stalks, persisting for some time.
• **NATIVE REGION** Japan.
• **HABITAT** Moist, sunny situations.

• *strong shoots have deeply lobed leaves*

small flowers carried on slender stalks

coarsely • *toothed lobes*

green stalks become • *red as fruits ripen*

Height 33 ft (10 m)	Shape Broadly weeping	Leaf persistence Deciduous	Leaf type

Family ROSACEAE	Species *Malus transitoria*	Author (Batalin) Schneider

MALUS TRANSITORIA

Leaves Variable, small and oblong, to 1 in (2.5 cm) long on short shoots, larger, to 3 in (7.5 cm) long and 2½ in (6 cm) across on vigorous shoots, deeply cut into three lobes, the central lobe with a lobe on each side, sharply toothed, bright green above, paler beneath, thinly hairy. **Bark** Purple-brown, cracking into smooth, vertical, rectangular plates. **Flowers** ¾ in (2 cm) across, white, with five petals, in small clusters in late spring. **Fruit** Tiny, yellow, ⁵⁄₁₆ in (8 mm) across, slightly flattened, carried on slender, red stalks.
• **NATIVE REGION** N.W. China.
• **HABITAT** Woods and thickets.

tiny fruits carried on thread-like stalks

small stipules at base of leaf stalk

pink flower buds

small clusters of narrow-petaled flowers

Height 33 ft (10 m)	Shape Broadly spreading	Leaf persistence Deciduous	Leaf type

Family ROSACEAE	Species *Malus trilobata*	Author (Labillardière) Schneider

MALUS TRILOBATA

Leaves To 3½ in (9 cm) long and 4¾ in (12 cm) across, with three deep lobes, the central lobe cut into three or more lobes, the basal lobes each with one or more lobes, glossy dark green and smooth above, paler and hairy beneath, turning yellow, red, and purple in autumn. **Bark** Dark gray-brown, cracking into numerous small squares, on a fluted trunk. **Flowers** 1½ in (4 cm) across, white, with five petals and yellow anthers, opening from woolly buds, borne in clusters at the ends of the shoots in summer. **Fruit** Small and hard, green or green flushed red, ¾ in (2 cm) across.
• **NATIVE REGION** S.W. Asia, Greece.
• **HABITAT** Woods and thickets.

bark cracks into many small plates

large flowers remain cup-shaped

deeply lobed leaves carried on slender stalks

Height 50 ft (15 m)	Shape Narrowly conical	Leaf persistence Deciduous	Leaf type

Family ROSACEAE	Species *Malus tschonoskii*	Author (Maximowicz) Schneider

MALUS TSCHONOSKII

Leaves Broadly ovate, to 4¾ in (12 cm) long and 3 in (7.5 cm) across, pointed, sharply toothed, gray and hairy becoming smooth and glossy above, thinly hairy beneath. **Bark** Purple-brown and smooth, becoming fissured and rough with age. **Flowers** 1¼ in (3 cm) across, white flushed pink, with five petals and yellow anthers, in clusters of up to five in late spring. **Fruit** Rounded, yellow-green flushed red, to 1¼ in (3 cm) across, speckled with lenticels.
• **NATIVE REGION** Japan.
• **HABITAT** Shallow, rocky soil in woods.

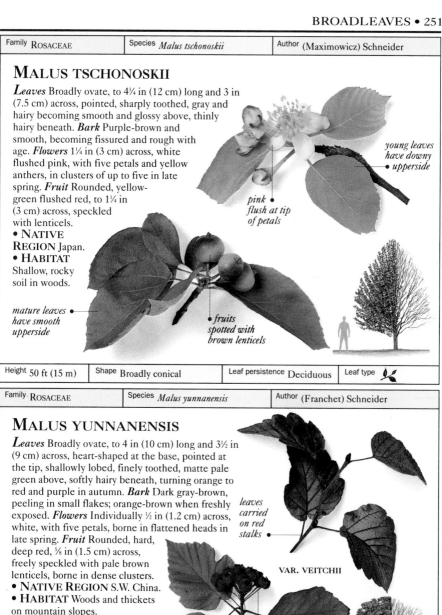

young leaves have downy upperside

pink flush at tip of petals

mature leaves have smooth upperside

fruits spotted with brown lenticels

Height 50 ft (15 m)	Shape Broadly conical	Leaf persistence Deciduous	Leaf type

Family ROSACEAE	Species *Malus yunnanensis*	Author (Franchet) Schneider

MALUS YUNNANENSIS

Leaves Broadly ovate, to 4 in (10 cm) long and 3½ in (9 cm) across, heart-shaped at the base, pointed at the tip, shallowly lobed, finely toothed, matte pale green above, softly hairy beneath, turning orange to red and purple in autumn. **Bark** Dark gray-brown, peeling in small flakes; orange-brown when freshly exposed. **Flowers** Individually ½ in (1.2 cm) across, white, with five petals, borne in flattened heads in late spring. **Fruit** Rounded, hard, deep red, ⅝ in (1.5 cm) across, freely speckled with pale brown lenticels, borne in dense clusters.
• **NATIVE REGION** S.W. China.
• **HABITAT** Woods and thickets on mountain slopes.
• **REMARK** The form shown, var. *veitchii*, differs in its brighter fruits, and in its leaves, which are heart shaped.

leaves carried on red stalks

VAR. VEITCHII

densely clustered, small fruits

leaf veins turn red in autumn

Height 33 ft (10 m)	Shape Broadly columnar	Leaf persistence Deciduous	Leaf type

Family ROSACEAE	Species *Malus* hybrids	Author None

CRAB APPLE HYBRIDS

pinkish flower buds

M any of the garden crab apples are hybrids between various species, raised in cultivation and grown for the beauty of their flowers or fruits; the attraction of some of these trees lies in both flowers and the fruits that follow in autumn. The plants usually make small, spreading trees, reaching about 20–26 ft (6-8 m) in height, and flowering in late spring and early summer. Several species have purplish leaves and flowers. This coloration arises as a result of hybridization with *Malus niedzwetzkyana*, a species found originally in the central Asian region of Turkestan.

◁ **'BUTTERBALL'**
This hybrid was raised in the United States. Rounded, yellowish fruits succeed the pink-flushed, white flowers.

▽ **'BUTTERBALL'**

fruits persist through autumn and winter

fruits mature to orange-yellow

◁ **'CRITTENDEN'**
This plant bears white flowers flushed slightly pink. They are followed by a profusion of bright scarlet fruits.

▽ **'CRITTENDEN'**

▽ **'DARTMOUTH'**
The small, white flowers of this form open from buds tinged faintly pink. The large fruits are 2 in (5 cm) across, red-purple and bloomy.

white flowers borne profusely

clustered flowers open after leaves unfold

• *fruits ripen from yellow to shades of purple and deep red*

◁ **'ELEYI'**
The fruits of this ornamental form are small, conical, and colored purple.

bronze-purple young leaves •

• *reddish purple flower petals narrow to white base*

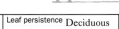

Height 26 ft (8 m)	Shape Broadly spreading	Leaf persistence Deciduous	Leaf type

• *white flowers open from deep pink buds*

▽ 'JOHN DOWNIE'
The soft pink buds of this form open into small white flowers with yellow anthers. The egg-shaped fruits are 1¼ in (3 cm) long and orange-yellow flushed red.

fruits ripen from green to yellow •

△ 'GOLDEN HORNET'
The flowers of this form are 1½ in (4 cm) across, pink in bud opening white flushed pink. The rounded, deep yellow fruits measure 1 in (2.5 cm) across.

• *pale pink buds open to white flowers*

'GOLDEN HORNET' ▷

purplish red flowers have broad petals •

• *distinctive egg-shaped fruits*

leaves can be unevenly lobed •

fruits carried on short stalks •   △ 'JOHN DOWNIE'

◁ 'LEMOINEI'
This colorful hybrid has deep bronze-purple young leaves, which mature to purplish green. The purplish red flowers are 1½ in (4 cm) across, and the deep purple fruits ⅝ in (1.5 cm) long.

flowers open as leaves mature •

cherrylike fruits •

▽ 'LISET'
The bronze-purple young leaves of this form become dark green, contrasting with the deep purple-pink flowers.

very dark red flower buds •

• *shiny shoots speckled with lenticels*   △ 'LISET'

Family ROSACEAE	Species *Malus* hybrids	Author None

• *small fruits carried on slender stalks*

◁ **'PROFUSION'**
The purplish red flowers of this plant are 1½ in (4 cm) across, borne profusely in large clusters. The dark green, red-veined leaves are bronze-purple when young. Deep reddish purple, rounded fruits, ½ in (1.2 cm) across, are produced in autumn.

• *leaves are often lobed on strong shoots*

fruits are red when ripe •

'RED SENTINEL' ▷
The pink buds of this hybrid open into white flowers 1¼ in (3 cm) across, which set rounded, long-persistent, glossy deep red fruits, 1 in (2.5 cm) across.

petals flushed pink at base •

△ **'RED JADE'**
This mushroom-shaped tree bears clusters of pink buds, which open to white flowers. The bright red fruits are carried on the branches into late autumn.

△ **'RED JADE'**

▽ **'ROYALTY'**
The glossy red-purple leaves of this compact tree turn red in late autumn. Deep red flower buds open deep red-purple.

'ROYALTY' ▷

double flowers have 15 petals each •

• *leaves still reddish as fruits ripen*

'VAN ESELTINE' ▷
This form is distinguished by its upright habit, double flowers, and the small, yellow or yellow flushed red fruits that follow in autumn.

Height To 26 ft (8 m)	Shape Variable	Leaf persistence Deciduous	Leaf type

Family ROSACEAE	Species *Mespilus germanica*	Author Linnaeus

MEDLAR

Leaves Elliptic to oblong, to 6 in (15 cm) long and 2 in (5 cm) across, untoothed or finely toothed, dark green above, usually hairy on both sides, turning yellow and brown in autumn, on very short stalks; shoots often thorny. *Bark* Gray-brown and smooth at first, cracking into thin plates with age; orange-brown when freshly exposed. *Flowers* To 2 in (5 cm) across, white, with five petals, borne singly on short stalks in late spring to early summer; vigorous plants often flower again in late summer. *Fruit* Rounded, flat-topped to pear-shaped, fleshy, brown, to 1¼ in (3 cm) across, with persistent sepals at the top.
• **NATIVE REGION**
S.W. Asia, S.E. Europe.
• **HABITAT** Forests, wood margins, and mountain thickets.
• **REMARK** Wild plants tend to be more shrubby than cultivated forms. The fruit becomes edible only after exposure to frost.

MESPILUS
GERMANICA ▷

finely toothed leaf margin •

untoothed leaf margin •

white flowers • borne singly

sepals remain • attached to fruits

'NOTTINGHAM' ▷

▽ 'NOTTINGHAM'
This cultivated form is selected for its large fruits.

cultivated form has larger leaves •

green sepals appear between petals •

Height 20 ft (6 m)	Shape Broadly spreading	Leaf persistence Deciduous	Leaf type

Family ROSACEAE	Species *Photinia beauverdiana*	Author Schneider

PHOTINIA BEAUVERDIANA

Leaves Elliptic to lanceolate, or obovate, to 4¾ in (12 cm) long and 2 in (5 cm) across, narrowed at the base, taper-pointed at the tip, sharply toothed, dark green above, smooth on both sides, turning red in autumn. *Bark* Gray and smooth, fluted at the base of the trunk. *Flowers* Individually ⅜ in (1 cm) across, white, with five petals, in flattened heads to 2 in (5 cm) across, in late spring. *Fruit* Egg-shaped, ³⁄₁₆ in (5 mm) across, green ripening to red.
• **NATIVE REGION** W. China.
• **HABITAT** Woods and thickets.

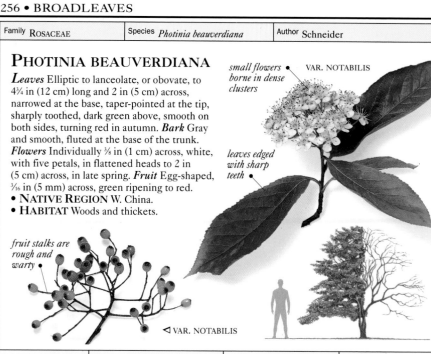

small flowers borne in dense clusters — VAR. NOTABILIS

leaves edged with sharp teeth •

fruit stalks are rough and warty •

◁ VAR. NOTABILIS

Height 20 ft (6 m)	Shape Broadly spreading	Leaf persistence Deciduous	Leaf type

Family ROSACEAE	Species *Photinia davidiana*	Author (Decaisne) Cardot

PHOTINIA DAVIDIANA

Leaves Elliptic to oblong or oblanceolate, to 4¾ in (12 cm) long and 1½ in (4 cm) across, taper-pointed at the tip, untoothed, dark green above, nearly smooth on both sides, turning red before falling. *Bark* Gray-brown and smooth. *Flowers* Individually ¼ in (6 mm) across, white, with five petals and pink anthers, in dense, rounded heads about 3 in (7.5 cm) across, in midsummer. *Fruit* Rounded and bright red, about ⁵⁄₁₆ in (8 mm) across, on long stalks, in small clusters.
• **NATIVE REGION** China, Vietnam.
• **HABITAT** Woods, thickets, and cliffs.

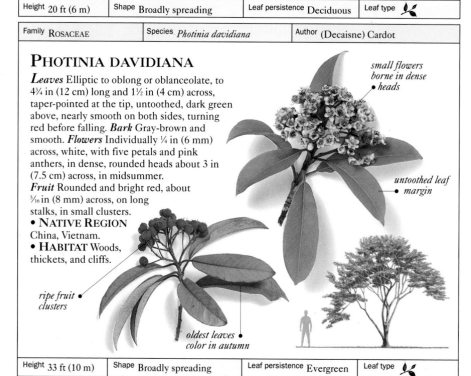

small flowers borne in dense • heads

untoothed leaf • margin

ripe fruit • clusters

oldest leaves • color in autumn

Height 33 ft (10 m)	Shape Broadly spreading	Leaf persistence Evergreen	Leaf type

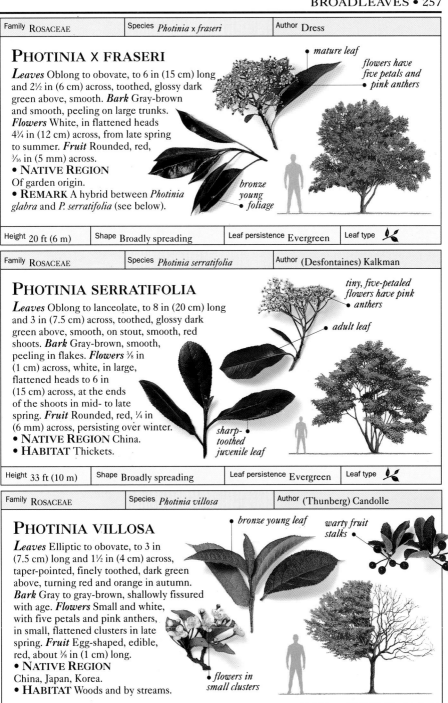

Family ROSACEAE	Species *Photinia x fraseri*	Author Dress

PHOTINIA X FRASERI

Leaves Oblong to obovate, to 6 in (15 cm) long and 2½ in (6 cm) across, toothed, glossy dark green above, smooth. **Bark** Gray-brown and smooth, peeling on large trunks. **Flowers** White, in flattened heads 4¾ in (12 cm) across, from late spring to summer. **Fruit** Rounded, red, ³⁄₁₆ in (5 mm) across.
• **NATIVE REGION** Of garden origin.
• **REMARK** A hybrid between *Photinia glabra* and *P. serratifolia* (see below).

mature leaf

flowers have five petals and pink anthers

bronze young foliage

Height 20 ft (6 m)	Shape Broadly spreading	Leaf persistence Evergreen	Leaf type

Family ROSACEAE	Species *Photinia serratifolia*	Author (Desfontaines) Kalkman

PHOTINIA SERRATIFOLIA

Leaves Oblong to lanceolate, to 8 in (20 cm) long and 3 in (7.5 cm) across, toothed, glossy dark green above, smooth, on stout, smooth, red shoots. **Bark** Gray-brown, smooth, peeling in flakes. **Flowers** ⅜ in (1 cm) across, white, in large, flattened heads to 6 in (15 cm) across, at the ends of the shoots in mid- to late spring. **Fruit** Rounded, red, ¼ in (6 mm) across, persisting over winter.
• **NATIVE REGION** China.
• **HABITAT** Thickets.

tiny, five-petaled flowers have pink anthers

adult leaf

sharp-toothed juvenile leaf

Height 33 ft (10 m)	Shape Broadly spreading	Leaf persistence Evergreen	Leaf type

Family ROSACEAE	Species *Photinia villosa*	Author (Thunberg) Candolle

PHOTINIA VILLOSA

Leaves Elliptic to obovate, to 3 in (7.5 cm) long and 1½ in (4 cm) across, taper-pointed, finely toothed, dark green above, turning red and orange in autumn. **Bark** Gray to gray-brown, shallowly fissured with age. **Flowers** Small and white, with five petals and pink anthers, in small, flattened clusters in late spring. **Fruit** Egg-shaped, edible, red, about ⅜ in (1 cm) long.
• **NATIVE REGION** China, Japan, Korea.
• **HABITAT** Woods and by streams.

bronze young leaf

warty fruit stalks

flowers in small clusters

Height 17 ft (5 m)	Shape Broadly spreading	Leaf persistence Deciduous	Leaf type

Family ROSACEAE	Species *Prunus armeniaca*	Author Linnaeus

APRICOT

Leaves Broadly ovate to rounded, to 4 in (10 cm) long and 2½ in (6 cm) across, with a usually rounded base, abruptly taper-pointed, finely toothed, glossy dark green. **Bark** Red-brown, smooth and glossy. **Flowers** 1 in (2.5 cm) across, pale pink or white, with five petals, nearly stalkless, usually borne singly on old shoots in early spring before the leaves emerge. **Fruit** Rounded and fleshy, edible, yellow sometimes flushed red, with a single hard, smooth stone enclosing an edible, white seed.
• **NATIVE REGION** C. Asia, N. China.
• **HABITAT** Hillsides and thickets.
• **REMARK** Naturalized in parts of Europe, and widely cultivated for its edible fruit.

bronze young leaves

sweet, edible flesh

hard stone has smooth surface

small glands along leaf stalk

Height 33 ft (10 m)	Shape Broadly spreading	Leaf persistence Deciduous	Leaf type

Family ROSACEAE	Species *Prunus avium*	Author Linnaeus

SWEET OR BIRD CHERRY

Leaves Elliptic to oblong, to 6 in (15 cm) long and 2½ in (6 cm) across, taper-pointed, sharply toothed, bronze when young becoming matte deep green above. **Bark** Glossy red-brown, peeling in horizontal bands. **Flowers** 1¼ in (3 cm) across, white, with five petals, borne in clusters in mid-spring just before or as the leaves emerge. **Fruit** A rounded, bitter or sweet, edible red berry, about ⅜ in (1 cm) across.
• **NATIVE REGION** Europe.
• **HABITAT** Woods and hedgerows.
• **REMARK** Also known as mazzard, gean, wild cherry. The species is most familiar in flower as a woodland tree. It may reach only 65 ft (20 m).

red fruits are edible

sharply toothed leaves

PRUNUS AVIUM

bronze-colored young leaves emerge with flowers

flower buds tinged pink

△ 'PLENA'
The large, double flowers of this smaller cultivar have numerous petals.

densely clustered flowers

Height 80 ft (25 m)	Shape Broadly columnar	Leaf persistence Deciduous	Leaf type

Family ROSACEAE	Species *Prunus cerasifera*	Author Ehrhart

CHERRY PLUM

Leaves Ovate to obovate, to 2½ in (6 cm) long and 1¼ in (6 cm) across, toothed at the margin, glossy dark green and smooth above, downy on the veins beneath. **Bark** Purple-brown, thinly scaly, with horizontal, orange lenticels, fissured with age. **Flowers** 1 in (2.5 cm) across, white, with five petals and reflexed sepals, borne singly or in small clusters in early spring before the leaves emerge. **Fruit** Rounded, plumlike, edible and red, 1¼ in (3 cm) across.
• **NATIVE REGION** Of garden origin.
• **REMARK** Also known as myrobalan. A similar species is the yellow-fruiting *Prunus divaricata*, which is native to S.E. Europe, and C. and S.W. Asia.

white flowers open before leaves •

PRUNUS CERASIFERA

very dark green shoots and leaves •

◁ **'NIGRA'**
Deep red-purple leaves and pink flowers distinguish this form.

pink flowers have dark • center

• stamens have pink anthers

△ **'PISSARDII'**
This form has pink flower buds, opening to white, and purple leaves.

△ **'ROSEA'**
This hybrid has red-purple foliage and small, pink flowers.

Height 26 ft (8 m)	Shape Broadly spreading	Leaf persistence Deciduous	Leaf type

Family ROSACEAE	Species *Prunus cerasus*	Author Linnaeus

SOUR CHERRY

Leaves Elliptic to ovate, to 3 in (7.5 cm) long and 2 in (5 cm) across, taper-pointed, sharply toothed, dark green above, smooth on both sides. **Bark** Purple-brown, with horizontal, orange-brown lenticels, peeling horizontally. **Flowers** ¾ in (2 cm) across, white, with five petals, in small clusters in mid-spring. **Fruit** An edible, red to black cherry, ¾ in (2 cm) across.
• **NATIVE REGION** Of garden origin.
• **REMARK** This species is related to sweet cherry *(Prunus avium*, see p.258).

leaves emerge • after flowers open

• ripe fruits remain sour

PRUNUS CERASUS

• green sepals

△ **'RHEXII'**
This form has large, rosettelike flowers.

Height 26 ft (8 m)	Shape Broadly spreading	Leaf persistence Deciduous	Leaf type

Family ROSACEAE	Species *Prunus domestica*	Author Linnaeus

PLUM

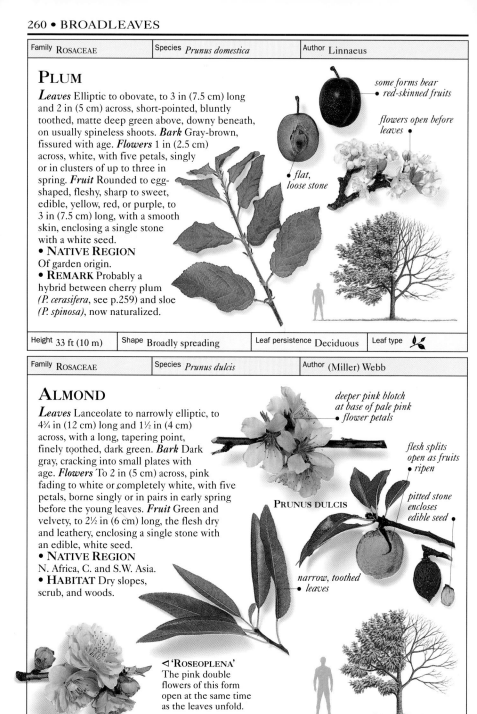

Leaves Elliptic to obovate, to 3 in (7.5 cm) long and 2 in (5 cm) across, short-pointed, bluntly toothed, matte deep green above, downy beneath, on usually spineless shoots. *Bark* Gray-brown, fissured with age. *Flowers* 1 in (2.5 cm) across, white, with five petals, singly or in clusters of up to three in spring. *Fruit* Rounded to egg-shaped, fleshy, sharp to sweet, edible, yellow, red, or purple, to 3 in (7.5 cm) long, with a smooth skin, enclosing a single stone with a white seed.
• NATIVE REGION
Of garden origin.
• REMARK Probably a hybrid between cherry plum *(P. cerasifera,* see p.259) and sloe *(P. spinosa),* now naturalized.

some forms bear red-skinned fruits

flowers open before leaves

flat, loose stone

Height 33 ft (10 m)	Shape Broadly spreading	Leaf persistence Deciduous	Leaf type

Family ROSACEAE	Species *Prunus dulcis*	Author (Miller) Webb

ALMOND

Leaves Lanceolate to narrowly elliptic, to 4¾ in (12 cm) long and 1½ in (4 cm) across, with a long, tapering point, finely toothed, dark green. *Bark* Dark gray, cracking into small plates with age. *Flowers* To 2 in (5 cm) across, pink fading to white or completely white, with five petals, borne singly or in pairs in early spring before the young leaves. *Fruit* Green and velvety, to 2½ in (6 cm) long, the flesh dry and leathery, enclosing a single stone with an edible, white seed.
• NATIVE REGION
N. Africa, C. and S.W. Asia.
• HABITAT Dry slopes, scrub, and woods.

deeper pink blotch at base of pale pink flower petals

PRUNUS DULCIS

flesh splits open as fruits ripen

pitted stone encloses edible seed

narrow, toothed leaves

◁ 'ROSEOPLENA'
The pink double flowers of this form open at the same time as the leaves unfold.

Height 26 ft (8 m)	Shape Broadly spreading	Leaf persistence Deciduous	Leaf type

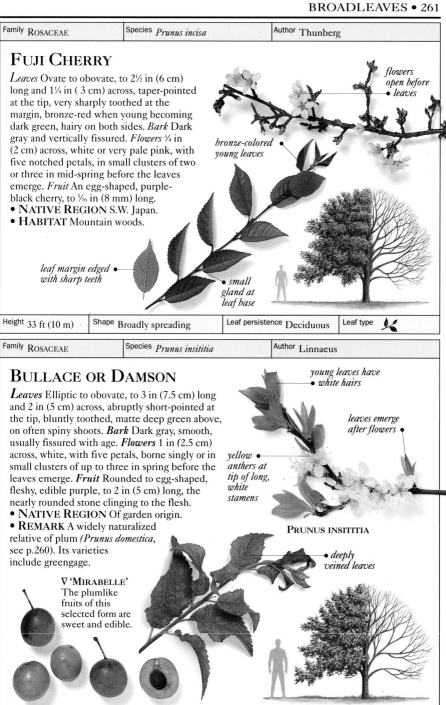

| Family ROSACEAE | Species *Prunus incisa* | Author Thunberg |

FUJI CHERRY

Leaves Ovate to obovate, to 2½ in (6 cm) long and 1¼ in (3 cm) across, taper-pointed at the tip, very sharply toothed at the margin, bronze-red when young becoming dark green, hairy on both sides. *Bark* Dark gray and vertically fissured. *Flowers* ¾ in (2 cm) across, white or very pale pink, with five notched petals, in small clusters of two or three in mid-spring before the leaves emerge. *Fruit* An egg-shaped, purple-black cherry, to ⁵⁄₁₆ in (8 mm) long.
• **NATIVE REGION** S.W. Japan.
• **HABITAT** Mountain woods.

flowers open before leaves

bronze-colored young leaves

leaf margin edged with sharp teeth

small gland at leaf base

| Height 33 ft (10 m) | Shape Broadly spreading | Leaf persistence Deciduous | Leaf type |

| Family ROSACEAE | Species *Prunus insititia* | Author Linnaeus |

BULLACE OR DAMSON

Leaves Elliptic to obovate, to 3 in (7.5 cm) long and 2 in (5 cm) across, abruptly short-pointed at the tip, bluntly toothed, matte deep green above, on often spiny shoots. *Bark* Dark gray, smooth, usually fissured with age. *Flowers* 1 in (2.5 cm) across, white, with five petals, borne singly or in small clusters of up to three in spring before the leaves emerge. *Fruit* Rounded to egg-shaped, fleshy, edible purple, to 2 in (5 cm) long, the nearly rounded stone clinging to the flesh.
• **NATIVE REGION** Of garden origin.
• **REMARK** A widely naturalized relative of plum *(Prunus domestica,* see p.260). Its varieties include greengage.

young leaves have white hairs

leaves emerge after flowers

yellow anthers at tip of long, white stamens

PRUNUS INSITITIA

deeply veined leaves

∇ 'MIRABELLE'
The plumlike fruits of this selected form are sweet and edible.

| Height 23 ft (7 m) | Shape Broadly spreading | Leaf persistence Deciduous | Leaf type |

Family ROSACEAE	Species *Prunus* forms or hybrids	Author None

JAPANESE CHERRIES

The Japanese cherries, or *Sato-zakura*, are ornamental, flowering garden trees raised or selected in Japan. They are thought to be forms or hybrids of two native Japanese species, the hill cherry *(Prunus jamasakura,* see p.265) and the Oshima cherry *(Prunus speciosa)*: trees similar to some of them grow wild in the hills and mountains of Japan. They have been cultivated in Japanese gardens for more than 1,500 years, yet are of relatively recent introduction to the West. Most have a spreading habit, but some are weeping or narrowly upright. The showy flowers are single to semidouble or fully double, and range from white to deep pink.

▽ 'AMANOGAWA'
A distinct tree of narrow, upright habit, to about 26 ft (8 m) in height. The pale pink double flowers are 1½ in (4 cm) across, and open in mid-spring before or with the young leaves.

pale pink flowers have yellow • anthers

deep bronze young leaves •

double flowers borne in dense • clusters

• sharply toothed leaves

double flowers have numerous • petals

bronze-green • young leaves

'KANZAN' OR
'SEK YOMA' △
This most popular and commonly planted Japanese cherry tree is vase shaped at first. Its branches spread and arch as the plant ages, to reach 33 ft (10 m) or more in height.

• teeth at leaf margin end in long, slender point

△ 'KANZAN'

△ 'CHEAL'S WEEPING' OR
'KIKU SHIDARE'
This form, which has long branches arching to the ground, usually reaches about 8 ft (2.5 m).

Height To 33 ft (10 m)	Shape Variable		Leaf persistence Deciduous	Leaf type

flowers fade to
white after
opening •

◁ 'SHIROFUGEN'
One of the most beautiful of
Japanese cherries, this spreading tree grows to 33 ft (10 m)
tall. The double flowers are
pink in bud, and open white
in late spring. They turn again
to pink before they fall.

flowers hang in
clusters beneath
• shoots

sharply toothed
• petals

young leaves mature
to dark green •

large white
flowers have
pink stamens •

△ 'SHOGETSU'
The large, white double
flowers of this spreading
tree open from pink-tinged
buds in late spring, and
form drooping clusters
among the pale green
young leaves.

'TAI HAKU' ▷
The great white
cherry was found in
an English garden
and reintroduced to
Japan, where at one
time it had been thought
lost to cultivation. Its
single flowers are the
largest of those of any
flowering cherry. They
open in mid-spring
among bronze-
colored
leaves.

petals tinged
green •

leaves edged
with fine-pointed
teeth

△ 'UKON'
The distinctive double flowers of
this form are pale yellow-green
flushed at first with pink. They
open in mid-spring with the
bronze-tinged young leaves.

Family ROSACEAE	Species *Prunus* hybrids	Author None

PRUNUS HYBRIDS

Apart from the Japanese cherries, there are many other hybrids between various species, either intentionally or accidentally raised and grown for their ornamental flowers and foliage. Their parentage involves several different species and hybrids, including *P. sargentii* (see p.268) and *P.* x *subhirtella* (see pp.270–271), and so these trees are more diverse than the Japanese cherries. They can be upright or spreading, usually reach no more than 33 ft (10 m), and are always deciduous; some produce good autumn color. The flowers are single to semidouble or fully double, usually opening in early to late spring.

• *double flowers have yellow anthers*

sharp-pointed, toothed leaves

△ 'ACCOLADE'
This small tree is thought to be a hybrid between *Prunus sargentii* (see p.268) and *Prunus* x *subhirtella* (see p.270).

• *small glands at base of leaf*

pink buds fade to nearly white on opening •

△ 'PANDORA'
This tree has pale pink single flowers, each with five petals. They open in early spring before the leaves emerge.

• *single-flower petals have notch at tip*

leaves end in short point •

leaf margin edged with coarse teeth •

△ 'SPIRE'
The matte dark green foliage of this form turns orange and red in autumn.

Height To 33 ft (10 m)	Shape Variable	Leaf persistence Deciduous	Leaf type

| Family ROSACEAE | Species *Prunus jamasakura* | Author Siebold ex Koidzumi |

HILL CHERRY

Leaves Oblong to obovate, to 4¾ in (12 cm) long and 2 in (5 cm) across, abruptly taper-pointed at the tip, sharply toothed, bronze or red becoming deep green above, blue-green beneath, smooth on both sides, turning yellow to red in autumn. **Bark** Purple-brown, with horizontal lenticels. **Flowers** 1¼ in (3 cm) across, pale pink to nearly white, with five petals notched at the tip, opening in small clusters in mid-spring as the young leaves emerge. **Fruit** A fleshy, deep purple-black berry, 1 in (2.5 cm) long.
• **NATIVE REGION** China, Japan, Korea.
• **HABITAT** Woods in hills and low mountains.
• **REMARK** Also known as *Prunus serrulata* var. *spontanea*.

notch at tip of petal

sharply toothed leaf margin

folded, soft young leaves

colored autumn leaves carried on red stalks

| Height 65 ft (20 m) | Shape Broadly spreading | Leaf persistence Deciduous | Leaf type |

| Family ROSACEAE | Species *Prunus laurocerasus* | Author Linnaeus |

CHERRY LAUREL

Leaves Elliptic to oblong or obovate, to 8 in (20 cm) long and 2½ in (6 cm) across, abruptly short-pointed, usually shallowly toothed at least above the middle, glossy yellowish to very dark green above, pale green beneath, smooth, on short, stout stalks. **Bark** Gray-brown and smooth. **Flowers** ⁵⁄₁₆ in (8 mm) across, white, with five petals, fragrant, in upright racemes to 4¾ in (12 cm) long, in the leaf axils in mid-spring, some-times flowering again in autumn. **Fruit** A rounded berry, ½ in (1.2 cm) across, green becoming red ripening to black.
• **NATIVE REGION** S.W. Asia, E. Europe.
• **HABITAT** Thickets in forests.

yellowish leaf stalks

fruits ripen from green through red to black

long flower clusters emerge from leaf axils

| Height 33 ft (10 m) | Shape Broadly spreading | Leaf persistence Evergreen | Leaf type |

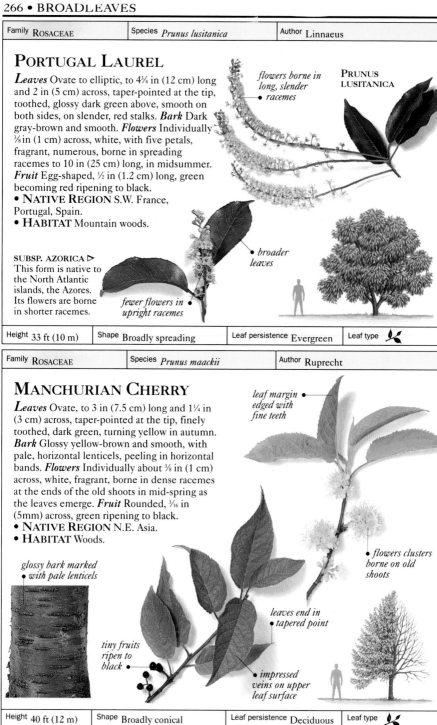

Family ROSACEAE	Species *Prunus lusitanica*	Author Linnaeus

PORTUGAL LAUREL

PRUNUS LUSITANICA

Leaves Ovate to elliptic, to 4¾ in (12 cm) long and 2 in (5 cm) across, taper-pointed at the tip, toothed, glossy dark green above, smooth on both sides, on slender, red stalks. *Bark* Dark gray-brown and smooth. *Flowers* Individually ⅜ in (1 cm) across, white, with five petals, fragrant, numerous, borne in spreading racemes to 10 in (25 cm) long, in midsummer. *Fruit* Egg-shaped, ½ in (1.2 cm) long, green becoming red ripening to black.
• **NATIVE REGION** S.W. France, Portugal, Spain.
• **HABITAT** Mountain woods.

flowers borne in long, slender • *racemes*

broader leaves

SUBSP. AZORICA ▷
This form is native to the North Atlantic islands, the Azores. Its flowers are borne in shorter racemes.

fewer flowers in • *upright racemes*

Height 33 ft (10 m)	Shape Broadly spreading	Leaf persistence Evergreen	Leaf type

Family ROSACEAE	Species *Prunus maackii*	Author Ruprecht

MANCHURIAN CHERRY

Leaves Ovate, to 3 in (7.5 cm) long and 1¼ in (3 cm) across, taper-pointed at the tip, finely toothed, dark green, turning yellow in autumn. *Bark* Glossy yellow-brown and smooth, with pale, horizontal lenticels, peeling in horizontal bands. *Flowers* Individually about ⅜ in (1 cm) across, white, fragrant, borne in dense racemes at the ends of the old shoots in mid-spring as the leaves emerge. *Fruit* Rounded, ³⁄₁₆ in (5mm) across, green ripening to black.
• **NATIVE REGION** N.E. Asia.
• **HABITAT** Woods.

leaf margin • *edged with fine teeth*

flowers clusters borne on old shoots

glossy bark marked • *with pale lenticels*

leaves end in • *tapered point*

tiny fruits ripen to black •

impressed veins on upper leaf surface

Height 40 ft (12 m)	Shape Broadly conical	Leaf persistence Deciduous	Leaf type

Family ROSACEAE	Species *Prunus padus*	Author Linnaeus

BIRD CHERRY

Leaves Elliptic, to 4 in (10 cm) long and 2½ in (6 cm) across, taper-pointed, finely toothed, matte dark green, usually turning red or yellow in autumn. *Bark* Dark gray and smooth. *Flowers* ⅜ in (1 cm) across, white, with five petals, fragrant, borne in upright, spreading, or drooping racemes to 6 in (15 cm) long, in mid- to late spring. *Fruit* A rounded to egg-shaped, glossy black berry, to ⁵⁄₁₆ in (8 mm) long.
• **NATIVE REGION**
N. Asia, Europe.
• **HABITAT**
Open places, by streams, woods.

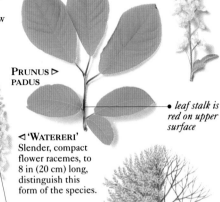

leaves end in abrupt point

PRUNUS ▷ PADUS

leaf stalk is red on upper surface

◁ **'WATERERI'**
Slender, compact flower racemes, to 8 in (20 cm) long, distinguish this form of the species.

'COLORATA' ▷
This form has red-purple young leaves, which mature to dark green above and red on the underside.

shorter-stalked flowers clustered in longer racemes

Height 50 ft (15 m)	Shape Broadly spreading	Leaf persistence Deciduous	Leaf type

Family ROSACEAE	Species *Prunus persica*	Author (Linnaeus) Batsch

PEACH

Leaves Narrowly elliptic to lanceolate, to 6 in (15 cm) long and 1½ in (4 cm) across, with a long, slender point at the tip, finely toothed, glossy dark green. *Bark* Dark gray, becoming fissured with age. *Flowers* To 1½ in (4 cm) across, pale to deep pink or red, sometimes white, short-stalked, borne singly or in pairs, in early spring. *Fruit* Rounded, fleshy, sweet, edible, usually orange-yellow flushed red, to 3 in (7.5 cm) across, enclosing a deeply pitted, furrowed stone with a white seed.
• **NATIVE REGION** China.
• **HABITAT** Mountains.

thin, velvety fruit skin

stone adheres to flesh

△ PRUNUS PERSICA

◁ **'PRINCE CHARMING'**
This form has double flowers.

▷ VAR. NECTARINA
The fruit of this variety has a smooth and slightly oily skin.

Height 26 ft (8 m)	Shape Broadly spreading	Leaf persistence Deciduous	Leaf type

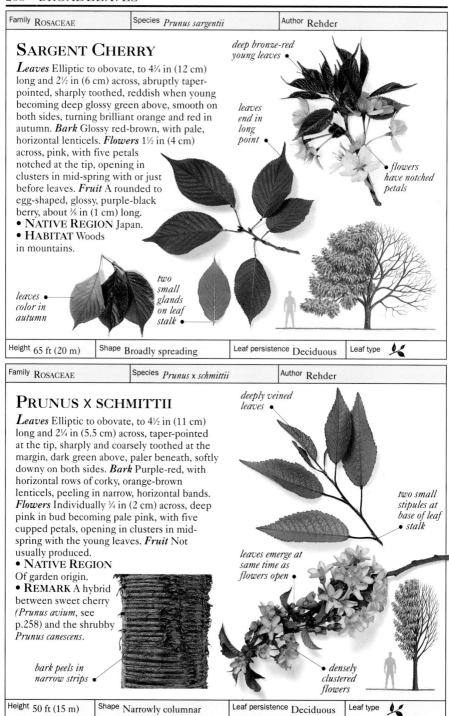

Family ROSACEAE	Species *Prunus sargentii*	Author Rehder

SARGENT CHERRY

Leaves Elliptic to obovate, to 4¾ in (12 cm) long and 2½ in (6 cm) across, abruptly taper-pointed, sharply toothed, reddish when young becoming deep glossy green above, smooth on both sides, turning brilliant orange and red in autumn. **Bark** Glossy red-brown, with pale, horizontal lenticels. **Flowers** 1½ in (4 cm) across, pink, with five petals notched at the tip, opening in clusters in mid-spring with or just before leaves. **Fruit** A rounded to egg-shaped, glossy, purple-black berry, about ⅜ in (1 cm) long.
• **NATIVE REGION** Japan.
• **HABITAT** Woods in mountains.

deep bronze-red young leaves

leaves end in long point

flowers have notched petals

leaves color in autumn

two small glands on leaf stalk

Height 65 ft (20 m)	Shape Broadly spreading	Leaf persistence Deciduous	Leaf type

Family ROSACEAE	Species *Prunus x schmittii*	Author Rehder

PRUNUS X SCHMITTII

Leaves Elliptic to obovate, to 4½ in (11 cm) long and 2¼ in (5.5 cm) across, taper-pointed at the tip, sharply and coarsely toothed at the margin, dark green above, paler beneath, softly downy on both sides. **Bark** Purple-red, with horizontal rows of corky, orange-brown lenticels, peeling in narrow, horizontal bands. **Flowers** Individually ¾ in (2 cm) across, deep pink in bud becoming pale pink, with five cupped petals, opening in clusters in mid-spring with the young leaves. **Fruit** Not usually produced.
• **NATIVE REGION** Of garden origin.
• **REMARK** A hybrid between sweet cherry *(Prunus avium,* see p.258) and the shrubby *Prunus canescens.*

deeply veined leaves

two small stipules at base of leaf stalk

leaves emerge at same time as flowers open

bark peels in narrow strips

densely clustered flowers

Height 50 ft (15 m)	Shape Narrowly columnar	Leaf persistence Deciduous	Leaf type

Family ROSACEAE	Species *Prunus serotina*	Author Ehrhart

BLACK CHERRY

Leaves Elliptic to lanceolate, to 4¾ in
(12 cm) long and 2 in (5 cm) across, taper-
pointed, finely toothed, glossy dark green
and smooth above, paler and smooth with
hairs along the midrib beneath, turning
yellow or red in autumn. **Bark** Dark gray,
smooth. **Flowers** ⅜ in (1 cm) across, white, in
spreading to drooping racemes to 6 in (15 cm)
long, at the ends of the shoots in late spring or
early summer. **Fruit** A rounded, edible cherry,
to ⅜ in (1 cm) across, red ripening to black.
• **NATIVE REGION** North America.
• **HABITAT** Woods, pastures, and roadsides.

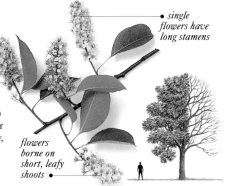

*single
flowers have
long stamens*

*flowers
borne on
short, leafy
shoots*

Height 80 ft (25 m)	Shape Broadly columnar	Leaf persistence Deciduous	Leaf type

Family ROSACEAE	Species *Prunus serrula*	Author Franchet

JAPANESE FLOWERING CHERRY

Leaves Lanceolate, to 4 in (10 cm) long and
1¼ in (3 cm) across, tapering to a slender point
at the tip, finely toothed at the margin, matte
dark green. **Bark** Glossy red-brown and
smooth, conspicuously banded with pale,
horizontal lenticels, peeling horizontally in
narrow strips. **Flowers** White, ¾ in (2 cm)
across, relatively inconspicuous, pendulous,
borne singly or in small clusters
of up to three in spring just
after the young leaves emerge.
Fruit Egg-shaped, about ⅜ in (1 cm)
long, yellow at first ripening to red.
• **NATIVE REGION** W. China.
• **HABITAT** Mountain woods.
• **REMARK** Also known as *Prunus
serrula* var. *tibetica*. This species is
easily distinguished by its
characteristic bark.

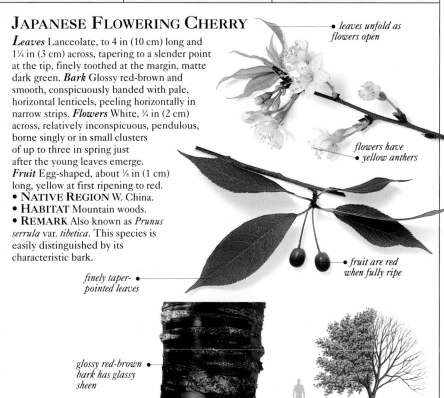

*leaves unfold as
flowers open*

*flowers have
yellow anthers*

*fruit are red
when fully ripe*

*finely taper-
pointed leaves*

*glossy red-brown
bark has glassy
sheen*

Height 50 ft (15 m)	Shape Broadly spreading	Leaf persistence Deciduous	Leaf type

Family ROSACEAE	Species *Prunus x subhirtella*	Author Miquel

SPRING CHERRY

Leaves Elliptic to ovate, to 3 in (7.5 cm) long and 2 in (5 cm) across, taper-pointed, sharply toothed, pale bronze when young becoming deep green above, paler beneath, turning yellow in autumn. *Bark* Gray-brown and smooth, banded with horizontal lenticels. *Flowers* Individually ¾ in (2 cm) across, pale pink or white, with five petals notched at the tip, opening from pink buds, in small clusters in early spring either before or as the young leaves emerge. *Fruit* A nearly black cherry, ⁵⁄₁₆ in (8 mm) across, sparsely borne.
• **NATIVE REGION** Japan.
• **HABITAT** In woods with the parents.
• **REMARK** A naturally occurring hybrid between Fuji cherry *(Prunus incisa, see p.261)* and *Prunus pendula*. It is seen only rarely in the wild, but has many garden forms. 'Autumnalis' is one of the most commonly cultivated varieties.

flowers open from pink buds

'AUTUMNALIS'

semidouble white flowers may open during winter

'AUTUMNALIS' ▷
The semidouble flowers of this form are white, tinged with pale pink. They open in autumn, during mild periods in winter, and in spring.

stipules at leaf base

bronze-green young leaves

sharply toothed leaf margin

leaves mature to dark green

△ **'AUTUMNALIS ROSEA'**
The semi-double flowers of this cultivar are very similar to those of 'Autumnalis,' but are deeper pink both in bud and when open. Like 'Autumnalis,' it flowers during mild weather in winter, and in spring.

spring flowers open as young leaves emerge

Height 20 ft (6 m)	Shape Broadly spreading	Leaf persistence Deciduous	Leaf type

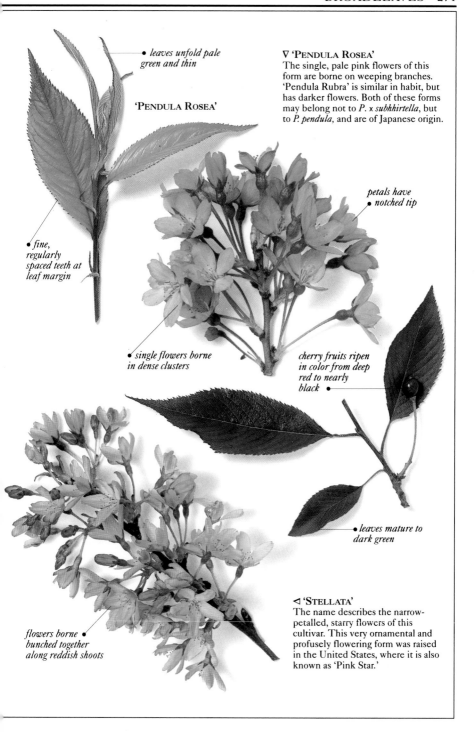

leaves unfold pale green and thin

'PENDULA ROSEA'

∇ 'PENDULA ROSEA'
The single, pale pink flowers of this form are borne on weeping branches. 'Pendula Rubra' is similar in habit, but has darker flowers. Both of these forms may belong not to *P.* x *subhhirtella*, but to *P. pendula*, and are of Japanese origin.

petals have notched tip

fine, regularly spaced teeth at leaf margin

single flowers borne in dense clusters

cherry fruits ripen in color from deep red to nearly black

leaves mature to dark green

flowers borne bunched together along reddish shoots

◁ 'STELLATA'
The name describes the narrow-petalled, starry flowers of this cultivar. This very ornamental and profusely flowering form was raised in the United States, where it is also known as 'Pink Star.'

Family ROSACEAE	Species *Prunus verecunda*	Author (Koidzumi) Koehne

KOREAN HILL CHERRY

Leaves Elliptic to obovate, to 4¾ in (12 cm) long and 2 in (5 cm) across, abruptly taper-pointed, sharply toothed, pale green to bronze when young becoming glossy green above, paler beneath, downy on one or both sides, turning red to purple in autumn. **Bark** Gray-brown, peeling in horizontal bands. **Flowers** 1¼ in (3 cm) across, white or pale pink, with five petals notched at the tip, borne in small clusters in mid-spring before or with the leaves. **Fruit** A red to purple cherry, to ⅜ in (1 cm) across.
• **NATIVE REGION** China, Japan, Korea.
• **HABITAT** Woods in hills and mountains.
• **REMARK** Also known as *Prunus serrulata* var. *pubescens*.

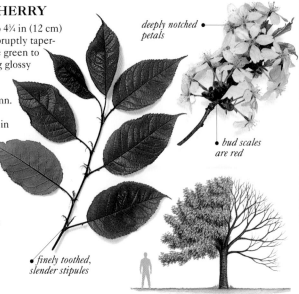

deeply notched petals

bud scales are red

finely toothed, slender stipules

Height 65 ft (20 m)	Shape Broadly spreading	Leaf persistence Deciduous	Leaf type

Family ROSACEAE	Species *Prunus x yedoensis*	Author Matsumura

YOSHINO CHERRY

Leaves Elliptic, to 4½ in (11 cm) long and 2½ in (6 cm) across, taper-pointed at the tip, sharply toothed at the margin, downy on both sides but particularly so when young beneath, becoming smooth and glossy above. **Bark** Purple-gray, with thick bands of corky lenticels. **Flowers** 1½ in (4 cm) across, pale pink fading to nearly white, with five petals notched at the tip, borne in small clusters in early spring before the young leaves emerge. **Fruit** A nearly rounded cherry, ½ in (1.2 cm) across, red ripening to black.
• **NATIVE REGION** Japan.
• **HABITAT** Woods in hills together with the parent plants.
• **REMARK** Probably a hybrid with several named cultivars. A major planting is at the Tidal Basin in Washington, D.C.

sharply toothed leaves

red unripe fruit

black ripe fruit

pale green young leaves

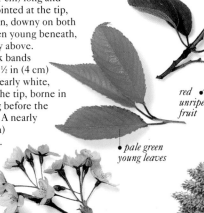

small, but plentiful, flowers

Height 40 ft (12 m)	Shape Broadly spreading	Leaf persistence Deciduous	Leaf type

Family ROSACEAE	Species *Pyrus calleryana*	Author Decaisne

CALLERY PEAR

Leaves Ovate to elliptic, to 3 in (7.5 cm) long and 2 in (5 cm) across, finely toothed, glossy above, smooth, turning red-purple in autumn or early winter. *Bark* Dark gray, cracking into scaly ridges; red-brown when freshly exposed. *Flowers* ⅜ in (1 cm) across, white, with five petals, in spring. *Fruit* Rounded to pear-shaped, fleshy, to ¾ in (2 cm) across, russet-brown spotted with white
• **NATIVE REGION** C. and S. China.
• **HABITAT** Thickets and alongside streams in mountains.

short-pointed leaves

clustered flowers

Height 50 ft (15 m)	Shape Broadly conical	Leaf persistence Deciduous	Leaf type

Family ROSACEAE	Species *Pyrus communis*	Author Linnaeus

COMMON PEAR

Leaves Ovate to elliptic, to 4 in (10 cm) long and 2 in (5 cm) across, rounded to heart-shaped at the base, taper-pointed, toothed, glossy deep green. *Bark* Dark gray, cracking into small plates. *Flowers* To 1½ in (4 cm) across, white, with five petals and deep pink anthers, in clusters in mid-spring. *Fruit* Rounded to pear-shaped, fleshy, sweet, edible, greenish to russet or yellow, sometimes flushed red, to 4 in (10 cm) long.
• **NATIVE REGION** Of garden origin.
• **REMARK** A hybrid involving several species, which probably originated in W. Asia.

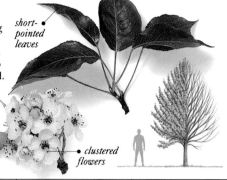

fruits vary in size, shape, and color

small, shallow teeth at leaf margin

long-stalked leaves

Height 50 ft (15 m)	Shape Broadly columnar	Leaf persistence Deciduous	Leaf type

Family ROSACEAE	Species *Pyrus salicifolia*	Author Pallas

WILLOW LEAF PEAR

Leaves Narrowly elliptic to narrowly lanceolate, to 3½ in (9 cm) long and ¾ in (2 cm) across, tapering at both ends, usually untoothed, becoming smooth above. *Bark* Pale gray-brown, cracking into smooth plates. *Flowers* ¾ in (2 cm) across, creamy white, five petals and deep pink anthers, in clusters in spring. *Fruit* Pear-shaped, hard, green, to 1¼ in (3 cm) long.
• **NATIVE REGION** Caucasus, N.E. Turkey.
• **HABITAT** Wood margins, thickets.

young leaves emerge with flowers

fruit has short, stout stalk

downy young leaves

Height 33 ft (10 m)	Shape Broadly weeping	Leaf persistence Deciduous	Leaf type

Family ROSACEAE	Species *Sorbus alnifolia*	Author (Siebold & Zuccarini) K. Koch

SORBUS ALNIFOLIA

Leaves Ovate to elliptic, to 4 in (10 cm) long and 1½ in (4 cm) across, pointed, toothed, dark green above, downy becoming smooth beneath, turning yellow, orange, or red in autumn. *Bark* Dark brown, smooth, with shallow fissures. *Flowers* ⅜ in (1 cm) across, white, in clusters in mid-spring. *Fruit* A rounded, reddish berry, about ⅜ in (1 cm) across.
• **NATIVE REGION** China, Japan, Korea, Taiwan.
• **HABITAT** Woods.

fruits marked with lenticels

five-petaled flowers

Height 65 ft (20 m)	Shape Broadly conical	Leaf persistence Deciduous	Leaf type

Family ROSACEAE	Species *Sorbus americana*	Author Marshall

AMERICAN MOUNTAIN ASH

Leaves Pinnate, to 10 in (25 cm) long, with about 15 oblong to lanceolate, pointed, toothed leaflets, to 4 in (10 cm) long and 1 in (2.5 cm) across, turning yellow or red in late autumn. *Bark* Gray and smooth. *Flowers* About ³⁄₁₆ in (5 mm) across, white, borne in dense heads to 8 in (20 cm) across, in late spring to early summer. *Fruit* An orange-red berry, ³⁄₁₆ in (5 mm) across.
• **NATIVE REGION** E. North America.
• **HABITAT** Woods.

fruit clusters hang down

pale green leaflets

Height 26 ft (8 m)	Shape Broadly spreading	Leaf persistence Deciduous	Leaf type

Family ROSACEAE	Species *Sorbus aria*	Author (Linnaeus) Crantz

WHITEBEAM

Leaves Elliptic to ovate, to 4¾ in (12 cm) long and 2½ in (6 cm) across, sharply toothed, pale green with hairs when young becoming glossy dark green above, white with hairs beneath. *Bark* Gray and smooth, developing rugged cracks with age. *Flowers* About ⅜ in (1 cm) across, white, with five petals, in flattened clusters in late spring. *Fruit* A rounded, bright red berry, about ½ in (1.2 cm) across, speckled with pale lenticels.
• **NATIVE REGION** Europe.
• **HABITAT** From lowland to mountains, on chalk and limestone.

clustered ripe fruits

mature leaves are glossy dark olive green

Height 50 ft (15 m)	Shape Broadly columnar	Leaf persistence Deciduous	Leaf type

Family ROSACEAE	Species *Sorbus aucuparia*	Author Linnaeus

ROWAN

Leaves Pinnate, to 8 in (20 cm) long, with up to 15 taper-pointed, sharply toothed leaflets, to 2½ in (6 cm) long, dark green and smooth above, blue-green and usually downy when young beneath, sometimes turning red in autumn. **Bark** Gray and smooth. **Flowers** ⁵⁄₁₆ in (8 mm) across, white, with five petals, in clusters to 6 in (15 cm) across, in late spring. **Fruit** A rounded, orange-red berry, ⁵⁄₁₆ in (8 mm) across, often forming heavy clusters.
• **NATIVE REGION** Asia, Europe.
• **HABITAT** Woods, heathland, moors, and mountains, on moist, acid soil.
• **REMARK** Also known as European mountain ash, mountain ash. The berries are used for making jellies and preserves, but can be poisonous if consumed raw.

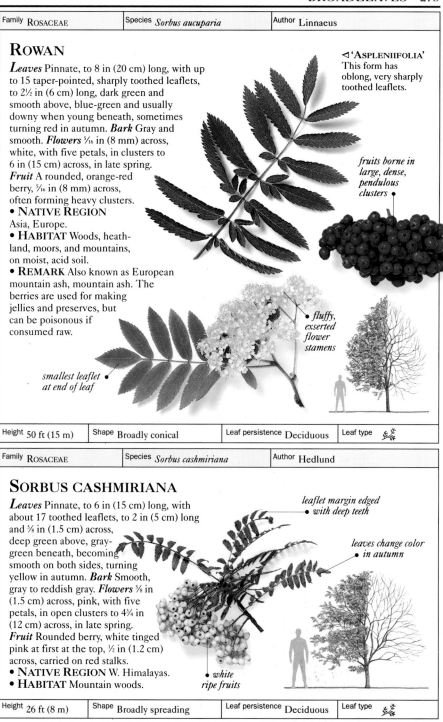

◁ '**ASPLENIIFOLIA**'
This form has oblong, very sharply toothed leaflets.

fruits borne in large, dense, pendulous clusters •

• *fluffy, exserted flower stamens*

smallest leaflet at end of leaf •

Height 50 ft (15 m)	Shape Broadly conical	Leaf persistence Deciduous	Leaf type

Family ROSACEAE	Species *Sorbus cashmiriana*	Author Hedlund

SORBUS CASHMIRIANA

Leaves Pinnate, to 6 in (15 cm) long, with about 17 toothed leaflets, to 2 in (5 cm) long and ⅝ in (1.5 cm) across, deep green above, gray-green beneath, becoming smooth on both sides, turning yellow in autumn. **Bark** Smooth, gray to reddish gray. **Flowers** ⅝ in (1.5 cm) across, pink, with five petals, in open clusters to 4¾ in (12 cm) across, in late spring. **Fruit** Rounded berry, white tinged pink at first at the top, ½ in (1.2 cm) across, carried on red stalks.
• **NATIVE REGION** W. Himalayas.
• **HABITAT** Mountain woods.

leaflet margin edged • with deep teeth

leaves change color • in autumn

• *white ripe fruits*

Height 26 ft (8 m)	Shape Broadly spreading	Leaf persistence Deciduous	Leaf type

Family ROSACEAE	Species *Sorbus commixta*	Author Hedlund

SORBUS COMMIXTA

Leaves Pinnate, to 8 in (20 cm) long, with up to 15 taper-pointed leaflets, to 3 in (7.5 cm) long and 1 in (2.5 cm) across, glossy above, blue-green beneath, turning yellow to reddish purple in autumn. **Bark** Gray and smooth. **Flowers** ⁵⁄₁₆ in (8 mm) across, white, with five petals, borne in clusters to 6 in (15 cm) across, in late spring. **Fruit** Orange-red, ⁵⁄₁₆ in (8 mm) across.
• **NATIVE REGION** Japan, Korea.
• **HABITAT** Mountain forests.

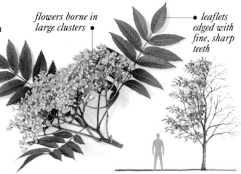

flowers borne in large clusters

leaflets edged with fine, sharp teeth

Height 33 ft (10 m)	Shape Broadly conical	Leaf persistence Deciduous	Leaf type

Family ROSACEAE	Species *Sorbus domestica*	Author Linnaeus

SERVICE TREE

Leaves Pinnate, to 8¾ in (22 cm) long, with up to 21 oblong, toothed leaflets, to 2½ in (6 cm) long and about ⅜ in (1 cm) across, yellow-green and smooth above, downy when young beneath, turning yellow or red in autumn. **Bark** Dark brown, scaly, cracking into plates. **Flowers** To ⅝ in (1.5 cm) across, white, with five petals, in rounded clusters about 4 in (10 cm) across, in late spring. **Fruit** Rounded or pear-shaped, yellow-green flushed red, to 1¼ in (3 cm) long.
• **NATIVE REGION** S.W. Asia, E. and S. Europe.
• **HABITAT** Mountain slopes, deciduous forests.

flowers borne in rounded heads

◁ **SORBUS DOMESTICA**

parallel-sided leaflets

fruits may be rounded or pear-shaped

VAR. PYRIFERA ▷
This form has bright red fruits shaped like miniature pears.

VAR. POMIFERA ▷
The fruits of this form resemble tiny apples.

fruits broaden above center

teeth at top half of leaflet margin point forward

Height 65 ft (20 m)	Shape Broadly columnar	Leaf persistence Deciduous	Leaf type

Family ROSACEAE	Species *Sorbus esserteauana*	Author Koehne

SORBUS ESSERTEAUANA

Leaves Pinnate, to 10 in (25 cm) long, with up to 15 taper-pointed leaflets, to 4 in (10 cm) long and 1½ in (4 cm) across, deep red-purple becoming glossy dark green and smooth above, gray-hairy when young beneath, turning red in autumn. **Bark** Gray-brown, thinly scaly. **Flowers** ⁵⁄₁₆ in (8 mm) across, white, with five petals, borne in heads to 4¾ in (12 cm) across, in late spring. **Fruit** Red, ⁵⁄₁₆ in (8 mm) across.
• NATIVE REGION S.W. China.
• HABITAT Mountains, cliffs, woods.

flowers borne in broad, flat heads

leaflets edged with sharp teeth

small berrylike fruits clustered in broad heads

Height 33 ft (10 m)	Shape Broadly spreading	Leaf persistence Deciduous	Leaf type

Family ROSACEAE	Species *Sorbus forrestii*	Author McAllister & Gillham

SORBUS FORRESTII

Leaves Pinnate, to 8 in (20 cm) long, with up to 17 leaflets, to 1½ in (4 cm) long and ⅝ in (1.5 cm) across, blue-green above, gray-green beneath, becoming smooth. **Bark** Purple-gray and smooth, with shallow, vertical fissures. **Flowers** ⅜ in (1 cm) across, white, with five petals, borne in flattened heads in late spring. **Fruit** Rounded, ⅜ in (1 cm) across, green ripening to white.
• NATIVE REGION S.W. China.
• HABITAT Mountain woods.

upper half of leaflets edged with small teeth

flowers borne in small, loose heads

lower half of leaflets has smooth margin

deep pink tinge around tip of fruit

Height 20 ft (6 m)	Shape Broadly spreading	Leaf persistence Deciduous	Leaf type

Family ROSACEAE	Species *Sorbus hupehensis*	Author Schneider

SORBUS HUPEHENSIS

Leaves Pinnate, to 6 in (15 cm) long, with up to 17 leaflets, to 2½ in (6 cm) long and ¾ in (2 cm) across, toothed towards the tip, blue-green above, blue-gray and smooth or nearly so beneath, turning red in autumn. **Bark** Gray and smooth. **Flowers** Individually ¼ in (6 mm) across, white, with five petals, in rounded clusters to 6 in (15 cm) across, in late spring. **Fruit** A rounded berry, about ⁵⁄₁₆ in (8 mm) across, white flushed pink at the top.
• **NATIVE REGION** China.
• **HABITAT** Mountain woods.

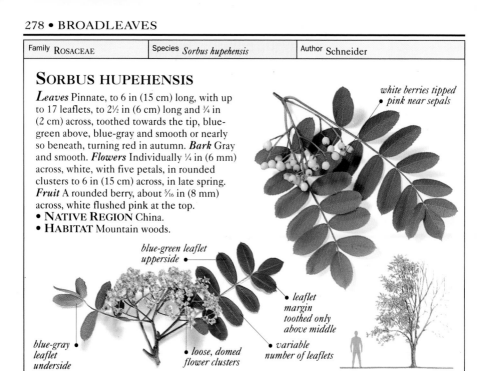

white berries tipped pink near sepals

blue-green leaflet upperside

leaflet margin toothed only above middle

blue-gray leaflet underside

loose, domed flower clusters

variable number of leaflets

Height 40 ft (12 m)	Shape Broadly columnar	Leaf persistence Deciduous	Leaf type

Family ROSACEAE	Species *Sorbus intermedia*	Author (Ehrhart) Persoon

SWEDISH WHITEBEAM

Leaves Ovate or broadly elliptic, to 4 in (10 cm) long and 2½ in (6 cm) across, lobed, more deeply lobed towards the base of the leaf, toothed, glossy dark green above, gray-green and hairy beneath. **Bark** Gray, cracking and flaking with age. **Flowers** Individually ¾ in (2 cm) across, white, with five petals, in large, dense clusters to 4¾ in (12 cm) across, in late spring. **Fruit** A broadly egg-shaped, bright red berry, to ⅝ in (1.5 cm) long, with few lenticels.
• **NATIVE REGION** N.W. Europe.
• **HABITAT** Woods.

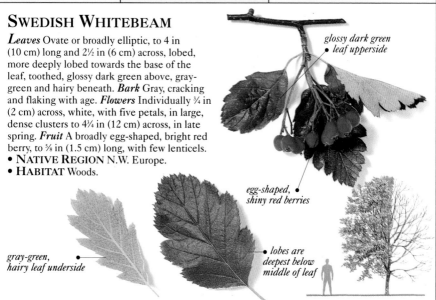

glossy dark green leaf upperside

egg-shaped, shiny red berries

gray-green, hairy leaf underside

lobes are deepest below middle of leaf

Height 50 ft (15 m)	Shape Broadly columnar	Leaf persistence Deciduous	Leaf type

Family ROSACEAE	Species *Sorbus* 'Joseph Rock'	Author None

SORBUS 'JOSEPH ROCK'

Leaves Pinnate, to 6 in (15 cm) long, with up to 17 sharply toothed leaflets, to 1½ in (4 cm) long and ½ in (1.2 cm) across, bright green above, gray-green beneath, becoming nearly smooth, turning orange, red, and purple in autumn. *Bark* Gray and nearly smooth, with small, orange lenticels. *Flowers* ⅜ in (1 cm) across, white, with five petals, borne in flattened heads 4 in (10 cm) across, in late spring to early summer. *Fruit* Rounded, ⅜ in (1 cm) across, green then yellow-white ripening to orange-yellow.
• **NATIVE REGION** Probably China.
• **HABITAT** May not occur in the wild.

fruits borne on red stalks

leaflets edged with small teeth

leaves change color in autumn

Height 33 ft (10 m)	Shape Broadly columnar	Leaf persistence Deciduous	Leaf type

Family ROSACEAE	Species *Sorbus latifolia*	Author (Lamarck) Persoon

SERVICE TREE OF FONTAINEBLEAU

Leaves Broadly ovate, to 4 in (10 cm) long and the same across, with shallow, pointed lobes towards the base, sharply toothed, glossy dark green above, gray and downy beneath. *Bark* Dark gray, cracked, flaking. *Flowers* Individually ⅝ in (1.5 cm) across, white, with five petals, borne in flattened heads in late spring. *Fruit* Rounded, yellow-brown, ½ in (1.2 cm) across, with conspicuous lenticels.
• **NATIVE REGION** C. and W. Europe.
• **HABITAT** Woods.
• **REMARK** This species probably originated as a hybrid between the whitebeam *(Sorbus aria,* see p.274) and the wild service tree *(Sorbus torminalis,* see p.282).

smooth leaf upperside

leaf underside felted with gray hairs

shallow leaf lobes edged with sharp teeth

leaves turn yellow in autumn

Height 40 ft (12 m)	Shape Broadly columnar	Leaf persistence Deciduous	Leaf type

Family ROSACEAE	Species *Sorbus sargentiana*	Author Koehne

SORBUS SARGENTIANA

Leaves Pinnate, to 14 in (35 cm) long, with about 11 oblong, taper-pointed, toothed leaflets, to 4¾ in (12 cm) long and 2 in (5 cm) across, matte deep green above, gray-green and hairy beneath, turning orange and red in autumn. **Bark** Purple-brown, cracked and flaking with age. **Flowers** ¼ in (6 mm) across, white, in rounded heads to 8 in (20 cm) across, in early summer. **Fruit** Rounded, bright red, ¼ in (6 mm) across, borne in large clusters.
• **NATIVE REGION** S.W. China.
• **HABITAT** Mountain woods.

terminal pair of leaflets points forward

small fruits borne in broad heads

Height 33 ft (10 m)	Shape Broadly columnar	Leaf persistence Deciduous	Leaf type

Family ROSACEAE	Species *Sorbus scalaris*	Author Koehne

SORBUS SCALARIS

Leaves Pinnate, to 8 in (20 cm) long, with numerous narrowly oblong leaflets, to 1½ in (4 cm) long and ⅜ in (1 cm) across, toothed towards the tip, glossy deep green above, gray and hairy beneath, turning red and purple in late autumn. **Bark** Smooth and gray, with shallow fissures. **Flowers** ¼ in (6 mm) across, white, with five petals, in broad, flattened heads to 6 in (15 cm) across, in late spring or early summer. **Fruit** Rounded, bright red, ¼ in (6 mm) across, in large clusters.
• **NATIVE REGION** S.W. China.
• **HABITAT** Mountain woods.

sparse, shallow teeth only at tip of leaflets

small flowers borne in dense clusters

small, deep red fruits

Height 33 ft (10 m)	Shape Broadly spreading	Leaf persistence Deciduous	Leaf type

Family ROSACEAE	Species *Sorbus thibetica*	Author (Cardot) Handel-Mazzetti

SORBUS THIBETICA

Leaves Elliptic to obovate or nearly rounded, to 6 in (15 cm) long and 4 in (10 cm) across, tapered at the base, pointed at the tip, sharply toothed, hairy becoming smooth or only thinly hairy and dark green above, densely covered in white hairs beneath, with up to 14 pairs of veins. **Bark** Gray-brown, thinly scaly, cracked, flaking at the base. **Flowers** White, with five petals, borne in clusters to 2½ in (6 cm) across, in late spring to early summer. **Fruit** A rounded, orange or yellow berry, ⅝ in (1.5 cm) across.
• **NATIVE REGION** S.W. China, Himalayas.
• **HABITAT** Evergreen and deciduous mountain forests.
• **REMARK** 'John Mitchell,' shown here, is the form seen most commonly.

large, glossy leaves

'JOHN MITCHELL'

gray, woolly flower stalks

leaves remain silvery on underside

Height 50 ft (15 m)	Shape Broadly conical	Leaf persistence Deciduous	Leaf type

Family ROSACEAE	Species *Sorbus x thuringiaca*	Author (Ilse) Fritsch

SORBUS X THURINGIACA

Leaves Narrowly ovate to elliptic, to 4 in (10 cm) long and 2½ in (6 cm) across, lobed except at the tip, more deeply lobed towards the base, toothed, glossy dark green above, gray and hairy beneath, often with several free leaflets at the base. **Bark** Purple-gray and smooth, cracking and flaking with age. **Flowers** ½ in (1.2 cm) across, white, with five petals, borne in dense clusters in late spring. **Fruit** A rounded, bright red berry, ⅜ in (1.2 cm) across.
• **NATIVE REGION** Europe.
• **HABITAT** Woods, together with the parent plants.
• **REMARK** A naturally occurring hybrid between the whitebeam *(Sorbus aria*, see p.274) and the rowan *(Sorbus aucuparia*, see p.275). The form shown here, 'Fastigiata,' is a commonly planted street tree, with upswept branches making a dense, broadly oval crown. Other forms are closer to *S. aucuparia*, and have more numerous free leaflets.

deepest lobes at leaf base

bright red fruits borne in arching clusters

leaf underside stays hairy

lobes become shallower towards leaf tip

'FASTIGIATA'

Height 40 ft (12 m)	Shape Broadly conical	Leaf persistence Deciduous	Leaf type

Family ROSACEAE	Species *Sorbus torminalis*	Author. (Linnaeus) Crantz

WILD SERVICE TREE

Leaves Broadly ovate, to 4 in (10 cm) long and nearly the same across, deeply cut into sharply toothed lobes, glossy dark green above, paler beneath, downy when young, turning yellow, red, or purple in autumn. **Bark** Dark brown, cracking into scaly plates. **Flowers** ½ in (1.2 cm) across, white, in flattened clusters in late spring to early summer. **Fruit** A rounded, russet-brown berry, ½ in (1.2 cm) long.
• **NATIVE REGION** N. Africa, S.W. Asia, Europe.
• **HABITAT** Woods.

ripe fruits speckled with lenticels

maplelike leaves

open flower clusters

Height 50 ft (15 m)	Shape Broadly columnar	Leaf persistence Deciduous	Leaf type

Family ROSACEAE	Species *Sorbus vestita*	Author (G. Don) Loddiges

SORBUS VESTITA

Leaves Elliptic, to 8 in (20 cm) or more long and 6 in (15 cm) across, sometimes with small lobes, sharply toothed, white-hairy when young becoming glossy dark green above, densely covered with white hairs beneath, with up to 11 pairs of veins. **Bark** Pale gray, peeling in thick flakes. **Flowers** ¼ in (2 cm) across, white, with five petals, in flattened clusters to 4 in (10 cm) across, in late spring to early summer. **Fruit** A rounded to pear-shaped berry, ¼ in (2 cm) across, green speckled with brown.
• **NATIVE REGION** The Himalayas.
• **HABITAT** Mountain forests.

fruits dotted with brown lenticels

fruits borne on stout stalks

Height 50 ft (15 m)	Shape Broadly conical	Leaf persistence Deciduous	Leaf type

Family ROSACEAE	Species *Sorbus vilmorinii*	Author Schneider

SORBUS VILMORINII

Leaves Pinnate, to 6 in (15 cm) long, with up to about 25 oblong leaflets, to ¼ in (2 cm) long, toothed towards the tip, glossy dark green above, gray-green beneath. **Bark** Smooth, dark gray. **Flowers** ¼ in (6 mm) across, white, with five petals, in clusters to 4 in (10 cm) across, in late spring to early summer. **Fruit** A roundish berry, ⅜ in (1 cm) long, deep red at first ripening to white.
• **NATIVE REGION** S.W. China.
• **HABITAT** Mountain woods.

crimson young fruits

fruits ripen through many shades of pink

Height 26 ft (8 m)	Shape Broadly spreading	Leaf persistence Deciduous	Leaf type

RUTACEAE

T HE 1,500 SPECIES OF TREES, shrubs, and climbing plants belonging to this family are contained in over 150 genera. They are found worldwide, but particularly in tropical and warm temperate regions. The leaves are usually alternate and often compound, and release an aromatic vapor when crushed. Flowers are green to white or yellow, usually with four or five petals.

Family RUTACEAE	Species *Phellodendron amurense*	Author Ruprecht

AMUR CORK TREE

Leaves Pinnate, to 14 in (35 cm) long, with up to 13 ovate to lanceolate, taper-pointed, untoothed or minutely toothed leaflets, to 4 in (10 cm) long and 2 in (5 cm) across, glossy deep green and smooth above, blue-green with hairs at the base of the midrib beneath, turning yellow in autumn. *Bark* Gray-brown, thick, corky, with prominent ridges. *Flowers* Males and females both small and greenish, males with yellow, protruding anthers, borne in conical clusters about 3 in (7.5 cm) long, on separate plants in mid-summer. *Fruit* Rounded, ⅜ in (1 cm) across, green ripening to black.
• **NATIVE REGION** N.E. Asia.
• **HABITAT** Moist places near streams in mountains.

bark furrowed with corky ridges

∇ **VAR. LAVALLEI**
Smooth, rather less glossy, leaflets, with a gray-green, hairy-veined underside, distinguish this form.

PHELLODENDRON
AMURENSE

• *leaflets have glossy green upperside*

• *aromatic fruits ripen from green to black*

PHELLODENDRON
AMURENSE

• *male flowers have exserted stamens*

• *leaflets have dull green upperside*

Height 40 ft (12 m)	Shape Broadly spreading	Leaf persistence Deciduous	Leaf type

Family RUTACEAE	Species *Ptelea trifoliata*	Author Linnaeus

HOP TREE

Leaves With three elliptic to ovate, untoothed or sparsely toothed leaflets, to 4 in (10 cm) long and 1½ in (4 cm) across, glossy dark green above, usually more or less smooth on both sides, turning yellow in autumn, aromatic when crushed. **Bark** Dark gray, nearly smooth. **Flowers** About ⅜ in (1 cm) across, yellow-green to green, with four or five petals, in clusters to 3 in (7.5 cm) across, at the ends of the shoots in early summer. **Fruit** With two seeds in the center of a broad, circular wing, to 1 in (2.5 cm) across, pale green ripening to pale brown.
• **NATIVE REGION** E. North America.
• **HABITAT** Moist woods, thickets, and rocky slopes.

PTELEA TRIFOLIATA

• seeds encircled by green wing

tiny, greenish flowers • borne in upright clusters

young leaves eventually become pale green •

glands on leaf • surface release aromatic oil

◁ '**AUREA**'
Viewed as a mass of foliage, the yellow young leaves of this form are quite striking.

Height 26 ft (8 m)	Shape Broadly spreading	Leaf persistence Deciduous	Leaf type

Family RUTACEAE	Species *Tetradium daniellii*	Author (Bennett) Hartley

TETRADIUM DANIELLII

Leaves Pinnate, to 12 in (30 cm) or more long, with up to 11 ovate or oblong, usually short-pointed, untoothed leaflets, to 4 in (10 cm) long and 1½ in (4 cm) across, glossy dark green and smooth above, blue-green and hairy at least when young beneath. **Bark** Gray and smooth. **Flowers** Small, white, aromatic, in broadly flattened heads to 6 in (15 cm) across, at the ends of the shoots in late summer to early autumn. **Fruit** A small, beaked, red-brown to nearly black capsule, ⁵⁄₁₆ in (8 mm) long, in dense clusters.
• **NATIVE REGION** China, Korea.
• **HABITAT** Mountain woods.
• **REMARK** Previously known as *Euodia daniellii*.

unequal-sided base of young leaflets •

male flowers have exserted • yellow anthers

Height 50 ft (15 m)	Shape Broadly spreading	Leaf persistence Deciduous	Leaf type

Family RUTACEAE	Species *Zanthoxylum ailanthoides*	Author Siebold & Zuccarini

ZANTHOXYLUM AILANTHOIDES

Leaves Pinnate, 12 in (30 cm) or more long, with up to 15 pairs of oblong, pointed leaflets, to 6 in (15 cm) long and 2 in (5 cm) across, light green above, blue-green beneath. *Bark* Gray and green, striped, with spiny pro-tuberances. *Flowers* Males and females yellow-green, in broad heads at the ends of the shoots, on separate plants in late summer. *Fruit* Small, green, with black seeds.
• **NATIVE REGION**
E. Asia.
• **HABITAT** Woods.

leaflets taper to finely pointed tip

very finely toothed leaflets

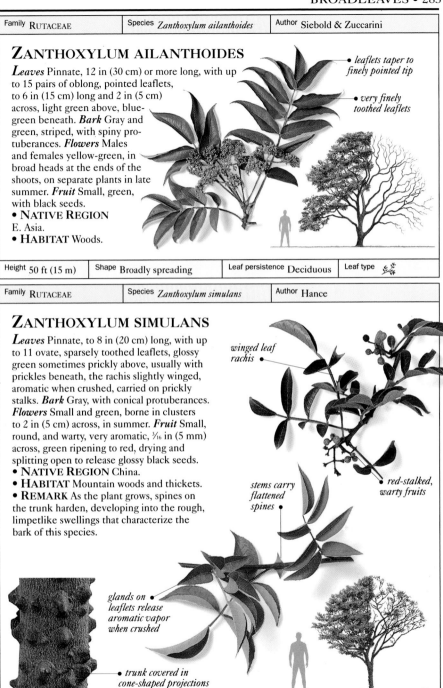

Height 50 ft (15 m)	Shape Broadly spreading	Leaf persistence Deciduous	Leaf type

Family RUTACEAE	Species *Zanthoxylum simulans*	Author Hance

ZANTHOXYLUM SIMULANS

Leaves Pinnate, to 8 in (20 cm) long, with up to 11 ovate, sparsely toothed leaflets, glossy green sometimes prickly above, usually with prickles beneath, the rachis slightly winged, aromatic when crushed, carried on prickly stalks. *Bark* Gray, with conical protuberances. *Flowers* Small and green, borne in clusters to 2 in (5 cm) across, in summer. *Fruit* Small, round, and warty, very aromatic, ³⁄₁₆ in (5 mm) across, green ripening to red, drying and splitting open to release glossy black seeds.
• **NATIVE REGION** China.
• **HABITAT** Mountain woods and thickets.
• **REMARK** As the plant grows, spines on the trunk harden, developing into the rough, limpetlike swellings that characterize the bark of this species.

winged leaf rachis

red-stalked, warty fruits

stems carry flattened spines

glands on leaflets release aromatic vapor when crushed

trunk covered in cone-shaped projections

Height 20 ft (6 m)	Shape Broadly spreading	Leaf persistence Deciduous	Leaf type

SALICACEAE

T HE TWO GENERA and about 350 species of trees and shrubs in this family occur throughout the world, except in Australasia, most commonly in northern temperate regions. Leaves are alternate or occasionally opposite. The tiny, petalless flowers are borne in catkins, males and females nearly always on separate plants. The fruit is a capsule containing small seeds.

Family SALICACEAE	Species *Populus alba*	Author Linnaeus

WHITE POPLAR

Leaves Variable, on vigorous shoots maplelike, with three to five lobes, to 4 in (10 cm) long and 3 in (7.5 cm) across, on short shoots shallowly lobed to wavy-edged, both types white with hairs when young becoming smooth and dark green above, densely covered in white hairs beneath. *Bark* Gray, fissured, dark at the base. *Flowers* In drooping catkins, males to 3 in (7.5 cm) long, gray with red anthers, females to 2 in (5 cm) long, green, on separate plants in early spring before the young leaves. *Fruit* Small, green capsules, borne in catkins to 4 in (10 cm) long, opening to release tiny seeds held in white, cotton wool-like hairs.
• **NATIVE REGION** N. Africa, C. and W. Asia, Europe.
• **HABITAT** Woods, in moist and dry places.
• **REMARK** Also known as abele.

white, hairy young leaves

mature leaves have smooth upper surface

strong shoots carry maplelike leaves

less vigorous shoots have shallowly-lobed leaves

dense, white hairs cover underside of leaves

Height 100 ft (30 m)	Shape Broadly columnar	Leaf persistence Deciduous	Leaf type

Family SALICACEAE	Species *Populus balsamifera*	Author Linnaeus

BALSAM POPLAR

Leaves Ovate, to 4¾ in (12 cm) long and 4 in (10 cm) across, taper-pointed, finely toothed, glossy green above, whitish and net-veined beneath, smooth on both sides, balsam-scented when young. *Bark* Gray, ridged. *Flowers* In catkins, males to 2 in (5 cm) long, females to 3 in (7.5 cm) long, green, on separate plants in early spring. *Fruit* Small green capsules, in catkins to 12 in (30 cm) long.
• **NATIVE REGION**
North America.
• **HABITAT** Moist woods.

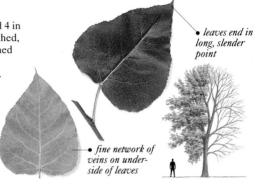

leaves end in long, slender point

• *fine network of veins on underside of leaves*

Height 100 ft (30 m)	Shape Broadly columnar	Leaf persistence Deciduous	Leaf type

Family SALICACEAE	Species *Populus x canadensis*	Author Moench

POPULUS X CANADENSIS

Leaves Broadly triangular, to 4 in (10 cm) long and across, with a short point at the tip, finely toothed, glossy green above. *Bark* Pale gray, with deep, vertical fissures. *Flowers* In catkins, males to 4 in (10 cm) long, females green, on separate plants in early spring before the leaves. *Fruit* Small green capsules, opening to release tiny seeds held in fluffy white hairs.
• **NATIVE REGION** Of garden origin.
• **REMARK** This group of hybrids between the North American species, cotton-wood *(Populus deltoides)*, and the black poplar *(Populus nigra*, see p.289), has many forms, including some of the most commonly grown poplars.

'MARILANDICA' ▷
Deep furrows give the bark of this form a craggy appearance.

• *irregularly ridged, pale gray bark*

leaves are edged with larger teeth towards base

◁ **'ROBUSTA'**
The bronze-red young leaves of this male form emerge in mid-spring, and mature by late summer to glossy deep green.

• *strikingly bright young leaves*

vertically ridged bark •

△ **'SEROTINA AUREA'**
This male form, which has bright yellow summer foliage, comes into leaf in late spring.

Height 100 ft (30 m)	Shape Broadly columnar	Leaf persistence Deciduous	Leaf type

Family SALICACEAE	Species *Populus* x *candicans*	Author Aiton

BALM OF GILEAD

Leaves Broadly ovate, to 6 in (15 cm) long
and 4 in (10 cm) across, usually heart-shaped
at the base, taper-pointed, toothed, dark
green above, whitish and net-veined
beneath, slightly downy on both sides.
Bark Gray and smooth, becoming ridged
with age. **Flowers** Females only,
green, in drooping catkins in
early spring. **Fruit** Small, green
capsules, borne in catkins to 6 in
(15 cm) long, opening to release tiny
seeds held in white, cotton wool-
like hairs.
• **NATIVE REGION**
Of garden origin.
• **REMARK** Also known as Ontario poplar.
This species is thought to be a hybrid of the
balsam poplar *(Populus balsamifera*, see
p.287), naturalized from gardens on
riverbanks in E. North America.
'Aurora,' a common form, has leaves
blotched white, cream, and pink.

leaves end in tapered point

variegation is strongest on vigorous shoots

△ **POPULUS** x **CANDICANS**

'AURORA' ▷

Height 100 ft (30 m)	Shape Broadly columnar	Leaf persistence Deciduous	Leaf type

Family SALICACEAE	Species *Populus* x *canescens*	Author (Aiton) P. Smith

GRAY POPLAR

Leaves Rounded to ovate, to 3 in (7.5 cm) long
and across, occasionally shallowly lobed,
toothed, densely covered in white hairs when
young becoming smooth and glossy deep green
above, gray and hairy beneath. **Bark** Pale gray,
with dark, diamond-shaped fissures when
young, becoming dark brown and deeply
furrowed with age. **Flowers** In drooping
catkins, males to 4 in (10 cm) long, gray
with red anthers, females to 4 in (10 cm)
long, green, on separate plants in early
spring. **Fruit** Small green capsules, borne
in catkins, opening to release tiny seeds
held in white, cotton wool-like hairs.
• **NATIVE REGION** Europe.
• **HABITAT** River valleys.
• **REMARK** A hybrid
between the white poplar
(Populus alba, see p.286)
and the aspen *(Populus
tremula*, see p.290),
widely naturalized
from cultivation.

upper leaf surface soon becomes smooth

rounded teeth at leaf margin

slender, flattened leaf stalks

young leaves have gray hairs on upper surface

gray-hairy leaf under-side

Height 100 ft (30 m)	Shape Broadly columnar	Leaf persistence Deciduous	Leaf type

Family SALICACEAE	Species *Populus lasiocarpa*	Author Oliver

CHINESE POPLAR

Leaves Broadly ovate, to 12 in (30 cm) long and 8 in (20 cm) across, deeply heart-shaped at the base, edged with small, rounded teeth at the margin, downy on both sides when young becoming deep green and smooth above, with red veins and stalk, carried on very stout shoots. **Bark** Gray-brown and vertically fissured. **Flowers** Males and females both yellow-green, males with red anthers, borne in stout, drooping catkins to 4 in (10 cm) long, sometimes on the same spike, usually on separate plants in mid-spring. **Fruit** Small, green capsules, borne in catkins, opening to release tiny seeds held in white, cotton wool-like hairs.
• **NATIVE REGION** C. China.
• **HABITAT** Moist woods in mountains.
• **REMARK** The very large, long-stalked leaves easily distinguish this species from others of its genus.

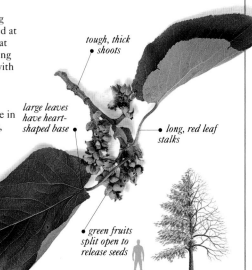

tough, thick shoots

large leaves have heart-shaped base

long, red leaf stalks

green fruits split open to release seeds

Height 65 ft (20 m)	Shape Broadly conical	Leaf persistence Deciduous	Leaf type

Family SALICACEAE	Species *Populus nigra*	Author Linnaeus

BLACK POPLAR

Leaves Triangular to ovate, to 4 in (10 cm) long and nearly the same across, larger on vigorous shoots, taper-pointed at the tip, bluntly toothed, with a narrow, translucent margin, bronze becoming glossy dark green above, paler beneath, smooth on both sides, turning yellow in autumn. **Bark** Dark gray-brown, coarsely fissured, often with large burrs. **Flowers** Males with red anthers, females green, in drooping catkins to 2 in (5 cm) long, on separate plants in early spring before the young leaves emerge. **Fruit** Small, green capsules, borne in catkins, opening to release tiny seeds held in white, cotton wool-like hairs.
• **NATIVE REGION** W. Asia, Europe.
• **HABITAT** River valleys.
• **REMARK** *Populus nigra* 'Italica,' the Lombardy poplar, is an upright form.

leaf tip usually has no teeth

slender, flattened leaf stalks

leaf base has no glands

Height 100 ft (30 m)	Shape Broadly spreading	Leaf persistence Deciduous	Leaf type

Family SALICACEAE	Species *Populus szechuanica*	Author Schneider

POPULUS SZECHUANICA

VAR. THIBETICA ▷

Leaves Ovate, to 12 in (30 cm) long and 8 in (20 cm) or more across on vigorous shoots, usually much smaller on short shoots, rounded to heart-shaped at the base, tapered at the tip, blunt-toothed, reddish to bronze-colored when young becoming dark green above, paler beneath, smooth on both sides. **Bark** Pinkish gray, cracking into large, smooth flakes with age. **Flowers** Small and without petals, males with deep red anthers, females green, borne in drooping catkins on separate plants in mid-spring before the young leaves emerge. **Fruit** Small, green capsules, in catkins to 6¼ in (16 cm) long, opening to release tiny seeds held in white, cotton wool-like hairs.
- **NATIVE REGION** W. China.
- **HABITAT** Moist mountain woods.
- **REMARK** The leaves of the form shown here, var. *thibetica*, are slightly hairy on the underside.

young leaves

softly hairy veins on leaf underside

◁ VAR. THIBETICA

red leaf stalks and midrib

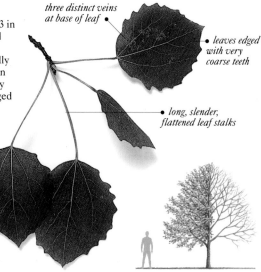

Height 100 ft (30 m)	Shape Broadly columnar	Leaf persistence Deciduous	Leaf type

Family SALICACEAE	Species *Populus tremula*	Author Linnaeus

EUROPEAN ASPEN

Leaves Rounded to broadly ovate, to 3 in (7.5 cm) long and across, with rounded teeth, bronze when young becoming gray-green above, paler beneath, usually smooth on both sides, turning yellow in autumn, on flattened stalks. **Bark** Gray and smooth, becoming darker and ridged at the base. **Flowers** Males with red anthers, females green, borne in drooping catkins to 3 in (7.5 cm) long, on separate plants in early spring before the young leaves emerge. **Fruit** Small, green capsules, in catkins, opening to release tiny seeds held in white, cotton wool-like hairs.
- **NATIVE REGION** Asia, N. Africa, Europe.
- **HABITAT** Woods and scrub on poor soil. In the south of its region, this species occurs in the mountains.

three distinct veins at base of leaf

leaves edged with very coarse teeth

long, slender, flattened leaf stalks

Height 65 ft (20 m)	Shape Broadly spreading	Leaf persistence Deciduous	Leaf type

| Family SALICACEAE | Species *Salix alba* | Author Linnaeus |

WHITE WILLOW

Leaves Lanceolate, to 4 in (10 cm) long and ⅝ in (1.5 cm) across, tapered at both ends, more slender at the tip, silvery-hairy when young becoming green above, gray or blue-green beneath. *Bark* Gray-brown, deeply fissured. *Flowers* Males and females both very small and without petals, clustered in slender, cylindrical, spreading to nearly upright catkins, males to 2 in (5 cm) long, yellow, females to 1½ in (4 cm) long, on separate plants in spring as the young leaves emerge. *Fruit* A small, green capsule, ³⁄₁₆ in (5 mm) long, opening to release fluffy, white seeds.
• **NATIVE REGION** W. Asia, Europe.
• **HABITAT** Riversides and meadows by water.
• **REMARK** This species is widely cultivated in its native region, where it is planted particularly in moist, coastal areas and by rivers.

male catkins have yellow anthers

green female catkins

SALIX ALBA

visibly hairy, silvery young foliage

leaves taper to fine point

dark green mature foliage

leaf buds on bare winter shoot

'BRITZENSIS' △
The young shoots of this form, which is commonly known as the scarlet willow, are bright orange-red during the winter months.

VAR. CAERULEA ▷
Cricket bats are traditionally made from this wood, hence the common name in Britain, cricket-bat willow.

blue-gray, slightly glaucous leaves

| Height 80 ft (25 m) | Shape Broadly columnar | Leaf persistence Deciduous | Leaf type |

Family SALICACEAE	Species *Salix babylonica*	Author Linnaeus

CHINESE OR WEEPING WILLOW

Leaves Lanceolate, to 4 in (10 cm) long and ¾ in (2 cm) across, tapering to a long, slender point, finely toothed at the margin, green above, bluish green and hairy when young becoming smooth beneath, on hanging, glossy brown shoots. *Bark* Gray-brown, fissured into rough, vertical ridges. *Flowers* Very small, without petals, borne in slender, cylindrical catkins, males to 2 in (5 cm) long, yellow, females to 1 in (2.5 cm) long, green, on separate plants in spring with the young leaves. *Fruit* A small green capsule, ³⁄₁₆ in (5 mm) long, opening to release fluffy, white seeds.
• **NATIVE REGION** N. China.
• **HABITAT** Now known only in cultivation.
• **REMARK** This species has been so long cultivated in North Africa, W. Asia, and E. Europe, that its original habitat cannot be determined.

male flowers, with yellow anthers, borne in catkins

◁ **SALIX BABYLONICA**

long, slender, drooping shoots

young leaves emerge with flowers

green female flowers, clustered in catkins

▽ **VAR. PEKINENSIS**
This form is also known as *Salix matsudana* and Pekin willow. It has a narrowly upright habit.

▽ **'PENDULA'**
This particularly graceful form of the weeping willow has typically long, drooping shoots and denser foliage.

visibly twisted shoots and leaves

finely taper-pointed, drooping leaves

'TORTUOSA' ▷
Commonly known as dragon's claw willow, this form has curiously contorted shoots and leaves.

Height 40 ft (12 m)	Shape Broadly weeping	Leaf persistence Deciduous	Leaf type

Family SALICACEAE	Species *Salix daphnoides*	Author Villars

VIOLET WILLOW

Leaves Narrowly elliptic, to 4¾ in (12 cm) long and 1¼ in (3 cm) across, taper-pointed, shallowly toothed, glossy dark green above, blue-green beneath, hairy becoming smooth on both sides, the shoots normally bloomy becoming glossy red-brown. **Bark** Gray and smooth. **Flowers** Males and females both very small and without petals, males with yellow anthers, borne in silky-hairy catkins to 1½ in (4 cm) long, in late winter to early spring before the leaves emerge. **Fruit** A small, green capsule, ³⁄₁₆ in (5 mm) long, opening to release fluffy, white seeds.
• **NATIVE REGION** Europe.
• **HABITAT** Moist woods.

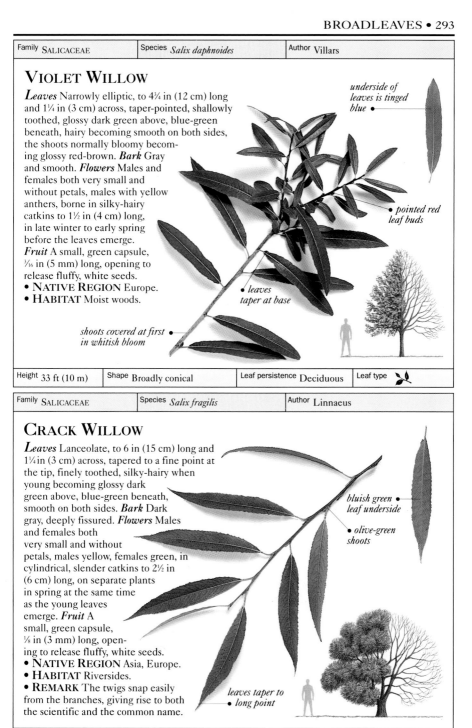

underside of leaves is tinged blue •

• pointed red leaf buds

• leaves taper at base

shoots covered at first • in whitish bloom

Height 33 ft (10 m)	Shape Broadly conical	Leaf persistence Deciduous	Leaf type

Family SALICACEAE	Species *Salix fragilis*	Author Linnaeus

CRACK WILLOW

Leaves Lanceolate, to 6 in (15 cm) long and 1¼ in (3 cm) across, tapered to a fine point at the tip, finely toothed, silky-hairy when young becoming glossy dark green above, blue-green beneath, smooth on both sides. **Bark** Dark gray, deeply fissured. **Flowers** Males and females both very small and without petals, males yellow, females green, in cylindrical, slender catkins to 2½ in (6 cm) long, on separate plants in spring at the same time as the young leaves emerge. **Fruit** A small, green capsule, ⅛ in (3 mm) long, opening to release fluffy, white seeds.
• **NATIVE REGION** Asia, Europe.
• **HABITAT** Riversides.
• **REMARK** The twigs snap easily from the branches, giving rise to both the scientific and the common name.

bluish green • leaf underside

• olive-green shoots

leaves taper to • long point

Height 50 ft (15 m)	Shape Broadly spreading	Leaf persistence Deciduous	Leaf type

Family SALICACEAE	Species *Salix pentandra*	Author Linnaeus

BAY WILLOW

Leaves Elliptic to narrowly ovate, to 4¾ in (12 cm) long and 2 in (5 cm) across, tapering to a short point, finely toothed, glossy very dark green above, paler beneath, smooth on both sides, slightly aromatic. **Bark** Gray-brown, with shallow fissures. **Flowers** Males and females both very small and without petals, males bright yellow, females green, in cylindrical catkins to 2 in (5 cm) long, on separate plants in early summer after the young leaves emerge. **Fruit** A small, green capsule, ¼ in (6 mm) long, opening to release fluffy, white seeds.
• **NATIVE REGION** Asia, Europe.
• **HABITAT** Riverbanks and meadows.

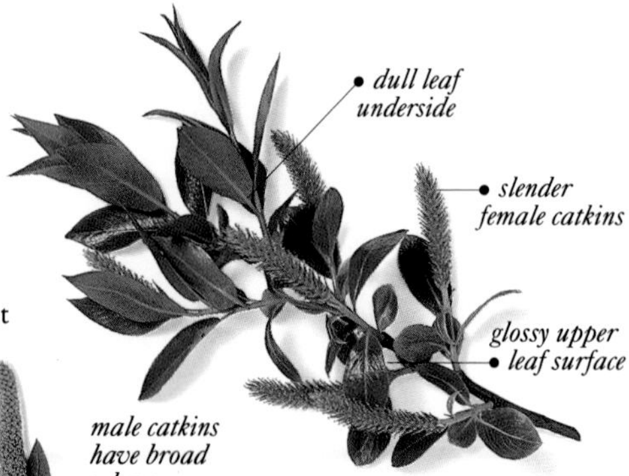

dull leaf underside

slender female catkins

glossy upper leaf surface

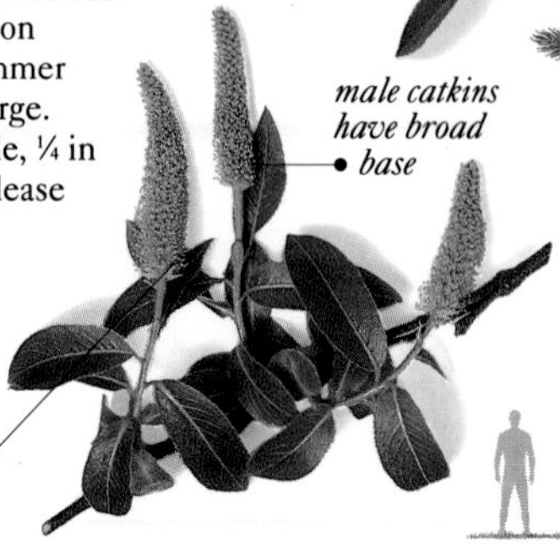

male catkins have broad base

catkins borne at end of leafy shoots

Height 50 ft (15 m)	Shape Broadly spreading	Leaf persistence Deciduous	Leaf type

Family SALICACEAE	Species *Salix x sepulcralis*	Author Simonkai

SALIX X SEPULCRALIS

'CHRYSOCOMA'

Leaves Narrowly lanceolate, to 4¾ in (12 cm) long and ¾ in (2 cm) across, taper-pointed, finely toothed, thinly hairy when young becoming bright green above, blue-green beneath, smooth, on slender, hanging, yellowish shoots. **Bark** Pale gray-brown, with shallow fissures. **Flowers** Small and without petals, in catkins to 3 in (7.5 cm) long, often on the same spike, in spring. **Fruit** A small green capsule, ⅛ in (3 mm) long, opening to release fluffy, white seeds.
• **NATIVE REGION** Of garden origin.
• **REMARK** A hybrid between white willow *(Salix alba, see p.291)* and Chinese weeping willow *(Salix babylonica, see p.292)*. Of its many different forms, 'Chrysocoma' – the familiar weeping willow shown here – is the best-known.

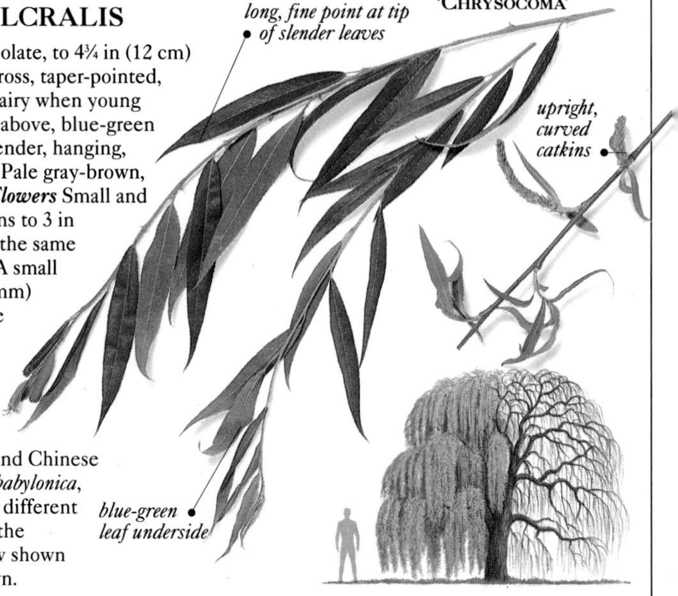

long, fine point at tip of slender leaves

upright, curved catkins

blue-green leaf underside

Height 65 ft (20 m)	Shape Broadly weeping	Leaf persistence Deciduous	Leaf type

SAPINDACEAE

W IDELY DISTRIBUTED MAINLY in tropical and subtropical regions, this family has 1,500 or so species of deciduous trees, shrubs, and climbers, collected in about 150 genera. The leaves are alternate, simple, pinnate, bipinnate, or with three leaflets. The small male or female flowers have usually five petals. The fruit is a dry and winged capsule, nut, or berry.

Family SAPINDACEAE	Species *Koelreuteria paniculata*	Author Laxmann

GOLDEN RAIN TREE

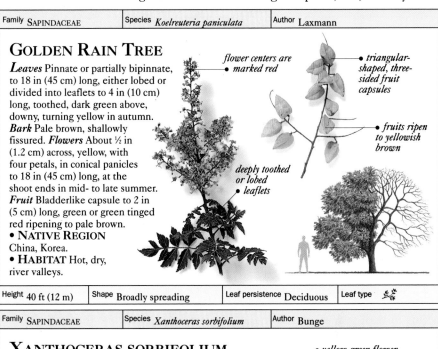

Leaves Pinnate or partially bipinnate, to 18 in (45 cm) long, either lobed or divided into leaflets to 4 in (10 cm) long, toothed, dark green above, downy, turning yellow in autumn. *Bark* Pale brown, shallowly fissured. *Flowers* About ½ in (1.2 cm) across, yellow, with four petals, in conical panicles to 18 in (45 cm) long, at the shoot ends in mid- to late summer. *Fruit* Bladderlike capsule to 2 in (5 cm) long, green or green tinged red ripening to pale brown.
• NATIVE REGION China, Korea.
• HABITAT Hot, dry, river valleys.

flower centers are marked red

triangular-shaped, three-sided fruit capsules

fruits ripen to yellowish brown

deeply toothed or lobed leaflets

Height 40 ft (12 m)	Shape Broadly spreading	Leaf persistence Deciduous	Leaf type

Family SAPINDACEAE	Species *Xanthoceras sorbifolium*	Author Bunge

XANTHOCERAS SORBIFOLIUM

Leaves Pinnate, to 12 in (30 cm) long, with up to 17 narrowly elliptic, toothed leaflets, to 2½ in (6 cm) long, glossy dark green above, smooth. *Bark* Gray-brown, fissured into scaly ridges. *Flowers* To 1¼ in (3 cm) across, white, with five petals, the petals blotched yellow-green becoming red at the base, in upright racemes to 10 in (25 cm) long, at the ends of the old shoots in late spring as or just after the young leaves emerge. *Fruit* A smooth, thick-walled, green capsule, to 2½ in (6 cm) across, broadest at the top, containing several pea-sized seeds.
• NATIVE REGION China.
• HABITAT Thickets.

yellow-green flower center eventually becomes red

leaflets edged with sharp teeth

flower petals curl backward

Height 26 ft (8 m)	Shape Broadly columnar	Leaf persistence Deciduous	Leaf type

SCROPHULARIACEAE

T HIS LARGE FAMILY has about 4,500 species and 220 genera of woody and herbaceous plants, found worldwide. The alternate or opposite leaves can be simple or lobed. The flowers have usually a five-lobed, two-lipped corolla. The fruit is a capsule. The trees are all in the genus *Paulownia*.

Family SCROPHULARIACEAE	Species *Paulownia tomentosa*	Author (Thunberg) Steudel

PAULOWNIA TOMENTOSA

Leaves Ovate, to 12 in (30 cm) long and 10 in (25 cm) across, heart-shaped at the base, taper-pointed, sometimes lobed, dark green and hairy above, hairy beneath. **Bark** Gray, smooth. **Flowers** To 2 in (5 cm) long, pale purple marked deeper purple and yellow inside, borne in upright panicles to 16 in (40 cm) long, in spring. **Fruit** A woody capsule, to 2 in (5 cm) long.
• **NATIVE REGION** China.
• **HABITAT** Mountains.

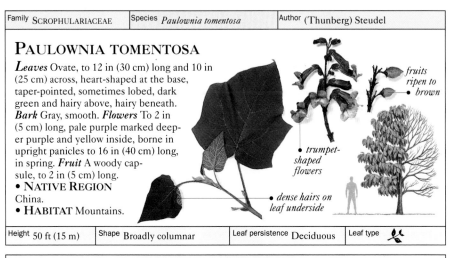

fruits ripen to brown

trumpet-shaped flowers

dense hairs on leaf underside

Height 50 ft (15 m)	Shape Broadly columnar	Leaf persistence Deciduous	Leaf type

SIMAROUBACEAE

T HIS FAMILY OF SOME 20 genera and 150 species of trees and shrubs occurs in both tropical and subtropical regions, and temperate regions of Asia. The alternate leaves are often pinnate. The small flowers have five petals; females develop into the fruit, which is dry and winged, or a capsule.

Family SIMAROUBACEAE	Species *Ailanthus altissima*	Author (Miller) Swingle

TREE OF HEAVEN

Leaves Pinnate, to 24 in (60 cm) long, with 15 or more pairs of leaflets, to 4¾ in (12 cm) long and 2 in (5 cm) across, glossy. **Bark** Gray-brown, with pale streaks. **Flowers** Males and females greenish yellow, with five or six petals, in large panicles at the ends of the shoots, usually on separate plants in mid to late summer. **Fruit** Winged, to 1½ in (4 cm) long.
• **NATIVE REGION** China.
• **HABITAT** Mountain woods.

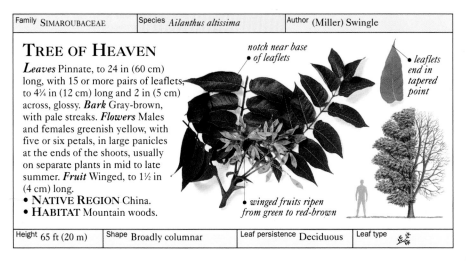

notch near base of leaflets

leaflets end in tapered point

winged fruits ripen from green to red-brown

Height 65 ft (20 m)	Shape Broadly columnar	Leaf persistence Deciduous	Leaf type

STYRACACEAE

T HERE ARE ABOUT 12 GENERA and 150 species of deciduous trees and shrubs in this family, found in east Asia, from the southern United States to Central and South America, with a single species in the Mediterranean. Leaves are alternate and simple. The flower corolla is tubular at the base, and is divided into five to seven lobes. The fruit is usually a capsule.

Family STYRACACEAE	Species *Halesia carolina*	Author Linnaeus

SNOWBELL TREE

Leaves Ovate-oblong, to 8 in (20 cm) long and 4 in (10 cm) across, taper-pointed at the tip, finely toothed, bright green above, paler beneath, thinly hairy on both sides, turning yellow in autumn. *Bark* Pale brown, with scaly, interlacing ridges. *Flowers* White or white flushed pink, drooping, the bell-shaped corolla ¼ in (2 cm) long, with four shallow lobes, in small clusters in mid- to late spring as the young leaves emerge. *Fruit* Pear-shaped, to 2 in (5 cm) long, with four wings, green at first ripening to pale brown.
• **NATIVE REGION** S.E. United States.
• **HABITAT** Rich, moist woods and alongside streams.
• **REMARK** In unfavorable conditions, this species reaches only about 33 ft (10 m).

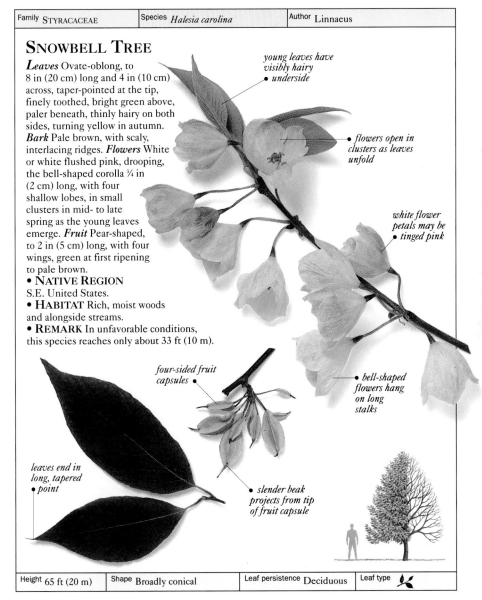

young leaves have visibly hairy • underside

flowers open in clusters as leaves unfold

white flower petals may be • tinged pink

four-sided fruit capsules •

bell-shaped flowers hang on long stalks

leaves end in long, tapered • point

slender beak projects from tip of fruit capsule

Height 65 ft (20 m)	Shape Broadly conical	Leaf persistence Deciduous	Leaf type

Family STYRACACEAE	Species *Pterostyrax hispida*	Author Siebold & Zuccarini

EPAULETTE TREE

Leaves Oblong to ovate, to 8 in (20 cm) long and 4 in (10 cm) across, tapered at the base, pointed at the tip, bright green and smooth or nearly so above, gray-green and more or less hairy beneath. **Bark** Pale gray-brown and corky, with orange fissures. **Flowers** Each about ¼ in (6 mm) long, white, fragrant, with conspicuous, exserted stamens, in hanging panicles to 8 in (20 cm) long, in early to midsummer. **Fruit** Small, gray, dry, about ½ in (1.2 cm) long, with five ribs, and yellow-brown bristles.
• **NATIVE REGION** China, Japan.
• **HABITAT** Woods and alongside mountain streams.

• *minutely-toothed leaf margin*

corolla at first closed over long, projecting • *stamens*

• *distinctively shaped drooping flower clusters*

Height 40 ft (12 m)	Shape Broadly spreading	Leaf persistence Deciduous	Leaf type

Family STYRACACEAE	Species *Styrax hemsleyana*	Author Diels

STYRAX HEMSLEYANA

Leaves Ovate to obovate, to 5 in (13 cm) long and 3¼ in (8 cm) across, oblique at the base, taper-pointed, sparsely toothed, smooth or nearly so. **Bark** Pale gray. **Flowers** About ⅝ in (1.5 cm) long, with a five-lobed corolla, white, with yellow anthers, the calyx densely covered with dark brown hairs, borne in upright to spreading racemes to 6 in (15 cm) long, emerging from the ends of short branches in early summer. **Fruit** Egg-shaped, gray and berrylike, ⅝ in (1.5 cm) long, enclosing a single seed.
• **NATIVE REGION** C. China.
• **HABITAT** Woods and thickets.
• **REMARK** Cultivated plants may grow taller than typical specimens found in the wild. This species is similar to *Styrax obassia* (see p.299), but has exposed brown leaf buds and less downy leaves.

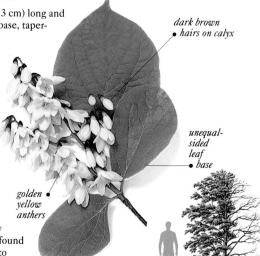

dark brown • *hairs on calyx*

unequal-sided leaf • *base*

golden • *yellow anthers*

Height 26 ft (8 m)	Shape Broadly columnar	Leaf persistence Deciduous	Leaf type

Family STYRACACEAE	Species *Styrax japonica*	Author Siebold & Zuccarini

JAPANESE SNOWBELL

Leaves Elliptic to ovate, to 4 in (10 cm) long and 2 in (5 cm) across, narrowed at the base, abruptly taper-pointed at the tip, with a finely or sparsely toothed margin, rich glossy green above, turning yellow or red in autumn. *Bark* Dark gray-brown and smooth, developing orange-brown fissures with age. *Flowers* About ⅝ in (1.5 cm) long, with a five-lobed corolla, white or pink-tinged, with yellow anthers, slightly fragrant, on slender stalks, in short racemes or hanging singly beneath the branches in early to midsummer. *Fruit* Rounded to egg-shaped, gray, and berrylike, to ⅝ in (1.5 cm) long, with a single seed.
• **NATIVE REGION** China, Japan, Korea.
• **HABITAT** Sunny places, usually on wet ground.
• **REMARK** This species makes a beautiful, elegant small tree or large shrub.

glossy green leaves have duller underside

bell-like flowers hang beneath branches

Height 33 ft (10 m)	Shape Broadly spreading	Leaf persistence Deciduous	Leaf type

Family STYRACACEAE	Species *Styrax obassia*	Author Siebold & Zuccarini

STYRAX OBASSIA

dense hairs cover underside of leaves

Leaves Variable, elliptic to rounded, to 8 in (20 cm) long and nearly the same across, dark green and smooth above, blue-gray and densely hairy beneath, turning yellow in autumn. *Bark* Gray-brown and smooth, becoming vertically fissured with age. *Flowers* Individually about 1 in (2.5 cm) long, with a five-lobed corolla, white, with yellow anthers, fragrant, borne in horizontally spreading racemes to 6 in (15 cm) long, in early to midsummer. *Fruit* Egg-shaped, gray, and berrylike, about ¾ in (2 cm) long, with a single seed.
• **NATIVE REGION** N. China, Japan, Korea.
• **HABITAT** Moist woods.
• **REMARK** The flower racemes are often almost hidden by the large, broad leaves.

largest leaves are carried at shoot end

loose racemes hang beneath leaves

Height 40 ft (12 m)	Shape Broadly columnar	Leaf persistence Deciduous	Leaf type

THEACEAE

T HE TEA FAMILY has 30 genera and over 600 species of deciduous trees and shrubs. They grow mainly in tropical regions, particularly Asia and the Americas, but also in temperate areas of east Asia and the southeast United States. Leaves are simple and usually alternate. Flowers are typically large and showy, with five petals. The fruit is most often a capsule.

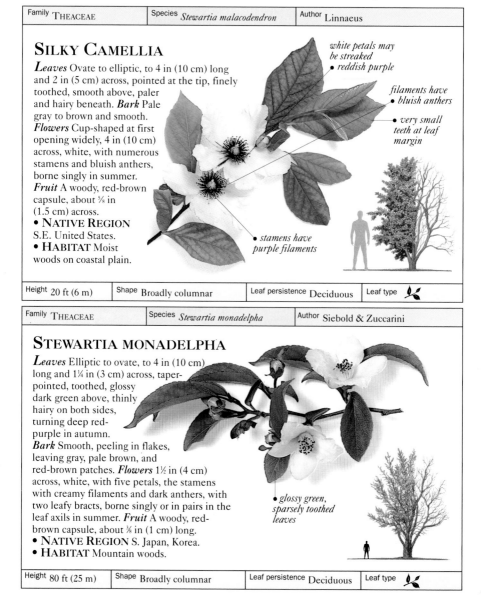

Family THEACEAE	Species *Stewartia malacodendron*	Author Linnaeus

SILKY CAMELLIA

Leaves Ovate to elliptic, to 4 in (10 cm) long and 2 in (5 cm) across, pointed at the tip, finely toothed, smooth above, paler and hairy beneath. **Bark** Pale gray to brown and smooth. **Flowers** Cup-shaped at first opening widely, 4 in (10 cm) across, white, with numerous stamens and bluish anthers, borne singly in summer. **Fruit** A woody, red-brown capsule, about ⅝ in (1.5 cm) across.
• **NATIVE REGION** S.E. United States.
• **HABITAT** Moist woods on coastal plain.

white petals may be streaked reddish purple

filaments have bluish anthers

very small teeth at leaf margin

stamens have purple filaments

Height 20 ft (6 m)	Shape Broadly columnar	Leaf persistence Deciduous	Leaf type

Family THEACEAE	Species *Stewartia monadelpha*	Author Siebold & Zuccarini

STEWARTIA MONADELPHA

Leaves Elliptic to ovate, to 4 in (10 cm) long and 1¼ in (3 cm) across, taper-pointed, toothed, glossy dark green above, thinly hairy on both sides, turning deep red-purple in autumn. **Bark** Smooth, peeling in flakes, leaving gray, pale brown, and red-brown patches. **Flowers** 1½ in (4 cm) across, white, with five petals, the stamens with creamy filaments and dark anthers, with two leafy bracts, borne singly or in pairs in the leaf axils in summer. **Fruit** A woody, red-brown capsule, about ⅜ in (1 cm) long.
• **NATIVE REGION** S. Japan, Korea.
• **HABITAT** Mountain woods.

glossy green, sparsely toothed leaves

Height 80 ft (25 m)	Shape Broadly columnar	Leaf persistence Deciduous	Leaf type

Family THEACEAE	Species *Stewartia pseudocamellia*	Author Maximowicz

STEWARTIA PSEUDOCAMELLIA

Leaves Broadly ovate to elliptic, to 4 in (10 cm) long and 2½ in (6 cm) across, tapered to a short point, finely toothed, dark green and smooth above, smooth or hairy beneath, turning yellow to orange or red in autumn. **Bark** Red-brown, peeling in thin, irregular plates, leaving gray and pink patches. **Flowers** 2½ in (6 cm) across, white, with five petals, the numerous stamens with yellow filaments and darker anthers, with two leafy bracts outside the sepals, borne singly or in pairs in the leaf axils in summer. **Fruit** A woody, red-brown capsule, about ¾ in (2 cm) long.
• **NATIVE REGION** Japan.
• **HABITAT** Mountain woods.
• **REMARK** As in other species of *Stewartia*, the five flower petals are joined together at the base and the flowers fall intact.

flaking bark creates pinkish gray patchwork effect

frilly-petaled flowers •

finely toothed leaf margin

flowers have bright yellow filaments •

▽ **STEWARTIA PSEUDOCAMELLIA**

△ **VAR. KOREANA**
The flowers of this native South Korean variety open more widely than those of the typical form. Its slightly larger leaves color just as well in autumn, however.

paler leaf underside may be smooth or hairy •

flower petals covered in silky hairs before opening •

dark green leaf upperside •

Height 65 ft (20 m)	Shape Broadly columnar	Leaf persistence Deciduous	Leaf type

TILIACEAE

T HE LIMES, or lindens, of the genus *Tilia* are well-loved members of this family, which includes more than 700 species of trees, shrubs, and herbaceous plants, in some 50 genera. Most are confined to the tropics, but the limes occur in temperate regions of the northern hemisphere. The leaves are alternate and sometimes lobed, frequently with starry hairs. The often fragrant flowers are small, usually with five petals and sepals, and numerous stamens. The fruit is variable, and may be woody, a dry capsule, or a berry.

Family TILIACEAE	Species *Tilia americana*	Author Linnaeus

AMERICAN LINDEN

Leaves Broadly ovate to nearly rounded, to 8 in (20 cm) long and 6 in (15 cm) across, abruptly tapered to a fine tip with coarse, pointed teeth, matte deep green above, paler and glossy beneath, becoming smooth on both sides except for tufts of brown hairs in the vein axils beneath. *Bark* Brown to gray, cracked into long, scaly ridges. *Flowers* ⅝ in (1.5 cm) across, pale yellow, with five petals, fragrant, in pendulous clusters of up to ten, each cluster with an oblong bract to 4 in (10 cm) long, in midsummer. *Fruit* Rounded, woody, pale gray-green, about ⅜ in (1 cm) across.
• **NATIVE REGION** E. North America.
• **HABITAT** Moist woods.
• **REMARK** Also known as basswood, lime, whitewood.

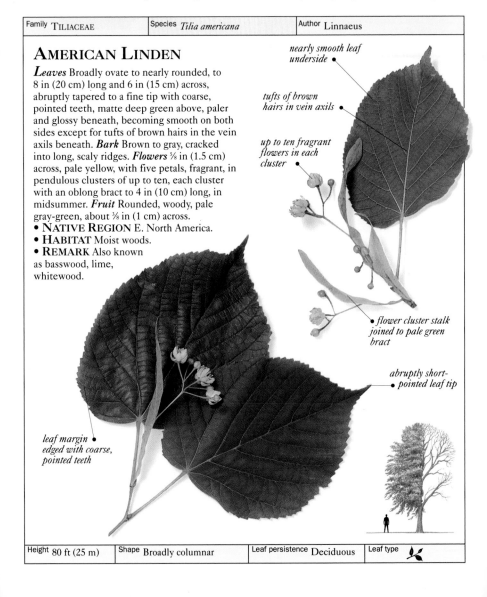

nearly smooth leaf underside

tufts of brown hairs in vein axils

up to ten fragrant flowers in each cluster

flower cluster stalk joined to pale green bract

abruptly short-pointed leaf tip

leaf margin edged with coarse, pointed teeth

Height 80 ft (25 m)	Shape Broadly columnar	Leaf persistence Deciduous	Leaf type

Family TILIACEAE	Species *Tilia cordata*	Author Miller

LITTLELEAF LINDEN

Leaves Rounded, to 3 in (7.5 cm) long and across, heart-shaped at the base, taper-pointed, toothed, glossy green above, blue-green beneath, smooth except for hairs in the vein axils beneath, turning yellow in autumn.
Bark Gray, smooth, becoming gray-brown and furrowed with age. ***Flowers*** ¾ in (2 cm) across, pale yellow, with five petals, fragrant, in clusters of up to ten, each with a green bract to 4 in (10 cm) long in midsummer.
Fruit Rounded, woody, gray-green, about ¼ in (6 mm) across.
• **NATIVE REGION** W. Asia, Europe.
• **HABITAT** On limestone.

small, glossy green leaves taper to long point at tip •

• up to ten flowers in each drooping or upright cluster

tufts of brown • hairs in vein axils on leaf underside

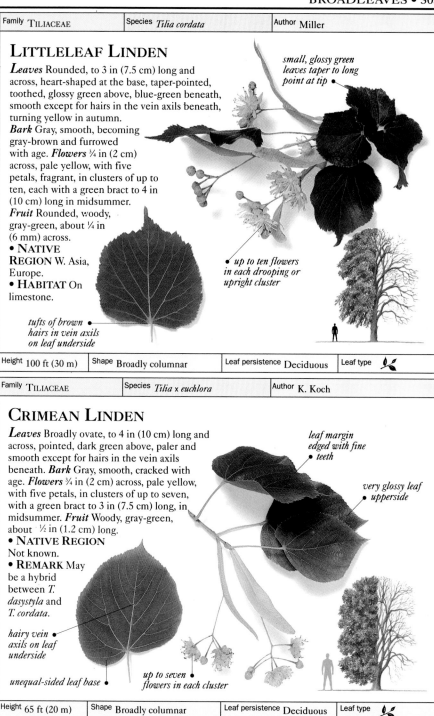

Height 100 ft (30 m)	Shape Broadly columnar	Leaf persistence Deciduous	Leaf type

Family TILIACEAE	Species *Tilia x euchlora*	Author K. Koch

CRIMEAN LINDEN

Leaves Broadly ovate, to 4 in (10 cm) long and across, pointed, dark green above, paler and smooth except for hairs in the vein axils beneath. ***Bark*** Gray, smooth, cracked with age. ***Flowers*** ¾ in (2 cm) across, pale yellow, with five petals, in clusters of up to seven, with a green bract to 3 in (7.5 cm) long, in midsummer. ***Fruit*** Woody, gray-green, about ½ in (1.2 cm) long.
• **NATIVE REGION** Not known.
• **REMARK** May be a hybrid between *T. dasystyla* and *T. cordata*.

leaf margin edged with fine • teeth

very glossy leaf • upperside

hairy vein • axils on leaf underside

unequal-sided leaf base •

up to seven • flowers in each cluster

Height 65 ft (20 m)	Shape Broadly columnar	Leaf persistence Deciduous	Leaf type

| Family TILIACEAE | Species *Tilia x europaea* | Author Linnaeus |

COMMON LINDEN

Leaves Broadly ovate to rounded, to 4 in (10 cm) long and across, heart-shaped at the base, abruptly short-pointed at the tip, coarsely toothed, dark green above, paler beneath, smooth except for tufts of hairs in the vein axils beneath. *Bark* Gray-brown, with shallow fissures. *Flowers* Small, ¼ in (2 cm) across, pale yellow, fragrant, with five petals, in clusters of up to ten, each cluster with a pale green bract to 4 in (10 cm) long, in midsummer. *Fruit* Egg-shaped, woody, gray-green, about ½ in (1.2 cm) long.
• **NATIVE REGION** Europe.
• **HABITAT** With the parents.
• **REMARK** Also known as *Tilia x vulgaris*. A hybrid between small-leaved lime (*Tilia cordata*, see p.303) and broad-leaved lime (*Tilia platyphyllos*, see p.305).

∇ TILIA X EUROPAEA

tufts of hairs in vein axils on leaf underside

each flower cluster has pale green bract

◁ 'WRATISLAVIENSIS'
The glowing, bright yellow young foliage of this form eventually matures to green.

| Height 130 ft (40 m) | Shape Broadly columnar | Leaf persistence Deciduous | Leaf type |

| Family TILIACEAE | Species *Tilia mongolica* | Author Maximowicz |

MONGOLIAN LINDEN

Leaves Broadly ovate, to 3 in (7.5 cm) long and across, with three to five lobes, taper-pointed at the tip, sharply toothed, reddish when young becoming glossy dark green above, blue-green beneath, smooth on both sides except for tufts of hair in the vein axis beneath, turning yellow in autumn, on red stalks. *Bark* Gray and smooth. *Flowers* Small, ¼ in (2 cm) across, pale yellow, fragrant, with five petals, borne in drooping clusters of up to 20, each clusters with a narrow, pale green bract to 4 in (10 cm) long, in mid-summer. *Fruit* Rounded, woody, gray-green, ½ in (1.2 cm) long.
• **NATIVE REGION** N.E. Asia.
• **HABITAT** Mountain slopes.
• **REMARK** Easily identified in season by its distinctively lobed, sharply toothed leaves.

lobed leaves edged with sharp teeth

upper leaf surface matures to dark green

tiny tufts of hairs in vein axis

| Height 50 ft (15 m) | Shape Broadly spreading | Leaf persistence Deciduous | Leaf type |

| Family TILIACEAE | Species *Tilia platyphyllos* | Author Scopoli |

BROAD-LEAVED LINDEN

TILIA PLATYPHYLLOS

Leaves Rounded to broadly ovate, to 4¾ in (12 cm) long and across, heart-shaped at the base, tapering to a short point at the tip, sharply toothed, dark green above, paler beneath, hairy on both sides especially beneath, turning yellow in autumn. **Bark** Gray, with shallow fissures. **Flowers** Small, ¾ in (2 cm) across, pale yellow, fragrant, with five petals, in drooping clusters of about five, each cluster with a pale green bract to 4¾ in (12 cm) long, in early to midsummer. **Fruit** Woody, gray-green, ½ in (1.2 cm) long, with five ribs.
• **NATIVE REGION** S.W. Asia, Europe.
• **HABITAT** Moist woods.

deeply veined leaves

flower clusters hang from pale green bracts

leaves edged with large, sharp teeth

◁ 'LACINIATA'
This unusual form has narrowly ovate, twisted leaves.

| Height 100 ft (30 m) | Shape Broadly columnar | Leaf persistence Deciduous | Leaf type |

| Family TILIACEAE | Species *Tilia tomentosa* | Author Moench |

SILVER LINDEN

leaves may be slightly lobed

Leaves Rounded, to 4¾ in (12 cm) long and 4 in (10 cm) across, often slightly lobed, usually obliquely heart-shaped at the base, tapering to a short point at the tip, sharply toothed, dark green above, white-hairy beneath. **Bark** Gray, with shallow ridges. **Flowers** Small, ¾ in (2 cm) across, pale yellow, highly fragrant, with five petals, in drooping clusters of up to ten, each cluster with a pale green bract to 4 in (10 cm) long, in mid- to late summer. **Fruit** Rounded to egg-shaped, woody, gray-green, to ½ in (1.2 cm) long.
• **NATIVE REGION** S.W. Asia, S.E. Europe.
• **HABITAT** Mixed deciduous and evergreen woods.
• **REMARK** Also known as *Tilia argentea*. The rich-scented flowers are lethal to bees.

flowers hang up to ten together

TILIA TOMENTOSA

distinctive silvery leaf underside

◁ 'PETIOLARIS'
The weeping silver lime is a form selected for its pendulous shoots and longer-stalked leaves.

| Height 80 ft (25 m) | Shape Broadly columnar | Leaf persistence Deciduous | Leaf type |

TROCHODENDRACEAE

A SINGLE GENUS WITH ONE species, described below, belongs to this family. Its affinities are uncertain, although is generally agreed to be relatively primitive among flowering plants. It is usually thought to be most closely related to either *Cercidiphyllum* (see p.133) or *Drimys* (see p.310).

Family TROCHODENDRACEAE	Species *Trochodendron aralioides*	Author Siebold & Zuccarini

TROCHODENDRON ARALIOIDES

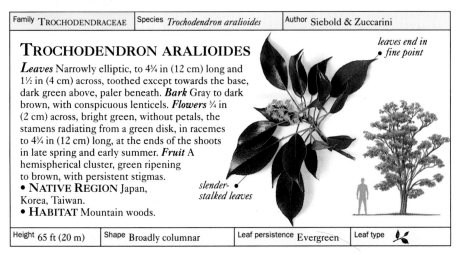

leaves end in
• fine point

Leaves Narrowly elliptic, to 4¾ in (12 cm) long and 1½ in (4 cm) across, toothed except towards the base, dark green above, paler beneath. **Bark** Gray to dark brown, with conspicuous lenticels. **Flowers** ¾ in (2 cm) across, bright green, without petals, the stamens radiating from a green disk, in racemes to 4¾ in (12 cm) long, at the ends of the shoots in late spring and early summer. **Fruit** A hemispherical cluster, green ripening to brown, with persistent stigmas.
• **NATIVE REGION** Japan, Korea, Taiwan.
• **HABITAT** Mountain woods.

slender-
stalked leaves

Height 65 ft (20 m)	Shape Broadly columnar	Leaf persistence Evergreen	Leaf type

ULMACEAE

T HE ELM FAMILY contains about 15 genera and 150 species of ever-green and deciduous trees and shrubs, growing wild in tropical and northern temperate regions. Leaves are usually alternate. The small flowers have no petals. The fruit may be winged and dry, fleshy with a single seed, or a nut.

Family ULMACEAE	Species *Celtis australis*	Author Linnaeus

SOUTHERN NETTLE TREE

rough upper
leaf surface •

base of leaf is
• three-veined

Leaves Lanceolate to ovate, to 6 in (15 cm) long and 2 in (5 cm) across, slender-pointed, rather light to dark green and roughly hairy above, gray-green and softly hairy beneath. **Bark** Pale gray, smooth. **Flowers** Males and females both small and green, without petals, either singly or in small clusters in the leaf axils, separately on the same plant in spring. **Fruit** Rounded, berrylike, about ⅜ in (1 cm) across, nearly black when ripe.
• **NATIVE REGION** S.W. Asia, S. Europe.
• **HABITAT** Warm, dry, rocky slopes.

leaves
edged with
sharp teeth

Height 65 ft (20 m)	Shape Broadly columnar	Leaf persistence Deciduous	Leaf type

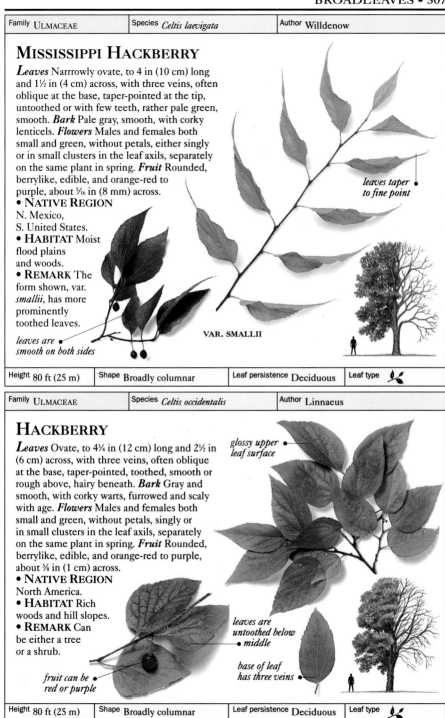

Family ULMACEAE	Species *Celtis laevigata*	Author Willdenow

MISSISSIPPI HACKBERRY

Leaves Narrrowly ovate, to 4 in (10 cm) long and 1½ in (4 cm) across, with three veins, often oblique at the base, taper-pointed at the tip, untoothed or with few teeth, rather pale green, smooth. **Bark** Pale gray, smooth, with corky lenticels. **Flowers** Males and females both small and green, without petals, either singly or in small clusters in the leaf axils, separately on the same plant in spring. **Fruit** Rounded, berrylike, edible, and orange-red to purple, about ⁵⁄₁₆ in (8 mm) across.
• **NATIVE REGION** N. Mexico, S. United States.
• **HABITAT** Moist flood plains and woods.
• **REMARK** The form shown, var. *smallii*, has more prominently toothed leaves.

leaves taper to fine point

leaves are smooth on both sides

VAR. SMALLII

Height 80 ft (25 m)	Shape Broadly columnar	Leaf persistence Deciduous	Leaf type

Family ULMACEAE	Species *Celtis occidentalis*	Author Linnaeus

HACKBERRY

Leaves Ovate, to 4¾ in (12 cm) long and 2½ in (6 cm) across, with three veins, often oblique at the base, taper-pointed, toothed, smooth or rough above, hairy beneath. **Bark** Gray and smooth, with corky warts, furrowed and scaly with age. **Flowers** Males and females both small and green, without petals, singly or in small clusters in the leaf axils, separately on the same plant in spring. **Fruit** Rounded, berrylike, edible, and orange-red to purple, about ⅜ in (1 cm) across.
• **NATIVE REGION** North America.
• **HABITAT** Rich woods and hill slopes.
• **REMARK** Can be either a tree or a shrub.

glossy upper leaf surface

leaves are untoothed below middle

base of leaf has three veins

fruit can be red or purple

Height 80 ft (25 m)	Shape Broadly columnar	Leaf persistence Deciduous	Leaf type

| Family ULMACEAE | Species *Ulmus x hollandica* | Author Miller |

ULMUS X HOLLANDICA

Leaves Ovate to elliptic, to 4¾ in (12 cm) long and 2½ in (6 cm) across, taper-pointed, toothed, usually hairy beneath. **Bark** Gray-brown, ridged. **Flowers** Tiny, red, borne in clusters on the shoots in early spring. **Fruit** A winged seed, to 1 in (2.5 cm) long.
• **NATIVE REGION** Europe.
• **HABITAT** Woods and hedgerows.
• **REMARK** A hybrid between wych elm *(Ulmus glabra)* and smooth-leaved elm *(Ulmus minor, see below)*.

unequal-sided • leaf base

glossy leaf • upperside

'KLEMMER'
This form was raised in Belgium. It is a narrowly conical tree.

| Height 100 ft (30 m) | Shape Broadly columnar | Leaf persistence Deciduous | Leaf type |

| Family ULMACEAE | Species *Ulmus japonica* | Author (Rehder) Sargent |

JAPANESE ELM

Leaves Elliptic to obovate, to 4 in (10 cm) long and 2½ in (6 cm) across, narrowed at the unequal base, taper-pointed at the tip, double-toothed, dark green and rough with hairs above, paler and downy at least on the veins beneath. **Bark** Pale gray-brown, fissured. **Flowers** Very small, red, in small clusters on the shoots in spring. **Fruit** A winged seed, ⅝ in (1.5 cm) long, ripening a few weeks after flowering time.
• **NATIVE REGION** N.E. Asia, Japan.
• **HABITAT** Woods, rocky places, and moors.

leaf base is only • slightly unequal

leaves end in abrupt • point

| Height 100 ft (30 m) | Shape Broadly spreading | Leaf persistence Deciduous | Leaf type |

| Family ULMACEAE | Species *Ulmus minor* | Author Miller |

SMOOTH-LEAVED ELM

rounded • leaves

VAR. VULGARIS

Leaves Elliptic to obovate, to 4¾ in (12 cm) long and 2½ in (6 cm) across, pointed, double-toothed, glossy bright green and smooth above, with hairs in the vein axils beneath. **Bark** Gray-brown, ridged. **Flowers** Tiny, red, in clusters in early spring. **Fruit** A small, winged seed.
• **NATIVE REGION** N. Africa, S.W. Asia, Europe.
• **HABITAT** Woods and hedgerows.
• **REMARK** The form shown, var. *vulgaris* (formerly *U. procera*), is the once-common English elm.

leaves edged • with sharp, double teeth

| Height 100 ft (30 m) | Shape Broadly columnar | Leaf persistence Deciduous | Leaf type |

Family ULMACEAE	Species *Ulmus parvifolia*	Author Jacquin

CHINESE ELM

Leaves Elliptic to ovate or obovate, to 2½ in (6 cm) long and 1½ in (4 cm) across, oblique at the base, pointed, sharply toothed, glossy dark green and sometimes rough above, with hairs in the vein axils beneath, turning yellow, red, or purple in autumn. **Bark** Gray-brown, peeling in scales. **Flowers** Tiny, red, in clusters in the leaf axils in early autumn. **Fruit** A small seed with a green wing, ⁵⁄₁₆ in (8 mm) long.
• **NATIVE REGION** E. Asia.
• **HABITAT** Rocky places.

leaves may persist into winter

oblique leaf base

Height 50 ft (15 m)	Shape Broadly spreading	Leaf persistence Deciduous	Leaf type

Family ULMACEAE	Species *Ulmus pumila*	Author Linnaeus

SIBERIAN ELM

Leaves Elliptic to narrowly ovate, to 2½ in (6 cm) long and 1 in (2.5 cm) across, nearly equal-sided at the base, taper-pointed, sharply toothed, dark green above, smooth on both sides. **Bark** Gray-brown, rough, corrugated. **Flowers** Very small, red, in clusters on the shoots in spring before leaves. **Fruit** A small seed surrounded by a rounded, notched, green wing, ½ in (1.2 cm) long.
• **NATIVE REGION** C. to E. Asia.
• **HABITAT** Sandy or stony soil.

curved point at leaf tip

nearly equal-sided leaf base

Height 65 ft (20 m)	Shape Broadly columnar	Leaf persistence Deciduous	Leaf type

Family ULMACEAE	Species *Zelkova carpinifolia*	Author (Pallas) K. Koch

ZELKOVA CARPINIFOLIA

Leaves Elliptic to oblong, to 4 in (10 cm) long and 2 in (5 cm) across, with about ten pairs of veins ending in triangular teeth, dark green and slightly rough above, hairy beneath, turning orange-brown in autumn. **Bark** Gray and smooth, flaking with age, on a fluted trunk. **Flowers** Males and females both small and green, in separate clusters on the same plant in spring. **Fruit** Small and rounded.
• **NATIVE REGION** Caucasus, N. Iran.
• **HABITAT** Forests.
• **REMARK** Easily distinguished by its short trunk divided into numerous upright branches.

short leaf stalk

leaf margin edged with large, broad teeth

Height 80 ft (25 m)	Shape Broadly columnar	Leaf persistence Deciduous	Leaf type

Family ULMACEAE	Species *Zelkova serrata*	Author (Thunberg) Makino

JAPANESE ZELKOVA (KEAKI)

Leaves Ovate to oblong-ovate, to 4¾ in (12 cm) long and 2 in (5 cm) across, rounded at the base, taper-pointed, sharply toothed, the teeth ending in a short point, dark green and slightly rough above, paler and nearly smooth beneath, turning yellow, orange, or red in autumn. **Bark** Pale gray and smooth, flaking with age. **Flowers** Males and females both small and green, on the young shoots on the same plant in spring. **Fruit** Small and rounded.
• **NATIVE REGION** China, Japan, Korea.
• **HABITAT** Moist soil near streams.

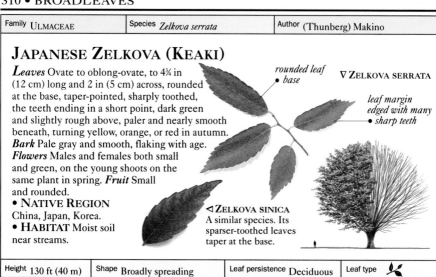

rounded leaf base

▽ ZELKOVA SERRATA

leaf margin edged with many sharp teeth

◁ ZELKOVA SINICA
A similar species. Its sparser-toothed leaves taper at the base.

Height 130 ft (40 m)	Shape Broadly spreading	Leaf persistence Deciduous	Leaf type

WINTERACEAE

A PRIMITIVE FAMILY, possibly related to the magnolias *(Magnolia,* see pp.202–215). About five genera and 60 species of evergreen trees and shrubs occur in Madagascar, and from Mexico to South America, and Southeast Asia to Australia and New Zealand. Plants have alternately arranged, untoothed leaves, five- or more petaled flowers, and small, berrylike clustered fruits.

Family WINTERACEAE	Species *Drimys winteri*	Author J. R. & J. G. Forster

WINTER'S BARK

Leaves Oblong to elliptic, to 8 in (20 cm) long and 2½ in (6 cm) across, untoothed, glossy dark green above, bluish green to bluish white beneath, leathery, aromatic when crushed. **Bark** Gray-brown and smooth, very aromatic. **Flowers** 1½ in (4 cm) across, white, fragrant, with numerous slender petals, borne in large clusters in spring to early summer. **Fruit** A small berry, green ripening to purple-black, in clusters at the end of long stalks.
• **NATIVE REGION** Mexico, South America.
• **HABITAT** Mountains.
• **REMARK** Named after Captain William Winter, who sailed with Sir Francis Drake in the sixteenth century. He used the bark (a source of vitamin C) to treat scurvy, a disease caused by a deficiency of the same vitamin.

flowers borne in dense, branched clusters

green unripe fruit

bloomy leaf underside

Height 50 ft (15 m)	Shape Narrowly conical	Leaf persistence Evergreen	Leaf type

GLOSSARY

TECHNICAL TERMS have been kept to a minimum, but a limited use of them is unavoidable in a book of this kind. Words in **bold** in the definitions are explained elsewhere in the glossary.

You may also find it useful to look at HYBRID PLANTS (p.8), A FAMILY TREE (p.9), WHAT IS A TREE? (pp.12–13), THE PARTS OF A TREE (pp.14–15), and CONIFER OR BROADLEAF? (pp.16–17).

- **ANTHER**
Part of a **stamen** that releases **pollen**.
- **ARIL**
Fleshy seed coat.
- **AURICLE**
Small, earlike **lobe**.
- **BIPINNATE**
Pinnate, with the divisions themselves pinnate.
- **BLOOMY**
Covered with a waxy or powdery blue-white deposit.
- **BRACT**
Leaflike structure below a flower or flower cluster.
- **CALYX**
Small part of a flower outside the petals, composed of **sepals**.
- **CAPSULE**
Dry fruit that splits open to release its seeds.
- **CATKIN**
Usually pendulous cluster of **bracts** and tiny flowers, most often of one sex.
- **COMPOUND LEAF**
One that is composed of two or more separate **leaflets**.
- **COROLLA**
Often showy and colored part of a flower, composed of petals.
- **DECIDUOUS**
Without leaves for part of each year.
- **ENTIRE**
Without teeth or **lobes**.
- **EVERGREEN**
Retaining leaves for more than one year.
- **EXSERTED**
Conspicuously protruding.
- **FILAMENT**
Stalk of an **anther**.

- **GLAUCOUS**
Bluish white.
- **HARDY**
Able to withstand winter temperatures.
- **HERBACEOUS PLANT**
Nonwoody plant that dies at the end of the growing season or overwinters by means of underground structures.
- **LEAF AXIL**
Angle formed between a leaf and its stem.
- **LEAFLET**
Single division of a **compound leaf**.
- **LENTICEL**
Usually corky area on a trunk that lets air through the bark.
- **LOBE**
Rounded segment or part.
- **MONOTYPIC**
Of a family: containing a single genus that contains only one species; of a genus: containing a single species.
- **NATIVE**
Growing naturally wild in a specific area.
- **NATURALIZED**
Introduced by man and growing as if naturally wild in a specific area.
- **OVARY**
Organ of a flower's female part that, in fruit, contains the seeds.
- **PALMATE**
Divided into **leaflets** or **lobes** in the manner of a hand.
- **PANICLE**
Raceme in which the branches are themselves branched.
- **PEALIKE**
Of a flower: similar in structure to that of a leguminous plant.

- **PERSISTENT**
Remaining attached.
- **PINNATE**
Compound leaf, with **leaflets** arranged on opposite sides of a common stalk.
- **POLLEN**
Spores or grains released from the **anthers**, containing the male reproductive element.
- **RACEME**
Stalked flowers borne singly along a central axis.
- **RACHIS**
Stalk of a **pinnate** leaf on which the **leaflets** are borne.
- **SEPAL**
Individual part of the **calyx**.
- **SIMPLE LEAF**
One that is not divided into **leaflets**.
- **SINUS**
Gap between two **lobes**.
- **SPIKE**
Raceme bearing unstalked flowers.
- **STAMEN**
Anther, usually on a **filament**. A variable number composes the male part of a flower.
- **STIGMA**
Organ of a flower's female part, borne at the tip of the **style**, on which the **pollen** is deposited.
- **STIPULE**
Small, leaflike structure, most often paired, borne where the leaf stalk joins the stem.
- **STYLE**
Organ of a flower's female part that bears the **stigma**.
- **TEPAL**
Petal or **sepal**, where there is no distinct difference between the two.

INDEX OF PLANTS

H

I

J

K

L

ACKNOWLEDGMENTS

THE AUTHOR AND PUBLISHER are greatly indebted to a number of institutions and people, without whom this book could not have been produced. The following supplied and/or collected plant material for photography: Barry Phillips (Curator), Bill George (Head Gardener), and all the staff of the Sir Harold Hillier Gardens and Arboretum, Ampfield, Hampshire; Robert Eburn, P.H.B. Gardner, Bernard and Letty Perrott, and Mrs Eve Taylor; Kate Haywood of The Royal Horticultural Society's Garden Wisley, Woking, Surrey; Hillier Nurseries (Winchester) Limited; Richard Johnston, Mount Annan section of the Royal Botanic Gardens, Sydney, Australia; Longstock Park Gardens; Mike Maunder and Melanie Thomas of the Royal Botanic Gardens, Kew, Surrey; Colin Morgan of the Forestry Commission Research Division, Bedgebury National Pinetum, Cranbrook, Kent; Andrew Pinder (Arboricultural Officer), London Borough of Richmond upon Thames; John White and Margaret Ruskin of the Forestry Commission, Westonbirt Arboretum, Tetbury, Gloucestershire.

The following helped to compile reference material for the illustrators: S. Andrews, T. Kirkham, and Mike Maunder of the Royal Botanic Gardens, Kew, Surrey; the Arnold Arboretum of Harvard University, Jamaica Plain, Massachusetts; Kathie Atkinson; S. Clark and S. Knees of the Royal Botanic Garden Edinburgh, Lothian, Scotland; D. Cooney of the Waite Arboretum, University of Adelaide, S. Australia; B. Davis; Dr. T.R. Dudley (Lead Scientist and Research Botanist) of the U.S. National Arboretum, Washington, D.C.; M. Flannagan of the Royal Botanic Gardens, Wakehurst Place, Ardingly, West Sussex; the Forestry Commission, Forest Research Station, Alice Holt Lodge, Farnham, Surrey; Anne James of the Parks Department, Dublin County Council, Irish Republic; Roy Lancaster; Scott Leathart; Alan Mitchell; K. Olver; The Royal Horticultural Society's Garden Wisley, Woking, Surrey; V. Schilling of the Tree Register of the British Isles (TROBI), Westmeston, West Sussex; T. Walker of the University of Oxford Botanic Gardens, Oxfordshire; John White and Margaret Ruskin of the Forestry Commission, Westonbirt Arboretum, Tetbury, Gloucestershire; P. Yeo of the University of Cambridge Botanic Garden, Cambridgeshire; Dennis Woodland.

The author would like to express his thanks to: the tremendous team at Dorling Kindersley, especially Vicki James, Gillian Roberts, and Mustafa Sami, for their diligence and commitment to the project; Matthew Ward, for his excellent photography; Roy Lancaster, for reading and commenting on the text; his wife Sue, and daughters Rachel and Ruth, for their support and encouragement.

We acknowledge the invaluable contributions of Mustafa Sami, who shepherded the illustrators with patient good humor, Spencer Holbrook, who gave him vital administrative support, and Donna Rispoli, who researched the references for the illustrators. Special thanks to Mel and Marianne, Witt and Kaye, whose generosity enabled the editor to take a holiday. Thanks also to Michael Allaby, for compiling the index and suggesting words for the glossary; Jane Cooke, for vital editorial assistance; Mike Darton, for reading page proofs, and for commenting on the glossary and introduction; Virginia Fitzgerald, for administrative help; Angeles Gavira and Ian Hambleton, for cataloguing all the transparencies; Steve Tilling, for commenting on the identification key; Helen Townsend, for caretaking the project while the editor was on holiday; Alastair Wardle, for his computer expertise.

Photographs by Matthew Ward, except: A–Z Botanical Collection 6, 8 *(top)*; Kathie Atkinson 190 *(right & below)*, 191; Bruce Coleman Ltd/Patrick Clement 167 *(Quercus petraea* acorns); Dorling Kindersley/ Peter Chadwick 12 (trunk), 15 (cone section, seed pods), 246 *(top left)*; Harry Smith Photographic Collection/ Polunin Collection 159 *(Quercus canariensis)* acorns), 169 *(Quercus pubescens* acorns). **Tree illustrations** by Laura Andrew 200, 201; Marion Appleton 132–143; David Ashby 118–125; Bob Bampton 258–273, 286–297; Anne Child 126, 127, 178–181; Tim Hayward 114–117, 128–131, 144, 145, 154–157, 202–211, 222–237, 274–283, 308–310; Janos Marffy 9, 17, 192–195; David More 158–173, 244-252; Sue Oldfield 12–13, 36–83, 108–113, 188, 189, 196–199, 213–215, 298, 299; Liz Pepperell 182–187, 190, 238–243; Michelle Ross 34, 35, 84–107, 146–152, 300–307; Gill Tomblin 174–177; Barbara Walker 216–221, 255–257, 284, 285. **Leaf type illustrations** by Paul Bailey. **Endpaper illustrations** by Caroline Church.